DEVOTIONS FOR

Growing
Strong

IN THE
Seasons OF Life

DEVOTIONS FOR

Growing Strong

IN THE Seasons OF Life

CHARLES R. SWINDOLL

FOREWORD BY
BILLY GRAHAM

ZondervanPublishingHouse
Grand Rapids, Michigan

A Division of HarperCollinsPublishers

Growing Strong in the Seasons of Life
Copyright © 1983 by Charles R. Swindoll, Inc.

Requests for information should be addressed to:
  Zondervan Publishing House
  Grand Rapids, Michigan 49530

Swindoll, Charles R.
  Growing strong in the seasons of life / Charles R. Swindoll : foreword by Billy
  Graham.
      p.   cm.
  Originally published: Portland, Or. : Multnomah Press. © 1983
  Includes bibliograhical references and index.
  ISBN 0-310-42141-1 (pbk.)
    1. Devotional exercises. 2. Devotional calendars. 3. Seasons—Religious
  aspects—Christianity.   I. Title.
  BV4832.2S885 1994
  242'.2—dc20   94-2775
                                                                   CIP

Scripture quotations, unless otherwise marked, are taken from the New American Standard Bible, © The Lockman Foundation 1960, 1962, 1968, 1971, 1972, 1973, 1975, 1977, and are used by permission.

Scripture references marked NIV are taken from the Holy Bible, New International Version®. NIV®. Copyright © 1973, 1978, 1984 by International Bible Society. Used by permission of Zondervan Publishing House. All rights reserved.

Scripture references marked MLB are taken from The Modern Language Bible: The New Berkeley Version in Modern English © 1959, 1969 by Zondervan Bible Publishers, and are used by permission.

Scripture references marked TLB are taken from The Living Bible, Copyright 1971 by Tyndale House Publishers, Wheaton, Illinois, and are used by permission.

Scripture references marked Phillips are taken from J. B. Phillips: The New Testament in Modern English, Revised Edition © J. B. Phillips 1958, 1960, 1972, and are used by permission of Macmillan Publishing Co. Inc., New York; and Collins Publishers, London.

Cover photo by AllStock
Cover design by Cindy Davis
Interior design by Cindy Davis

Printed in the United States of America

  95 96 97 98 99 / DH / 10 9 8 7 6 5 4 3 2

*With gratitude and delight I dedicate this volume to
Edgar and Can Dee Neuenschwander
who have been loving and supportive during
the cold winters, the changing springs, the hot
summers, and the busy autumns of the past
twelve years of my life. Through it all they have
proven themselves faithful friends both
in season and out of season.*

CONTENTS

Foreword 13
Introduction 15
Prelude 17

Winter
A Season of Reverence

December
Consistency 23
The Tongue... 26
Dealing with Disillusionment 29
Zeal behind the Wheel 33
Please, Not So Serious 35
Expecting Perfection and Accepting Humanity.............. 38
A Birth.. 42
Prophetic Momentum 44
The Lonely Trail of the Gimper 47
No Place for Pride.. 50
Depression... 53
Finishing the Course 55

January
Thoroughness 59
Memorizing Scripture 61
Habits 63
Monday Morning Pulpits 66
Dialogues of the Deaf 69
Admiration 71
Love without a Net 74
The Dark Side of Greatness 77
Clear View from Mt. Perspective 80
Expectations 84
Secret Wounds, Silent Cries 87
Benedictions 90

February

Quietness 93
Solving Problems 95
You Are Not a Nobody 98
Cool Skepticism 101
Asking Why 103
Erosion 105
Friendly — Inside Out 108
A Parable: Saving Lives 110
The Winsome Witness 112
Rumors 117
You Are Important 120
Tears 123

Spring
A Season of Renewal

March

Roots 129
Newborn 131
A Cure for Tunnel Vision 133
Orderliness 136
Impatience 139
When Following Seems Unfair 142
Better than Sacrifice 145
A Way in the Storm 147
An Antidote for Weariness 150
Destination Unknown 153
Loneliness 156
Be an Encourager! 158

April

Hidden Saints 161
Watch Out for Fakes 164
Clichés 167
A Sheltering Tree 170
The Law of Echoes 172

Tomorrow 175
Illogical Logic 178
The Sting of Pearls 181
Bitterness 184
Stumbling 187
Comforting 189
Call for Help! 192

May

Trophies 195
Fulfillment 198
Procrastination 201
Impacting Lives 204
Luxuries 207
Holding Things Loosely 209
Meditation 211
Famine 214
Externals and Internals 217
Simplicity 220
Keeping Your Word 223
Surprises 226

Summer
A Season of Rest

June

Building Memories 233
Living It Up 236
Man's Quest 239
Fathers 242
Anniversaries 244
Overexpecting 247
In the Shade of a Juniper 250
Insight 252
Appraising Life 254
Acting Medium 257
A Rare and Remarkable Virtue 259
Take Time to Be Tender 261

July

Risking Liberty 264
Compromise and Consequence 267
Worm Theology 270
Failures 273
The Broken Wing 275
Searching for Shelter 278
Manipulation 283
Disorientation 286
Relaying the Truth 289
God's Control 292
Very Thin Wires 294
"Final Descent . . . Commence Prayer" 297

August

Restraint 301
Modeling God's Message 304
Comparison 306
Choosing Your Words 309
Nit-Picking 311
Staying Alert 314
The Case Against Vanilla 316
Rationalization 318
Long Winds, Deep Roots 320
Taking Time 323
Of Roots and Wings 325
Operation Relaxation 327

Autumn
A Season of Reflection

September

Doing vs. Being 335
The Final Priority 338
A Rabbit on the Swim Team 340
Self-Praise 343
Monuments 345
Cracks in the Wall 348

Time 351
The Plug-in Drug 354
Please Be Careful 357
Resentment 360
Health 362
Isolation and Involvement 365

October

"The Opra Ain't Over" 368
Presumption 371
Designer-label Planet 374
Growing Old 377
Reality 379
Lifelines 382
Adversity and Prosperity 385
Unambitious Leadership 388
Pharisaism 390
Fear 394
Courage 397
Songless Saints 399

November

Back to the Basics 402
Busyness 405
Spiritual Leadership 408
A Fire for Cold Hearts 411
Biblical Illiteracy 413
Taking God Seriously 415
Nostalgia 418
Grace Revisited 420
Thanksgiving 423
Gentleness 427
One Long Extended Gift 429
Year-end Reflections 431

Conclusion **435**
Footnotes **437**
Scripture Index **439**
Subject Index **446**

FOREWORD

On various occasions popular musical artists will release special albums that represent their best efforts. The titles are familiar to all of us: "The Best of Sinatra" . . . "The Best of Streisand" . . . "The Best of Neil Diamond." It is not uncommon for these albums to push their way quickly to the top of the hit parade as music lovers listen again and again to their favorite artists doing their best work.

This volume by your friend and mine could be called "The Best of Charles Swindoll." For almost twenty years this man has ministered to our world through books, several of which have become (and still are) bestsellers. All of us have come to expect high quality and unusual insights as we pick up another book to which he has put his pen . . . and we have not once been disappointed.

Here is another winner. *Growing Strong in the Seasons of Life* is not only a beautiful statement about four distinct "seasons," it is also a healthy and balanced diet of hope for the discouraged, a refuge for the hurting, a challenge for the weary, and a friend for the lonely. You will smile with understanding and you may even weep with compassion. You will appreciate how carefully Scripture is woven into the fabric of each page, sometimes boldly, but more often softly, artistically.

May you find the living Lord opening His arms of love to you as you move through each of these four seasons. Take your time. Walk slowly. Feel God's presence as you consider the days and weeks and years that He has given to you. Ask Him to bring new strength to your soul.

With delight I recommend "The Best of Charles Swindoll" to you. Here is a combination of words, phrases, and ideas you'll want to read again and again. A book for all seasons.

Billy Graham

INTRODUCTION

I am glad God changes the times and the seasons, aren't you?

Just think how dull things would become if He didn't paint nature's scenes in different colors several times a year. With infinite creativity and remarkable regularity, He splashes white over brown and orange over green, giving such attention to detail that we are often stunned with amazement.

Each of the four seasons offers fresh and vital insights for those who take the time to look and to think. Hidden beneath the surface are colorful yet silent truths that touch most every area across the landscape of our lives. As each three-month segment of every year holds its own mysteries and plays its own melodies, offering sights and smells, feelings and fantasies altogether distinct, so it is in the seasons of life. The Master is neither mute nor careless as He alters our times and changes our seasons. How wrong to trudge blindly and routinely through a lifetime of changing seasons without discovering answers to the new mysteries and learning to sing the new melodies! Seasons are designed to deepen us, to instruct us in the wisdom and ways of our God. To help us grow strong . . . like a tree planted by the rivers of water.

This is a book about the recurring seasons of life. It offers a series of suggestions and ideas to help you read God's signals with a sensitive heart. Quietly and deliberately, we'll walk together through each scene, pondering the subtle shading as well as the obvious broad brush strokes from the Artist's hand. Let's take our time and leave room for our feelings to emerge. Let's sing in harmony with the Composer's music. Let's drink in the beauty of His handiwork. It will take time, so let's not hurry.

Our journey begins in the winter, a season of quiet *reverence*. This is followed by spring, a season of refreshing and encouraging *renewal*. Then comes summer, a season of enjoyable and much-needed *rest*. Finally, we'll stroll through autumn, a season of nostalgic *reflection*. Our hope is to grow stronger and taller as our roots dig deeper in the soft soil along the banks of the river of life. And let's not fear the winds of adversity! The gnarled old twisted trees, beaten and buffeted by wind and weather along the ocean shores, tell their own stories of consistent courage. May God make us strong as the winds whip against us, my friend. Roots grow deep when the winds are strong. Let's commit ourselves to growing strong in the seasons of life.

Just before we embark on our journey, allow me a final few paragraphs concerning the composition of these thoughts.

When my family and I moved to Fullerton in the summer of 1971, I immediately began writing a weekly column in our church newsletter, which I called "Think It Over." I have continued that discipline to this day. Little did I realize the far-reaching effect these provocative articles would some day have on our generation! I must express my gratitude to the staff of Multnomah Press for their creative sensitivity and bold vision to publish this material in various formats and titles since 1977. *For Those Who Hurt; Starting Over; Standing Out; Killing Giants, Pulling Thorns; Make Up Your Mind;* and *Encourage Me* have emerged from the original "Think It Over" articles. We have all been amazed to see how broadly God has used and continues to use each one of those books in peoples' lives. I confess, *I have been the most surprised of all!* (I've been tempted to publish the letters from those who wrote me, describing how God used the books in their lives.) This volume is a compilation of several previously published articles that first appeared in those books, plus numerous other columns never before published. I am especially indebted to Julie Cave and Larry Libby for their loving friendship over the years. Because of their skilled insight and creative editorial assistance, I was able to see how such varied columns fit so beautifully into the theme of the seasons.

And once again, I declare my gratitude to Helen Peters, my personal secretary, for her unselfish patience with me, along with her relentless devotion to the task of typing and retyping the original manuscript.

Now . . . let's walk together as God escorts us through the seasons. Let's listen closely to His voice as we observe the changing scenery. It might be wise for us to brace ourselves against those strong gusts of wind that inevitably accompany each season. But even the storms bear a message of encouragement for us:

Deeper roots make for stronger lives.

Charles R. Swindoll

PRELUDE

*L*et's face it: Most of us could use a little encouragement when it comes to consistency in our walk with Christ. Right? We could all use a trusted friend who could be available several times a week to offer a little friendly prompting. To check in on our progress.

This is a book to give to yourself.

Oh, you can give a copy to someone else, too. But save one — for you. It's a book to read in, write on, and companion with. Sorry, but it simply wasn't designed for a shelf in the library or a parking space on the coffee table. It's a book that was meant to be *used.* And if the cover gets bent, the margins get scribbled, and the once white pages betray a coffee stain or two — so much the better.

Here's how the book can work for you: The pages of this volume contain 144 individual articles — which works out to about 3 per week (Monday, Wednesday, Friday, perhaps). Just the number most of us can handle without falling behind if we decide to use this book as as devotional aid.

Following each article, a "Deepening Your Roots" section suggests Scripture that relates to the day's reading. This may vary from just a verse or two to a longer passage when it's important to understand the full context.

Following this, "Branching Out" suggests one to four practical assignments to help you put principles from the article into action. Try at least one assignment per reading. Many of them are fun!

At the end of the week (after every three articles) is a short "Growing Strong" section. At this point (probably Saturday or Sunday) you're ready to take a break, review how your week went, and reflect back on the various assignments.

The seasons of life roll by at an astonishing rate. Only our great God and His Word remain unchanged. As we invest time and energy in that Word, we drink from the well of eternity.

All of us will grow old in the seasons of life.

By His grace, we may also grow strong.

Winter

A Season of Reverence

WINTER

Just the sound of the word whistling through our lips puts a mental chill up our spines. Winter seems to speak of barrenness, frigid feelings of discomfort and discontent, icy shadows sprawled across frozen ponds, naked branches reaching up as if in supplication for relief. Short days, long nights. Fast-fading memories of yesterday's fun in the sun, bike rides along the beach, the World Series, Thanksgiving. Heavy, gray clouds and harsh winds sting our faces and steal our smiles. With grim determination we trudge on, sometimes alone and isolated, within our own little world of heavy garb and frosty windows. "The dead of winter"—ah, an apt description!

Not all agree. Ski buffs and snow lovers resent such a depressing portrayal of their favorite season. So do artists who prefer a quaint cottage in New Hampshire rather than an ocean view at Malibu or a sandy beach at St. Thomas. For many, a year without winter would be a devastating disappointment. What better time to warm up alongside a crackling fire, listen to some fine music, and stare away an evening? Toss in the joy of Christmas, the celebration of New Year's Eve, the Super Bowl, a Valentine's Day kiss . . . and you've got enough to make anybody forget ninety-five degree days, along with flies and mosquitoes at an August picnic. What a difference perspective makes!

Winter . . . the ideal occasion to slow down. To invest a few extra hours in quiet reverence. To take a long walk over the freshly fallen white manna delivered earlier that day. To remind ourselves that "our God is in the heavens; He does whatever He pleases" (Psalm 115:3).

Is it winter right now in the season of your life? Are you feeling depressed . . . alone . . . overlooked . . . spiritually on "hold" . . . cold . . . barren? Beginning to wonder if your soul will ever thaw? Entertaining doubts that behind those thick, gray clouds there exists a personal, caring God?

Take it by faith, friend; He is there, and furthermore, He is neither dead nor deaf. What you are enduring is one of those dry-spell times when you'd rather curl up and cry than stand up and sing. That's okay. Those times come.

They also pass.

When this winter season ends, you'll be wiser, deeper, stronger. Therefore, in reverence, look up. Be still and discover anew that He is God. That He is doing "whatever He pleases" in your life.

Maybe the following "winter thoughts" will change your perspective and help convince you.

CONSISTENCY

*T*he questions are different, but each answer is the same.

> What will guard us against foolish extremes?
> What characterizes those who are habitually successful in sports or sales or some skill?
> What single quality in a business builds respect deeper than any other?
> What brings security in relationships?
> What makes us choose a particular brand name over all others?
> What's needed most by parents in the home?
> What draws you to the same restaurant time and again?
> What do you want most from your paperboy . . . or milkman . . . or postman?
> What will add more weight to your witness for Christ than anything else?

CONSISTENCY. That's the answer to all nine questions, and you know it's true. Steadiness. You can count on it. It'll be there tomorrow just like it was yesterday . . . free from silly moods, sudden changes, or fickle fads. Early in the day or late at night, consistency stands firm. When pain or hardship bites, consistency doesn't bleed. When the majority is tired and irritable, consistency is stable and resilient. Not insensitive, boring . . . but reliable, faithful. Not opposed to change or reason, but trustworthy. Not stubborn, but solid. Yes, that's it: solid.

It's the stuff most mothers are made of when their little ones get sick . . . and missionaries who lose themselves in their labor even though it yields limited fruit. It reveals itself in faithful employees who show up on time, roll up their sleeves, and commit themselves more to doing the job than watching the clock. Diligence is its brother . . . dependability, its partner . . . discipline, its parent.

CONSISTENCY. A living model of patience, determination, and strength — regardless of shifty, rootless times. The blasts of ridicule and criticism may punch it in the face — but consistency stands and takes it as silently as a bronze statue takes the tempest. One poet calls it "a jewel," another "an anchor of iron." It knows little of ups or downs, highs or lows, blue Mondays or holiday hangovers. It hates tardiness and absenteeism. It thrives on sacrifice and unselfishness. It's an obvious mark of maturity. It's hanging in there day in and day out in spite of everything that could get you sidetracked.

In biblical terms, consistency is a subtle, supple thread woven into the fabric of scriptural truth. Paul had it in mind when he told Timothy to

> . . . be ready in season and out of season . . . (2 Timothy 4:2);

and when he exhorted the Galatians

> . . . let us not lose heart . . . for in due time we shall reap if we
> do not grow weary (Galatians 6:9).

James saw it as a stabilizing trait, which he called

> . . . endurance. And let endurance have its perfect result, that
> you may be perfect . . . (James 1:3b – 4).

We are reminded that Abraham was consistent when it came to believing God's promise to him, because

> . . . he did not waver . . . (Romans 4:20).

But best of all,

> Jesus Christ is the same yesterday and today, yes and forever
> (Hebrews 13:8).

One of the most attractive, magnetic characteristics of the Christ is His consistency. When you need Him, He is there. He's there even when you don't think you need Him! You're never too early or too late. He's never in a lousy mood nor will He ask you to call back during office hours. He's available . . . because He's immutable. With Him, there's no new year or old year. He is "the same," regardless.

CONSISTENCY.
>It's the jewel worth wearing . . .
>>It's the anchor worth weighing . . .
>>>It's the thread worth weaving . . .
>>>>It's the battle worth winning.

Deepening Your Roots

Romans 4; 1 Timothy 4:15–16; Hebrews 6:1–12

Branching Out

1. Show up early at work every day this week.
2. Be happy (positive) every day. Work at being consistent.
3. What's something you consistently do that irritates others, and is something you could change? How about working on changing it?

The Tongue

On a windswept hill in an English country churchyard stands a drab, gray slate tombstone. Bleak and unpretentious, it leans slightly to one side, beaten slick and thin by the blast of time. The quaint stone bears an epitaph not easily seen unless you stoop over and look closely. The faint etchings read:

> BENEATH THIS STONE, A LUMP OF CLAY,
> LIES ARABELLA YOUNG,
> WHO ON THE TWENTY-FOURTH OF MAY,
> BEGAN TO HOLD HER TONGUE.

The tongue — what a study in contrasts! To the physician it's merely a two-ounce slab of mucous membrane enclosing a complex array of muscles and nerves that enable our bodies to chew, taste, and swallow. How helpful! Equally significant, it is the major organ of communication that enables us to articulate distinct sounds so we can understand each other. How essential!

Without the tongue no mother could sing her baby to sleep tonight. No ambassador could adequately represent our nation. No teacher could stretch the minds of students. No officer could lead his fighting men in battle. No attorney could defend the truth in court. No pastor could comfort troubled souls. No complicated, controversial issue could *ever* be discussed and solved. Our entire world would be reduced to unintelligible grunts and shrugs. Seldom do we pause to realize just how valuable this strange muscle in our mouths really is.

But the tongue is as volatile as it is vital. It was Washington Irving who first said, "A sharp tongue is the only edge tool that grows keener with constant use." It was James, the half brother of Jesus, who first warned:

> The tongue is a fire . . . a restless evil and full of deadly poison
> (James 3:6, 8).

Verbal cyanide. A lethal, relentless, flaming missile which assaults with hellish power, blistering and destroying at will.

And yet it doesn't look anything like the brutal beast it is. Neatly hidden behind ivory palace gates, its movements are an intriguing study of coordination. It can curl itself either into a cheery whistle or manipulate a lazy, afternoon yawn. With no difficulty it can flick a husk of popcorn from between two jaw teeth or hold a thermometer just so. And it is *tricky!* It can help you enjoy the flavor of a stick of peppermint as it switches from side to side without once getting nipped. Moments later it can follow the directions of a trumpeter, allowing him to play "Flight of the Bumblebee" without a single miscue.

But watch out! Let your thumb get smashed with a hammer or your toe get clobbered on a chair and that slippery creature in your mouth will suddenly play the flip side of its nature.

Not only is the tongue untamed, it's *untamable!* Meaning what? Meaning as long as you live it will never gain control of itself. It defies being tamed. Incredible! We can tame Flipper and Trigger and Shamu and Lassie. We can train falcons to land on our wrists, pigeons to carry our messages, dogs to fetch the paper, elephants to stand on rolling balls, tigers to sit on stools, and alligators to turn over and get their bellies rubbed. But the tongue? Impossible to train!

Many men before me have offered counsel on how to keep our tongues checked and caged. One was William Norris, the American journalist who specialized in simple rhymes that packed a wallop. He once wrote:

> If your lips would keep from slips,
> Five things observe with care:
> To whom you speak; of whom you speak;
> And how, and when, and where.

Publius, the Greek sage, put his finger on another technique we tend to forget when he admitted:

> I have often regretted my speech, never my silence.

King David put it even more bluntly in Psalm 39:

> I will guard my ways,
> That I may not sin with my tongue;
> I will guard my mouth as with a muzzle (v.1).

That's what it takes. A tight, conscious muzzle on the muscle in your mouth. Harnessing such a wily creature requires a determined mindset. With your Lord's help, take these three first steps:

Think first. Before your lips start moving, pause ten seconds and mentally preview your words. Are they accurate or exaggerated? Kind or cutting? Necessary or needless? Wholesome or vile? Grateful or complaining?

Talk less. Your chances of blowing it are directly proportional to the amount of time you spend with your mouth open. Try closing it for a while. Compulsive talkers find it difficult to keep friends. They're irritating. So conserve your verbal energy!

Start today. Fit that muzzle on your mouth *now*. It's a project you've put off long enough. Arabella Young waited too long.

Deepening Your Roots
Proverbs 12:18, 21:23; Ephesians 4:29

Branching Out
Work on the two suggestions given in today's article: Think first. Talk less.

DEALING WITH DISILLUSIONMENT

The prophet was in the pits. Literally. Like Poe's fanciful character, he was "sick, sick unto death." Swamped with disillusionment and drowning in despair, he cursed the day he was born and wondered why an abortion wasn't performed, killing him prior to his birth.

He screamed:

> Why did I ever come forth from the womb to look on trouble and sorrow, so that my days have been spent in shame? (Jeremiah 20:18).

An exaggeration? Not hardly. Read the record for yourself. Jeremiah's journal holds nothing back. In chapter 20 the chief officer in the temple had him beaten (forty lashes), then placed in stocks. That means his feet, hands, and neck were secured in a torturous device that caused the body to be bent almost double. That happened after he was beaten! Why? Had he committed some crime? No. He had simply declared the truth. He had done what was right — and this is what he got in return. It hurt him deeply.

On top of all that, sarcastic whisperings swirled about. His once-trusted friends tagged him with a nickname — Magor-Missabib — meaning "terror on every side." That also hurt. He must have felt like a limp rag doll in the mouth of a snarling Doberman.

His prayers became laced with loneliness and bold complaints:

> O LORD, Thou hast deceived me and I was deceived; Thou hast overcome me and prevailed. I have become a laughingstock all day long; everyone mocks me. . . . for me the word of the Lord has resulted in reproach and derision all day long (Jeremiah 20:7 – 8).

The man is in anguish. Prophet or not, he is struggling with God's justice, His strange treatment. Deep down he is questioning His presence.

"Where is He? Why has Jehovah vanished at a time when I need Him the most?"

The ancient man of God is not alone with feelings like that. Who hasn't wrestled with similar questions and doubts? Few express it more vividly than Elie Wiesel in the terse, tightly packed sentences of his book, *Night*. Wiesel, a Jew, spent his teenage years in a Nazi death camp at Birkenbau. His young eyes witnessed tragedies too horrible to repeat. The toll it took on him is best described in the foreword by French Nobel-prize-winning author François Mauriac:

> For him (Wiesel), Nietzsche's cry expressed an almost physi-cal reality: God is dead, the God of love, of gentleness, of comfort . . . has vanished forevermore. . . . And how many pious Jews have experienced this death. On that day, horrible even among those days of horror, when the child watched the hanging of another child, who, he tells us, had the face of a sad angel, he heard someone behind him groan: "Where is God? Where is He? Where can He be now?"

What desperate feelings!

And one need not be in a concentration camp to have those thoughts. Or doubled over in stocks and beaten with rods. No, sometimes they come in the long, dark tunnel of suffering when the pain won't go away. Or when a marriage partner who promised to stay "for better or for worse" breaks that vow. Or when a long-sought-after dream goes up in smoke. Or when we kiss a loved one goodbye for the last time.

Not always . . . but sometimes (usually unuttered and hidden away in the secret vaults of our minds) we question Jehovah's justice. We ask, "Is He absent today?" Personally, I cannot bring myself to chide Jeremiah. The heavens above him appeared as brass. His Lord's passivity disillu-sioned him. The silence of God was more than he could take. There are such times, I openly confess, when I, too, wonder about why He permits certain things to occur that seemingly defy His character.

At those times I'm tempted to say what the prophet said:

> I will not remember Him or speak anymore in His name . . .
> (20:9a).

"That's it! I'm tossing in my collar. No more sermons and devotion-als for this preacher. Secular job here I come!" But right about the time I start to jump, I experience what Jeremiah admitted:

. . . Then in my heart it becomes like a burning fire shut up in my bones; and I am weary of holding it in, and I cannot endure it (20:9b).

Directly sent from God is this strong surge of hope, this cleansing fire of confidence, this renewed sense of determination swelling up within me. And the disillusionment is quietly replaced with His reassurance as He reminds me of that glorious climax to the hymn I often sing back to Him in full volume:

"All is well, all is well!"

Thank God, it is. Recently, I doubted that — like Jeremiah. But not today. Reassurance has returned. Divine perspective has provided a fresh breeze of hope in the pits. I have determined that disillusionment must go. Now . . . not later.

Like Magor-Missabib, I ain't about to quit! God has broken through the brass above. With antiphonal voice His angels answer, "All is well, all is well!"

Deepening Your Roots
Psalm 37:1 – 13; Jeremiah 32:17 – 42; Lamentations 3:19 – 32; John 16:33

Branching Out

1. Write out John 16:33 and put it in your wallet to look at whenever you become disillusioned.
2. Have you ever complained to God like Jeremiah did? If not, maybe you should. And, like the prophet, WAIT and see how God brings new hope to your soul. When that happens jot a note to yourself (maybe in your Bible) to remind you — next time you want to throw in the towel — that God will see you through.
3. Name a towel in your closet "Jeremiah" so that whenever you see it you'll remember it "pays to WAIT on God."

🐦 🐦 🐦

Growing Strong

Bet I touched upon some painful spots this week. Aggravated? Glad I zeroed in on some areas that need attention? Good. Growing isn't always smooth and pain-free, is it? But isn't it a healthy sensation! What excites you as you think about this book and what is taking place in your heart or life?

_____

_____

_____

_____

ZEAL BEHIND THE WHEEL

When Jehu was born, he hit the dirt running. Throughout life, he had one speed — *wide open*. Sired by a cyclone, nursed by thunder, reared on grits and cornbread, and enthroned through a blood-bath revolution King Jehu became a byword for recklessness and aggression. His dynasty has been called by the experts the "Execution Dynasty," since they killed kings about like you'd flick flies off the kitchen table. Read his biography for yourself, you'll see (2 Kings 9:11–10:36).

Jehu drove a wild chariot and spent more time raising dust in the two-wheel wonder than he did raising money on the throne. In fact, his entire reputation revolved around his *driving*. On one occasion he sealed a friendship by a maddening chariot ride, during which he demonstrated his "zeal for the Lord" (2 Kings 10:15–16). Read and picture the following. You'll smile.

> . . . he met Jehonadab the son of Rechab coming to meet him; and he greeted him and said to him, "Is your heart right, as my heart is with your heart?" And Jehonadab answered, "It is." Jehu said, "If it is, give me your hand." And he gave him his hand, and he took him up to him into the chariot. And he said, "Come with me and see my zeal for the Lord." So he made him ride in his chariot.

That story makes me laugh out loud! I'm convinced Jehonadab was never quite the same. He probably died on his feet with his eyes open, his knuckles white as rice, and bug stains all over his face. His bones are still shaking. Jehonadab will probably stutter throughout eternity.

But more picturesque is a previous scene portrayed for us in 9:20 as Jehu is approaching two godless kings, Joram and Ahaziah (who were, no doubt, scared to death). The verse describes his coming in the distance:

> And the watchman reported: "He came even to them, and he did not return; and the driving is like the driving of Jehu the son of Nimshi, for he drives furiously."

You see, by that time the national byword for fast and furious driving was "driving like the driving of Jehu." The New International Version says, ". . . he drives like a madman."

Sons and daughters of Jehu live on. Polished cedar chariots pulled by lathered-up stallions have changed into a sleek, slick, four-on-the-floor job or a neat little sports car or handsome sedan. But there's an amazing similarity between the drivers and their reputations. What is most remarkable is that the century-twenty Jehus are not always wild-eyed Jacks with one arm around a girl. Sometimes they are little old ladies in tennis outfits and sneakers . . . or middle-aged homemakers with a station wagon full of kiddos . . . or well-dressed executives late for lunch . . . or preoccupied preachers taking their half of the road out of the middle . . . or Sunday drivers jockeying for a slot in the church parking lot.

God's work of grace moves downward, have you noticed? The last part of us to experience full salvation is our *right foot,* which is filled with the sinew of selfishness. The way we act behind the wheel is far more indicative of our walk with God than the way we act praying in a pew or smiling over a well-marked Bible. Why don't you and I commit ourselves to a little less speed and (unlike Jehu) a lot less "furious" reputation.

And if we occasionally *must* speed, maybe it would help to sing loudly:

At 45 mph . . . "God Will Take Care of You"
At 55 mph . . . "Guide Me, O Thou Great Jehovah"
At 65 mph . . . "Nearer, My God, to Thee"
At 75 mph . . . "Nearer, Still Nearer!"
At 85 mph . . . "This World Is Not My Home"
At 95 mph . . . "Lord, I'm Coming Home"
Over 100- . . . "Precious Memories"

One thing for sure, we oughta peel off all bumper stickers and window stickums that announce our faith. It's tough explaining doves and fish and stuff written in Greek to cops who read only English and have never heard of Jehu.

Deepening Your Roots
2 Kings 10; John 13:34; 1 Peter 2:11–16

Branching Out
1. Don't exceed any speed limits this week!
2. Ask five other people to describe your driving.

PLEASE, NOT SO SERIOUS

Recently, I happened upon a brief column on one of my favorite characters out of American history, the "Wizard of Menlo Park" — Thomas Alva Edison, the inventor. He was, in fact, the man who had almost eleven hundred (!) of his inventions patented.

Thanks to that curious, insightful genius, we have a light over our shoulders, sound emerging from grooved platters, small boxes that store enough energy to start our cars, movies that include sound tracks, small metal cylinders that allow one person's voice to be heard by tens of thousands . . . and hundreds of other devices we now take for granted. We don't live one day without enjoying the fruit of Edison's life.

Not everyone is so fortunate. Or practical. Between 1962 and 1977, Arthur Pedrick patented 162 inventions. Sounds impressive until you understand that none of them were taken up commercially. Not one.

Among his greatest inventions were:

- A bicycle with amphibious capability.
- An arrangement whereby a car could be driven from the back seat.
- Several golf inventions, including a golf ball that could be steered in flight.

The grandest scheme of Pedrick, who described himself as the "One-Man-Think-Tank Basic Research Laboratories of Sussex," was to irrigate deserts of the world by sending a constant supply of snowballs from the polar region through a massive network of giant peashooters.

You're smiling. You're also thinking, "Swindoll is making this up." Wrong. It's all documented in a book I read by Stephen Pile, appropriately entitled *The Book of Failures*. It's got unbelievable stuff in it.

Like that time back in 1978 during the fireman's strike in England. It made possible one of the greatest animal rescue attempts of all time. Valiantly, the British Army had taken over emergency firefighting. On January 14 they were called out by an elderly lady in South London to retrieve her cat. They arrived with impressive haste, very cleverly and carefully rescued the cat, and started to drive away. But the lady was so grateful she invited the squad of heroes in for tea. Driving off later with fond farewells and warm waving of arms, they ran over the cat and killed it.

The prize for the most useless weapon of all times goes to the Russians. They invented the "dog mine." The plan was to train the dogs to associate food with the undersides of tanks, in the hope that they would run hungrily beneath advancing Panzer divisions. Bombs were then strapped to the dogs' backs, which endangered the dogs to the point where no insurance company would look at them.

Unfortunately, the dogs associated food solely with *Russian* tanks. The plan was begun the first day of the Russian involvement in World War II . . . and abandoned on day two. The dogs with bombs on their backs forced an entire Soviet division to retreat.

All of which brings me to two very brief and simple points:

1. No matter how sincere we may be or how hard we may work, some days are best forgotten. Murphy's Law, remember?

2. Some things that seemed terribly important and serious at the time become absolutely hilarious after a little time passes.

Perhaps that's why Psalm 90:12 encourages us to "number our days." The verse goes on to promise that when we do that we get wiser. I take it to mean we *gain* wisdom when we lengthen our view of life.

Does something seem terribly important to you today? Extremely, vitally serious? Almost to the point of distraction? Number your days. Get a little perspective. Realize that it won't be long before you will look back on that up-tight, high-powered, super-charged issue with a whole new outlook. To be quite candid with you, you may laugh out loud in the future at something you're eating your heart out over today.

Don't sweat the small stuff. Nobody bats one thousand. Not even Edison . . . or Pedrick . . . or Russian eggheads . . . or the British Army.

Let's learn a lesson from those dogs with bombs on their backs. Some of the best-laid plans blow up in our faces. So when the smoke clears, try smiling instead of crying.

Deepening Your Roots

Psalm 90:12, 145:1 – 14; Ecclesiastes 3:1 – 4; Luke 6:20 – 23

Branching Out

1. Rather than complaining, try *laughing* today when something goes wrong.
2. When something disappoints or discourages you today, write down what happened on a piece of paper, put the paper in an envelope, seal it, and place the envelope in a drawer or cupboard to open up some other day.

EXPECTING PERFECTION AND ACCEPTING HUMANITY

Not being a bumper-sticker freak, I find myself turned off by most of the stuff people announce on rear windows and back bumpers. I've had to do a lot of explaining to my younger kids . . . and sometimes they have had to help *me* out! Much of the junk is just plain repulsive — even some of the religious jargon.

But a couple of years ago I noticed a new one. For some reason it stuck in my cranium as firmly as on chrome.

CHRISTIANS ARE NOT PERFECT, JUST FORGIVEN.

The last time I saw it was on the back of the car that passed me while I was doing about 65. It fit. The time before that, I saw it on a VW bug (God love him) that had a ticket under the wiper because the meter was red. I tried to imagine the cop who checked the license number and saw the sticker. He was probably surprised Christians overpark!

Now before I emote all over this page, I need to set the record straight. There is no way we are *ever* going to convince all those outside the family of God that this is true. A few unbelievers understand, but most will *never* get that wired correctly. Instead, they will continue until their dying day being shocked and angered and offended whenever a Christian shows cracks in his or her life. Of all the things they can't seem to grasp, these two issues confuse them the most: God's grace and human depravity.

- How can something as marvelous as forgiveness of sins and eternal salvation be *free?*
- How can *that* person claim to be a Christian and act like that?

If you've done much witnessing, you know how often those two questions are asked. Non-Christians are stumped when it comes to the grace of God and the humanity of Christians. Why? Because their whole perspective is horizontal. Things that are valuable are costly. Therefore, it is inconceivable that something as priceless as heaven could be offered as a free gift. There isn't much grace running loose on the horizontal plane. And since their whole frame of reference is so mancentered, it's virtually impossible for them to imagine an individual who claims he belongs to God as one who still struggles with imperfection. After all, if you say God has come into your life and Christ has wiped your slate clean, how come you aren't perfect?

That's the non-Christian's way of thinking, and I accept that. They equate salvation with perfection — no wonder they're confused! But the Christian? Hey, we know better . . . or we certainly *should.* Being fellow members of one another, we understand that becoming a Christian in no way ushers us into a life of perfection, erasing our humanity and eradicating our depravity. If all that actually happened, then why in the world is the Bible filled with counsel on forgiving others, understanding their failures, accepting their cracks, and focusing on their strengths (few though they may be)? It's one thing for an unbeliever to expect perfection — I can live with that and tolerate it fairly well — but it's *most* disconcerting to be pushed into a perfection mold by brothers and sisters!

Oh, I understand that our example is in Christ . . . and that our standard is high . . . and that our motives are often good. But it needs to be said again and again and again and again.

CHRISTIANS ARE NOT PERFECT, JUST FORGIVEN.

How very easy it is to manipulate and even victimize our brothers and sisters! How quickly the thin thread of freedom snaps as heavy weights of perfectionistic expectations are placed on us! Christ Jesus never did that with His own. When people were near Him there was this incredible magnetism because of an absence of unrealistic expectations and subtle demands and manipulative devices. He did not use pressure tactics. He simply accepted people as they were.

A paralysis sets in when we operate in the choking context of the perfection-expectation syndrome. Fed by fear and guilt, the Christian becomes a victim of others rather than a victor in Christ. You see, we ultimately act out those pressures and thereby limit our potential.

In one of Wayne Dyer's bestselling works, he talks about how outside forces can limit our ability to achieve.

> In the 1960's a teacher was given a roster showing the actual I.Q. test scores of the students of one class, and for another class a roster in which the I.Q. column had been [mistakenly] filled in with the students' locker numbers. The teacher

assumed that the locker numbers were the actual I.Q.s of the students when the rosters were posted at the beginning of the semester. After a year it was discovered that in the first class the students with high actual I.Q. scores had performed better than those with low ones. But in the second class the students with higher locker numbers scored significantly higher than those with lower locker numbers!

Believe me, if locker numbers can do it, so can the guilt brought on by Christians expecting perfection from one another. Let's back off! Let's relax the strangle hold on each others' necks. Let's allow the Lord to do the criticizing and finger-pointing and the demanding and the judging. Let's grow up and stop being so fragile and nitpicking. I love what Ruth Graham once so wisely said:

It's my job to love Billy. It's God's job to make him good.

Replace the name *Billy* with the name of your mate, your parent, your friend, your boss, your neighbor, your missionary, and especially your pastor, and you'll begin to get the drift of the bumper sticker's message. What's more, you'll be a lot easier to be around.

Remember, we've got to live with you, too.

Deepening Your Roots
Romans 2:1 – 4, 14 – 15:7; Ephesians 4:32

Branching Out
1. Memorize Ephesians 4:32 this week.
2. What are some expectations you have of your spouse, or a friend, or a child that show your demanding attitude? _____

_____

Work on your attitude by not forcing that person to meet your demands.

ભ ભ ભ

Growing Strong

If you "branched out" this week, I commend you! You grew ten inches this week if you managed to go light on that gas pedal or eased up on the demands you place on others. How do you rate your week?

_____

_____

_____

_____

A BIRTH

If Dan Rather had been living in 1809, his evening news broadcasts would have concentrated on Austria . . . not Britain or America. The attention of the entire world was on Napoleon as he swept across helpless hamlets like fire across a Kansas wheat field. Nothing else was half as significant on the international scene. The broad brush strokes on the historian's canvas gave singular emphasis to the bloody scenes of tyranny created by the diminutive dictator of France. From Trafalgar to Waterloo, his name was a synonym for superiority.

At that time of invasions and battles, babies were being born in Britain and America. But who was interested in babies and bottles, cradles and cribs while history was being made? What could possibly be more important in 1809 than the fall of Austria? Who cared about English-speaking infants that year Europe was in the limelight?

Somebody should have. A veritable host of thinkers and statesmen drew their first breath in 1809.

- *William Gladstone* was born in Liverpool.
- *Alfred Tennyson* began his life in Lincolnshire.
- *Oliver Wendell Holmes* cried out in Cambridge, Massachusetts.
- *Edgar Alan Poe,* a few miles away in Boston, started his brief and tragic life.
- A physician named Darwin and his wife called their infant son *Charles Robert.*
- *Robert Charles Winthrop* wore his first diapers.
- A rugged log cabin in Hardin County, Kentucky, owned by an illiterate wandering laborer, was filled with the infant screams of a newborn boy named *Abraham Lincoln.*

All that (and more) happened in 1809 . . . but who cared? The destiny of the world was being shaped on battlefields in Austria — *or was it?* No, indeed!

Only a handful of history buffs today could name even one Austrian campaign — but who can measure the impact of those other lives? What appeared to be super-significant to the world has proven to be no more exciting than a Sunday afternoon yawn. What seemed to be totally *insignificant* was, in fact, the genesis of an era.

Go back eighteen centuries before that. Who could have cared about the birth of a baby while the world was watching Rome in all her splendor? Bounded on the west by the Atlantic . . . on the east by the Euphrates . . . on the north by the Rhine and Danube . . . on the south by the Sahara Desert, the Roman Empire was as vast as it was vicious. Political intrigue, racial tension, increased immorality, and enormous military might occupied everyone's attention and conversation. Palestine existed under the crush of Rome's heavy boot. All eyes were on Augustus, the cynical Caesar who demanded a census so as to determine a measurement to enlarge taxes. At that time who was interested in a couple making an eighty-mile trip south from Nazareth? What could possibly be more important than Caesar's decisions in Rome? Who cared about a Jewish baby born in Bethlehem?

God did. Without realizing it, mighty Augustus was only an errand boy for the fulfillment of Micah's prediction . . . a pawn in the hand of Jehovah . . . a piece of lint on the pages of prophecy. While Rome was busy making history, God arrived. He pitched His fleshly tent in silence on straw . . . in a stable . . . under a star. The world didn't even notice. Reeling from the wake of Alexander the Great . . . Herod the Great . . . Augustus the Great, the world overlooked Mary's little Lamb.

It still does.

Deepening Your Roots
Matthew 1:18 – 25, 2:1 – 23

Branching Out

1. What was a significant news event the year you were born?_____

_____

(If you don't know, ask your parents or older relatives.) Name three other people who were born the same year you were: _____

_____

2. Look at your baby pictures sometime this week or, if possible, drive by the house where you grew up as a child.

3. Find someone else and then one of you read the Christmas story aloud.

PROPHETIC MOMENTUM

I spoke to the Rams one Monday afternoon. That night they went out and creamed the Cowboys.

I spoke to the Steelers the evening before Super Bowl XIV. They ripped the Rams the next day.

I spoke to the Dodgers the following summer before they took the field against the Reds. They whupped 'em!

I spoke to the Angels that same season. They actually went out and won a game! They, in fact, beat the reigning World Series champs, the Kansas City Royals, that afternoon.

It's a lot of fun when you get a winning streak going. Sportscasters call it athletic momentum when it happens in sports events, meaning that surge of assurance, the sixth sense of confidence that says, "No doubt about it, we're on the move. We're gonna win this thing!" If I didn't know better, I could call my pre-game chapel service winning streak *prophetic momentum.* I could lead myself to believe that I have such a gift — "You guys wanna win? Just invite me over a few hours before the game, and it's in the bag. When I speak, you win!"

No way! No reason to kid ourselves. In the long run I'm about as prophetically gifted as the local weathercaster. And my momentum is about as surging as a poached egg. Whatever tie there is between my speaking and somebody's winning is purely coincidental. Prophetic utterance is not my bag.

True prophets — the authentic variety — have long since fled the scene. But they once walked like giants on this earth's landscape. Daring men. Willing to stake their lives on the absolute truth of their claims. No margin for error in judgment or mental mistake in the smallest detail. And they didn't predict obvious generalities like, "Tomorrow the sun will rise," or "Tonight it's going to be dark." No, these guys were risky. I mean, some were downright scary. Their credentials were not gathered from stuffy, Middle-East graduate schools, nor were they all old men who came up through the ranks and slowly earned the right to be heard.

A prophet was a prophet back then because he passed a very simple (yet exacting) test: Whatever he predicted, that very thing would happen. If he was a phony, it wouldn't. Moses laid down that precept:

> And you may say in your heart, "How shall we know the word which the LORD has not spoken?" When a prophet speaks in the name of the LORD, if the thing does not come about or come true, that is the thing which the LORD has not spoken. The prophet has spoken it presumptuously; you shall not be afraid of him (Deuteronomy 18:21 – 22).

As a prophet, there were only two possible grades he could make on a test — 100 or zero. A straight 'A' report card or he flat out flunked. Worse than that, the fake was stoned by the people (Deuteronomy 13) if he predicted stuff that didn't happen. But if God's hand was on that man . . . if he was indeed Jehovah's throat . . . stand back in fear. His momentum was awesome. And I do mean *awesome!* Every one of them was a summa cum laude graduate of the SCHOOL OF DIVINE PRESENCE. They didn't mess around. They never missed.

Take Isaiah, the brilliant son of Amoz, who passed Moses's test with flying colors. Around 710 B.C., a strong Assyrian army commanded by a vicious king named Sennacherib besieged Jerusalem. Intimidated and paralyzed with fear, the citizens believed the propaganda a fellow named Rabshakeh began to feed them. When good King Hezekiah heard how his people were getting brainwashed, he pled with Isaiah, the prophet, to pray for deliverance. Isaiah did one better. He made some short-range predictions that a rumor would reach King Sennacherib of internal trouble in his kingdom, causing him to return without attacking Jerusalem. You guessed it. That's exactly what happened (Isaiah 37:36 – 38).

The same gifted prophet also predicted that Babylon would completely destroy Judah and haul out all the treasures of the Jews. He even foretold that the surviving sons of the royal family would become eunuchs in the Babylonian palace. A little over 100 years later, guess what? Yep, Isaiah 39:5 – 7 . . . Daniel 1.

Isaiah also predicted invincible Babylon would later be conquered and annihilated by the Medes . . . and that Babylon would never be inhabited again. Only the lonely howl of hyenas would be heard on that day (Isaiah 13:17 – 22). "Preposterous!" some must have screamed. Remember, Babylon (one of the seven wonders) was considered impregnable. In approximately 150 years after God's mouthpiece had spoken, Babylon fell. Daniel 5:1 – 31 says it all.

He even announced that a certain king named Cyrus would see that Jerusalem and her Temple were rebuilt by allowing those who wished to do this work to return to their homeland. Again, right on target . . . Isaiah 44:28 – 45:1 and Ezra 1:1 – 11. It took about 200 years before it occurred, but it did. Isaiah was right on.

Now that's *prophetic momentum,* folks.

So what's the big deal? Well, first of all it means Isaiah was no rookie, carrying out a hit-and-miss pre-game chapel program for a few teams in Israel. And second, when he talked about "a virgin" some day being "with child" and calling his name "Immanuel," it was no fluke. And when he predicted . . .

> For a child will be born to us, a son will be given to us; and the government will rest on His shoulders; and His name will be called Wonderful Counselor, Mighty God, Eternal Father, Prince of Peace (Isaiah 9:6).

. . . everybody *should* have listened, but they didn't.

Most still don't.

But *we* do.

The incredible reached zenith proportions 800 years later (!) in a feeding trough in lowly Bethlehem . . . and the cry from the Infant's throat broke the centuries of silence. For the first time in time, God's voice could actually be heard coming from human vocal cords. Everybody should have believed, but they didn't. Strangely, they must not have realized that prophetic momentum had led to prophetic fulfillment.

Most still don't.

But *we* do. Immanuel has come!

Deepening Your Roots
Ezra 1:1 – 11; Isaiah 44:24 – 45; Luke 1:26 – 38

Branching Out

1. What's something in Scripture that you find hard to believe? Try accepting it, without question, and see what it does for you. _____

_____

2. Try to predict who your next phone call will be from: _____

3. Bethlehem. Look it up on a map and dwell upon the fact that it is the city where Christ was born. Find out something about that city.

THE LONELY TRAIL OF THE GIMPER

You won't find one in the National Wildlife Federation's Manual of Rare Species. But rare it is.

Like the bald eagle, the prairie bison, and the whooping crane, *gimpers* are seldom seen on our landscapes. Occasional sightings, however, have reportedly occurred on college campuses, business offices, rest homes, athletic teams, and among groups of salesmen. Look closely, and you may even run across a few in some churches. In fact, though their appearances are seldom, *gimpers* form the backbone of whatever they're a part of. One of the reasons they're so hard to spot is that they never run in packs. They're loners.

Okay, so what is a gimper, anyway? Plug these clues into your computer program and see if you can come up with a revealing readout:

- In the '76 Summer Olympics, Bruce Jenner was a *gimper.*
- In the six-day war, so was Moshe Dayan.
- As a football strategist, Vince Lombardi qualified.
- A *gimper* of motherhood was Susanna Wesley.
- Donald Barnhouse was a *gimper* preacher.
- As a creative thinker, da Vinci belonged to the club.
- A *gimper* president was Abe Lincoln.
- Thomas Edison was a *gimper* inventor.
- Jim Elliot and Nate Saint were *gimper* missionaries.

And there are others much less famous but equally impressive. You might even have one in your own family and not know it. Jesse's youngest son David was one — but it caught his dad unaware.

Still can't figure it out? Maybe you'd better huddle with Webster for a minute or two. No, scratch that. Don't bother. It isn't there. A few dictionaries include *gimp,* however, which means "spirit, vim, vigor, ambition."

My own first encounter with *gimper* was many years ago in the writing of Dr. M. R. DeHaan. The gravel-voiced, great-hearted teacher of the Radio Bible Class mentioned a gimper as "one who aspired to excel, to be different." A gimper is committed to the core — thoroughly and unequivocally. His roots of dedication result in the rich fruit of determination, excellence, and achievement. Setting their sights high, gimpers drive toward the goal, absorbed in the passion of quality — accomplished at almost any cost.

Now you're getting the picture. Right? Your mind is probably leaping to that graphic Old Testament gimper . . . Jabez. First Chronicles 4:9 – 10 records the compelling prayer of a unique man who refused to be satisfied with an ordinary, brand-x, milk-toast life. You'd never catch Jabez praying, "Dear God, help me to balance my status with my quo. Keep me satisfied in Dullsville, Israel." Not a chance. He pleaded with the Lord to bless him *indeed* . . . to *enlarge* the borders of his perspective . . . and God did just that! It pleased Jehovah to break the predictable mold and launch into society a visionary missile named Jabez.

Did the Lord Jesus make reference to gimpers? No doubt about it. In no uncertain terms He implied how important these rare individuals were to Him when He delivered His immortal Mountain Message. People ask you to go a mile? Be a gimper, go *two*. Others love their friends and hate their enemies? Gimpers love their enemies and pray for their persecutors! And catch this:

> . . . if you greet your brothers only, what do you do more than
> others? (Matthew 5:47).

Read that one again. That's what gimpers ask. It's the first question in the Gimper's Manual: "What do you do *more* than others?"

Dotted through the New Testament are references to *abounding* and *excelling*. Each time I run my finger across one of those power lines, I'm challenged to be a gimper.

We are to be gimper givers (2 Corinthians 8:7).

Our walk is to be a gimper walk (1 Thessalonians 4:1).

We should have a gimper love for others (1 Thessalonians 4:10).

The average Christian rejoices; gimper Christians "rejoice *always*." Most of us pray; gimpers "pray *without ceasing*." It's common to give thanks; gimpers "give thanks *in everything*." The basic believer wants to refrain from evil; gimper believers "abstain from *every form* of evil" (1 Thessalonians 5:15 – 22).

At age twenty-five, Amaziah was crowned king over Jerusalem. At age fifty-four, he died. For twenty-nine years he did right, according to 2 Chronicles 25:1 – 2. That's correct — he did right. Stuck to the rules, made all the necessary appearances, smiled when he was supposed to, and looked dignified when protocol required it. As a king, he did right. But God candidly adds, ". . . yet not with a whole heart." He wasn't *whole-heartedly*, hook-line-and-sinker sold out to righteousness. He got by. He yawned his way through almost three decades of history. He punched in at eight o'clock sharp, took a half hour for lunch and punched out at five. For twenty-nine years. Like the muddy Mississippi, he just kept rolling along.

How different Paul was! In his own words, "steadfast, immovable, always abounding . . ." Unlike the river, he didn't just roll — he *ricocheted!* He didn't just live life — he *attacked* it. Paul made slothful saints about as comfortable as sleeping on a coat hanger. Nobody ever wanted to "gimp" as much as he.

Unless it be thee. Or me.

Wanna race?

Deepening Your Roots

1 Chronicles 4:9 – 10; 1 Corinthians 9:24 – 27; 1 Thessalonians 5:15 – 22

Branching Out

1. In what way do you desire to excel or stand out? What kind of gimper would you like to be? _____
2. Be a gimper today. Love someone who is your enemy and pray for that person.
3. Get someone to take a quiz; ask him to define "gimper." Give him a treat if his answer is anywhere close to the definition.

❧ ❧ ❧

Growing Strong

The countdown is over. Christmas has come and gone. But what about the last few days? Did they leave any lasting impact on you or your family? Whether good or bad, put in writing how this year's Christmas went for you.

_____

_____

_____

_____

NO PLACE FOR PRIDE

Marian Anderson, the black American contralto who deserved and won worldwide acclaim as a concert soloist, didn't simply grow great; she grew great simply. In spite of her fame, she remained the same gracious, approachable lady . . . never one to "put on airs." A beautiful model of humility.

A reporter, while interviewing Miss Anderson, asked her to name the greatest moment in her life. She had had many big moments. The choice seemed difficult to others who were in the room that day. For example:

- There was the night conductor Arturo Toscanini announced, "A voice like hers comes once in a century."
- Furthermore, in 1955 she became the first Negro to sing with the Metropolitan Opera Company in New York.
- The following year her autobiography, *My Lord, What a Morning,* was published . . . a best seller.
- In 1958 she became a United States delegate to the United Nations.
- On several occasions during her illustrious career, she received medals from various countries around the world.
- Then there was that memorable time she gave a private concert at the White House for the Roosevelts and the King and Queen of England.
- Her home town, Philadelphia, had, on one occasion, awarded her the $10,000 Bok Award as the person who had done the most for that city.
- And in 1963 she was awarded the coveted Presidential Medal of Freedom.
- To top it all, there was that Easter Sunday in Washington D.C. when she stood beneath the Lincoln statue and sang for a crowd of 75,000, which included Cabinet members, Supreme Court Justices, and most members of Congress.

Which of those big moments did she choose? *None of them.* Miss Anderson quietly told the reporter that the greatest moment of her life was the day she went home and told her mother she wouldn't have to take in washing anymore.

Some folks go to great lengths to hide their humble origins. We often think we should mask the truth of our past lest people think less of us — especially if our today is much more respectable than our yesterday. But the truth is, when we peel off our masks, others are usually not repelled; they are drawn closer to us. And frequently, the more painful or embarrassing the past, the *greater* are others' appreciation and respect. Marian Anderson's candid remark simply increases our admiration of her.

A while back I learned that a man I have known for quite some time had suffered an emotional breakdown earlier in his life. He had been hospitalized. He went through great struggles getting back on his feet. When that news reached me, I immediately felt a compelling urge to embrace him, to express a profound and renewed respect for the man. But to him it represented a spot on his record, a scar too ugly to expose.

The prophet Isaiah mentions this very thing as he reminds us to:

> . . . Look to the rock from which you were hewn, and to the quarry from which you were dug (51:1).

That sounds much more noble and respectable than its literal meaning. The word "quarry" actually refers to "a hole" in the Hebrew text. The old King James Version doesn't miss it far: "the hole of the pit from which ye are digged." Never forget "the hole of the pit."

What excellent advice! Before we get all enamored with our high-and-mighty importance, it's a good idea to take a backward glance at the "hole of the pit" from which Christ lifted us. And let's not just *think* about it; let's admit it. It has a way of keeping us all on the same level — recipients of grace. And don't kid yourself, even those who are extolled and admired have "holes" from which they were dug.

With Moses it was murder.
With Elijah it was deep depression.
With Peter it was public denial.
With Samson it was recurring lust.
With Thomas it was cynical doubting.
With Jacob it was deception.
With Rahab it was prostitution.
With Jephthah it was his illegitimate birth.

Not even that bold body of reformers had lily-white pasts. Why, some of them had crawled out of the deepest, dirtiest, most scandalous "holes" you could imagine. And it was *that* which kept them humble, honest men . . . unwilling to be glorified or idolized. As they took Isaiah's advice and looked at "the hole of the pit," they found no place whatsoever for pride.

Marian Anderson never forgot that her roots reached back into poverty. No amount of public acclaim ever caused her to forget that her mama took in washing to put food in little Marian's tummy. I have the feeling that every time she started to entertain exaggerated ideas of her own importance, a quick backward glance at her humble beginnings was all it took. And the best part of all was that she didn't hide it.

The next time we're tempted to believe our own stuff, let's just look back to the pit from which we were dug. It has a way of shooting holes in our pride.

Deepening Your Roots

Exodus 2; Judges 11 and 12; Mark 14:27 – 31, 66 – 72

Branching Out

1. In one word, describe your days/years as a child: _____
   What value/contribution have those years made as to who you are today?

   _____

   _____

2. Admit something from your "quarry" to a dear friend.
3. If a reporter asked you: "What was the greatest moment in your life?" what would be your answer? _____

   _____

ᴅEPRESSION

The smoky tones of Peggy Lee's voice occasionally blow across my mind like a sea breeze over a dry, sun-washed beach:

Is that all . . . is that all there is . . .?

With no bitterness intended, I ask that haunting question in the backwash of certain situations — and so do most of you. How much like the tide we are! When our spirits are high, we are flooded with optimism, hope, and pleasant expectations. But when low, with our jagged barnacles of disappointment and discouragement exposed, we entertain feelings of raw disillusionment. We usually hide the plunging inner tideline from others, protecting ourselves with a thick coat of public image shined to a high-gloss finish with the wax of superficiality . . . embellished with a religious cliché or two. But all the while, at ebb tide within, cold winds blow across the empty, empty sand.

Now if you're the type who *honestly and truly* never gets low — never feels the oppressive pang of periodic depression (I'm sure there are a few), then you'll not understand my paintings or choice of frames. But if you're like me, you'll need no guide to help you through this gallery where shadows cast their debilitating aura.

There are peculiar low tides that often follow a great victory.

Is that all . . . is that all there is to victory?

Elijah asked that. Fresh off a stunning victory at Carmel, the prophet became vulnerable and frightened. Alone under the gnarled limbs of a twisted juniper tree, he cried out to God — not in spontaneous praise but overwhelmed with self-pity. Elijah suffered the low tide that often follows victory.

Then there are special low tides that accompany great vision.

Is that all . . . is that all there is to vision?

Paul asked that. Having taken gigantic strides into the vast regions of Asia and having forged out an impeccable theology that was to serve the church for centuries — the apostle was caught at low tide. He freely admits this in his second letter to friends at Corinth:

> We do not want you to be uninformed, brothers, about the hardships we suffered in the province of Asia. We were under

great pressure, far beyond our ability to endure, so that we despaired even of life (2 Corinthians 1:8, NIV).

While in the heights of accomplishing a vast encompassing vision, Paul tripped and fell into a deep well of sudden despair. Weary, lonely, and emotionally drained, the seasoned apostle hit bottom. Low tide occasionally accompanies vision, a malady not limited to century-one saints.

And there are those low tides that attach themselves to great valor.

Is that all . . . is that all there is to valor?

David asked that. He had killed a giant and married a princess. He was a fierce and resourceful front-line fighter but found himself the target of his own king's spear. Although a proven and dedicated warrior, unmatched in Israel's ranks for bravery, he was forced to flee. This sent him reeling, appearing insane before the king of Gath. The once-exalted man of valor now "scribbled on the doors of the gate, and let his saliva run down into his beard" (1 Samuel 21:13). David had wrestled with bears, tackled sinewy lions, and leveled a 9-foot-9 Philistine . . . but was now rendered helpless by a low tide. All his valor seemed only a cheap, empty dream.

Low tide . . . how painful *yet how essential.* Without it the changing ocean becomes a predictable, boring body of water with no mysterious marriage to the moon, lacking its romantic, magnetic appeal. Without it there would be no need for Elishas to minister to anguished Elijahs . . . no need for visionaries to fall in dependence on their faces before God . . . no need for the valiant to be reminded of their source of strength.

Is that all . . . is that all there is to low tides?

No, there is more, much more, most of which can never be described . . . only discovered.

Deepening Your Roots
1 Kings 19:1 – 7; 2 Corinthians 1:1 – 11, 4:1 – 18

Branching Out

1. Console someone today (by phone or in person) who is having a low-tide season. Care for him in a loving way, maybe just by filling up his lonely evening, bringing flowers or uplifting music, or taking him out for a surprise dinner.
2. Be prepared for your low-tide moments. Look at your upcoming commitments and anticipate ahead of time when you might feel "down."
3. Read more about depression so you can better understand it and perhaps help someone who may be experiencing one of life's deepest struggles.

FINISHING THE COURSE

Not enough is said or written today about *finishing* well.

Lots and lots of material is available on motivation to get started and creative ways to spark initiative. Plenty of advice is floating around on setting goals and establishing priorities and developing a game plan. All of it is insightful and needed. Getting off the dime is often a herculean task. Starting well is Plan "A," no doubt about it.

But let's hear it for the opposite end for a change. Let's extol the virtues of sticking with something until it's *done*. Of hanging tough when the excitement and fun fade into discipline and guts. You know, being just as determined eight minutes into the fourth quarter as at the kickoff. Not losing heart even though the project has lost its appeal. In his fine book, *A Long Obedience in the Same Direction,* Eugene Peterson expresses the same concern with these insightful words:

> Our attention spans have been conditioned by thirty-second commercials. Our sense of reality has been flattened by thirty-page abridgments.
>
> It is not difficult in such a world to get a person interested in the message of the gospel; it is terrifically difficult to sustain the interest. Millions of people in our culture make decisions for Christ, but there is a dreadful attrition rate . . . In our kind of culture anything, even news about God, can be sold if it is packaged freshly; but when it loses its novelty, it goes on the garbage heap. There is a great market for religious experience in our world; there is little enthusiasm for the patient acquisition of virtue, little inclination to sign up for a long apprenticeship in what earlier generations of Christians called holiness.

I fear our generation has come dangerously near the "I'm-getting-tired-so-let's-just-quit" mentality. And not just in the spiritual realm. Dieting is a discipline, so we stay fat. Finishing school is a hassle, so we bail out. Cultivating a close relationship is painful, so we back off. Getting a book written is demanding, so we stop short. Working through conflicts in a marriage is a tiring struggle, so we walk away. Sticking with an occupation is tough, so we start looking elsewhere. This reminds me of something my sister passed along to me, entitled *Six Phases of a Project:*

- Enthusiasm
  - Disillusionment
    - Panic
      - Search for the guilty
        - Punishment of the innocent
          - Praise and honors for the nonparticipants.

By the time a project has run its crazy course, confusion has replaced accomplishment. Participants have changed to spectators. The "let's-just-quit" mentality is upon us.

Ignace Jan Paderewski, the famous composer-pianist, was scheduled to perform at a great concert hall in America. It was an evening to remember — black tuxedos and long evening dresses, a high-society extravaganza. Present in the audience that evening was a mother with her fidgety nine-year-old son. Weary of waiting, he squirmed constantly in his seat. His mother was in hopes that her boy would be encouraged to practice the piano if he could just hear the immortal Paderewski at the keyboard. So — against his wishes — he had come.

As she turned to talk with friends, her son could stay seated no longer. He slipped away from her side, strangely drawn to the ebony concert grand Steinway and its leather tufted stool on the huge stage flooded with blinding lights. Without much notice from the sophisticated audience, the boy sat down at the stool, staring wide-eyed at the black and white keys. He placed his small, trembling fingers in the right location and began to play "chopsticks." The roar of the crowd was hushed as hundreds of frowning faces turned in his direction. Irritated and embarrassed, they began to shout:

> *"Get that boy away from there!"*
> *"Who'd bring a kid that young in here?"*
> *"Where's his mother?"*
> *"Somebody stop him!"*

Backstage, the master overheard the sounds out front and quickly put together in his mind what was happening. Hurriedly, he grabbed his coat and rushed toward the stage. Without one word of announcement he stooped over behind the boy, reached around both sides, and began to improvise a countermelody to harmonize with and enhance "chopsticks." As the two of them played together, Paderewski kept whispering in the boy's ear:

> *Keep going. Don't quit, son. Keep on playing . . . don't stop . . . don't quit.*

And so it is with us. We hammer away on our project, which seems about as significant as "chopsticks" in a concert hall. And about the time we are ready to give it up, along comes the Master, who leans over and whispers:

> *Now keep going; don't quit. Keep on . . . don't stop; don't quit,*

as He improvises on our behalf, providing just the right touch at just the right moment.

Do I write today to a few weary pilgrims? Is the road getting long and hope wearing a little thin? Or to a few parents who are beginning to wonder if it's worth it all — this exacting business of rearing children, which includes cleaning up daily messes and living with all that responsibility? Or to you who have a dream, but seeing it accomplished seems too long to wait? Listen to the Master's whispering:

> Let us not lose heart in doing good, for in due time we shall reap if we do not grow weary (Galatians 6:9).

> Therefore . . . be steadfast, immovable . . . your toil is not in vain in the Lord (1 Corinthians 15:58).

> Be of sober spirit, be on the alert . . . . And after you have suffered for a little while, the God of all grace . . . will Himself perfect, confirm, strengthen and establish you (1 Peter 5:8, 10).

So many start the Christian life like a lightning flash — hot, fast, and dazzling. But how many people (aged sixty and over) can you name who are finishing the course with sustained enthusiasm and vigor? Oh, there are some, I realize, *but why so few?* What happens along the way that swells the ranks of quitters? I really wish I knew that answer. If I did, I'd shout warnings from the pulpit Sunday after Sunday. No, better than that,

I'd stoop over and whisper them to every discouraged person I meet. Before it's too late . . . before he quits, and, instead of mastering the *Minuet* or *Concerto in A Minor,* settles for "chopsticks."

Deepening Your Roots
Nehemiah 2:17 – 20, 6:15 – 16; Galatians 6:7 – 10

Branching Out

1. Go back and finish something you quit too soon.
2. Next time you see a piano, play chopsticks and tell the story above to someone nearby. Encourage the individual to finish an undone project or to keep at something he's engaged in.
3. Make a list of projects you are working on. Post it where you will see it each day. Check off each project you finish. When all projects are done, reward yourself with an evening of fun. Take a friend to help celebrate.

❧ ❧ ❧

Growing Strong

We've come to the close of another week . . . and another year. But what a feeling to know you're getting stronger and growing tall in God! Who wants to stay the same? I sure don't. Ready for a new year, more of this book, and a heart and body that are improving with age? Tell me why . . .

_____

_____

_____

_____

THOROUGHNESS

I have just taken my Webster's Dictionary off the shelf and looked up "thorough." He says it means "carried through to completion, careful about detail, complete in all respects."

That's convicting! Few indeed are the people who finish what they start — and do a complete job of it. Now I'm not referring to a neurotic fanaticism of extreme, unpractical, and unbalanced pre-occupation with only the details. Not the trees-in-the-forest syndrome. I'm talking about the rare but beautiful experience of carrying out a responsibility to its completion. I'll name a few:

1. *A course at school.* Doing the very best you can to the peak of your performance capacity — for the sheer joy of total fulfillment.

2. *A project at home.* Mapping out a plan, then tackling the task with abandoned energy, dedicated to the goal of "doing the job right."

3. *In occupation.* The fine art of *working* is a lost art today — really getting in there and studying the job, reading and expanding your knowledge. Becoming an expert in your field — for the simple delight of accomplishment!

4. *Everyday duties.* Is there the telltale sign "unfinished" written across your housework ladies? Is your trademark "mañana," or the cliché, "someday, I'll have to get that done?"

Why not dig right in and refuse to give up until that task is *done?* Why not tighten your belt a notch and wade into that unpleasant job with renewed determination to write "finished" over it?

There is a verse in Proverbs that is commonly quoted around the Swindoll house when we *really* finish a job like it should be done.

Desire accomplished is sweet to the soul (Proverbs 13:19a, KJV).

When you have accomplished or thoroughly fulfilled a task, there is a feeling of satisfaction that cannot be expressed in words.

Listen to another Proverb:

> The soul of the sluggard craves and gets nothing, but the soul of the diligent is made fat (13:4).

The sluggard longingly craves but because he is "allergic to work," he gets nothing in return! (Proverbs 20:4 makes this clear.)

So what are you waiting for? Does it need painting? Paint it — and do a thorough job! Does it need cleaning? Clean it — thoroughly! Does it need ironing? Iron it — wrinkle free, with gusto! Does it need attention? Give it thorough, unrestrained attention! Stop being satisfied with a half-hearted, incomplete job! Stun those around you with a thorough, finished product! AND STOP PUTTING IT OFF! As a music teacher of mine used to say when I'd stare in disbelief at the difficulty of a piece before me, "Attack it, boy!"

I close with a simple reminder. *The difference between something good and something great is attention to detail.*

That's true of a delicious meal, a musical production, a play, a new automobile, a well-kept home, a church, our attire, a business, a lovely garden, a sermon, a teacher, a well-disciplined family.

Let's launch into the remainder of this week with an intense interest in quality control. Let's move out of thick ranks of the mediocre . . . and join the thin ranks of excellence.

Deepening Your Roots

Genesis 2:2 – 3:15, 31:38 – 42; Colossians 3:22 – 25

Branching Out

1. What are three projects you've put off for a long time?

    1. _____

    2. _____

    3. _____

    Select one to accomplish this week.

2. Help a friend by offering to assist him in finishing a task.

3. Read at least one chapter of a book this week that relates to your job and would enhance your knowledge and productivity.

MEMORIZING SCRIPTURE

I know of no other single practice in the Christian life more rewarding, practically speaking, than memorizing Scripture. That's right. No other single discipline is more useful and rewarding than this. No other single exercise pays greater spiritual dividends! Your *prayer life* will be strengthened. Your *witnessing* will be sharper and much more effective. Your *counseling* will be in demand. Your *attitudes* and *outlook* will begin to change. Your *mind* will become alert and observant. Your *confidence* and *assurance* will be enhanced. Your *faith* will be solidified.

God's Word is filled with exhortations to implant His truth in our hearts. David says that a young man can keep his life pure by treasuring God's Word in his heart (Psalm 37:31; 119:9 – 11). Solomon refers to this in Proverbs 4:4:

> . . . let your heart hold fast my words; keep my command-
> ments and live.

The words "hold fast" come from a single Hebrew term, meaning "to grasp, seize, lay hold of." Scripture memory gives you a firm grasp of the Word — and allows the Word to get a firm grasp of *you!* Solomon also mentions writing the Word "on the tablet of your heart" (Proverbs 7:3) and having Scriptures kept within you so "they may be ready on your lips" (Proverbs 22:18).

Now, I know you've been challenged to do this before. But is it happening? Perhaps you have procrastinated because you have mental blocks against it. Maybe you tried, but you either did not see the value or could not get beyond the method that was demanded by some memory program — little cards, booklets, check-up techniques, hearers, etc. Perhaps that seemed elementary and insulted your intelligence. I understand.

Okay . . . forget the methods . . . but don't throw the baby out with the bath water. Take your Bible, turn to a passage that's been especially helpful . . . and commit that passage to memory — all on your own. Don't learn just isolated verses here and there. Bite off whole *chunks* of Scripture. That way you can get the flow of thought God had in mind.

Here are seven things I have found helpful:

1. Choose a time when your mind is free from outside distractions . . . perhaps soon after getting up in the morning.

2. Learn the reference by repeating it every time you say the verse(s). Numbers are more difficult to remember than words.

3. Read each verse through several times — both in a whisper and aloud. Hearing yourself say the words helps cement them into your mind.

4. Break the passage into its natural phrases. Learn the reference and then the first phrase. Then repeat the reference and first phrase as you go to the second phrase. Continue adding phrases one by one.

5. Learn a little bit *perfectly* rather than a great deal *poorly.* Do not go on to the next verse until you can say the previous one(s) perfectly, without a glance at your Bible.

6. Review the verse(s) immediately after you have gone through this process. Twenty to thirty minutes later, repeat what you've memorized. Before the day has ended, firmly fix the verse(s) in your mind by going over it fifteen to twenty times. (You can do this as you drive or do your job.)

7. Use the verse(s) orally as soon as possible. After all, the purpose of Scripture memory is a practical one, not academic. Use the verses in conversation, in correspondence, in teaching, in counseling, in everyday opportunities. Relate what you've learned to your daily situation. You'll be thrilled with the results.

Deepening Your Roots
Psalm 37:30 – 31, 119:9 – 16; Matthew 4:1 – 10

Branching Out

1. Try to memorize three verses (or one paragraph) of Scripture that you like.
2. Write out the verses you chose on a 3×5 card and post it on your bathroom mirror. Read these verses (aloud) each time your eye catches a glimpse of the card.
3. Once you've learned your verses, ask a friend who knows how to do calligraphy (fancy writing) to pen them for you. If you have the money, have the piece framed to mark this important event in your life: the day you learned an entire passage of God's Word.

HABITS

I used to bite my fingernails right down to the quick. I'd rip off those babies just as soon as the first signs of new growth would appear. For well over twenty years I carried around ten ugly stumps which resulted in two miserable experiences:

Personal embarrassment. I was always afraid of such things as "clean hands inspection" at school and summer camps. And doctor's exams where the man would look down and groan at my mitts.

Physical limitations. If I ever dropped a dime — *forget it!* The same for trying to pick up a tooth-pick, pluck out splinters, or put in tiny screws. My mom tried all sorts of gimmicks to make me stop: money bribes, red-hot-burn-your-mouth-stuff painted on my nails, wearing gloves day and night, public embarrassment and private reminders. But nothing worked, and I mean *nothing.* I'd go right on and bite them off until they'd bleed. I remember having dates and keeping my hands in my pockets the whole time so the girl wouldn't notice. I avoided card games, skipped piano lessons, refused to try on rings and stayed away from hand-craft projects. How I hated that habit! I wanted so badly to stop I would stay awake at night thinking about it. But the simple fact was *I couldn't.* In spite of the pain and the pressure, that habit, like all habits, had me in its grip.

As the American educator, Horace Mann, once described the predicament:

> Habit is a cable: we weave a thread of it every day, and at last
> we cannot break it.

But God began to convict me about my nail-nibbling ways. It took Him nearly a decade to bring about a final and complete victory, ashamed as I am to admit it. During the process He gently, yet pointedly, caused me to see that this was an area of my life much deeper than eight fingers and a couple of thumbs. I was being enslaved — mastered and manipulated by the beast of habit. I was a living contradiction to the liberating truth of 1 Corinthians 6:12:

> All things are lawful for me, but not all things are profitable. All
> things are lawful for me, but I will not be mastered by anything.

You can't believe the fire of conviction this verse once set ablaze within me. The Greek word translated "mastered" means "to be held under the authority of something." A close look reveals that this isn't a verse talking about something lawless or wicked, but something that is actually *lawful . . . but not profitable.* My first encounter with the verse was not my final encounter with this painful habit. But it was certainly a turning point toward change, thank God.

The backwash of this nail-biting testimony has far-reaching effects. Not a person who reads this book is completely free from bad habits, whether lawless or lawful. That's the price we pay for being human. Some are wrestling with a habit as accepted and common as overeating or exaggerating or cheating or procrastinating. Others, by habit, are negative and suspicious, resulting in habitually closed minded responses. While some are ungrateful and demanding, others are continually extravagant and undiscerning.

Some of you feel trapped by overt dependence on alcohol consumption, addition to drugs, cravings for nicotine and caffeine, the lure of sensual lust, or a pill for every ill. Habits like gossip, worry, irritability and profanity are often practiced without guilt, justified through cleverly devised mental schemes.

The list is endless, for habits are as numerous as every detail of life. Rather than enlarging the list, let's focus on five suggestions that will help us blend 1 Corinthians 6:12 into our lives.

Stop rationalizing. Refuse to make comments like: "Oh, that's just me. I'm just like that — always have been, always will be. After all, nobody's perfect." Such excuses take the edge off disobedience and encourage you to diminish or completely ignore the Spirit's work of conviction.

Apply strategy. Approach your target with a rifle, not a shotgun. Take on each habit one at a time, not all at once.

Be realistic. It won't happen fast. It won't be easy. Nor will your resolve be permanent overnight. Periodic failures, however, are still better than habitual slavery.

Be encouraged. Realize you're on the road to ultimate triumph . . . for the first time in years! Enthusiasm strengthens self-discipline and prompts an attitude of stick-to-itiveness.

Start today. This is the very best moment thus far in your life. To put it off is an admission of defeat and will only intensify and prolong the self-confidence battle.

Extracting the hurtful thorns of habit enables the pilgrim to focus less attention on himself and more attention on the One who is worthy. And the most exciting thought of all is that He will be right there in the morning ready to help you through the day with all the power you will need, one moment at a time.

Need proof? How about ten fingernails and an emery board?

Deepening Your Roots
Matthew 6:24; 1 Corinthians 6; Hebrews 10:19 – 25

Branching Out

1. Name three habits you'd like to get rid of:

   1. _____

   2. _____

   3. _____

   Choose one and start applying the five steps mentioned in today's article.

2. Make yourself accountable to someone and tell him the habit you want to leave behind you. Ask that person to call you daily to see how you're doing and to encourage you.

3. Write down ten reasons why you should stop your habit, and ten benefits if you do stop. Post these reasons and benefits in a conspicuous place to encourage you throughout the week.

ℤ ℤ ℤ

Growing Strong

I know, you're probably feeling I've come down hard on you! I understand. But why not start the new year off by wrestling with some tough topics or habits? And speaking of habits . . . what are you working on to overcome? Making headway? I knew you could do it!

_____

_____

_____

_____

MONDAY MORNING PULPITS

*T*wo things bother me a lot when the subject of Christians and their work is mentioned. First, how few are genuinely happy in their jobs. Second, how frequently I hear about Christians who are poor workers on their jobs. Some employers have even told me that they prefer to *not* hire Christians. Wow . . . That's quite an indictment! As I probe for reasons, here's what is said. These are actual statements I've heard:

> They tend to be presumptuous — they take advantage of a Christian boss. . . .

> It's the old problem of attitude. I find them negative, critical, and resistant to change. . . .

> Incompetence. It seems to me that the last several I've hired simply could not (or *would* not) do the job. . . .

> They are often preoccupied with other things — witnessing, church, whatever. . . .

> Frankly . . . I can't trust them when I'm not around. The last one I hired was just plain dishonest. . . .

Okay, so these may be the exceptions . . . so this represents a very small minority. I'm *still* bothered. For every "exception" there's a host of offenses and a lot of hard feelings created. A minority apple can still spoil a majority barrel . . . if it's rotten. Show me a lazy, irritating Christian on the job and I'll show you an office or store or customer or shop that isn't interested in his message. Like it or not, the world watches us with the scrutiny of a sea gull peering at a shrimp in shallow water. The believer at work is under constant surveillance. That's our number one occupational hazard. And when we speak of our Savior and the life He offers, everything we say is filtered through that which has been observed by others.

The very best platform upon which we may build a case for Christianity at work rests on six massive pillars: integrity, faithfulness, punctuality, quality workmanship, a pleasant attitude, and enthusiasm. Hire such a person and it will only be a matter of time before business will improve . . . people will be impressed . . . and Christianity will begin to seem important.

Scripture for that? Sure. How about 1 Corinthians 10:31:

> Whether, then, you eat or drink or whatever you do, do all to the glory of God.

or Colossians 3:17:

> And whatever you do in word or deed, do all in the name of the Lord Jesus, giving thanks through Him to God the Father.

or Matthew 5:16:

> Let your light shine before men in such a way that they may see your good works, and glorify your Father who is in heaven.

or a whole bunch in James's letter that say, in effect, genuine faith is validated by solid works. Right belief and right behavior go hand in hand.

It will help you do a super job if you will remember that there's no sacred-secular distinction supported in Scripture. Titus 1:15 says:

> To the pure, all things are pure. . . .

That means your Monday-through-Friday employment is pure, it's *sacred* — just as sacred as your Sunday activities. To the Christian all of life is sacred! Paul wasn't writing only to preachers when he expressed these immortal words:

> I, therefore . . . entreat you to walk in a manner worthy of the calling with which you have been called (Ephesians 4:1).

At a Bible conference for laymen this very point was emphasized again and again. Each individual was made aware that he or she was called by God into a profession or work. Regardless of the employment it was "sacred," it was God's calling. At the close of the conference one was asked, "Say, Tom what's your job?" With wisdom he answered, "I'm an ordained plumber."

Christian friend, your work is your calling . . . it's your *ordained* responsibility . . . it's your pulpit. Say, how's the ministry coming along?

Deepening Your Roots

1 Thessalonians 4:11 – 12; 2 Thessalonians 3:6 – 13; James 1:14 – 24

Branching Out

1. Listen to your speech today and watch to see if you complain a little or a lot. Ask someone what he thinks of your attitude.

2. Rate yourself in each of these areas; then take your weakest area and try to improve it:

   ☐ integrity   ☐ punctuality   ☐ faithfulness
   ☐ attitude   ☐ productivity   ☐ enthusiasm

DIALOGUES OF THE DEAF

"It is impossible to overemphasize the immense need humans have to be really listened to, to be taken seriously, to be understood. No one can develop freely in this world and find a full life without feeling understood by at least one other person . . . .

"Listen to the conversations of our world, between nations as well as those between couples. They are for the most part dialogues of the deaf."

So wrote Dr. Paul Tournier, the eminent Swiss psychiatrist and author. His words convict me. They usually do . . . but *these* especially. Because they probe at an area of weakness in my own life. Not a glaring weakness; a subtle one. One that I'm able to hide from most folks because I'm often the one who's expected to talk. But some time ago it began to dawn on me that I needed to cultivate a discipline far more difficult than talking . . . and one that required an exceptional amount of skill.

Listening.

I don't mean just hearing. Not simply smiling and nodding while somebody's mouth is moving. Not merely staying quiet until it's "your turn" to say something. All of us are good at that game—cultivated in the grocery store, local laundromat, or on the front steps of the church building.

Dialogues of the deaf! Sounds come from voice boxes; guttural noises are shaped into words by tongues and lips. But so little is listened to—I mean *really* taken in. As Samuel Butler once stated: "It takes two people to say a thing—a sayer and a sayee. The one is just as essential to any true saying as the other."[2]

Illustration: *Children.* They express their feelings. Deep down in their fragile, inner wells are a multitude of needs, questions, hurts, and longings. Like a tiny bucket, their tongues splash out these things. The busy, insensitive, preoccupied parent, steamrolling through the day, misses many a cue and sails right past choice moments never to be repeated.

Or how about the person we spot without Christ? Have you ever practiced *listening evangelism?* Unless we're careful we usually unload the goods and go for the scalp. But people bruise easily. Sometimes irreparably. We must take care not to fold, spindle, mutilate, or assault! Sure, the gospel must ultimately be shared, but taking the time to listen patiently and respond calmly is an essential part of the process. I nodded with agreement when I read the admonishment of a rough and ready tycoon as he began the meeting with: "Now listen slowly!"

Check out Christ with the woman at the well (John 4). He could have blown her away with an endless barrage of verbal artillery. He didn't. He genuinely listened when she spoke; He "listened slowly." He read the lines of anxiety on her face and felt the weight of guilt in her heart. As she talked, He peered deeply into the well of her soul. It wasn't long before she found herself completely open, yet not once did she feel forced or needlessly embarrassed. His secret? He listened. He studied every word, each expression. Even the tone of her voice.

What does it take? Several things. Rare qualities. Like caring. Time. Unselfishness. Concentration. Holding the other person in high esteem. Sensitivity. Tolerance. Patience. Self-control. And — perhaps most of all — allowing room for silence while the other person is thinking and trying to get the words out. Wise is the listener who doesn't feel compelled to fill up all the blank spaces with verbiage.

Solomon said it clearly in Proverbs 20:12:

> The hearing ear and the seeing eye, The LORD has made both
> of them.

Two ears. Two eyes. Only one mouth. Maybe that should tell us something. I challenge you to join me in becoming a better listener. With your mate. Your friends. Your kids. Your boss. Your teacher. Your pupils. Your clients. Your fellow Christians as well as those who need to meet Christ.

If those who battle with blindness need Seeing Eye Dogs, we can be certain that those who struggle through dialogues of the deaf need Hearing Ear friends.

Deepening Your Roots

Leviticus 26:14, 18, 21, 27, 40 – 46; Luke 8:4 – 18; John 4:1 – 26; James 1:19

Branching Out

1. Force yourself to be quiet in a meeting today and practice careful listening.
2. Take your spouse, or friend, or child out for a special treat and (without telling them) get them to talk. You listen.

ADMIRATION

An usher met me as I was leaving the church several Sundays ago. He had been involved in counting the morning offering. He smiled as he walked up to me, stuck out his hand, and said, "I've got something for you. It came in the offering."

Here was a little hand-scribbled note from a child who had been in our worship service. It read:

TO PASTER CHUCK SWINDOL

I don't think you know me, but I shure know you. You are a very good speeker for Jesus Christ, I think your neet.

I even understand what you are saying and that's how it should be.

I LOVE YOU!

Guess what was attached to the note. A chocolate sucker, all wrapped in cellophane ready to be enjoyed.

Now friend, that's admiration. When a darling little kid will surrender his prized possession . . . wow! That sucker means more to me than most any honor I could ever receive, because it represents something no amount of money can buy. A child's respect. Personal admiration. To some busy, active youngster tucked away in our vast congregation, I represent somebody he or she looks up to. And believes in.

I'm honest, it chokes me up. It also keeps me on my toes. Somewhere out there is a child whose eyes are on me . . . whose ears are tuned in . . . who's also pretty choosy. After all, that sucker was wrapped in cellophane and tied with ribbon . . . and it hadn't even been licked (so far as I could tell).

Admiration. There's not much of it today. Maybe that explains the inordinate hunger for fantasy heroes like Batman, Superman, Luke Skywalker, E.T., and Rocky. There has never been a day when the athletic prima donnas have had larger fan clubs or bizarre musical groups bigger crowds. There was a time when patriotism provided us with all the models we needed. Remember? Why, who ever had the audacity to suggest a hint of suspicion against MacArthur . . . or "Ike" . . . or the local police department, or the *FBI,* for that matter? The cop on the corner may have been stared at, but it was out of respect, not rebellion. Physicians were also admired. So were teachers. And lawyers. And preachers. And hard workers. And mothers.

What's happened? Why the low regard for leaders? Especially the outspoken ones who stand for decency and integrity and love for the country, the flag, human dignity, and a wholesome respect for the family.

Have recent political scandals raped everyone's trust in anyone? Are all police officers suspect? Is it necessary for every surgeon to conduct his profession more concerned about a malpractice lawsuit than the gall bladder operation? Is corruption now so prevalent in government that young men and women with integrity no longer consider political science a viable major? Has the Vietnam thing soured everybody against the military? I mean, where are the heroes?

Hymn-writer Isaac Watts's question should be changed from, "Are there no foes for me to face?" to "Are there no models for me to follow?" And it would be a right-on query. Foes to face we have. Models to admire, we don't. At least it seems that way. Now we are like the best-sellers — *Looking Out for No. 1* and *Pulling Your Own Strings.*

Funny thing, when you write stuff like this, you feel a little dated. . . . Somewhat soap boxish. You sense there's a whole gang of quasi-sophisticates thinking, "There's the old *Marine* coming out in Swindoll again. Shades of Guadalcanal gung-ho . . . Americanism on parade." Well, if a confession will help, I openly admit I still get a chill down my spine when they play our national anthem at the Olympics. I also confess getting a little misty when I recall standing at ramrod attention saying the pledge of allegiance as a barefoot fourth-grader at Southmayd Elementary . . . then praying for a crippled president I had never seen, but admired more than words could say.

Our cynical, self-centered society would do well to restore an invaluable antique that has been cast aside, forgotten like a dust-covered treasure: admiration. As that restoration occurs, so will the *esprit de corps* of our nation, the morale that once gave us pride to pull together and passion to stand alone. Our children need it. So do our youth, as well as adults. Individuals we hold in high esteem, in whom the qualities of greatness are incarnated. People who mirror the bedrock principle of solid Christian character. Those things can neither be purchased nor inherited. Slowly, almost unawares, admiration becomes the carbon paper that transfers character qualities by the rubbing of one life against another.

Like Christ with His guys. Like a godly coach with the team. Like an authentic Christian businessman with his peers. Like a faithful dad with his family. Usually the model doesn't even consider himself such until something little happens.

Something as little as a chocolate sucker in the church offering plate on Sunday morning.

Deepening Your Roots
John 13:1 – 17; 1 Corinthians 10:23 – 11:1; Titus 2:1 – 8

Branching Out

1. Think of a person you look to for advice and then jot down one to three ways he or she provided a model for you.

   1. _____
   2. _____
   3. _____

2. Send a note and special gift (how about a chocolate sucker!) to someone who has impacted your life. Encourage him today. He just may be wondering if he has ever influenced anyone.

℞ ℞ ℞

Growing Strong

Hey, I'm really interested in this past week and what you learned from that person you "listened" to. Feeling more sensitive these days and aware of people's voices? That's a sign of growing stronger! So that you don't forget what you learned this week, write out something you gained from one of your Branching Out assignments.

_____

_____

_____

_____

LOVE WITHOUT A NET

Anne Morrow was shy and delicate. Butterfly-like.

Not dull or stupid or incompetent, just a quiet specimen of timidity. Her dad was ambassador to Mexico when she met an adventurous young fellow who visited south of the border for the U.S. State Department. The man was flying from place to place promoting aviation. Everywhere he went he drew capacity crowds. You see, he had just won $40,000 for being the first to cross the Atlantic by air. The strong pilot and the shy princess fell deeply in love.

When she became Mrs. Charles Lindbergh, Anne could have easily been eclipsed by her husband's shadow. She wasn't, however. The love that bound the two together for the next forty-seven years was tough love, mature love, tested by triumph and tragedy alike. They would never know the quiet comfort of being an anonymous couple in a crowd. The Lindbergh name didn't allow that luxury. Her man, no matter where he went, was news, forever in the limelight . . . clearly a national hero. But rather than becoming a resentful recluse or another nameless face in a crowd of admirers, Anne Morrow Lindbergh emerged to become one of America's most popular authors, a woman highly admired for her own accomplishments.

How? Let's let her give us the clue to the success of her career.

> To be deeply in love is, of course, a great liberating force and the most common experience that frees. . . . Ideally, both members of a couple in love free each other to new and different worlds. I was no exception to the general rule. The sheer fact of finding myself loved was unbelievable and changed my world, my feelings about life and myself. I was given confidence, strength, and almost a new character. The man I was to marry believed in me and what I could do, and consequently I found I could do more than I realized.

Charles did believe in Anne to an extraordinary degree. He saw beneath her shy surface. He realized that down in her innermost well was a wealth of wisdom, a deep, profound, untapped reservoir of ability.

Within the security of his love she was freed — *released* — to discover and develop her own capacity, to get in touch with her own feelings, to cultivate her own skills, and to emerge from that cocoon of shyness a beautiful, ever-delicate butterfly whose presence would enhance many lives far beyond the perimeter of her husband's shadow. He encouraged her to do her own kind of flying and he admired her for it.

Does that imply she was a wild, determined, independent wife, bent on "doing her own thing," regardless? Am I leaving that impression? If so, I'm not communicating clearly. Such would be an inaccurate pen portrait of Anne Morrow Lindbergh. She was a butterfly, remember . . . not a hawk.

Make no mistake about it, this lady was inseparably linked in love to her man. In fact, it was within the comfort of his love that she gleaned the confidence to reach out, far beyond her limited, shy world.

We're talking roots and wings. A husband's love that is strong enough to reassure yet unthreatened enough to release. Tight enough to embrace yet loose enough to enjoy. Magnetic enough to hold, yet magnanimous enough to allow for flight . . . with an absence of jealousy as others applaud *her* accomplishments and admire *her* competence. Charles, the secure, put away the net so Anne, the shy, could flutter and fly.

Isn't this the essence of that finest essay ever written on love . . . the *sine qua non* of true agape?

> Love . . . is kind, never jealous . . . never haughty or selfish . . .
> If you love someone you will be loyal . . . no matter what the
> cost. You will always believe in him, always expect the best
> . . . always stand your ground defending him [or her] (from 1
> Corinthians 13, TLB).

It's a lot like Roy Croft's words:

> I love you, / Not only for what you are
> But for what I am / When I am with you.
>
> I love you, / Not only for what
> You have made of yourself
> But for what / You are making of me.
>
> I love you, / For the part of me / That you bring out;
> I love you, / For putting your hand
> Into my heaped-up heart
> And passing over / All the foolish, weak things

That you can't help / Dimly seeing there,
And for drawing out / Into the light
All the beautiful belongings
That no one else had looked / Quite far enough to find.
I love you because you
Are helping me to make / Of the lumber of my life
Not a tavern / But a temple;
Out of works / Of my every day
Not a reproach / But a song.[3]

Have you a fragile butterfly who needs reassurance, room to become, space to spread her wings outside the cocoon of fear and timidity? Is she in need of realizing she has color all her own, and beauty and grace and style to be appreciated beyond the fence surrounding your own garden? Are you generous enough to put away the net and let others enjoy her too? She's the Lord's you know . . . not *your* possession. And since that is true, if you release her to spread her lovely wings for His glory, she won't fly away forgetting and forsaking her roots. She will flutter and flourish, adding dimensions of delight you would never otherwise know.

But if you're not careful, fellow husband, you'll be so busy flying from place to place yourself that you won't stop to appreciate that shy, delicate thing of beauty God has given you. You will forget she lives in the cocoon eclipsed beneath the shadow of your life . . . still, silent, looking very much like a butterfly in flight, but feeling more like a specimen under glass.

Deepening Your Roots

1 Corinthians 13; Galatians 5:1, 13 – 15; Philemon 8 – 18

Branching Out

1. Ask your wife/husband or a friend to tell you of a time when he felt trapped by you, and when you made him feel free.
2. Ask someone what quality he enjoys the most about your spouse or a close friend. Then tell your spouse (or friend) what that person said and compliment your mate or friend on a character trait that *you* like.
3. What's something you would like to be encouraged to do, but haven't done?

Why not try to do it?

THE DARK SIDE OF GREATNESS

"There lies the most perfect ruler of men the world has
ever seen . . . [and] now he belongs to the ages."

Of whom was this said?

One of the Caesars? No. Napoleon? No. Alexander the Great? No.
Eisenhower? Patton? MacArthur . . . or some earlier military strategist
like Grant or Lee or Pershing? No, none of the above. How about Rockne
or Lombardi? No. Or Luther? Calvin? Knox? Wesley? Spurgeon? Again,
the answer is no.

Well, it was no doubt said of a great leader, a powerful and persuasive
personality, was it not? Certainly one admired for his success. That
depends, I suppose.

When he was seven years old, his family was forced out of their home
because of a legal technicality. He had to work to help support them.

At age nine, while still a backward, shy little boy, his mother died.

At twenty-two, he lost his job as a store clerk. He wanted to go to law
school, but his education was not good enough.

At twenty-three, he went into debt to become a partner in a small
store. Three years later his business partner died, leaving him a huge debt
that took years to repay.

At twenty-eight, after developing a romantic relationship with a
young lady for four years, he asked her to marry him. She said no. An earlier youthful love he shared with a lovely girl ended in heartache at her
death.

At thirty-seven, on his *third* try, he was finally elected to Congress.
Two years later he ran again and failed to be reelected. I should add it was
about this time he had what some today would call a nervous breakdown.

At forty-one, adding additional heartache to an already unhappy marriage, his four-year-old son died.

The next year he was rejected for Land Officer.

At forty-five, he ran for the Senate and lost.

Two years later, he was defeated for nomination for Vice President.

At forty-nine, he ran for the Senate again . . . and lost again.

Add to this an endless barrage of criticism, misunderstanding, ugly and false rumors, and deep periods of depression and you realize it's no wonder he was snubbed by his peers and despised by multitudes, hardly the envy of his day.

At fifty-one, however, he was elected President of the United States . . . but his second term in office was cut short by his assassination. As he lay dying in a little rooming house across from the place where he was shot, a former detractor (Edwin Stanton), spoke the fitting tribute I quoted at the top of this column. By now you know it was spoken of the most inspirational and highly regarded president in American history. Abraham Lincoln, the man whose birthday we soon will celebrate.

What a strange lot we are! Enamored of the dazzling lights, the fickle applause of the public, the splash of success, we seldom trace the lines that led to that flimsy and fleeting pinnacle. Bitter hardship. Unfair and undeserved abuses. Loneliness and loss. Humiliating failures. Debilitating disappointments. Agony beyond comprehension suffered in the valleys and crevices of the climb from bottom to top.

How shortsighted! Instead of accepting the fact that no one deserves the right to lead without first persevering through pain and heartache and failure, we resent those intruders. We treat them as enemies, not friends. We forget that the marks of greatness are not delivered in a paper sack by capricious gods. They are not hurriedly stuck onto skin like a tattoo.

No, those who are really worth following have paid their dues. They have come through the furnace melted, beaten, reshaped, and tempered. To use the words of the teacher from Tarsus, they bear in their bodies "the brand-marks of Jesus" (Galatians 6:17). Or, as one paraphrases it, they carry "the scars of the whippings and wounds" which link them to all mankind.

Small wonder when such people move from time to eternity they "belong to the ages."

Deepening Your Roots

Genesis 39:19 – 21, 41:50 – 52, 45:4 – 8; Proverbs 18:12; 1 Peter 1:3 – 9

Branching Out

1. Write down five painful times from your life which have contributed towards who you are today. Thank God for what those trials produced in you.
2. In memory of Lincoln, freely give someone $5.00. Or, if you're rich, hand 'em a $50 bill.

CLEAR VIEW FROM MT. PERSPECTIVE

The coed had two problems common to many students: low grades and no money. She was forced to communicate both to her parents, who she knew would have trouble understanding. After considerable thought she used a creative approach to soften the blows of reality and wrote:

> Dear Mom and Dad,
>
> Just thought I'd drop you a note to clue you in on my plans. I've fallen in love with a guy named Jim. He quit high school after grade eleven to get married. About a year ago he got a divorce.
>
> We've been going steady for two months and plan to get married in the fall. Until then, I've decided to move into his apartment (I think I might be pregnant).
>
> At any rate, I dropped out of school last week, although I'd like to finish college sometime in the future.

On the next page she continued:

> Mom and Dad, I just want you to know that everything I've written so far in this letter is false. NONE of it is true.
>
> But Mom and Dad, it IS true that I got a C in French and flunked Math. It IS true that I'm going to need some more money for my tuition payments.

Pretty sharp coed! Even bad news can sound like good news if it is seen from a certain vantage point. So much in life depends on "where you're coming from" as you face your circumstances. The secret, of course, is perspective.

And what *is* perspective? Obviously, it's related to the way we view something. The term literally suggests "looking through . . . seeing clearly." One who views life through perspective lenses has the capacity to see things in their true relations or relative importance. He scopes in on the big picture. He distinguishes the incidental from the essential . . . the temporary from the eternal . . . the partial from the whole . . . the trees from the forest.

For the next few minutes, snap a telescopic lens on your perspective and pull yourself up close. Close enough to see the *real* you. Study what you see. Like a physician giving you a physical. Like an artist painting your portrait. Like a biographer writing your story. From the reflection in your mental mirror, pay close attention to your life. Try your best to examine the inner "you" on the basis of *time*.

Lift yourself above the smothering details of today's tangled thicket and breathe the crisp, fresh air that surrounds the clear view high up on Mt. Perspective. Seems to me the only way to carry out this project is to look in two directions . . . back, then ahead. In many ways what we see in our past and visualize in our future determines how we view ourselves today . . . right now . . . that depth-yielding third dimension we call "the present."

As we look *back,* one overriding thought eclipses all others. It's not very new, nor very profound, but few would debate its truth: LIFE IS SHORT. That's not only a valid observation from experience, it's a constant beacon reflecting from the pages of the Bible. Psalm 90 flashes that truth again and again. Listen to some of the analogies employed by the composer.

> Life is short . . .
> . . . like yesterday when it passes by (v. 4a).
> . . . as a watch in the night (v. 4b).
> . . . like grass . . . it sprouts and withers (vv. 5 – 6).
> . . . like a sigh (v. 9).
> . . . soon it is gone (v. 10).

Wistful scenes looking back from Mt. Perspective. Standing on that silent summit brings a subtle, perhaps painful reminder that we aren't getting any younger. Life indeed is short.

Shifting our position and looking *ahead* at the opposite horizon we discern another singular message. Again, the words are neither unique nor scholarly — but they echo back repeatedly: LIFE IS UNCERTAIN. A single adjective could precede most every event in our future: unexpected. Unexpected . . . surgery, transfer, change, accomplishment, loss, benefit, sickness, promotion, demotion, death. Life indeed, is uncertain.

Well, then — what about today?

I suggest there are three words which adequately and accurately describe the present. They do not contradict either of the lessons we've learned on the peaks of Mt. Perspective. Nor do they require rose-colored glasses. Neither do they agree with the futile meanderings of modern philosophy. Looking to the present, we discover: LIFE IS CHALLENGING. Because it is short, every moment wells up challenging possibilities. Because it is uncertain, it's filled with challenging adjustments. Could this be what Jesus referred to when He promised an *abundant* life? Abundant with challenges, brimming with possibilities, spilling over with opportunities to adapt, shift, alter, and change. This is the perspective that keeps people young. It is also the path that leads to optimism and motivation.

Every new dawn, before you awaken, life makes a delivery to your front door, rings the doorbell, and runs. Each package is cleverly wrapped. Put together they comprise a series of challenging opportunities brilliantly disguised as unsolvable problems. They are wrapped in paper with big print. One package reads: "Watch out — better worry about this!" Another: "Danger: this will bring fear!" And another: "Impossible, you'll never handle this one!"

When you hear the ring in the morning, try something new.

Have Jesus Christ answer the door for you.

Deepening Your Roots
1 Chronicles 28:9 – 20; Luke 12:22 – 34; Colossians 4:5

Branching Out

1. No challenges in your life? Ask God for one that will give you opportunity to grow, contribute, and learn He is dependable.
2. Too many challenges? Pray before you move out that door and ask God for the ability to see them as opportunities, not obstacles. Allow Him to help you enjoy each one.

ઌ ઌ ઌ

Growing Strong

Know what I enjoyed most about this week? The emphasis on prayer. We can never do too much of it. It's vital if we want to keep strong and keep growing. Why not take a moment now to write out a prayer, telling God why you love Him, or thanking Him for something He did for you this week?

ＥXPECTATIONS

There is a fly in the ointment of disappointments. We put it there. So there's nobody to blame but ourselves. By doing so we set ourselves up for a jolt . . . a period of frustration we could have otherwise missed. I'm referring to the disease-carrying insect of *expectations*.

Stop and think it over. What causes you to experience disappointment? Someone or something has failed to fulfill your expectations. Right? You had it all set up in your mind: the way a certain situation would work out, the way a certain person was going to respond. But it never materialized. Your wish fell fast and hard against stone-cold reality. Your desire dissolved into an empty, unfulfilled dream.

After you've heard a few stories of disappointment, they begin to sound painfully similar. As I spin some records in my memory, I hear several sad songs from different voices. Listen with me for a moment to their wistful echoes:

> I'm not happy in my work. When I got the job, I never realized it would be like this.

> Marriage has become a drag! On our wedding day I thought it would all be so different. It's nothing like I imagined at all.

> She was once a friend of mine. I reached out, helped her, loved her, and gave myself to her. I thought the least she would do was respond the same way to me.

> We had them over for dinner more than once and they never did reciprocate. We didn't even get a thank-you note. Talk about disappointment!

> He asked me out several times. I felt I was more than just another date to him. I really anticipated a deepening romance . . . but it never occurred. I was hurt.

> Man, I chose this college thinking it would provide me with an ideal education. Now here I am a senior — but I'm not nearly as prepared as I thought I would be.

The discipleship group was nothing like I expected. I anticipated one thing and got another.

We came to this church with high hopes. Expecting great things, we threw ourselves into the program without reservation. Now we're disillusioned with the whole thing.

Glad we had children? Hardly. You know, we thought having kids was going to be fun — a downhill slide. You can't imagine how happy we are to see them leave the nest. They really let us down.

God called me into the ministry. He later led my family and me into the pastorate. We were burning with zeal and bursting with hope. But after ten years, the fire's gone out. The delight just isn't there anymore. I'm frustrated.

Yeah, we just got back from Europe. No, it wasn't that great. Nothing like we thought it would be.

Recognize the tune? The scratchy sounds on the disappointment side of the disk are well-worn. Self-made bitterness, resentment, and pessimism ooze from the grooves. It's played year after year and we've all heard it — or sung it.

It's time we switched to the flip-side. We need to take an honest look at this painful thorn that blurs our vision and conceives our disappointments. *Expectations.* We erect mental images which are either unrealistic, unfair, or biased. Those phantom images become our inner focus, rigidly and traditionally maintained. Leaving no room for flexibility on the part of the other person (allowing no place for circumstantial change or surprise) we set in mental concrete the way things *must* go. When they *don't,* we either tumble or grumble . . . or both.

The result is tragic. As our radius of toleration is reduced, our willingness to accept others' imperfections or a less-than-ideal circumstance is short-circuited. And, worst of all, the delightful spontaneity of a friendship is strained. The chain of obligation, built with the links of expectation, binds us in the dungeon of disappointment.

With all due respect to the beloved hymn we've sung half our lives, I'd suggest we change the title to "Blest Be the Tie that *Frees.*"

We need to give one another stretching space — the room to respond and react in a variety of ways, even as our infinite Creator molded a variety of personalities. This will require a ritual burning of our list of

expectations. For some of us, it could make quite a bonfire. It will also mean we stop anticipating the *ideal* and start living with the real — which is always checkered with failure, imperfection, and even *wrong.* So instead of biting and devouring one another (Galatians 5:15), let's support individual freedom as we serve one another in love (Galatians 5:13).

I don't know of a better way to kill the flies that spread the disease of disappointment.

Deepening Your Roots

Psalm 5:3; Matthew 20:1 – 16; Colossians 3:12 – 17

Branching Out

1. Name three expectations you have of your spouse, yourself, a child, or a friend.

   1. _____
   2. _____
   3. _____

   Now, remove those expectations (mentally) and let the relationship be.
2. Ask a close friend what he expects of you and your friendship. Talk about those expectations.
3. Set aside an evening in which you have no expectations and enjoy the time, regardless of what takes place.

SECRET WOUNDS, SILENT CRIES

Tucked away in a quiet corner of Scripture is a verse that brims with emotion. Read thoughtfully these ancient words from the pen of Job:

> From the city men groan, and the souls of the wounded cry out . . . (Job 24:12).

Slip into that scene . . . a busy metropolis . . . speed . . . movement . . . noise. Rows of buildings, acres of apartments, miles of houses, restaurants, stores, cars, bikes, kids. All of that is obvious. Any city-dweller could describe the scene, delineate the action.

But there is more. Behind and beneath the loud splash of human activity are invisible aches. Job calls them "groans." In Hebrew, the word suggests that this groan comes from one who has been *wounded.* Perhaps that is why Job adds the next line in poetic form, "the souls of the wounded cry out. . . ." In that line, "wounded" comes from a term that means "pierced" *as if stabbed.* Not a physical stabbing — for it is "the soul" that is crying out. What does he mean?

There are those who suffer from the blows of "soul stabbings," wounds which can be far more painful and devastating than "body stabbings." Job has reference to deep lacerations of the heart — invisible, internal injuries no surgeon in the world could detect. The city is full of such hurts. It's a desolate, disturbing scene . . . but painfully true. Wounded, broken, bruised, many a person cries out with groans from the innermost being.

Perhaps that described *you* today. You may be "groaning" because you've been misunderstood, or treated unfairly. The injury is deep because the blow landed from someone you trust and respect . . . someone you are vulnerable to . . . someone you love. It is possible that your pain was inflicted by the stabbing of someone's tongue. An individual who said things that are simply untrue. Perhaps the comment was made only in passing, but it cut into the tissue, it pierced you deeply. The person who made the remark will never know. But you will . . . as you endure . . . keep quiet . . . and bleed.

Quite probably others of you are living with scars brought on by past sins or failures. Although you have confessed and forsaken those ugly, bitter days, you can't seem to erase the backwash. Sometimes when you're alone the past slips up from behind like a freak ocean wave and overwhelms you. The scab is jarred loose. The wound stays inflamed and tender and you wonder if it will *ever* go away. Although it is unknown to others, you live in the fear of being found out . . . and rejected.

It was Amy Carmichael who once helped heal a wound within me and turn it into a scar of beauty instead of disgrace. I share with you her words:

NO SCAR?

Hast thou no scar?
No hidden scar on foot, or side, or hand?
I hear thee sung as mighty in the land,
I hear them hail thy bright ascendant star,
Hast thou no scar?

Hast thou no wound?
Yet I was wounded by the archers, spent,
Leaned Me against a tree to die; and rent
By ravening beasts that compassed Me, I swooned:
Hast thou no wound?

No wound, no scar?
Yet, as the Master shall the servant be,
And, pierced are the feet that follow Me;
But thine are whole: can he have followed far
Who has no wound nor scar?

Tucked away in a quiet corner of *every* life are wounds and scars. If they were not there, we would need no Physician. Nor would we need one another.

Deepening Your Roots

Psalm 109:21 – 31, 147:1 – 11; Isaiah 53:1 – 12

Branching Out

1. Choose three people whom you can encourage by saying healing words.
2. Trust someone by letting him know of your hurt and allowing him to aid you in the healing process.

BENEDICTIONS

During my years of growing up, I sat through hundreds of sermons from dozens of preachers. My family skipped from church to church trying to find one that would meet our needs — Baptist, Methodist, Lutheran, Presbyterian, Brethren, Independent . . . you name it, we attended it. As I recall those years, one thing stands out in my mind as the best part of almost every sermon I heard — *the end!* I remember so clearly that no matter how strong or weak, how exciting or dull, how long or short the message may have been, the most beautiful words of the day were uttered as the man would bow his head and give a brief closing prayer. It wasn't until I was nearly grown that I realized he was actually quoting a passage of Scripture to which had been given the name "benediction."

There are three prominent benedictions in the New Testament, each one equally familiar to our ears. As soon as you read them, you will be reminded of how well-acquainted you are with them:

> The grace of the Lord Jesus Christ, and the love of God, and the fellowship of the Holy Spirit, be with you all (2 Corinthians 13:14).

> Now the God of peace, who brought up from the dead the great Shepherd of the sheep through the blood of the eternal covenant, even Jesus our Lord, equip you in every good thing to do His will, working in us that which is pleasing in His sight, through Jesus Christ, to whom be the glory forever and ever. Amen (Hebrews 13:20, 21).

> Now to Him who is able to keep you from stumbling, and to make you stand in the presence of His glory blameless with great joy, to the only God our Savior, through Jesus Christ our Lord, be glory, majesty, dominion and authority, before all time and now and forever. Amen (Jude 24 – 25).

These inspired expressions of praise were once in vogue more than they are now in our day of spontaneity and freedom. In fact, it was considered an *expected* part of a dignified worship service . . . the minister was not through until he closed the sermon by quoting (with a pardonable flair of eloquence) his favorite "benediction." Who can fault such a custom? After all, he was declaring the Word of God — and we can never get too much of that! There are occasions that arise in our church where a "benediction" seems most appropriate, and I will use one with delight to close the service. It seems to give a final voice in a fitting fashion, far more significant than a casual prayer could provide.

Unfortunately, however, familiarity with our hearing these lovely statements has resulted in our missing their depth of meaning. Let me choose Jude's words as an example. Look back and read again the third quotation you read earlier.

What a powerful promise! If you'd take the time to turn in your Bible to Jude's letter, you'd notice that just before those closing words he refers to our Savior's coming in mercy for His own. This "benediction" builds upon that thought as it tells us something our Lord is doing for us now as well as something He will do for us then, when He comes back for us.

Now: He is "keeping us from stumbling."

Then: He will "present us blameless with great joy."

Currently — during the interval between our new birth and His sudden appearance — He is guarding us, keeping us, protecting us, securing us, helping us not to stumble. How He cares for His sheep! How He loves us and rescues us! How often He lifts us when we are low and supports us when we are weak! As long as we rely on Him, He *guards us from stumbling*. But, alas, we do not always rely on Him . . . so we stumble and we *continue* to do so. In fact, we frequently look back over a week that's passed and feel that's all we did — stumble.

Here's where the second part fits so perfectly. When our dear Lord will one day reach down and snatch us up — up before Him *blameless* . . . faultless . . . flawless, He will be no peeved deity, angry because of our failures and ready to strike us because they were many. David ratifies that fact in Psalm 103:10 and 14.

> He has not dealt with us according to our sins, nor rewarded us according to our iniquities. For He Himself knows our frame; He is mindful that we are but dust.

Picture yourself before God as Tennyson describes it:

> . . . in that fierce light which beats upon a throne, and blackens every blot.

You would think it a natural thing for the Almighty to frown and draw from His records a legal-size clipboard with your name at the top upon which would be listed the numerous times you stumbled. How depressing a thought! No — a thousand times, no! God keeps no such records to be used against you.

He will accept you in that day, being fully aware that you are but dust . . . and He will escort you into the presence of His glory BLAMELESS. I invite you to stop at this moment and think that over. It's not possible to imagine the scene without smiling, seized with inexpressible joy.

Today: Kept from stumbling.

Tomorrow: Accepted as blameless.

Now, there's a benediction that'll do more than end my sermon. It ought to make your day.

Deepening Your Roots
Psalm 103:1 – 14; James 3:2; Jude 1 – 24

Branching Out

1. How did you stumble last week? Now say to yourself: "Even though I've stumbled, God has forgiven me and will call me blameless one day."
2. How did God guard you from stumbling last week?
3. Before you go to bed tonight, say Jude's benediction out loud and thank God for His care for you.

જી જી જી

Growing Strong

How's it going, my friend? Was your week filled with friends and activity or was it a span of time that contained mostly quiet moments by yourself? Right now, how are you doing?

If that answer conveys a happy heart, great! If not, then do me and yourself a favor — go out and have some fun today *with a friend.* Do something that will cause you both to smile. Have fun.

_____

_____

_____

_____

QUIETNESS

*I*t is almost 10:00, Monday night. Aside from a few outside noises — a passing car . . . a barking dog . . . a few, faint voices in the distance — all's quiet on our Fullerton, California, front. That wonderful, much-needed presence has again come for a visit — *quietness*. Oh, how I love it . . . how I need it. The last time it was this quiet was a few weeks ago when I was walking with a friend along the sandy shores at Carmel. The silence of that early dawn was broken only by the rhythmic roar of the rolling surf and the cry of a few gulls floating overhead. The same thought I had then I have now: *I cannot be the man I should be without times of quietness.* Stillness is an essential part of our growing deeper as we grow older. Or — in the words of a man who helped shape my life perhaps more than any other:

> We will not become men of God without the presence of solitude.

Those words haunt me when I get caught in the treadmill of time schedules . . . when I make my turn toward the homestretch of the week and try to meet the deadline of demands, just like you. Alas, we are simply geared too high. Thanks to "Alka Seltzer," "Excedrin," "Sleep Eze," and "Compoz," we repeat our nonproductive haste with monotonous regularity. As Peter Marshall put it:

> We are in such a hurry, we hate to miss one panel of a revolving door.

Talk about pollution! I want you to think about what our nervous systems undergo just to stay afloat: *Noise* (music, news, talk, laughter, machinery, appliances, phones, and traffic) from 6:00 A.M. 'til midnight. *Speed* (bumper to bumper at 65 m.p.h., on-ramps and off-ramps, deadlines and appointments) that makes us frown rather than smile . . . that causes us to check our watches more often than checking in with our Lord. *Activities* (meetings, services, suppers, luncheons, breakfasts, rallies, and clubs — all "necessary" and "nice") that have a way of dismissing quietness like an unwanted guest. Sure — some things are important — super, in fact — but not *everything*. Listen, if you and I *really* treasure quietness, we will have to make time for it. When you feed it only the "left overs" from the schedule, it always goes hungry.

Now, believe me, I'm not bitter. I'm just being direct and honest with you about an ingredient that cannot be ignored much longer in our lives without our paying a dear, dear price. I am jealous that we: "Be still and know that I am God." I am desperately concerned that we slow down and quiet down and gear down our lives so that intermittently each week we carve out time for quietness, solitude, thought, prayer, meditation, and soul searching. Oh, how much agitation will begin to fade away . . . how insignificant petty differences will seem . . . how big God will become and how small our troubles will appear! Security, peace, and confidence will move right on in.

This is what Isaiah, the prophet, meant when he wrote:

> And the work of righteousness will be peace,
> And the service of righteousness, quietness and confidence
>   forever.
> Then my people will live in a peaceful habitation,
> And in secure dwellings and in undisturbed resting places . . .
>   (32:17 – 18).

You know something? That still, small voice will never shout. God's methods don't change because we are so noisy and busy. He is longing for your attention, your undivided and full attention. He wants to talk with you in times of quietness (with the TV *off*) about your need for understanding, love, compassion, patience, self-control, a calm spirit, genuine humility . . . and wisdom. But He won't run to catch up. He will wait and wait until you finally sit in silence and listen.

Deepening Your Roots
Psalm 46, 131; Isaiah 30:15 – 18; Mark 6:30 – 32

Branching Out

1. Set aside one evening this week when you will unplug the TV. Spend at least sixty minutes being quiet. (Read the Bible, think about God and you, pray, etc.)
2. Take at least a fifteen-minute walk by yourself and look for these items as you stroll down the sidewalk or road: a bird, a flower, and a child at play.
3. While the kids take a nap, take fifteen minutes for yourself and just be "still" awhile. Listen to God speak to you.

SOLVING PROBLEMS

*E*dward Roy had a problem. Earthy, but not earth-shattering. Not very enjoyable to talk about at dinner either, but big enough to make the man struggle through a few sleepless nights.

He ran a lowly business — *Jiffy Johns* of Pompano Beach, Florida. Five hundred portable toilets for rent. Band concerts, construction sites, church picnics, outdoor gatherings of any size could rent his product. But that wasn't Ed's problem. As expected, when he started his business in 1982, lots of folks in Florida needed a place to be alone when they were caught out in the open. Rentals were up. That was good and bad.

Now he had to figure out what to do with all the sewage . . . *that* was the problem.

Many a man would've thrown his hands in the air in exasperation and spent half his profit to have somebody haul off his product's product. Not Ed. There had to be a better way.

In his search for a solution, he found a solar-heating process that turned sewage into fertilizer. Then came a masterstroke of marketing: instead of trying to sell the technology directly to local Florida communities, his company expanded and began to operate three three-million-dollar plants itself. Under this new arrangement, the company would treat sewage for a fee and convert it into fertilizer, which was, in turn, sold for a substantial profit. A limited partnership soon produced the cash — the *Jiffy Industries, Inc.* (new name) provided a good tax shelter. I suppose we could say Edward Roy *literally* turned his problem into a project.

And what a project! Jiffy stock turned in the year's best performance on any American exchange, rising from 92¢ a share to a whopping $16.50 — a spectacular 1,693 percent gain. Newsweek magazine recently reported that "with dozens of states suffering from a surfeit of sewage . . . Jiffy's 'Anaerobic Digester' is catching on everywhere." One reputable stockbroker predicts the stock will be selling for $25 a share within six months.

Gross though it may seem, I doubt that I'll ever forget the problem Edward Roy had with his johns. He simply refused to let all that stuff get the best of him. What a lesson for all of us!

Life is difficult . . . really very little more than an endless series of problems. Do we want to moan and groan about them or face them? Do we want to teach the next generation the disciplines involved in accepting and solving them or encourage them to run and hide from them?

I appreciate and agree with M. Scott Peck, M.D., who wrote:

> . . . it is in this whole process of meeting and solving problems that life has meaning. Problems are the cutting edge that distinguishes between success and failure. Problems call forth our courage and our wisdom; indeed they create our courage and our wisdom. It is only because of problems that we grow mentally and spiritually. . . . It is through the pain of confronting and resolving problems that we learn. As Benjamin Franklin said, "Those things that hurt, instruct."
>
> Fearing the pain involved, almost all of us . . . attempt to avoid problems. We procrastinate, forget them, pretend they do not exist. We even take drugs to assist us in ignoring them, so that by deadening ourselves to the pain we can forget the problems that cause the pain (*The Road Less Traveled,* p. 16).

And then the clincher. Dr. Peck suggests:

> This tendency to avoid problems and the emotional suffering inherent in them is the primary basis of all human mental illness.

When I read this statement, it reminded me of a similar comment the renowned physician Carl Jung once wrote:

> Neurosis is always a substitute for legitimate suffering.

The tragedy, of course, is that the substitute itself ultimately becomes more painful than the "legitimate suffering" it was trying to avoid. And, adding insult to injury, the avoidance of legitimate suffering means we also avoid the *growth* that problems demand of us. Our determination to push pain away instead of meeting it head on creates a vicious circle.

Could this explain why God's wisest saints are often people who endure pain rather than escape it? Like their Savior, they are men and women "acquainted with grief." I recall that Jesus "learned obedience *from* the things which he suffered" (Hebrews 5:8), not *in spite of* those things.

Do you have a problem? You're smiling back at me. "A problem? Would you believe *several dozen* problems?" If you listen to the voices around you, you'll search for a substitute — an escape route. You'll miss the fact that each one of those problems is a God-appointed instructor ready to stretch you and challenge you and deepen your walk with Him. Growth and wisdom await you at the solution of each one, the pain and mess notwithstanding.

What may seem today as lowly, repulsive, and useless as sewage can become the most significant distinctive of your life. Furthermore, your stock will go up! But you'll never know until you go into partnership with the Son.

Deepening Your Roots
1 Peter 4:12 – 19; James 1:1 – 12

Branching Out

1. List three problems you are facing today and the escape route you usually take. Then list after each problem these words: WAIT ON GOD.

   1. _____
   2. _____
   3. _____

2. Read the stock exchange and find the going rate for Jiffy Industries, Inc.

3. Name a problem you have: _____
   Decide to endure it rather than run from it. What was the outcome?

YOU ARE NOT A NOBODY

*L*et's take a quiz.

Pull a sheet of scratch paper out of your memory bank and see how well you do with the following questions:

1. Who taught Martin Luther his theology and inspired his translation of the New Testament?

2. Who visited Dwight L. Moody at a shoe store and spoke to him about Christ?

3. Who worked alongside and encouraged Harry Ironside as his associate pastor?

4. Who was the wife of Charles Haddon Spurgeon?

5. Who was the elderly woman who prayed faithfully for Billy Graham for over twenty years?

6. Who financed William Carey's ministry in India?

7. Who refreshed the Apostle Paul in that Roman dungeon as he wrote his last letter to Timothy?

8. Who helped Charles Wesley get underway as a composer of hymns?

9. Who found the Dead Sea Scrolls?

10. Who personally taught G. Campbell Morgan, the "peerless expositor," his techniques in the pulpit?

11. Who were the parents of the godly and gifted prophet Daniel?

Okay, how did you do? Over fifty percent? Maybe twenty-five percent? Not quite that good?

Before you excuse your inability to answer the questions by calling the quiz "trivia," better stop and think. Had it not been for those unknown people — those "nobodies" —- a huge chunk of church history would be missing. And a lot of lives would have been untouched.

Nobodies.

What was it Jim Elliot, the martyred messenger of the gospel to the Aucas, once called missionaries? Something like a *bunch of nobodies trying to exalt Somebody.*

But don't mistake anonymous for *unnecessary.* Otherwise, the whole Body gets crippled . . . even paralyzed . . . or, at best, terribly dizzy as the majority of the members within the Body become diseased with self-pity and discouragement. Face it, friend, the Head of the Body calls the shots. It is His prerogative to publicize some and hide others.

If it's His desire to use you as a Melanchthon rather than a Luther . . . or a Kimball rather than a Moody . . . or an Onesiphorus rather than a Paul . . . or a Hoste rather than a Taylor, relax!

Better than that, give God praise! You're among that elite group mentioned in 1 Corinthians 12 as:

> . . . some of the parts that seem weakest and least important are really the most necessary. . . . So God has put the body together in such a way that extra honor and care are given to those parts that might otherwise seem less important (vv. 22, 24, TLB).

If it weren't for the heroic "nobodies," we wouldn't have top-notch officers to give a church its leadership. Or quality sound when everyone shows up to worship. Or janitors who clean when everyone is long gone. Or committees to provide dozens of services behind the scenes. Or mission volunteers who staff offices at home or work in obscurity overseas with only a handful of people. Come to think of it, if it weren't for the faithful "nobodies," you wouldn't have this book in your hands right now.

Nobodies . . . exalting Somebody.

Are you one? Listen to me! It's the "nobodies" Somebody chooses so carefully. And when *He* has selected you for that role, He does not consider you a nobody.

Be encouraged!

Deepening Your Roots

Proverbs 27:2; 1 Corinthians 12:12 – 26; Hebrews 11

Branching Out

1. Study in depth a character from the Hebrews 11 passage.
2. Look around and praise three people who are never in the limelight.

❧ ❧ ❧

Growing Strong

Another week down! How'd it go? Tell me about your most positive incident from the past few days. What did you gain from it? What did you learn about yourself while experiencing it?

_____

_____

_____

_____

COOL SKEPTICISM

Nine-year-old Danny came bursting out of Sunday school like a wild stallion. His eyes were darting in every direction as he tried to locate either mom or dad. Finally, after a quick search, he grabbed his daddy by the leg and yelled, "Man, that story of Moses and all those people crossing the Red Sea was great!" His father looked down, smiled, and asked the boy to tell him about it.

"Well, the Israelites got out of Egypt, but Pharaoh and his army chased after them. So the Jews ran as fast as they could until they got to the Red Sea. The Egyptian Army was gettin' closer and closer. So Moses got on his walkie-talkie and told the Israeli Air Force to bomb the Egyptians. While that was happening, the Israeli Navy built a pontoon bridge so the people could cross over. They made it!"

By now old dad was shocked. "Is *that* the way they taught you the story?"

"Well, no, not exactly," Danny admitted, "but if I told it to you the way they told it to us, you'd *never* believe it, Dad."

With childlike innocence the little guy put his finger on the pulse of our sophisticated adult world where cool skepticism reigns supreme. It's becoming increasingly more popular to operate in the black-and-white world of facts . . . and, of course, to leave no space for the miraculous.

It's really not a new mentality. Peter mentions it in one of his letters:

> . . . I want to remind you that in the last days there will come scoffers who will . . . laugh at the truth. This will be their line of argument: "So Jesus promised to come back, did he? Then where is he? He'll never come! Why, as far back as anyone can remember everything has remained exactly as it was since the first day of creation" (2 Peter 3:3 – 4, TLB).

Skeptics think like that. If they could choose their favorite hymn, it would certainly include the words, "As it was in the beginning, it is now and ever shall be. . . ."

Take gravity. Heavy objects fall toward earth. Always. So a builder can construct a house and never worry about his materials floating away. Count on it. *Take chemistry.* Mixing certain elements in precise proportions yields the same result. Always. So a doctor can prescribe a medication with predictable confidence. *Take astronomy.* The sun, the moon, those stars work in perfect harmony. Always. Even the mysterious eclipse comes as no surprise. *Take anatomy.* Whether it's the pupil of the eye expanding and contracting in response to light or our skin regulating our body temperature or our built-in defense mechanism fighting disease, we operate strictly on the basis of facts. Hard, immutable, stubborn facts. Reliable as the sunset. Real as a toothache. Clear as an X-ray. Absolute, unbending, undeniable.

People who conduct their lives according to such thinking are called smart. They haven't a fraction of tolerance for the supernatural. To them it is sloppy to think in terms of the unexplainable, the "miraculous." If insurance companies choose to leave room for "acts of God," that's their business ... but those are fightin' words in laboratories and operating rooms and scientific rap sessions and among newspaper editors.

Then what about miracles? Well, let's limit them to a child's world of fiction and fables. And, if necessary, to stained-glass sanctuaries where emotion runs high and imagination is needed to make all those stories interesting. After all, what's a little religion without a pocketful of miracles? And if we started trying to account for all those things in the Bible, think of the time it would take to explain stuff like how the sun stood still, or why all those fish filled the disciples' nets, or what brought Lazarus back from beyond, or why Jesus' body has never been found, or how the death of Christ cleans up lives year after year, or how come the Bible is still around.

Smart, keen-thinking skeptics don't have to worry about explaining little things like that. It's easier to simply embrace a wholesale denial of the miraculous ... which is fine and dandy ... until they themselves get sick, face death, and need miraculous help crossing that final river.

What happens then? Hey, if I told you what the Bible really says, you'd *never* believe it.

Deepening Your Roots
Exodus 14; Luke 9:10 – 17; 2 Peter 3

Branching Out

1. Name something you'd like to see change in your life (maybe an attitude or habit), and ask God to perform a miracle in you.
2. Read through a newspaper and see if you can find the word "miracle" used.

ASKING WHY

*T*he sound was deafening.

Although no one was near enough to hear it, it ultimately echoed around the world. None of the passengers in the DC-4 ever knew what happened . . . they died instantly. That was February 15, 1947. The Avianca Airline flight bound for Quito, Ecuador, crashed clumsily into the 14,000 foot-high towering peak of El Tablazo not far from Bogota . . . then dropped, a flaming mass of metal, into a ravine far below. A young New Yorker, Glenn Chambers, was one of the victims. He planned to begin a ministry with the *Voice of the Andes,* a life-long dream that suddenly aborted into a nightmare.

Before leaving the Miami airport earlier that day, Chambers hurriedly dashed off a note to his mom on a piece of paper he found on the floor of the terminal. That scrap of paper was once a printed piece of advertisement with the single word *WHY* sprawled across the center. But between the mailing and the delivery of that note, Chambers was killed. When the letter did arrive, there staring up at his mom was that haunting question — *WHY?*

Of all questions it is the most searching, the most tormenting. It falls from the lips of the mother who delivers a stillborn . . . the parent who hears that dreaded diagnosis, "It's leukemia," . . . the wife who learns of her husband's tragic death . . . the overseas serviceman who gets a "Dear John" . . . the struggling father of five who loses his job . . . the close friend of one who commits suicide.

Why? Why me? Why now? Why this? No manmade gauge can measure the shock and horror that strike the nervous system as ill-fated news travels into the human ear. No preparation can fully ready us for such moments. Few thoughts can steady us afterward . . . perhaps only one.

Consider Job . . . imagine his feelings when he heard these words: "You've lost your livestock, they've been stolen. Your sheep and camels were also destroyed. Your employees were murdered, Job. One more thing — your children were crushed in a freak windstorm . . . they are dead, my friend, all *ten* of them."

That actually happened. Job got the news in one, five-minute period of panic. Shortly thereafter he came down with the most painful disease imaginable . . . *boils* from head to toe. Grief-stricken. Stunned. Confused.

Reeling. Stinging. Standing beside ten fresh graves. At a total loss to explain even *one* tragedy, to say nothing of five. It was naked, raw agony. And the heavens were mute. No explanation thundered across the celestial chasm. Not one reason. Not one. It was sufficient to give a cynic her vicious, vocal day in court.

"Curse God and die!" (signed — Mrs. Job)

Boldly, he snapped, "You sound like a fool, woman!" Wisely, he stated, "Shall we accept only good from God and never adversity?" Notice very carefully what Job claimed that day. Don't miss the thing that carried him through. Unlike the stance of the stoic ("Grin and bear it . . . or, at least, grit your teeth and endure it"), Job grabbed one great principle and held on to it. It formed the knot at the end of his rope . . . it steadied his step . . . it kept him from cursing. It was the same knot a broken-hearted mother in New York tied the winter of 1947. No single truth removes the need to ask *Why?* like this one. Here it is:

GOD IS TOO KIND TO DO ANYTHING CRUEL . . .
TOO WISE TO MAKE A MISTAKE . . .
TOO DEEP TO EXPLAIN HIMSELF.

It's remarkable how believing that one profound statement erases the *Why?* from earth's inequities. Paul declared it in other terms.

Oh, the depth . . . of the wisdom and knowledge of God! How unsearchable are His judgments and unfathomable His ways! (Romans 11:33).

That's it! Job rested his case there. Mrs. Chambers stopped asking *Why?* when she saw the *Who* behind the scene. All other sounds are muffled when we claim His absolute sovereignty.

Even the deafening sound of a crashing DC-4.

Deepening Your Roots

Job 40; Psalm 84:10 – 12; Romans 9:1 – 21

Branching Out

1. If you found out today that your spouse or best friend had been killed in a car accident, what would you say to God?
2. What is something you need to trust God about?

EROSION

I remember only two things from my high school chemistry class. First, I got rid of a wart on the back of my right hand through applications of sulfuric acid for thirty-three consecutive days. Second, I watched the slow death of a frog in an unforgettable experiment.

My teacher placed the hapless creature in an oversized beaker of cool water. Beneath the beaker he moved a Bunsen burner with a very low flame so that the water heated very slowly — something like .017 of a degree Fahrenheit per second. In fact, the temperature rose so gradually that the frog was never aware of the change. Two and a half hours later the frog was dead . . . *boiled to death.* The change occurred so slowly that the frog neither tried to jump out nor released a complaining kick.

Attentive as I was to the gruesome demonstration, I never realized I was witnessing a profound principle that would remind me of that frog for the rest of my life. The principle, in a word, is *erosion.*

The first eleven chapters of 1 Kings record the erosion of a great man, in fact, *the* greatest of his day. Blessed with royal blood and an abundance of brains, Solomon was a natural for the throne of David. He was tutored at the feet of Nathan, groomed through the heart of Bathsheba, polished under the eyes of David, and matured by the hand of God. The mark of excellence was upon him.

Wisdom, loyalty, diplomacy, faithfulness and efficiency characterized the attitudes and acts of David's gifted son for the first few years of his kingship. Best of all, "Solomon loved the Lord" (1 Kings 3:3) and carefully walked in His ways. His achievements, power, international influence, and wealth were nothing short of phenomenal:

> Now God gave Solomon wisdom and very great discernment and breadth of mind, like the sand that is on the seashore. And Solomon's wisdom surpassed the wisdom of all the sons of the east and all the wisdom of Egypt. For he was wiser than all men . . . and his fame was known in all the surrounding nations. So King Solomon became greater than all the kings of the earth in riches and in wisdom. . . . And all the earth was seeking the presence of Solomon (1 Kings 4:29 – 31, 10:23 – 24a).

It has been proved that his annual income reached well into the millions. The unparalleled achievement of his life was the design and construction of Solomon's Temple, one of the seven wonders of the ancient world. After the suspicious queen of Sheba came to visit his kingdom to satisfy her mind that all she had heard was not merely an exaggeration, she humbly admitted:

> . . . I did not believe the reports, until I came and my eyes had seen it. And behold, the half was not told me. You exceed in wisdom and prosperity the report which I heard (1 Kings 10:7).

Candidly, Solomon had it all.

Things slowly began to change, however. Almost as if he had attained the mastery of man and God, he seized the reins of compromise and wrong, and drove himself to the misty flats of licentiousness, pride, lust, and idolatry. Like insane Nero in later history, Solomon became irrational, sensual, and even skeptical of things he once held precious.

Layers of dust collected in the majestic temple he had built, now that the monarch had turned his attention to another project: the building of strange edifices for the strange gods he and his strange wives were now serving. Solomon (like many another absolute monarch, super salesman, top business executive, athletic prima donna, or filmstar playboy) simply drove too fast and traveled too far. The vultures of his own vulnerability soon spotted his carnal carcass and began to feed upon his vitals. The termination of his now sterile life came prematurely.

The son of David died a debauched, effeminate cynic, so satiated with materialism that life was all "vanity and striving after wind" (Ecclesiastes 2:26b). He left a nation confused, in conflict, and soon to be fractured by civil war.

Deterioration is never sudden. No garden "suddenly" overgrows with thorns. No church "suddenly" splits. No building "suddenly" crumbles. No marriage "suddenly" breaks down. No nation "suddenly" becomes a mediocre power. No person "suddenly" becomes base. Slowly, almost imperceptibly, certain things are accepted that once were rejected. Things once considered hurtful are now secretly tolerated. At the outset it appears harmless, perhaps even exciting, but the wedge it brings leaves a gap that grows wider as moral erosion joins hands with spiritual decay. The gap becomes a canyon. That "way which seems right" becomes, in fact, "the way of death." Solomon wrote that. He ought to know.

Take heed, you who stand: take heed, lest *you* fall! Be careful about changing your standard so that it corresponds with your desires. Be very cautious about becoming inflated with thoughts of your own importance. Be alert to the pitfalls of prosperity and success. Should God grant riches, fame, and success, don't run scared or feel guilty. Just stay balanced. Remember Solomon, who deteriorated from a humble man of wisdom to a vain fool in a rather brief span of time.

I'm now grateful for that chemistry class experiment I witnessed back in 1951. At the time I kept thinking, "What a drag." No longer. The memory of that frog has kept me out of a lot of hot water.

Deepening Your Roots

1 Kings 9:1 – 9; Proverbs 3:1 – 15; 1 Corinthians 10:1 – 13; Hebrews 2:18

Branching Out

1. What's a wrong area of thought or action that you've begun to tolerate in your life? Spend at least one hour this week reading Scripture that talks about it to get God's perspective on the matter.
2. Write out five standards by which you live your life. Use this list as a reference mark when you feel attracted by the world's standards.

   1. _____
   2. _____
   3. _____
   4. _____
   5. _____

ℛ ℛ ℛ

Growing Strong

We talked over some serious things this week. Remember? What's a phrase, verse, question, or illustration from this book that still sticks out in your mind? How has it helped you in the "dailyness" of living this past week?

_____
_____
_____
_____

FRIENDLY — INSIDE OUT

Are you attractive? I'm not referring to external beauty nor facial features. I'm asking if you are attractive — magnetic, winsome, charming, friendly. Listen to Proverbs 18:24a (KJV):

> A man that hath friends must show *himself* friendly.

Do you see the point of the proverb? To have friends we must *be* friendly. Friendliness is a matter of being someone ... more than it is doing something.

A prerequisite to friendliness is a positive, healthy self-image. Ephesians 5:29 suggests this fact in a context dealing with a man's love for his wife.

> For no one ever hated his own flesh, but nourishes and cherishes it, just as Christ also does the church. (Read also Romans 12:3.)

A healthy attitude toward ourselves is necessary before there can be a healthy attitude toward others ... and attract them as friends. To encourage you toward that vital objective, let me remind you of three simple, yet wonderful facts:

> 1. God originally designed and "prescribed" you (Psalm 139:13 – 17).
>
> 2. God is not through — He hasn't completed His work in you (Romans 8:29; Ephesians 2:10).
>
> 3. The *real* you — that which God develops — is *within* you (1 Samuel 16:7).

Far more than your outward size, shape, features, and dress, your *inner* qualities are the things that make you attractive and friendly. First Peter 3:1 – 6 makes this abundantly clear.

So — rather than feeling obligated to "glad hand" everyone you see at church and work up an outward appearance of friendliness, take a long look at the *inner* you, the real you. Call to mind those qualities He has developed within you. Find encouragement in the fact that you have a unique combination of inner qualities found in no one else — so you have a contribution to make in just being yourself!

Ask God to give you the ability to be positive, honest, and open (and comfortable doing so!) at all times. Ask Him to use you to *be* a friend to someone who is needing a friend. Personally, I think that makes a lot more sense than feeling we have to walk around with a grin twenty-four hours a day!

I agree with John R. Mott:

> Rule by the heart. When logic and argument and other forms of persuasion fail, fall back on the heart-genuine friendship.

Deepening Your Roots
1 Samuel 16:1 – 7; 1 Kings 5:1 – 12; John 15:15

Branching Out
1. Choose an acquaintance to befriend this week.
2. What is an inner quality you like about yourself that makes you unique?
3. Show yourself friendly today by (you fill in the blank) _____

_____

A Parable: Saving Lives

On a dangerous seacoast notorious for shipwrecks, there was a crude little lifesaving station. Actually, the station was merely a hut with only one boat . . . but the few devoted members kept a constant watch over the turbulent sea. With little thought for themselves, they would go out day and night tirelessly searching for those in danger as well as the lost. Many, many lives were saved by this brave band of men who faithfully worked as a team in and out of the lifesaving station. By and by, it became a famous place.

Some of those who had been saved as well as others along the seacoast wanted to become associated with this little station. They were willing to give their time and energy and money in support of its objectives. New boats were purchased. New crews were trained. The station that was once obscure and crude and virtually insignificant began to grow. Some of its members were unhappy that the hut was so unattractive and poorly equipped. They felt a more comfortable place should be provided. Emergency cots were replaced with lovely furniture. Rough, hand-made equipment was discarded and sophisticated, classy systems were installed. The hut, of course, had to be torn down to make room for all the additional equipment, furniture, systems, and appointments. By its completion, the life-saving station had become a popular gathering place, and its objectives had begun to shift. It was now used as sort of a clubhouse, an attractive building for public gatherings. Saving lives, feeding the hungry, strengthening the fearful, and calming the disturbed rarely occurred by now.

Fewer members were now interested in braving the sea on lifesaving missions, so they hired professional lifeboat crews to do this work. The original goal of the station wasn't altogether forgotten, however. The lifesaving motifs still prevailed in the club's decorations. In fact, there was a liturgical lifeboat preserved in the *Room of Sweet Memories* with soft, indirect lighting, which helped hide the layer of dust upon the once-used vessel.

About this time a large ship was wrecked off the coast and the boat crews brought in loads of cold, wet, half-drowned people. They were dirty, some terribly sick and lonely. Others were black and "different" from the majority of the club members. The beautiful new club suddenly became messy and cluttered. A special committee saw to it that a shower house was immediately built *outside* and *away from* the club so victims of shipwreck could be cleaned up *before* coming inside.

At the next meeting there were strong words and angry feelings, which resulted in a division among the members. Most of the people wanted to stop the club's lifesaving activities and all involvements with shipwreck victims . . . ("it's too unpleasant, it's a hindrance to our social life, it's opening the door to folks who are not *our kind*"). As you'd expect, some still insisted upon saving lives, that this was their primary objective — that their only reason for existence was ministering to *anyone* needing help regardless of their club's beauty or size or decorations. They were voted down and told if they wanted to save the lives of various kinds of people who were shipwrecked in those waters, they could begin their own lifesaving station down the coast! They did.

As years passed, the new station experienced the same old changes. It evolved into another club . . . and yet another lifesaving station was begun. History continued to repeat itself . . . and if you visit that coast today you'll find a large number of exclusive, impressive clubs along the shoreline owned and operated by slick professionals who have lost all involvement with the saving of lives.

Shipwrecks still occur in those waters, but now, most of the victims are not saved. Every day they drown at sea, and so few seem to care . . . so very few.

Do you?

Deepening Your Roots
Colossians 4:2 – 6; Matthew 5:13 – 16; Ephesians 5:1 – 33

Branching Out

1. Take time today to pray for someone you know is shipwrecked.
2. Look for someone in need this week and be his "salvation" by meeting his need.
3. Keep your porch light on all week (day and night) to remind yourself that you and your home are to be a lighthouse for the world.

THE WINSOME WITNESS

*T*onight was fun 'n' games night around the supper table in our house. It was wild. First of all, one of the kids snickered during the prayer (which isn't that unusual) and that tipped the first domino. Then a humorous incident from school was shared and the event (as well as how it was told) triggered havoc around the table. That was the beginning of twenty to thirty minutes of the loudest, silliest, most enjoyable laughter you can imagine. At one point I watched my oldest literally fall off his chair in hysterics, my youngest doubled over in his chair as his face wound up in his plate with corn chips stuck to his cheeks . . . and my two girls leaning back, lost and preoccupied in the most beautiful and beneficial therapy God ever granted humanity: *laughter.*

What is so amazing is that everything seemed far less serious and heavy. Irritability and impatience were ignored like unwanted guests. For example, during the meal little Chuck spilled his drink twice . . . and even *that* brought the house down. If I remember correctly, that made six times during the day he accidentally spilled his drink, but nobody bothered to count.

All is quiet now, a rather unusual phenomenon around here. It's almost midnight and although my bones are weary, I'm filled and thrilled with the most pleasant memories a father can enjoy — a healthy, happy, laughing family. What a treasure! The load that often weighs heavily upon my shoulders about this time each week seems light and insignificant now. Laughter, the needed friend, has paid another dividend.

If you ask me, I think it is often just as sacred to laugh as it is to pray . . . or preach . . . or witness. But then — laughter *is* a witness in many ways. We have been misled by a twisted, unbalanced mind if we have come to think of laughter and fun as being carnal or even questionable. This is one of Satan's sharpest darts and from the looks and long lines on our faces, some of us have been punctured too many times. Pathetic indeed is the stern, somber Christian who has developed the look of an old basset hound through long hours of practice in restraining humor and squelching laughs.

Looking stern and severe is nothing new. The frowning fraternity of the sour set got started in the first century. Its charter members were a scowling band of religious stuffed shirts called Pharisees. I hardly need to remind you that Jesus' strongest words were directed at them. Their super-serious, ritually rigid life style nauseated our Lord. This brings me to a related point of contention I have with artists who portray Jesus Christ perpetually somber, often depressed. You simply cannot convince me that during thirty-three years as a carpenter and discipler of the Twelve He never enjoyed a long, side-splitting laugh. Wouldn't it be refreshing to see a few pictures of Jesus leaning back with His companions, thoroughly enjoying a few minutes of fun with them? Surely that isn't heresy!

Picture in your mind Martin Luther, the reformer. What do you see? A stern-faced, steel-jawed, frowning fighter with his German fist clenched and raised against wrong? *Wrong!*

Several of his biographers inform us that he *abounded* in an unguarded, transparent sincerity . . . plain and pleasant honesty . . . playful humor and mirth. Small wonder he attracted the oppressed, browbeaten people of his day like flies and honey. The reformer, you see, wasn't afraid to laugh. In one word, surprising though it may seem, Luther was *winsome*.

Let's try another famous name: Charles Haddon Spurgeon, the great preacher of London. What do you see? A sober, stoop-shouldered pastor who dragged the weight of sinful England around with a rope? Try again!

Spurgeon was a character. His style was so loose he was criticized again and again for bordering on frivolity in the Tabernacle pulpit. Certain incensed fellow clergymen railed against his habit of introducing humor into his sermons. With a twinkle in his eye, he once replied:

> "If only you knew how much I hold back, you would commend me. . . . This preacher thinks it less a crime to cause a momentary laughter than a half-hour of profound slumber."[4]

Spurgeon dearly loved life. His favorite sound was laughter — and frequently he leaned back in the pulpit and *roared aloud* over something that struck him funny. He infected people with cheer germs. Those who caught the disease found their load lighter and their Christianity brighter. Like Luther, Spurgeon was *winsome*.

Winsomeness. That tasteful, appealing, ultra-magnetic quality . . . that charisma . . . that ability to cause joy and genuine pleasure in the thick of it all. When a teacher has it, students line up for the course. When a dentist or physician has it, his practice stays full. When a salesman has it, he gets writer's cramp filling out orders. When an usher has it, the church is considered friendly. When a college president has it, the public relations department has a downhill slide. When a coach has it, the team shows it. When a restaurant owner has it, the public knows it. When parents have it, kids grow it.

Winsomeness *motivates.* It releases the stranglehold grip of the daily grind. It takes the sting out of reality. Winsomeness *simplifies.* Things suddenly become less complicated . . . less severe . . . less bothersome. The hole at the end of the tunnel becomes far more significant than the dark passage leading to it. Winsomeness *encourages.* Without ignoring the wrong, winsomeness focuses on the benefits, the hopes, the answers. Even when it must deal with jagged disappointment or inescapable negatives, winsomeness stands tall and refuses to spend the night in such dwellings.

Winsome humor is an asset beyond value in the life of a missionary. Indeed, it is a most serious deficiency if a missionary lacks the ability to find something to smile about in diverse and difficult situations. I recently read of a Swede who was urged by friends to give up the idea of returning to India as a missionary because it was so hot there. "Man," he was exhorted, "it's 120 degrees in the shade!" "Vell," countered the Swede in noble contempt, "ve don't alvays have to stay in the shade, do ve?"[5]

Some frowning, neurotic soul is reading this and saying, "Well, somebody's got to do the job. Life is more than a merry-go-round. Laughter is all right for schoolgirls — but adults, especially *Christian adults,* have a task to perform that's deadly serious." Okay, pal. So it's serious. So it isn't all a joke. Nobody's going to argue that life has its demands and that being mature involves discipline and responsibility. But who says we have to have an ulcer and drive ourselves (and each other) to distraction in the process of fulfilling our God-given role? No one is less efficient or more incompetent than the person on the brink of a breakdown, who has stopped having fun, who is nursing a bleeding ulcer, who has become a pawn in the brutal hands of relentless responsibilities, who has begun a one-man crusade for *whatever,* who has lost the ability to relax and laugh and "blow it" without guilt. Our hospitals are full — literally jammed — with victims of the let's-cut-the-fun philosophy of life. And today, quite frankly, they really aren't much of an asset to society — nor to the cause of Christ. That is not a criticism — it's reality.

By a sense of humor, I am neither referring to distasteful, inappropriate, vulgar jesting, nor foolish and silly talk that is ill-timed, offensive, and tactless. I mean that necessary ingredient of wit — enjoyable, delightful expressions or thoughts — which lifts our spirits and lightens our day.

How is such winsomeness cultivated — and communicated — in our homes and among our other contacts? What practical steps can be taken to yank us out of the doldrums? I suggest three specific projects:

1. Start each day with pleasant words. Your family will be the first to benefit (better have the glycerin tablets ready). No need to dance around like Bozo the Clown or force jokes into your sleepy mate's ears. Just be pleasant in your remarks, cheerful with your greetings. As you are slipping out of bed, thank God for His love . . . His calm, fresh reminders that this new day is under His control. Quietly state the encouraging truth: God loves me.

2. Smile more often. I cannot think of many occasions when a smile is out of place. Develop a cheerful countenance. A frowning face repels. A smile reaches out and attracts. God gave you this gift that radiates encouragement. Don't fence it in . . . loosen up, break that concrete mask — *smile*. You might even release a laugh or two this month if you want to get fanatical about it.

3. Express at least one honest comment of appreciation or encouraging remark to each person you are with during the day. As a Christian, you want to share Christ's love. You want to lift up hearts that are heavy. Spot strengths — and say so. Steadfastly decline to camp on other's weaknesses. Ask the Lord to make you genuinely interested in others instead of so occupied with yourself. Ask Him to enable you to take the risk and reach out. Ask Him to be winsome through you.

In spite of bleak and serious surroundings about us, I firmly believe we need another good dose of Solomon's counsel. Listen to David's wisest son:

> A joyful heart makes a cheerful face, but when the heart is sad, the spirit is broken. All the days of the afflicted are bad, but a cheerful heart has a continual feast (Proverbs 15:13, 15).

> A joyful heart is good medicine [the Hebrew says, ". . . causes good healing . . ."] but a broken spirit dries up the bones (Proverbs 17:22).

Honestly now . . . how's your sense of humor? Are the times in which we live beginning to tell on you — your attitude, your face, your outlook? If you aren't sure, ask those who live under your roof, they'll tell you! Solomon talks straight, too. He (under the Holy Spirit's direction) says that three things will occur in the lives of those who have lost their capacity to enjoy life: (1) a broken spirit, (2) a lack of inner healing, and (3) dried-up bones. What a barren portrait of the believer!

Have you begun to shrivel into a bitter, impatient, critical Christian? Is your family starting to resemble employees at a local mortuary? The Lord points to a better way — the way of joyful winsomeness. "A joyful heart" is what we need . . . and if ever we needed it, it is now.

Deepening Your Roots
Genesis 21:6; Psalm 126:1 – 6

Branching Out

1. At 3:30 p.m. every day this week take a creativity break (stop what you're doing and find another person, if possible) and have five minutes of some light-heartedness or laughter. Shoot rubber bands at a target, read the comics, or — better still — speak with someone you don't know very well.
2. Laugh, just to laugh, and see if others join in.
3. Offer a smile and a pleasant word to each person you see this morning.

❧ ❧ ❧

Growing Strong

"On the lookout for others" could easily describe the emphasis of this past week's thoughts. Doesn't it feel good to put others and their needs before your own? I thought so. Describe how you felt after accomplishing one of the Branching Out assignments:

_____

_____

_____

_____

RUMORS

Abraham Lincoln's coffin was pried open twice.

The first occasion was in 1887, twenty-two long years after his assassination. Why? You may be surprised to know it was *not* to determine if he had died of a bullet fired from John Wilkes Booth's derringer. Then *why?* Because a rumor was sweeping the country that his coffin was empty. A select group of witnesses observed that the rumor was totally false, then watched as the casket was resealed with lead.

A second time, fourteen years later, the martyred man's withered body was viewed again — this time by even more witnesses. Why *again?* For the same grim purpose! Rumors of the same nature had again implanted doubts in the public's mind. The pressure mounted to such proportions, that the same ghoulish, grotesque ceremony had to be carried out. In spite of the strong protests of Lincoln's son Robert, the body was exposed a second time. Officials felt the rumors should be laid to rest along with the Civil War president. Finally — the corpse was permanently embedded in a crypt at Springfield.

"How unfair!" you say. "Cruel" is a better word. But, you see, rumors are like that. Lacking authoritative facts and direct source, information is loosely disseminated, creating unrest and harm. It is pandered by busybodies who cater to the sick appetite in petty people. Those who feed on rumors are small, suspicious souls. They find satisfaction in trafficking in poorly-lit alleys, dropping subtle bombs that explode in others' minds by lighting the fuse of suggestion. They find comfort in being only an "innocent" channel of the unsure information . . . *never* the source. The ubiquitous "They say" or "Have you heard?" or "I understand from others" provides safety for the rumor-spreader.

> "Have you heard that the Hysterical Concrete Memorial Church is about to split?"

> "I understand Ferdinand and Flo are divorcing . . . they say she was unfaithful."

> "They say his parents have a lot of money."

"Did you hear that Pastor Elphinstonsky was asked to leave his former church?"

"I was told their son is taking dope . . . got picked up for shoplifting."

"Someone said they *had* to get married."

"Somebody mentioned he is a heavy drinker."

"I heard she's a flirt . . . watch out for her!"

"The word is out — he finally cheated his way to the top."

"It's a concern to several people that he can't be trusted."

Shakespeare does a super job of portraying the truth about rumors in *King Henry IV:*

> Rumor is a pipe
> Blown by surmises, jealousies, conjectures,
> And of so easy and so plain a stop
> That the blunt monster with uncounted heads
> The still-discordant wavering multitude
> Can play upon it (II, induction, line 15).

And how certain Christians can play that pipe! The sour melodies penetrate many a phone conversation . . . or mealtime discussion . . . or after-church "fellowship times" (what a name!) . . . or a leisurely evening with friends. The tongue is capable of prying open more caskets, exposing more skeletons in the closet, and stirring up more choking, scandalous dust than any other tool on earth.

With this in view, I submit four suggestions for silencing rumor-mongers:

1. Identify sources *by name.* If someone is determined to share information that is damaging or hurtful, request that the source be specifically stated.

2. Support evidence *with facts.* Do not accept hearsay. Refuse to listen unless honest-to-goodness *truth* is being communicated. You can tell. Truth is rarely veiled or uncertain. Rumors fade when exposed to the light.

3. Ask the person, *"May I quote you?"* It's remarkable how quickly rumor-spreaders can turn four shades of red! Equally remarkable is the speed with which they can backpedal.

4. Openly admit, *"I don't appreciate hearing that."* This approach is for the strong. It might drive a wedge between you and the guilty . . . but it's a sure way to halt the regular garbage delivery to your ears.

Deepening Your Roots

Proverbs 10:11 – 21, 15:1 – 7; James 3:1 – 12

Branching Out

1. After dinner tonight write down those things you talked about during the meal and determine if you gossiped about someone. Be honest.
2. Can you name a rumor you heard recently? Do something to stop it from spreading.

You Are Important

There is only one YOU.

Think about that. Your face and features, your voice, your style, your background, your characteristics and peculiarities, your abilities, your smile, your walk, your handshake, your manner of expression, your viewpoint . . . everything about you is found in only one individual *since man first began* — YOU.

How does that make you feel? Frankly, I'm elated!

Dig as deeply as you please in the ancient, dusty archives of *Homo sapiens* and you'll not find another YOU in the whole lot. And that, by the way, did not "just happen"; it was planned that way. Why? Because God wanted you to be YOU, that's why. He designed you to be a unique, distinct, significant person unlike any other individual on the face of the earth, throughout the vast expanse of time. In your case, as in the case of every other human being, the mold was broken, never to be used again, once you entered the flow of mankind.

Listen to David's perspective on that subject:

> You made all the delicate, inner parts of my body, and knit them together in my mother's womb. Thank you for making me so wonderfully complex! It is amazing to think about. Your workmanship is marvelous — and how well I know it. You were there while I was being formed in utter seclusion! You saw me before I was born and scheduled each day of my life before I began to breathe. Every day was recorded in your Book! (Psalm 139:13 – 16, TLB).

If I read this astounding statement correctly, you were prescribed and then presented to this world exactly as God arranged it.

Reflect on that truth, discouraged friend.

Read David's words one more time, and don't miss the comment that God is personally involved in the very days and details of your life. Great thought!

In our overly-populated, identity-crisis era, it is easy to forget this. Individuality is played down. We are asked to conform to the "system."

Group opinion is considered superior to personal conviction and everything from the college fraternity to the businessman's service club tends to encourage our blending into the mold of the masses.

It's okay to "do your thing" just so long as it is similar to others when they do "their thing." Any other thing is the wrong thing. Hogwash!

This results in what I'd call an *image syndrome,* especially among the members of God's family called Christians. There is an "image" the church must maintain. The pastor (and his staff) should "fit the image" in the eyes of the public. So should all those in leadership. Youth programs and mission conferences and evangelistic emphases dare not drift too far from the expected image established back when. Nobody can say exactly when.

Our fellowship must be warm, but filled with clichés. Our love must be expressed, but not without its cool boundaries. The creative, free, and sometimes completely different approach so threatens the keepers of the "image syndrome" that one wonders how we retain *any* draft of fresh air blown through the windows of flexibility and spontaneity.

My mind lands upon a fig-picker from Tekoa . . . a rough, raw-boned shepherd who was about as subtle as a Mack truck on the Los Angeles-Santa Ana freeway. He was tactless, unsophisticated, loud, uneducated, and uncooperative. His name was Amos. That was no problem. He was a preacher. That *was* a problem. He didn't fit the image . . . but he refused to let that bother him.

He was called (of all things) to bring the morning messages in the king's sanctuary. And bring them he did. His words penetrated those vaulted ceilings and icy pews like flaming arrows. In his own way, believing firmly in his message, he pounced upon sin like a hen on a June bug . . . and the "image keepers" of Israel told him to be silent, to peddle his doctrine of doom in the backwoods of Judah. His rugged style didn't fit in with the plush, "royal residence" at Bethel (Amos 7:12 – 13).

Aware of their attempt to strait-jacket his method and restructure his message, Amos replied:

> I was neither a prophet nor a prophet's son, but I was a shepherd, and I also took care of sycamore-fig trees. But the LORD took me from tending the flock and said to me, "Go, prophesy to my people Israel" (Amos 7:14 – 15, NIV).

Amos was not about to be something he wasn't! God made him, God called him, and God gave him a message to be communicated in his own, unique way. A Tekoa High dropout had no business trying to sound or look like a Princeton grad.

Do I write to an Amos? You don't "fit the mold"? Is that what sent you down into the valley of discouragement? You don't *sound* like every other Christian or *look* like the "standard" saint . . . or *act* like the majority?

Hallelujah! Don't sweat it, my friend. And don't you dare change just because you're outnumbered. Then you wouldn't be YOU.

What the church needs is a lot more faithful fig-pickers who have the courage to simply be themselves, regardless. Whoever is responsible for standardizing the ranks of Christians ought to be shot at dawn. In so doing they completely ignored the value of variety, which God planned for His church when He *"arranged the parts in the body, every one of them, just as He wanted them to be"* (1 Corinthians 12:18).

You are YOU. There is only one YOU. And YOU are important.

Want to start feeling better? Really desire to dispel discouragement? I can say it all in three words:

Start being YOU.

Deepening Your Roots
Genesis 37:19, 40:1 – 8; Romans 12:3 – 8; Philippians 2:1 – 4

Branching Out

1. Name five things you like about yourself that are unique to you:

    1. _____
    2. _____
    3. _____
    4. _____
    5. _____

2. Name someone you don't like or enjoy being around. Now, name three positive things about that person that says he is a special individual:

    1. _____
    2. _____
    3. _____

3. Write a friend and tell him three things you like about him that make him a unique person.

TEARS

When words fail, tears flow.

Tears have a language all their own, a tongue that needs no interpreter. In some mysterious way, our complex inner-communication system knows when to admit its verbal limitations . . . and the tears come.

Eyes that flashed and sparkled only moments before are flooded from a secret reservoir. We try in vain to restrain the flow, but even strong men falter.

Tears are not self-conscious. They can spring upon us when we are speaking in public, or standing beside others who look to us for strength. Most often they appear when our soul is overwhelmed with feelings that words cannot describe.

Our tears may flow during the singing of a great, majestic hymn, or when we are alone, lost in some vivid memory or wrestling in prayer.

Did you know that God takes special notice of those tears of yours? Psalm 56:8 tells that He puts them in His bottle and enters them into the record He keeps on our lives.

David said, "The Lord has heard the voice of my weeping."

A teardrop on earth summons the King of Heaven. Rather than being ashamed or disappointed, the Lord takes note of our inner friction when hard times are oiled by tears. He turns these situations into moments of tenderness; He never forgets those crises in our lives where tears were shed.

One of the great drawbacks of our cold, sophisticated society is its reluctance to show tears. For some strange reason, men feel that tears are a sign of weakness . . . and many an adult feels to cry is to be immature. How silly! How unfortunate! The consequence is that we place a watchdog named "restraint" before our hearts. This animal is trained to bark, snap, and scare away any unexpected guest who seeks entrance.

The ultimate result is a well-guarded, highly respectable, uninvolved heart surrounded by heavy bars of confinement. Such a structure resembles a prison more than a home where the tender Spirit of Christ resides.

Jeremiah lived in no such dwelling. His transparent tent was so tender and sensitive he could not preach a sermon without the interruption of tears. "The weeping prophet" became his nickname and even though he didn't always have the words to describe his feelings, he was never at a loss to communicate his convictions. You could always count on Jeremiah to bury his head in his hands and sob aloud.

Strange that this man was selected by God to be His personal spokesman at the most critical time in Israel's history. Seems like an unlikely choice — unless you value tears as God does. I wonder how many tear bottles in heaven are marked with his name.

I wonder how many of them bear *your* initials. You'll never have many until you impound restraint and let a little tenderness run loose. You might lose a little of your polished respectability, but you'll have a lot more freedom. And a lot less pride.

Deepening Your Roots

Lamentations 1:12 – 16, 3:46 – 50; Jeremiah 50:4; Luke 7:36 – 50

Branching Out

1. When's the last time you cried? _____
   If it has been months or years, ask God to bring something your way this week that could be the catalyst to cause tear drops to form and flow from your eyes.
2. Have you ever cried alongside someone else as he experienced grief or joy? Ask God to make your heart tender enough to hurt with others and free enough to cry with them.
3. If you find yourself crying this week, don't try to hide the tears from those around you. Tears are beautiful to God! And to God's people.

☙ ☙ ☙

Growing Strong

The weeks go by so fast. The cold of winter is about to release itself to spring, the season of renewal. Hope! How wonderful to feel a sense of hope inside that says, "Even though I've failed, God still loves me." Are you ready for what's ahead? Eager for spring to come? I'm glad to hear that. Before you turn the page — take time to tell me what you hope our spring together in this book will produce:

_____

_____

_____

_____

Spring

A Season of Renewal

SPRING

As I sit here in my home writing these words, it is the first day of spring. Literally. I'm ready for a new season, aren't you? Especially spring.

Colorful little pansy blooms are fluttering in the breeze alongside the winding brick walkway out front. I can see them through my study window. Two sparrows (I guess that's what they are) are playing fly 'n seek. They are either madly in love or really ticked off at each other. They've built a tiny nest in the streetlight near the mailbox. Tiny pink buds now cover our ruby-leaf plum tree up near the window, and the grass is decidedly greener than it was a couple of months ago. God's private urban renewal program is happening before my very eyes in my yard. I was wrong again. Just when I was convinced everything was doomed to perpetual drab, it's become rainbow city out there. Amazing!

Reminds me of a slice of my life . . . how about you? The blizzard blast of winter does a numbing number on our minds, have you noticed? Feelings of helplessness settle in. The fragrance of blossoms seems buried forever, smothered beneath the cold, snuffed out in the root system . . . never again to emerge. Makes us wonder if we'll ever run free again, if the sod will ever soften, if we'll ever again feel warmly embraced by the rays of the sun as it smiles on us through cloudless days. Bottom line: Will change ever occur?

Suddenly, God pushes back the gate and in marches March to the cadence of the Conductor's command. Happens every year. Enter: renewal. Exit: doubt. Hello hope, good-bye despair.

O spring, how we missed you!

How much we need your gracious nudging! Stir us from our slumber. Bring back the color. Add a little shower now and then to clean things up. Blow away those threatening clouds with your sweet, gentle breezes so we can see again the mountains of challenge that make us want to climb higher. They've been there all winter, but we've been inside a long, long

time. It's easy to lose sight of the beautiful peaks and the lovely meadows when we reduce life to "Operation Survival."

Is it springtime right now in your season of life? Perhaps you're awakening from spiritual hibernation, crawling slowly out of a dark cave of disillusionment and discouragement. Don't be afraid to try again. That's the sun out there! It invites you to try out its splendor . . . to believe anew. To realize that the same Lord who renews the trees with buds and blossoms, who renews the grass with green in place of brown, is ready to renew your life with hope and courage (April 15, notwithstanding!).

The promise of change is all around. If you are ready to believe that, read on. The following "spring thoughts" have been designed with you in mind.

Roots

There's this tree in my front yard that gives me fits several times a year. It leans. No, it never breaks or stops growing . . . it just leans. It's attractive, deep green, nicely shaped, and annually bears fragrant blossoms. But let a good, healthy gust give it a shove — and over it goes. Like, *fast.*

It happened today. Right now the thing is tilted on about a forty-five degree angle towards the north. Stake and all, over it went. Seems such a shame this good-looking, charming tree can't hold its own. Take away the support ropes and it's only a matter of time . . . no match against the invisible slugger with a wild haymaker. Unless I lift it up, it will stay down for the full count. Every time.

Why? Well, in layman's language, it's top-heavy. Lots of leafy branches and heavy foliage above ground (which all of us appreciate and enjoy), but down underneath, weak roots. Little shoots here and there, reaching out for water and nutrients . . . but insufficient to support the fast-growing stuff up above. And the thing doesn't have sense enough to lay back on the new leaves until the roots catch up!

So out I go in the morning to bring it back up straight. I'll talk to it, give it a piece of my mind I can't afford to lose, and with a jerk, tell it to "straighten up." But let another blustery bully come roarin' out of his corner and I'll guarantee you it will fall victim to a sucker punch before the third round.

If nothing else, that overgrown, ornery perennial has provided me with an object lesson I can't ignore any longer: Strong roots stabilize growth. If that's true of trees it is certainly crucial for Christians. Roots strengthen and support us against the prevailing winds of persuasion. When the mind-bending gales attack without warning, it's the network of solid roots that holds us firm and keeps us straight. Beautiful branches and lacy leaves, no matter how attractive, fail to fortify us as the velocity increases. It takes roots, stubborn, deep, powerful roots, to keep us standing.

That explains why the Savior said what He did about the plant that withered. It had a root problem (Mark 4:6), so it couldn't handle the blistering rays of the sun. And why Paul's prayer for those young, energetic

Ephesian believers included the thought of "being rooted and grounded . . ." (3:17). And why the apostle urged the Colossian Christians to be "firmly rooted . . . built up and established" in their faith (2:7). Strong roots stabilize growth. That's the reason they are so very important. Without them we lean and sometimes snap.

But before you get excited about whipping up a strong set of roots, better remember this: It takes time. There's no instant route to roots. And it isn't fun 'n games either. It's hard work. Nor is it a high-profile process. Nobody spends much time digging around a tree trunk, admiring: *"What neat roots you have!"* No, the stronger and deeper the roots, the less visible they are. The less noticed.

Mark it down — there won't be a seminar next week that promises "Strong roots in five days or your money back." The process is slow. Neither will there ever be a lot of noise and smoke surrounding their growth. The process is silent. But in the long run the final product will be irreplaceable . . . invaluable.

If you're looking for a showy, shallow, get-up-there-quick kind of growth, then I've got the answer. Drop by soon and I'll sell you a perfect specimen — ropes and all.

Cheap.

Deepening Your Roots
Mark 4:1 – 41; Ephesians 3:1 – 21; Colossians 2:1 – 23

Branching Out

1. Deepen your roots today by spending one solid hour reading Scripture. Then write (in the space below) one key thought or promise that strengthened you out of that reading. _____

   _____

2. Buy a tree, plant it in your yard, and let it be a constant reminder of your need to grow deep roots.

NEWBORN

*T*wo hours away from our own front door we traveled completely around the world. We didn't miss a continent. From Paraguay to the Congo. From the Serengeti Plains of Tanzania into the tropical rain forests of Malagasy, across the Indian Ocean to mysterious Malaya. Then it was the tundra of the Arctic Circle, Scandinavia to Mesopotamia, Egypt to China, Manchuria to Siberia. From the icy heights of the Himalayan peaks, across the vast outback of Australia, on deep into the tangled jungles of New Guinea. . . .

By bus.

In only forty-five minutes.

We *ooohd* and *ahhhd* our way through every conceivable scent, sight, and sound. Nothing was the same, except the small familiar sign that kept popping up on the trails and the trees: Please Don't Feed the Animals.

You guessed it. The famed San Diego Zoo earned another blue ribbon. Where else can a family hear the shrill scream of peacocks running free, touch an elephant's snout, study in detail the colorful crest of a rare cockatoo, look into the ceaseless stare of a silvery gray koala perched on the forked branches of a eucalyptus, or stand eighteen inches from a cobra . . . all in one afternoon? I'll tell you, it makes the child come out from inside us. As we marvel at God's handiwork among His creatures, we gain a renewed respect for His creative genius. Who else could ever come up with a fat-tailed *gecko?* Or the two-toned *tapir?* Or that weird, long-tongued *okapi* . . . part horse and part giraffe(!) . . . with fur like velvet and enormous ears?

Above and beyond all this, we had a rare treat seldom witnessed in that hundred-acre nucleus of Balboa Park. It was *so* unusual that our salty guide was suddenly mute. We happened upon a newborn. Can't remember the four-footed species, but the tiny thing was no more than two minutes old. There it lay out in the open. Still curled as though in the womb. Wet, wide-eyed, and flop-eared, that awkward, fuzzy ball of new life was blinking at its very first glimpse of dirt, rock, sun, and water. Standing over it was its mama, fresh blood on her strong hind legs as she proudly licked away the afterbirth and the cord. The other animals? Hardly a second glance. They milled around totally unconcerned.

We could stay no longer. We had to "stay on schedule," so we roared off, leaving a choking cloud of diesel exhaust in our wake.

Many moons have passed since that memorable episode, yet I can't get over the analogy. What happened down there is an amazingly accurate scenario of what happens every day around our world. Not physically, but spiritually. Not among caged animals, but in human hearts. Whether in Madagascar or Monterrey, Zaire or Zurich, Belfast or Birmingham, as traffic swirls by and the pace increases and pressure mounts . . . a new birth from heaven suddenly transpires. For some, it's in the heat of the day and for others it happens toward evening or in the dead of night. Some newborns take their first breath in a small church on a windswept hill after hearing the simple yet stirring story of the Savior's death. Others are in a lonely prison cell sitting beside a radio. Still others are on a campus surrounded by a few Christians who care.

God steps in. Unannounced, He bursts into the soul, bringing forgiveness, cleansing, peace, a whole new perspective and dimension. He calls it "eternal life." And the newborn? Whether an ignorant savage in West Irian or an influential statesman on Capitol Hill, it really doesn't matter. The Scriptures paint the same portrait for all newborns:

> . . . a new creature . . . old things passed away . . . new things have come (2 Corinthians 5:17).

New hope. New attitudes. New feelings. New direction. New destiny. The newborn shakes his head, blinks, looks around at his first glimpse of new life, and he can hardly believe it. And the world? Why, of course, it rushes on. Unconcerned, busy, preoccupied; it has to "stay on schedule." Someone's eternal new birth has occurred. Although it doesn't attract a second glance from those standing around, God's kingdom is being silently enlarged.

It happens every day in our vast world. It even happened *today*. For all you know, maybe two minutes away from your own front door.

Deepening Your Roots
John 3:1 – 17; 2 Corinthians 5:17; 1 Peter 1:1 – 5

Branching Out

1. Sometime this week hold a baby in your arms.
2. Pray for a young Christian every day this week.

A Cure for Tunnel Vision

*T*he splinter in my thumb this morning brings back pleasant memories of yesterday's diversion. Cranking up the old radial arm saw in my garage, I wound up with two pecky cedar window box planters. I plunged into the project with the zeal of a paratrooper, ecstatic over the airborne sawdust, delighting over every angle, every nail, every hammer blow, even the feel of the wood and the scream of the saw. I caught myself thinking about nothing but the next cut . . . the exhilaration of accomplishment . . . the sheer joy of doing something totally opposite of my career and completely different from my calling.

Periodically, I looked up through the sawdust and prayed, "Lord, I sure do like doing this!" In this terror-filled aspirin age, my saw and I gave each other wide, toothy grins.

It was Sir William Osler, the Canadian-born physician and distinguished professor of medicine at Johns Hopkins University, who once told an audience of medical men:

> No man is really happy or safe without a hobby, and it makes precious little difference what the outside interest may be — botany, beetles or butterflies; roses, tulips or irises; fishing, mountaineering or antiques — anything will do as long as he straddles a hobby and rides it hard.[6]

A worthier prescription was never penned. Diversions are as essential to our health and personal development as schools are to our education, or as food is to our nourishment. And it's funny — you can always tell when it's time to shift gears and change hats. The frown gets deeper . . . the inner spirit gets irritable . . . the jaw gets set . . . the mind gets fatigued — these are God's signals to you that say, "Don't abort, divert! Don't cave in, get away! Don't crumble, create!" The saddest believers I know — those most bored, most lonely, most miserable, most filled with self-pity — are those who have never developed interests outside the realm of their work.

The only vision they possess is *tunnel vision,* the most significant thing they've ever created is an *ulcer,* the only thing they can discuss in depth is their old nine-to-five routine. No thanks! That's not a career, it's a sentence. It may be fulfilling the demands of an occupation, but you'll never convince me it's the experience of "abundant life" our Lord talked about.

Ladies and girls, sit down this very evening and read Proverbs 31:10–31. This passage describes a woman of great worth—a valuable human being. The interesting thing to note is that she has such balance. She is *not* locked into the dull demands of a routine existence. She is notably efficient in several areas *outside* the home and *beyond* the church.

Men, give attention to such characters as Nehemiah or Job (when he was healthy) or David or Paul. Mark these names down on the ledger of guys who recognized the value and joy of involvement and accomplishment outside the boundaries of their "stated" occupations. One used his hands in construction, another composed music, another raised cattle.

Before you shelve this discussion, try answering these questions:

> Can you name at least one area of interest (outside the limits of your "calling") which you are presently developing?
>
> Do you experience as much satisfaction in your diversion as you do in your occupation (sometimes more!)?
>
> Whenever you plunge into your diversion, is it without guilt and without anxiety?
>
> Are you aware that your diversion is as significant to God and to your own happiness as your actual vocation?

If your answer to any of the above is no, you need a few splinters in your thumb. They may help you forget the worries in your head.

Deepening Your Roots

1 Samuel 16:18 – 23; 2 Samuel 22:1; Proverbs 31:1 – 31

Branching Out

1. Spend at least three hours this week working on one of your hobbies, or finding one!
2. Start a new hobby that forces you to be with new people.

❧ ❧ ❧

Growing Strong

You had lots to do this week. How'd it go? Accomplish any of the Branching Out assignments? Tell me about one important thing you learned this week:

_____

_____

_____

_____

ORDERLINESS

*D*oing all things "decently and in order" applies to a lot more areas than theology. It's remarkable how many guys who have the ability to articulate the most exacting nuances of their expertise never get their desks cleared off. The last time a lot of them picked up their socks was when they were finishing a week at summer camp. They're brainy enough to understand Einstein's law of relativity or figure out the answers to computer foul-ups . . . but the trash under the kitchen sink can overflow until it's ankle deep without their awareness. Isn't it amazing how many men have quiz-kid heads and pig-pen habits?

And it's not limited to the male species. Some women have the toughest time just keeping a path clear from the front door to the den. I heard last week about a gal who was such a lousy housekeeper *Good Housekeeping* canceled her subscription!

She must have been a friend of Erma Bombeck. Erma's the one who says that her idea of being organized is hauling in the garden hose before winter. She's the one who admits that her cupboard shelves are lined with newspapers that read MALARIA STOPS WORK ON THE CANAL.

Of course, it's possible to become a "neatness neurotic." Like the fastidious wife of that poor fella who got hungry late one night and got out of bed for a midnight snack. When he came back to bed, she had it made.

Certainly there are ridiculous extremes. People who can't stand having a thing out of place are as bad off (maybe worse!) as those whose family at supper time resembles a Chinese fire drill. The answer to disorderliness is not vacuuming four times a day or running around the house nervously clicking off lights and tightening faucets or setting up your monthly bills according to the Dewey Decimal System. They put folks away who must have things that perfect. Furthermore, nobody likes to be around an individual so super structured. Once again — the secret is *balance.*

If the truth could be told, however, most of us don't struggle with being TOO orderly. Our problem is the other side of the coin. And the result is predictable: We burn up valuable energy and lose precious time because of it. Spending what it takes to become a little more efficient is an investment that pays rich dividends. Because we are reluctant to do so, our lives are marked by mediocrity, haphazardness, and putting out need-less fires.

Stop and think that over. Maybe a few questions will help prime the pump of self-analysis:

- Do you often lose things?
- Are you usually late for appointments and meetings?
- Do you put off doing your homework until late?
- Are you a time waster . . . like on the phone or with TV?
- Is your reading limited to only the essentials rather than heavier works?
- Are you prompt in paying bills and answering mail?
- Is your attire attractive? Things match? Clothing pressed? Shoes shined?
- Many unfinished projects lying around?
- Does your desk stay cluttered? How about the tops of tables and counters?
- Can you put your hands on important documents right away?
- Do you have a will? Is it in a protected place?
- Can you concentrate and think through decisions in a logical, well-arranged manner?

Stab, stab. Twist, twist. Even though those questions hit below the belt, they reveal the pulse of your efficiency heartbeat. Before you get all hot and bothered, fearing some gigantic plan only an efficiency expert with a Master's in business could pull off, relax. If you're like me, life is too busy to add some unrealistic, humongous program.

Let's deal with the problem in a simplified manner. First off, admit to yourself that you could stand a change here and there. Try to be specific enough to pinpoint a couple of particular areas that keep bugging you. Don't bite off too much, just one or two trouble spots you plan to deal with first.

Now then, *write down* your problem. Maybe it would be:

> *I am usually late to a meeting. More often than not, I have to hurry . . . and even then, I am five to ten minutes late.*

Once this is done, think about several practical ways you can conquer the habit pattern you've fallen into. Again, *write down* the plan for cor-rection. One final suggestion — work on only one or two projects a month. Too many targets will frustrate you. Don't forget to pray, by the way.

Proverbs is a book that puts a high priority on orderliness. We can't read it without getting motivated ... and convicted! Take 24:30 – 34, where inefficiency is personified as a "sluggard."

> I passed by the field of the sluggard, and by the vineyard of the man lacking sense; and behold, it was completely overgrown with thistles, its surface was covered with nettles, and its stone wall was broken down. When I saw, I reflected upon it; I looked, and received instruction. "A little sleep, a little slumber, a little folding of the hands to rest," then your poverty will come as a robber, and your want like an armed man.

How can this happen to us? The answer is given a couple of chapters later:

> The sluggard says, "There is a lion in the road! A Lion is in the open square!" As the door turns on its hinges, so does the sluggard on his bed. The sluggard buries his hand in the dish; he is weary of bringing it to his mouth again. The sluggard is wiser in his own eyes than seven men who can give a discreet answer (26:13 – 16).

The syndrome is painfully clear:
1. We see danger ... but we don't care (the lion).
2. We are concerned ... but too lazy to change (the bed).
3. We become victims of habit (the dish).
4. We rationalize around our failures.

"Decently and in order." That's our goal, remember. Most of us are a lot more decent than we are orderly. Which means we qualify as highly moral, modestly clothed, well-behaved sluggards.

Deepening Your Roots

1 Corinthians 14:40; Colossians 2:1 – 7

Branching Out

1. Take one of the items I asked you to "stop and think over," and make it an area you'll work on this week.
2. Identify two "messy" areas in your home:

   1. _____
   2. _____

   Choose one of them and clean it up by Sunday.

1MPATIENCE

As I write this I'm at 35,000 feet. It's 5:45 p.m., Saturday. It should be 4:15. The airliner was an hour and a half late. People are grumpy. Some are downright mad. Stewardesses are apologizing, promising extra booze to take off the edge. To complicate matters, a Japanese man across the aisle has a rather severe nosebleed and they're trying to instruct the poor chap . . . *but he doesn't speak a word of English!*

So now the meal is late. The lady on my left has a cold and makes an enormous sound when she sneezes (about every ninety seconds — I've timed her). It's something like a dying calf in a hail storm or a bull moose with one leg in a trap. Oh, one more thing. The sports film on golf just broke down and so did the nervous systems of half the men on board. It's a zoo!

It all started with the *delay.* "Mechanical trouble," they said. "Inexcusable," responded a couple of passengers. Frankly, I'd rather they fix it before we leave than decide to do something about it en route. But we Americans don't like to wait. Delays are irritating. Aggravating. Nerve-jangling. With impatient predictability we are consistently — and I might add *obnoxiously* — demanding. We want what we want *when* we want it. Not a one of us finds a delay easy to accept.

Do you question that? Put yourself into these situations:

- You're at the grocery store. Busy evening ahead. Long lines. Shopping cart has a wheel that drags. You finally finish and choose a stall with only two ahead of you. The checker is new on the job . . . her hands tremble . . . beads of perspiration dot her brow. Slowly she gets to you. Her cash register tape runs out. She isn't sure how to change it. You're delayed. How's your response?
- It's dinner-out-with-the-family night. That special place. You've fasted most of the day so you can gorge tonight. You're given a booth and a menu but the place is terribly busy and two waitresses short. So there you sit, hungry as a buffalo in winter with a glass of water and a menu you've begun to gnaw on. You're delayed. How's your response?

- You're a little late to work. The freeway's full so you decide to slip through traffic using a rarely-known shortcut only Daniel Boone could have figured out. You hit all green lights as you slide around trucks and slow drivers. Just about the time you start feeling foxy, an ominous clang, clang, clang strikes your ears. A train! You're delayed. How's your response?

The rubber of Christianity meets the road of proof at just such intersections in life. As the expression goes, our faith is "fleshed out" at times like that. The best test of my Christian growth occurs in the mainstream of life, not in the quietness of my study. *Anybody* can walk in victory when surrounded by books, silence, and the warm waves of sunshine splashing through the window. But those late takeoffs, those grocery lines, those busy restaurants, those trains! That's where faith is usually "flushed out."

The stewardess on this plane couldn't care less that I'm a "pretribulational rapturist." Your waitress will not likely be impressed that you can prove the authorship of the Pentateuch. Nor will the gal at the checkstand stare in awe as you inform her of the distinctive characteristics of biblical infallibility which you embrace.

One quality, however — a single, rare virtue scarce as diamonds and twice as precious — will immediately attract them to you and soften their spirits. That quality? The ability to accept delay graciously. Calmly. Quietly. Understandingly. With a smile. If the robe of purity is far above rubies, the garment of patience is even beyond that. Why? Because its threads of unselfishness and kindness are woven on the Lord's loom, guided within our lives by the Spirit of God. But, alas, the garment seldom clothes us!

Remember the verse?

> But the fruit of the Spirit is love, joy, peace . . .

And what else? The first three are the necessary style along with the buttons and zipper of the garment. The rest give it color and beauty:

> . . . patience, kindness, goodness, faithfulness, gentleness, self-control . . . (Galatians 5:22 – 23).

The ability to accept delay. Or disappointment. To smile back at setbacks and respond with a pleasant, understanding spirit. To cool it while others around you curse it. For a change, I refused to be hassled by today's delay. I asked God to keep me calm and cheerful, relaxed and refreshed. Know what? He did. He *really* did. No pills. No booze. No hocus-pocus. Just relaxing in the power of Jesus.

I can't promise you that others will understand. You see, I've got another problem now. Ever since takeoff I've been smiling at the stewardesses, hoping to encourage them. Just now I overheard one of them say to the other, "Watch that guy wearing glasses. I think he's had too much to drink."

<u>Deepening Your Roots</u>

Proverbs 14:29, 19:11; Romans 12:9 – 13; 2 Corinthians 6:1 – 13; Ephesians 4:1 – 3

<u>Branching Out</u>

1. When you wait in line this week, offer to let the person behind you go ahead of you, or give a compliment to the person waiting on you behind the counter or checkout area.
2. As you wait to see the doctor, or to get a check cashed or car filled with gasoline, etc., use those minutes to do some creative thinking rather than add fuel to your anger. Think about twenty things you can be thankful for. Here's one to start you off: (1) life!
3. When you are waiting for someone who is late, take that time to *pray* for him!

WHEN FOLLOWING
SEEMS UNFAIR

They were sitting around a charcoal fire at the edge of the Sea of Galilee. Jesus and over half of His chosen disciples. It was dawn; quiet and cool. Smoke drifted lazily from the fire as well as the aroma of freshly toasted bread and smoked fish. Perhaps the fog hung low. No doubt small talk and a few laughs occurred as they breakfasted. Surely someone commented on how good it was to catch over 150 fish so *quickly*.

The sounds of these hungry men must have echoed across the placid waters of Galilee. How delightful it must have been to know they were reclining on sand with the resurrected Savior in their midst.

Suddenly the conversation ceased. Jesus turned to Simon Peter. Their eyes met. For a few moments they talked together about the depth of Simon's love for his Lord. It must have been painful for the rough-hewn disciple, but he answered Jesus with honesty and humility.

Then, as abruptly as that conversation had begun, it ended — with a command. From Jesus to Peter, "Follow Me!" (John 21:19). Simple; easily understood; heard by everyone, especially Simon. The Lord wanted Simon's heart — without a single reservation. Jesus realized that His disciple was affectionately drawn to Him and greatly admired Him. But Jesus now told him to be totally available, fully committed with no strings attached. His command was perfectly calculated to get the fisherman off the fence.

Simon's response was classic. Verses 20 and 21 tell the story.

> Peter, turning around, saw the disciple whom Jesus loved [John] . . . [and] seeing him said to Jesus, "Lord, and what about this man?"

Isn't that typical? The finger was on Peter and he attempted to dodge some of its pointed direction by asking Jesus about John. "What about John, Lord? You're asking me to follow you . . . how about *him?* Aren't you going to give him the same kind of command? After all, he's a disciple, too!"

Notice Jesus' reply in the very next verse. It must have stung.

> Jesus said to him, "If I want him to remain until I come, what is that to you? You follow Me!"

This entire dialogue became permanently etched in Peter's memory. I am certain he *never* forgot the reproof.

Now what does this say to us — and what does it say to the members of our family? Simply this: Following Christ is an *individual* matter. The Lord saves us individually. He gifts and commissions us individually. He speaks to us and directs us individually. Peter momentarily forgot this fact. He became overtly interested in the will of God for *John's* life.

Does that sound a little like you? It may be that God is putting you through an experience that seems terribly demanding, even humiliating. You are facing the rigors of an obedient walk . . . and you may be looking over the fence or across the dining room table, wondering about *his* life, or *her* commitment. You're entertaining the thought, "It simply is not fair."

"What is that to you?" asks Christ. When it comes to this matter of doing His will, God has not said that you must answer for anyone else except yourself. Quit looking around for equality! Stop concerning yourself with the need of others to do what you are doing. Or endure what you have been called to endure. God chooses the roles we play. Each part is unique.

Some couples seem uniquely allowed by God to endure hardship — the loss of a child, a lingering and crippling illness, financial bankruptcy, a fire that levels everything to ashes, an unexplainable series of tragedies — while others are hardly touched by difficulty. It's so very easy for the Peter within us to lash out and bitterly lobby for an Equal Wrongs Amendment before the Judge. His response remains the same: "My child, just follow Me. Remember you're not John . . . you're Peter."

Has God called you to a difficult or demanding mission field . . . or occupation . . . or type of ministry . . . or home situation? Has He led you to live sacrificially . . . or pass up a few pleasures? If He has — *follow Him!* And forget about *John*, okay? If Jesus is big enough to prod the *Peters*, then He is also big enough to judge the *Johns*.

Deepening Your Roots
Mark 1:14 – 20, 10:21 – 31; Luke 14:25 – 35

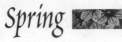

Branching Out

1. Who or what do you usually blame for keeping you from following Christ?

   _____

   Decide to blame no one, or thing, but instead be responsible for your own commitment.

2. What sacrifices have you made in order to follow Christ? _____

   _____

   What new sacrifices are you confronted with today? _____

   _____

≈ ≈ ≈

Growing Strong

Another week has quickly gone by. Seven days that you'll never recapture. Were they growth-producing days? Good. What was the toughest and yet most rewarding event of your week?

_____

_____

_____

_____

BETTER THAN SACRIFICE

The bleating sheep on the slopes of Carmel brought a frown to Samuel's brow. The movement of oxen and donkeys in the sultry valley made his stomach turn.

But when his eyes fell upon two men in the distance, walking and talking together like friends, that was the last straw! As he approached them, he remembered his earlier instruction to Saul:

> The LORD sent me to anoint you as king over His people, over Israel; now therefore, listen to the words of the LORD . . . "Now go and strike Amalek and utterly destroy all that he has, and do not spare him; but put to death both man and woman, child and infant, ox and sheep, camel and donkey" (1 Samuel 15:1, 3).

The words had been unmistakably clear and direct. King Saul was to carry out God's plans. It was an open-and-shut case of divine *extermination* without options and without opinions. The Sovereign of heaven had spoken . . . and there was to be absolute, instant obedience by King Saul. There wasn't. That's what angered Samuel when he visited the scene of slaughter and was met by the sounds and smile of life rather than the silence and stench of death.

With the severity of a submachine gun, the prophet faced the king.

"What's going on? Why do I hear and see these evidences of life? Who gave you the OK to erect a monument to yourself on the mountain? Where did you get the right to alter the command of God?"

Instead of admitting his disobedience, Saul stammered and stuttered three alternate routes:

First, he *lied.* "I have carried out the command of the LORD" (v. 13).

Second, he *rationalized.* "[We] spared the best of the sheep and oxen, to sacrifice to the LORD . . ." (v. 15).

Third, he *passed the buck.* "I did obey the voice of the LORD . . . but the people took some of the spoil, sheep and oxen . . ." (vv. 20 – 21).

Samuel was not impressed. He stared at King Saul and his buddy, Agag (who should have been a corpse by now), and then rebuked the stubborn king as few men in Scripture were rebuked:

> Has the LORD as much delight in burnt offerings and sacrifices as in obeying the voice of the LORD? Behold, to obey is better

than sacrifice, and to heed than the fat of rams. For rebellion is as the sin of divination, and insubordination is as iniquity and idolatry. Because you have rejected the word of the LORD, He has also rejected you from being king (1 Samuel 15:22, 23).

Finally, we read Saul *confessed,* "I have sinned" (v. 24).

The sands of time have covered over this ancient scene, but our bent to disobey is still present. With this in mind, take a long look at Samuel's rebuke once again. In summary, he said three serious things to Saul:

- To obey is better than all sorts of sacrificial activities.
- To rebel is similar to involving yourself in demonism.
- To disobey is no better than worshiping an idol.

Powerful words! Let's apply them in a few details of life.

Has the Lord clearly led you to do something and yet you are saying "No" or "Not now"? Maybe you're trying to bargain with Him, substituting something else in place of His direct advice . . . like Saul. WAIT NO LONGER — OBEY!

Is there within you a stubborn spirit that causes you rebel, argue, and fight back, even though you *know* it's against His leading? Perhaps you've bragged about your strong will or have cultivated the habit of resistance . . . like Saul. REBEL NO MORE — OBEY!

Have you developed the deceitful technique of hiding your disobedience behind the human masks of lies or rationalization or manipulation or blame . . . like Saul? DECEIVE NO FURTHER — OBEY!

The very best proof of your love for your Lord is *obedience* . . . nothing more, nothing less, nothing else.

Deepening Your Roots

1 Samuel 15; Proverbs 19:23, 29:25; 1 John 3:21 – 24, 5:1 – 4

Branching Out

1. What's an area in your life you have a tough time conquering or letting God control? _____

   Next time you face that area, action, or thought, tell yourself, "I will not succumb. God, I need Your strength to overpower this temptation."

2. Memorize one of the verses you read today that will strengthen your desire to obey God and help you resist Satan.

A WAY IN THE STORM

*B*low that layer of dust off the book of Nahum in your Bible and catch a glimpse of the last part of verse 3, chapter 1:

> The way of the LORD is in the whirlwind and in the storm . . .
> (MLB).

That's good to remember when you're in a rip-snortin', Texas frog-strangler as I was some years back. I nudged myself to remember God's presence as the rain-heavy, charcoal clouds hemorrhaged in eerie, aerial explosions of saw-toothed lightning and reverberating thunder. Witnessing that atmospheric drama, I reminded myself of its Director who was, once again, having His way in the whirlwind and the storm. Nahum and I took the Texas highway through Weatherford, Cisco, Abilene, and Sweetwater. There was no doubt but that the Lord, the God of the heavens, was in the storm. Nature refuses to let you forget her Artist.

But life has its storms. Hurricanes that descend from blue, sun-drenched skies or clear, starry nights. What about the whirlwinds of disease, disaster, and death? What about the storms of interruptions, irritations, and ill treatment? If Nahum's words apply to the heavenly sphere, do they also apply to the earthly? Surely if God's way is in the murky, threatening sky, it is also in the difficult, heart-straining contingencies of daily living. The Director of the heavenly and earthly theaters is One . . . and the same. The cast may be different, the plot may be altered, the props may be rearranged, but just offstage stands the Head, the Chief . . . overseeing every act, every scene, every line.

Ask Nebuchadnezzar. He would reply:

> And all the inhabitants of the earth are accounted as nothing, but He does according to His will in the host of heaven and among the inhabitants of earth; and no one can ward off His hand or say to Him, "What hast Thou done?" (Daniel 4:35).

David, if asked, would answer:

> But our God is in the heavens; He does whatever He pleases (Psalm 115:3).

Paul would add:

> For it is God who is at work in you, both to will and to work
> for His good pleasure (Philippians 2:13).

Moses nailed it down with his comment:

> When you are in distress and all these things have come upon
> you . . . you will return to the LORD your God and listen to His
> voice (Deuteronomy 4:30).

Life is literally filled with God-appointed storms. It would take several volumes much bulkier than this one to list the whirlwinds in the walk of a Christian. But two things should comfort us in the midst of daily lightning and thunder and rain and wind. First, these squalls surge across *everyone's* horizon. God has no favorite actors who always get the leading role. Second, we all *need* them. God has no other method more effective. The massive blows and shattering blasts (not to mention the little, constant irritations) smooth us, humble us, and compel us to submit to *His* script and *His* chosen role for our lives.

William Cowper could take the stand in defense of all I have written. During one period of his life, heavy, persistent clouds choked out all sunlight and hope. He tried to end it all one bleak morning by swallowing poison. The attempt at suicide failed. He then hired a coach, was driven to the Thames River, intending to hurl himself over a bridge . . . but was "strangely restrained." The next morning he fell on a sharp knife — and broke the blade! Failing in this method, he tried to hang himself but was found and taken down unconscious . . . still alive. Some time later he picked up a Bible and began to read the book of Romans. It was there Cowper finally met the God of storms, submitting to the One who had pursued him through so many desolate days and windy nights. In the center of the storm, he found peace.

After a rich life of Christian experiences — but not without whirlwind and storm — Cowper sat down and recorded his summary of the Lord's dealings with familiar words:

> God moves in a mysterious way
>   His wonders to perform;
> He plants His footsteps in the sea,
>   And rides upon the storm.
> Deep in unfathomable mines
>   Of never-failing skill

He treasures up His bright designs,
And works His sovereign will.

Before the dust settles, why not ask God to have His way in today's whirlwind? The play is so much more enjoyable when the cast cooperates with the Director.

Deepening Your Roots

Deuteronomy 4:27 – 31; Daniel 4:28 – 37; Nahum 1:1 – 3

Branching Out

1. Think back to a stormy time in your life. Did God use that storm to draw you near to Him, or show you something about His character? _____
   _____

2. Feel caught up in a whirlwind? Name it: _____
   _____

   Ask God to have His way in your dustbowl of life.

3. Cut out a weather map from the paper and post it somewhere in your house to trigger your mind to think again of God and His sovereignty.

An Antidote for Weariness

It was over thirty years ago that my brother, then on the mission field, introduced a hymn to me I'd not heard before. He loves to play the piano — and plays it beautifully — so he sat at the keyboard and played the simple melody and sang the beloved words of a hymn I have since committed to memory.

The melodic strains of this piece often accompany me as I drive or take a walk in solitude or return late from a day of pressure and demands. Actually the hymn is not new; it's an old piece based on an early Greek hymn that dates as far back as the eighth century.

> Art thou weary, art thou languid,
>   Art thou sore distressed?
> "Come to me," saith One, "And coming
>   Be at rest."
> Hath He marks to lead me to Him
>   If He be my Guide?
> In His feet and hands are wound-prints,
>   And His side.
> Finding, following, keeping, struggling,
>   Is He sure to bless?
> Saints, apostles, prophets, martyrs,
>   Answer, "Yes."[7]

Surely in the home and heart of some soul who reads this book, there is a silent sigh, a twinge of spiritual fatigue . . . a deep and abiding weariness. It's no wonder! Our pace, the incessant activity, the noise, the interruptions, the deadlines and demands, the daily schedule, and the periodic feelings of failure and futility bombard our beings like the shelling of a beachhead. Our natural tendency is to wave a white flag, shouting, "I give up! I surrender!" This, of course, is the dangerous extreme of being weary — the decision to bail out, to throw in the towel, to give in to discouragement and give up. There is nothing wrong with feeling weary, but there is everything wrong with abandoning ship in the midst of the fight.

Growing weary is the consequence of many experiences — none of them bad, but all of them exhausting. To name just a few:

We can be weary of *waiting.* "I am weary with my crying; my thought is parched; my eyes fail while I wait for my God" (Psalm 69:3).

We can be weary of *studying and learning.* "Of making many books there is no end, and much study wearies the body" (Ecclesiastes 12:12, NIV).

We can be weary of *fighting the enemy.* "He arose and struck the Philistines until his hand was weary and clung to the sword" (2 Samuel 23:10).

We can be weary of *criticism and persecution.*

> I am weary with my sighing;
> Every night I make my bed swim,
> I dissolve my couch with my tears.
> My eye has wasted away with grief;
> It has become old because of all my adversaries (Psalm 6:6 – 7).

Lots of things are fine in themselves, but our strength has its limits . . . and before long fatigue cuts our feet out from beneath us. The longer the weariness lingers, the more we face the danger of that weary condition clutching our inner man by the throat and strangling our hope, our motivation, our spark, our optimism, our encouragement.

Like Isaiah, I want to "sustain the weary" with a word of encouragement (Isaiah 50:4). Since our Lord never grows weary, He is able to give strength to the weary — He really is! If you question that, you *must* stop and read Isaiah 40:28 – 31. Do that right now.

But let's understand that God does not dispense strength and encouragement like a druggist fills your prescription. The Lord doesn't promise to give us something to *take* so we can handle our weary moments. He promises us *Himself.* That is all. And that is enough.

The Savior says:

> Come to me, all you who are weary and burdened, and I will give you rest. Take my yoke upon you and learn from me, for I am gentle and humble in heart, and you will find rest for your souls. For my yoke is easy and my burden is light (Matthew 11:28 – 30, NIV).

And Paul writes:

> For he himself is our peace . . . (Ephesians 2:14, NIV).

In place of our exhaustion and spiritual fatigue, He will give us rest. All He asks is that we come to Him . . . that we spend awhile thinking about Him, meditating on Him, talking to Him, listening in silence, occupying ourselves with Him — totally and thoroughly lost in the hiding place of His presence.

> Consider him . . . so that you will not grow weary and lose heart (Hebrews 12:3, NIV).

Growing weary, please observe, can result in losing heart.

Art thou weary? Heavy laden? Distressed? Come to the Savior. Come immediately, come repeatedly, come boldly. And be at rest.

When was the last time you came to the Lord, all alone, and gave Him your load of care?

No wonder you are weary!

Deepening Your Roots
Isaiah 40:28 – 31; 2 Corinthians 12:7 – 10; 1 Thessalonians 5:12 – 14

Branching Out

1. Set aside one hour today (make it a priority) and a place where you can get away from everyone, from work, from noise, etc., and pour your heart out to God. Be honest.
2. Mark a day on your calendar (must be by next month) when you (your spouse may come, but no children) will take off (you cannot stay at home) and retreat somewhere to relax, read the Word, talk, pray, etc. Don't allow anything to interfere with this commitment. It's a must.
3. Find a way to relieve someone who is weary. Here are some ideas: babysit without charge, to allow a mother or father to shop or rest; help a friend finish a project; plant some flowers or weed a yard; mow a lawn or clean out a garage, etc.

❧ ❧ ❧

Growing Strong

Some weeks you just can't win — everything goes wrong. And some weeks you just can't lose — everything goes your way. And some weeks you win and lose. What was your week like? Ho-hum? Exciting? Full of struggles, but plenty of growth? Hey, that's great. You're getting stronger. Feel it? In what way?

DESTINATION UNKNOWN

So you know where you are going?

The place? Dublin, Ireland. The time? Toward the end of the nineteenth century. The event? A series of blistering attacks on Christianity, especially the "alleged resurrection" of Jesus of Nazareth. The person? Thomas Henry Huxley.

You remember Huxley. Devoted disciple of Darwin. Famous biologist, teacher, and author. Defender of the theory of evolution. Bold, convincing self-avowed humanist. Traveling lecturer.

Having finished another series of public assaults against several truths Christians held sacred, Huxley was in a hurry the following morning to catch his train to the next city. He took one of Dublin's famous horse-drawn taxis and settled back with his eyes closed to rest himself for a few minutes. He assumed the driver had been told the destination by the hotel doorman, so all he said as he got in was, "Hurry . . . I'm almost late. *Drive fast!*" The horses lurched forward and galloped across Dublin at a vigorous pace. Before long Huxley glanced out the window and frowned as he realized they were going west, *away* from the sun, not toward it.

Leaning forward, the scholar shouted, "Do you know where you are going?" Without looking back, the driver yelled a classic line, not meant to be humorous, "No, your honor! But I'm driving *very* fast!"

That true story is more than a story. It's an apt summary not only of the spirit of Huxley and his followers in the nineteenth century but of many in our own day. Great speed, much motion, rapid movement, but an unknown destination. As Rollo May, the contemporary psychologist, once admitted:

> It is an old and ironic habit of human beings to run faster when
> we have lost our way.

Maybe that describes you. It can happen to anyone — strong, aggressive individuals as well as quiet, passive types. Even people like Rabbi Saul. Back in the first century he, like Huxley, was engaged in a mission of assault. Bold, dogmatic, sincere, and scholarly, the Jew from Tarsus was busy putting Christians where he felt they belonged, out of circulation! Until . . . well, until he met the very Man he was trying to convince others was a fraud. The results? A changed life. A changed man. A changed mind. A changed mission. Even a changed name. Enter Paul the apologist.

Several years later he (of all people) stumbled into Athens (of all places). The scriptural record puts it mildly, calling Athens "a city full of idols." Pausanius, who wrote fifty years after Paul was there, states, "Athens had more images than all the rest of Greece put together." Pliny adds, "In the time of Nero, Athens had well over twenty-five to thirty thousand public statues." (He didn't include *another* thirty thousand in the Parthenon.) Petronius once sneered, "It is easier to find a god than a man in Athens."

By and by, monotheistic rabbi and polytheistic philosopher stood nose to nose in the ancient oval office of the world, the famed *Areopagus*. A lonely stranger facing an intimidating body of powerful men. Those eggheads had the appearance of brilliance. Like Huxley's driver, however, they didn't know where they were going. But they were driving *very* fast. In an impromptu speech of remarkable logic and brevity — a mere six sentences that takes only two minutes to read — the Jew became a Greek to the Greeks that he might win the Greeks. Read it for yourself in Acts 17:22 – 31.

After quoting (from memory!) one of their own poets, Paul referred to their "unknown god" and spoke not only of Zeus but Jehovah . . . not about shrugging their shoulders at tomorrow *a la* the old Epicurean song, but about "judgement . . . through a Man whom He [God] has appointed," having raised Him from the dead.

Boom! That did it. End of speech at Athens. Some began to sneer. Others mumbled, "Mmmm . . . interesting. Let's meet again and dialogue together." Still others — perhaps only a few — stopped right then and there and believed in the One whom God raised from the dead.

In a big hurry these days? Driving yourself at breakneck speed? Working up lots of lather . . . but unaware of your destination? Easter is God's annual question. All across the world on Sunday morning Christ will lean forward and shout, "Do you know where you are going?" Wonder how many will be honest enough to answer, "No, your honor! But I am driving *very* fast!" Perhaps many.

But a few will stop, turn around, and head toward the Son.

Deepening Your Roots

1 Kings 1:20 – 39; Proverbs 14:12; Acts 17:22 – 31

Branching Out

1. Get up early and watch the sun rise, or catch a sunset in some quiet spot.
2. Now look again (in several Bible versions) at the sermon in Acts 17:22 – 31. Is the "unknown God" your God?

LONELINESS

It is the most desolate word in all human language. It is capable of hurling the heaviest weights the heart can endure. It plays no favorites, ignores all rules of courtesy, knows neither border nor barrier, yields no mercy, refuses all bargains, and holds the clock in utter contempt. It cannot be bribed; it will not be left behind. Crowds only make it worse, activity simply drives it deeper. Silent and destructive as a flooding river in the night, it leaves its slimy banks, seeps into our dwelling, and rises to a crest of despair. Tears fall from our eyes as groans fall from our lips — but loneliness, that uninvited guest of the soul, arrives at dusk and stays for dinner.

You have not known the bottom rung of melancholia until loneliness pays you a lengthy visit. Peter Tchaikovsky knew. The composer wrote the following words in a minor key:

None but the lonely heart can feel my anguish . . .

There is simply no other anguish like the consuming anguish of loneliness. Ask the inmate in prison this evening . . . or the uniformed man thousands of miles at sea or in some bar tonight . . . or the divorcée in that apartment . . . or the one who just buried his or her life's companion . . . or the couple whose arms ache for the child recently taken . . . or even the single, career-minded person who prepares a meal for one and goes to bed early, *alone,* surrounded by the mute memory of yesterday's song and today's disappointment.

I've crossed paths with many who could echo Tchaikovsky's lament . . . like the little Norwegian widow in Boston who now lives alone with only pictures of him whom God took . . . like the young nurse in 1967 who, after a shattered romance and broken engagement, went back to the Midwest to start over . . . like the alcoholic who wept on my desk one wintry morning clutching the bitter note left by his wife and kids: "Goodbye, forever" . . . like the husband beside the fresh grave on a windswept hill, who sobbed on my shoulder, "What now?" . . . like the disillusioned teenaged girl, away from home and heavy with child — wondering, "How can I face tomorrow?"

Some time ago someone placed this ad in a Kansas newspaper:

I will listen to you talk for 30 minutes without comment for $5.00.

Sounds like a hoax, doesn't it? But the person was serious. Did anybody call? You bet! It wasn't long before this individual was receiving ten to twenty calls a day. The pang of loneliness was so sharp that some were willing to try *anything* for a half hour of companionship.

God knows, my friend, and He *does* care. Please believe that! He not only knows and cares — He understands, He is touched, He is moved. Entering into every pulse of anguish, He longs to sustain and deliver us.

In the strangling grip of Golgotha, our Savior experienced the maximum impact of loneliness. For an undisclosed period of time, the Father forsook Him. His friends had already fled. One had betrayed Him. Now the Father turned away. In the bottomless agony of that moment, our Lord cried — He literally screamed aloud (Matthew 27:45 – 46). The loneliness of those dark moments as our Savior carried our sin cannot be adequately pictured on paper. Cold print cannot convey it. But is it any wonder that He is now able to sympathize and enter in as we battle feelings of loneliness? Those who bear the scars of that silent warfare need no explanation of the pain — only an invitation to share in the wound and, if possible, help in the healing.

When we are lonely, we need an understanding friend. *Jesus* is the One who "sticks closer than a brother." When we are lonely, we need strength to keep putting one foot in front of the other — *Jesus* is the One "who strengthens me." When we are lonely, we need to lift our eyes off ourselves. *Jesus,* the "Founder and Finisher" of the life of faith, invites us to fix our eyes on Him (Hebrews 12:1 – 3) and refuse to succumb.

God is a Specialist when the anguish is deep. His ability to heal the soul is profound . . . but only those who rely on His wounded Son will experience relief. Jesus answers Tchaikovsky with these words in a major key:

None but the trusting heart can feel My deliverance.

Deepening Your Roots
Psalm 25:16 – 22; Matthew 27:45 – 46; Hebrews 12:1 – 3

Branching Out

1. Consider someone you know who is possibly lonely. Call him up or go over and visit with him with the express purpose of "cheering him up."
2. Feeling lonely? Let's change that. Spontaneously drop by a friend's house and take the person out for pie and coffee, or breakfast (if it is early in the morning when you're reading this).

BE AN ENCOURAGER!

*H*enry Drummond's remark haunts me at times:

> How many prodigals are kept out of the kingdom of God by
> the unlovely characters of those who profess to be inside!

Will you allow me in this private chat with you to pick out one "unlovely" characteristic frequently found in Christian circles . . . and develop it from a positive point of view? I'm thinking of the *lack of encouragement* in our relationships with others. It's almost an epidemic!

To illustrate this point, when did *you* last encourage someone else? I firmly believe that an individual is never more Christlike than when full of compassion for those who are down, needy, discouraged, or forgotten. How terribly essential is our commitment to encouragement!

Woven into the fabric of the book of Acts is the quiet yet penetrating life of a man who is a stranger to most Christians. Barnabas emerged from the island of Cyprus, destined to an abstruse role of "minister of encouragement." In fact, his name means "Son of Encouragement" according to Acts 4:36. In comparison to the brilliant spotlights of this book — Peter, Paul, Silas, James, and Apollos — Barnabas appears as a flickering flame . . . but, oh, how essential his light was. How warm . . . how inviting!

Journey with me through chapter 4. The young, persecuted assembly at Jerusalem was literally "under the gun." If ever they needed encouragement, it was then. They were backed to the wall and financially stripped. Many were pressed, the needs were desperate. The comforter from Cyprus spontaneously gave all he had. He sold a tract of land and demonstrated that he was living for others by bringing the proceeds to this band of believers (vv. 32 – 37). That's what we might call: *encouragement in finances.*

The next time Barnabas appears, he's at it again! In chapter 11 the Body is growing and the Word is spreading like a flame. It's too big for the leaders to handle. Assistance is needed: gifted assistance. What does Barnabas do? He searches for and finds Saul of Tarsus (v. 25) who was an outcast because of his former life. Not afraid to stick his neck out for a new Christian who was suspect in the eyes of the public, Barnabas took him by the hand and brought him to Antioch. Before the entire assembly, the "Son of Encouragement" gave his new friend a push into a priority position . . . in fact, it was into the very place where Barnabas himself had been experiencing remarkable blessing as a church leader (vv. 22 – 23, 26).

Without a thought of jealousy, he later allowed Saul to take the leadership and set the pace for the first missionary journey (chapter 13). It is interesting to note the names were soon switched from "Barnabas . . . and Saul" (13:1), to "Paul and Barnabas" (13:42). This is the supreme test. It takes a great person to recognize that a man younger than he has God-given abilities and to encourage him to move ahead with full support. This we might call: *encouragement of fellowship and followship.*

The curtain comes down upon Barnabas's life in chapter 15. Journey two is about to begin. He and Paul discuss the possibility of taking John Mark, a young man who earlier had chosen not to encounter the rigors of that first missionary journey (13:13). Can you imagine that discussion?

"No," said Paul. "He failed once . . . he will again!"

"Yes," insisted Barnabas. "He can and will succeed with encouragement."

Paul would not withdraw his no vote. Barnabas stood his ground, believing in the young man's life, in spite of what happened before. Same style as always. You know the outcome (vv. 36 – 39). Barnabas demonstrated: *encouragement in spite of failure.*

Oh, the need for this ministry today! Is there some soul known to you in need of *financial* encouragement? A student off at school . . . a young couple up against it . . . a divorcée struggling to gain back self-acceptance . . . a forgotten servant of God laboring in an obscure and difficult ministry . . .? Encourage generously!

Do you know of someone who could and should be promoted to a place of greater usefulness, but is presently in need of your companionship and confidence? Go to bat for him! Stand in his stead . . . give him a boost. He needs your *fellowship.* How about someone who is better qualified than yourself? You would be amazed at the blessing God would pour out upon you if you'd really back him with *followship.*

Then there are the failures. The Lots, the Samsons, the Jonahs, the Demases, the John Marks. Yes, they failed. They blew it. Are you big enough to extend a hand of encouragement and genuine love? Lift up the *failure* with encouragement. It pays off! It did in John's case. He wrote the Gospel of Mark and ultimately proved to be very useful to Paul's ministry (2 Timothy 4:11b).

To Henry Drummond's indictment, I suggest a solution. A new watchword for our times.

ENCOURAGEMENT!

Shout it out. Pass it around.

Deepening Your Roots

Acts 4:32 – 37, 13:1 – 39; 1 Thessalonians 5:1 – 12

Branching Out

1. Next time you go to church, sit by someone you don't know and ask God for an opportunity to speak an encouraging word, or invite him to eat with you at your home, or treat him to dinner.
2. Look for someone at work, or among your family, or a friend, who has failed. Rather than condemn the person, encourage him by believing in him and telling him so.
3. While everyone else finds fault in someone, you be different. Find something good to say to, or about, the individual.

☙ ☙ ☙

Growing Strong

What a week! It had to be super if you worked at encouraging others, celebrated Christ's resurrection, and made an effort to brighten someone's lonely day — maybe even your own. Good job if you did that. Now, what's the most memorable happening of the past few days?

_____

_____

_____

_____

HIDDEN SAINTS

Place: O'Hare Field, Chicago. Busiest airport in the world.
Time: Late Friday afternoon. Busiest time in the day.
Scene: American Airlines terminal. Busiest area in the building.
Location: Central concourse. Busiest traffic in the terminal.
People: Three preachers. Busiest mouths in the place.

Enter—one small, smiling airline stewardess who isn't too busy to notice a paperback copy of *The Amplified Bible* in one of our hands. "Hey," she shouted with a grin, "are you guys Christians?" "Yes we are," we answered in unison. "Praise the Lord!" was her quick reply as hundreds of hurrying, preoccupied travelers brushed by. There we stood. Having never met, we were suddenly one in the Spirit. Place, time, scene, location, people were reduced to insignificance as we stood together no more than five minutes and encouraged one another in the faith. Our earthly destinations were hundreds of miles apart—Buffalo . . . Tucson . . . Fullerton—but our eternal destination was identical. For one brief interlude we were locked together as family members . . . even though physical strangers. Then we were off on our separate ways.

Several unrelated Scriptures flashed across my mind following that encounter. First, I thought of God's announcement to Elijah when He mentioned seven thousand hidden, unknown yet available believers who had not bowed to Baal (1 Kings 19:18). Second, I thought of the unnamed, hidden saints in Caesar's household who never made the headlines but were, nevertheless, counting for Christ (Philippians 4:22). Next, I remembered the long list of unheard-of Christians Paul listed in Romans 16—hidden saints like Junias, Ampliatus, Urbanus, Stachys, Apelles, Andronicus, Aristobulus, Phlegon, Hermes . . . and on and on (vv. 7–15)! You won't find a familiar name in the bunch, but they still belonged to the Savior.

Hidden saints—how many there are! Not insignificant nor reluctant, just *unknown* to us. If we could see as our Father sees, I'm convinced we would be amazed at the size of His family. If the spiritual iceberg were

suddenly turned upside down and exposed for all to view, the magnitude of the Church He is building would literally take our breath away.

Isaac Watts caught a mental glimpse of such a scene after he had meditated on Psalm 72. He recorded his thoughts:

> From north to south the princes meet
>> To pay their homage at His feet;
> While western empires own their Lord,
>> And savage tribes attend His Word.
>
> People and realms of every tongue
>> Dwell on His love with sweetest song,
> And infant voices shall proclaim
>> Their early blessings on His name.

How short-sighted we are. How restricted in our vision. Our God has planted His people all over this globe. The iron curtain, the bamboo curtain, the prosperity curtain, the poverty curtain notwithstanding. He has His prepared and appointed instruments. As yet the shafts are hidden in His quiver, in the shadow of His hand; but at the precise moment at which they will tell with the greatest effect, He draws them out and launches them in the air. History—biblical and otherwise—is replete with illustrations of unknown, hidden saints emerging from the woodwork and etching their mark upon humanity.

In unpretentious fashion, in subtle ways, many reveal their spiritual identity to those who can decipher the code: an *ICHTHUS* on the back window or around the neck . . . a well-used Testament in the pocket or worn Bible beside the hospital bed . . . an attitude of forgiveness when an offense is committed . . . a spirit of acceptance when death invades. Ah, there are dozens of ways hidden saints are brought out of hiding, but more often than not, their identity is neither displayed nor acknowledged.

My point is a simple one: *We are not alone.* To be sure, we are not all alike nor in the majority. We never will be! But neither are we an insignificant, struggling handful of nobodies stumbling and groping our way through life. We may be overlooked, but we're not overwhelmed. We may be unknown, but we're not unnoticed. We may be outnumbered, but we're not outclassed. We may be hidden, but we're not lost.

Never forget, we're the ones who belong to the King.

Deepening Your Roots

Psalm 72; Romans 16:1 – 27; Philippians 4:21 – 22

Branching Out

1. Look for some hidden saints this week and note any that are new to you.
2. Have you been hiding on purpose? If so, take a step this week and let others know you are a Christian.

WATCH OUT FOR FAKES

A friend of mine ate dog food one evening. No, he wasn't at a fraternity initiation or a hobo party . . . he was actually at an elegant student reception in a physician's home near Miami. The dog food was served on delicate little crackers with a wedge of imported cheese, bacon chips, an olive, and a sliver of pimento on top. That's right, friends and neighbors, it was hors d'oevres *á la Alpo.*

The hostess is a first-class nut! You gotta know her to appreciate the story. She had just graduated from a gourmet cooking course, and so she decided it was time to put her skill to the ultimate test. Did she ever! After doctoring up those miserable morsels and putting them on a couple of silver trays, with a sly grin she watched them disappear. One guy (my friend) couldn't get enough. He kept coming back for more. I don't recall how they broke the news to him . . . but when he found out the truth, he probably barked and bit her on the leg! He certainly must have gagged a little.

Ever since hearing that story — it is actually the truth — I've thought about how perfectly it illustrates something that transpires *daily* in another realm. I'm referring to religious fakes . . . professional charlatans . . . frauds . . . counterfeit Christians who market their wares on shiny platters decorated with tasty persuasion and impressive appearance. Being masters of deceit, they serve up delectable dishes camouflaged by logical-sounding phrases.

Hey, that's smart! If you want to make a counterfeit dollar bill, you don't use yellow construction paper, cut it in the shape of a triangle, put the Lone Ranger's picture in the center, and stamp "3" on each corner. That deceives nobody. Deception comes in *convincing* fashion, wearing the garb of authenticity, supported by the credentials of intelligence, popularity, and even a touch of class. By the millions, gullible gluttons are duped into swallowing lies, thinking all the while they are digesting the truth. In reality they are underscoring the well-worn words of Phineas Taylor Barnum: *"There's a sucker born every minute."*

> For such men are false apostles, deceitful workers, disguising themselves as apostles of Christ. And no wonder, for even

> Satan disguises himself as an angel of light. Therefore it is not
> surprising if his servants also disguise themselves as servants
> of righteousness . . . (2 Corinthians 11:13 – 15).

A glance at the silver platter and everything looks delicious: "apostles
of Christ . . . angels of light . . . servants of righteousness." Through the
genius of disguise, they not only look good, they *feel* good, they *smell*
good! The media serves them under your nose.

Testimonies abound! Listen to some:

"This is new . . . it has changed my life!"

Others say, "I did what he said . . . and now God speaks to me directly.
I see visions. I can *feel* God."

Over two million freely shout, "Eternity is *now* . . . materialism is
godly. Getting rich is a sign of spirituality."

A larger band of followers claim, "We own nothing. Everything goes
to the guru."

You find them everywhere. On street corners with little magazines,
looking ever so dedicated to God. Staring up at the stars, discovering the
future. Sitting in small groups on hillsides, eating canary mix, refusing to
shave or bathe lest they interrupt their "communion with God." The platter is filled with variety! You find some attending religious pep rallies led
by flamboyant cheerleaders in $800 orange suits and diamond-studded
shoes. On the opposite extreme are mystical dreamers who prefer seclu-
sion as they squat in silence.

They may have a "new" look — feel and taste like the real thing —
but they are not. As Screwtape once quoted to Wormwood their father's
couplet:

> Old error in new dress is ever error nonetheless.[8]

Which is another way of saying, "Dog food is dog food, no matter
how you decorate it." Or, as Paul put it so pointedly, "They are false . . .
deceitful . . . disguising themselves as apostles of Christ." They may not
look like it, but they are as phony as a yellow three-dollar bill.

Unfortunately, as long as there are hands to pick from the platter, there
will be good-looking, sweet-smelling tidbits available. But some day,
some dreadful day, the final Judge will determine and declare the truth
from error. There will be a lot of gagging and choking . . . and it will no
longer taste good.

Nothing tastes good in hell.

Deepening Your Roots

Luke 21:5 – 19; 1 John 1:5 – 10; Philippians 1:9 – 11

Branching Out

1. How does Satan try to deceive you? _____
   _____

2. Ask God to help you be discerning in all your decisions today; to know what
   is *best*. Note below a decision you made today that you sought God's counsel
   on: _____
   _____
   _____

CLICHÉS

I'd like to start a club. But not just any club. I've had the name and membership requirements for this particular organization tattooed on the underside of my eyelids for a long time.

It's going to be called a *DWAC Club:* Down With All Clichés! Getting in won't be easy. In order to become a member, you'll have to pledge yourself to a life of verbal discipline. You'll have to promise a bold breakout from the penitentiary of worn out expressions where you've been imprisoned for too many years.

But that's not all. You will have to promise to express yourself in fresh, penetrating ways to both God and fellow man. Before getting in line to join DWAC, let me warn you: The dues are high. *First,* you will have to put the torch to much of your "spiritual language," throwing into the bonfire your treasured list of pet expressions. *Second,* you will be required to stretch your mental muscles as you force yourself to substitute meaningful terms in place of religious-sounding ad lib.

Still want to sign up? A *third* bylaw insists that you learn to adjust to a world free from the security of such threadbare clichés as:

    . . . lead, guide, and direct us
    . . . I trust this will be a blessing to your heart and life . . . (yawn)
    . . . just trust the Lord
    . . . share my testimony
    . . . bless all the missionaries
    . . . wonderful message in song . . . (sigh)
    . . . bless the gift and the giver
    . . . shall we bow our hearts together?
    . . . a time of food, fun, and fellowship . . . (zzz)
    . . . bless this food to our bodies
    . . . ad infinitum, AD NAUSEUM!

Now wait — stop and think before you pick up rocks to stone me. Haven't you heard those weather-beaten phrases so long you could scream? Or worse — maybe you're so mesmerized or embalmed that you don't even hear them anymore. Christians seem to have developed the use of trite, hackneyed words and phrases into an art. *Cliché* is a French term, really. Originally, it meant "stereotype," and Mr. Webster defines stereotype: "To repeat without variation; frequent and almost mechanical repetition of the same thing . . . something conforming to a fixed pattern." Like a broken record . . . a pull-string doll with ten pre-recorded phrases . . . the ceaseless droning of parking regulations at an airport.

Our Lord once told the Pharisees they were guilty of using "meaningless repetition" when they prayed (Matthew 6:7). *Don't we?* Are we qualified to sit in judgment? On another occasion Jesus rebuked them for appearing and sounding righteous before men when they were inwardly full of hypocrisy (Matthew 23:27 – 28). All right, which one of us is going to cast the first stone at those Pharisees?

Without wanting to sound like an ultra-critical heretic, I will name a few places where twentieth-century clichés abound:

- In stale, cranked-out testimonies, lacking relevance and fresh thinking.
- In public prayers, particularly in groups where we "take turns" around the circle, or in pastoral and pre-offering prayers.
- In religious radio and television broadcasts, especially when the announcer or preacher is unprepared, lapsing into his shopworn stock of religious jargon.
- In old sermons warmed over in late Saturday night's oven, served the next morning.
- In missions conferences, Bible conferences, men's conferences, couples' conferences, prophetic conferences, family life conferences, most all conferences!
- In answers to standard questions about God, the Bible, and doubtful things.
- In pat, "doctrinal advice" to the sick, sinful, and sorrowing.
- In weddings and funerals.
- In lengthy devotionals tacked on at the end of a "fun" gathering.
- In public announcements made during "opening exercises" (cliché!) and church services.
- In seasonal greetings at Christmas, Easter, Mother's Day, Groundhog Day, etc.
- In cranked-out invocations and benedictions.

Honestly, I am not condemning. *I am pleading.*

We are witnesses and spokesmen for the God of infinite variety, boundless creativity, indescribable majesty and beauty. We hold in our possession a white-hot message of hope, a pulsating invitation to approach a living Savior. Can we justify garbing this hope in faded sackcloth, delivering it in a predictable monotone? I am longing for those of us afflicted with anemic phraseology to step forward for a transfusion. I am asking for a frank admission that our assembly-line answers and stale statements are covered with the cobweb of tradition spun by the spider of laziness. Many of our words lost their impact years ago, suffering for decades from the public abuse of overuse.

Before five separate groups, one after another, Paul described his life and service for the Great King. Yet each time he stayed creative. You won't find a single cliché in the inspired record of the battered apostle's words (Acts 22 – 26). If Paul could do it, so should we.

At this point, I openly submit a confession. *Preachers are the worst offenders.* If $5.00 fines were issued for each cliché that escapes over the pulpit, most of us would be broke at the end of each month. So let's sign a pact together, and call it a mutual DWAC project, okay? I will do everything in my power to tune up my communications . . . if you will, too. Let's fumigate our phrases, destroying forever that plague of verbal locusts which threatens to consume the freshness of our all-important message.

All potential DWAC clubbers: sign that membership card today. I've got my pen out, too.

Deepening Your Roots

Job 15:3, 18:2; Matthew 6:5 – 15, 23:27 – 39; Acts 5:40 – 7:22

Branching Out

1. Pay someone $5.00 for every cliché you use in a two-hour period.
2. Listen carefully to some children this week and catch a vision to be fresh and real. Write down the favorite phrase you heard one of them use: _____

   _____

3. Eliminate a cliché from your speech.

ऌ ऌ ऌ

Growing Strong

Those were tough assignments this week. It's not easy to be discerning twenty-four hours a day, and to stop those clichés before they roll off that tongue requires alertness and determination. Your growth this week may not be noticed by others, but you and God know how far you've come. Jot down one attempt you made in seeking to fulfill this week's assignments: _____

A SHELTERING TREE

Shortly before his death, Samuel Taylor Coleridge wrote *Youth and Age* in which he reflected over his past and strength of his earlier years. He wrote, for example:

> Nought cared this body for wind or weather,
> When youth and I lived in it together. . . .

But, to me, the most moving line in this quaint work is the statement:

> Friendship is a sheltering tree. . . .

How true . . . how terribly true! When the searing rays of adversity's sun burn their way into our day, there's nothing quite like a sheltering tree — a true friend — to give us relief in its cool shade. Its massive trunk of understanding gives security as its thick leaves of love wash our face and wipe our brow. Beneath its branches have rested many a discouraged soul!

Let me name a few. Elijah was ready to quit. Depressed and threatened, he turned in his prophet's badge and wrote out his resignation. God refused to accept either. He gave him rest, good food, and a tree named Elisha — who, according to Elijah's own testimony, "ministered to him" (1 Kings 19:19 – 21). In the analogy of Coleridge, Elijah rested in the shade of Elisha's "sheltering tree."

Paul had a similar experience. In fact, the trees in his life significantly sustained him. There was Barnabas who stood by him when everyone else ran from him (Acts 9:26 – 27; 11:25 – 26). There was Silas, his traveling companion over many an otherwise lonely mile (Acts 15:40 – 41). When you add Dr. Luke and Timothy and Onesiphorus and Epaphroditus and Aquila and Priscilla, you find a veritable *forest* of sheltering trees in that great man's life. Even Jesus enjoyed Lazarus, Martha, and Mary. Even *He* was refreshed beneath those sheltering branches from Bethany (John 11:5).

But of all the trees that God placed beside His choice servants, one human redwood looms the largest, in my opinion. David was hunted and haunted by madman Saul. The king's single objective was to witness with his own eyes David's corpse. Between Saul and David, however, stood a sheltering tree named Jonathan, who neither shook nor shed in that precarious place. No matter how hard he tried, Saul could not chop down that tree! Loyal and dependable, Jonathan assured David, "Whatever you say, I will do for you" (1 Samuel 20:4). No limits. No conditions. No bargains. No reservations. Best of all, when things were at their worst, he "went to David . . . and encouraged him in God" (1 Samuel 23:16). Why? Why would he provide such a refreshment? Because he was committed to the basic principles of a friendship. Because "he loved him as he loved himself" (1 Samuel 18:1). It was love that knit their hearts together. The kind of love that causes men to lay down their lives for their friends, as Jesus put it (John 15:13). No greater love exists on this globe.

Beneath whose branches are *you* refreshed, dear reader? Or, dare I ask, who rests beneath *yours?* Occasionally, I run across an independent soul who shuns the idea that he needs such a shelter, feeling that trees are for the immature, the spiritual babes, or those who haven't learned to trust only in the Lord. It is *that* person I most pity, for his horizontal contacts are invariably superficial and shallow. Worst of all, his closing years on earth will be spent in the loneliest spot imaginable — a hot, treeless desert.

So, then, let's be busy about the business of watering and pruning and cultivating our trees, shall we? Would I be more accurate if I added *planting* a few? Growing them takes time, you know . . . and you may really need a few when the heat rises and the winds begin to blow.

But I should remind you that a real, genuine, deep, solid friend is exceedingly rare. Either you're still looking through the forest . . . or, like me (thank God), you're enjoying shade and shelter today beside your God-given tree.

Deepening Your Roots
1 Kings 19:19 – 21; Proverbs 18:24, 27:9 – 10

Branching Out

1. Do something special for one of your close friends this week.
2. Send a card to a friend and let him know you cherish his friendship.
3. Make something for a close friend which will be a constant reminder of your friendship. (Ideas: picture album, pillow, name plaque, painting, etc.)

THE LAW OF ECHOES

A young boy lived with his grandfather on the top of a mountain in the Swiss Alps. Often, just to hear the sound of his own voice echoing back to him, he would go outside, cup his hands around his mouth, and shout, "HELLO!" Up from the canyons the reply reverberated, "HELLO . . . HELLO . . . hello . . . hello. . . ." Then he would call out, "I LOVE YOU . . . I LOVE YOU . . . I love you . . . I love you . . . love you. . . ."

One day the boy seriously misbehaved and his grandfather disciplined him severely. Reacting violently, the child shook his fist and screamed, "I HATE YOU!" To his surprise, the rocks and boulders across the mountainside responded in kind: "I HATE YOU . . . I HATE YOU . . . I hate you . . . hate you . . . hate you. . . ."

And so it is in life. Call it one of the immutable laws of human nature. We get in return exactly what we give. It all comes back. Incredible echoes mirror our actions to an emphatic degree, sometimes in greater measure than we give. The results are often embarrassing, or tragic.

What was it Jesus once said? Luke tells us:

> Treat men exactly as you like them to treat you. . . . Don't judge other people and you will not be judged yourselves. Don't condemn and you will not be condemned. Make allowances for others and people will make allowances for you. Give and men will give to you. . . . For whatever measure you use with other people they will use in their dealings with you (Luke 6:31, 37 – 38, Phillips).

Let's call it the law of echoes. Tennyson said:

> Our echoes roll from soul to soul and grow forever and forever.

The law of echoes applies to a marriage. You want a wife who is gracious, forgiving, tolerant, and supportive? Start with her husband! It will roll from your soul to hers, my friend. As our Savior puts it, "Treat her exactly as you would like her to treat you." That's quite a promise. But it rests on quite an assignment.

The law of echoes applies to our work as well. The rocky canyons within the lives of others are ready to echo back the identical attitudes and actions we initiate. Want your associates at work to be cheery, unselfish, free from catty, caustic comments and ugly glares? The place to begin is with that person who glares back at you from the bathroom mirror every morning.

The law is remarkably consistent. Children echo their parents; pupils in a classroom are usually echoes of teachers; a congregation of worshipers is more often than not a reflection of the pastor. If the one communicating is negative, severe, blunt, and demanding . . . guess what? The echo reflects those same characteristics, almost without exception.

I read recently about a teacher who asked her students to jot down, in thirty seconds, names of people they really disliked. Some students could think of only one person during that half minute. Others listed as many as fourteen. The interesting fact that emerged from the research was — *those who disliked the most people were themselves the most widely disliked.*

The law of echoes. If you want others to judge and condemn you, you start it. If you want them to be understanding, broad-minded, allowing you room to be you — then begin by being that way yourself. Like begets like. Smiles breed smiles. A positive attitude is as contagious as Hong Kong flu. Unfortunately, so are frowns, sighs, and harsh words. Whatever you deposit in the echo bank, you draw in return. *Sometimes* with interest.

A missionary was sitting at her second-story window when she was handed a letter from home. As she opened the letter, a crisp, new, ten-dollar bill fell out. She was pleasantly surprised, but as she read the letter her eyes were distracted by the movement of a shabbily dressed stranger down below, leaning against a post in front of the building. She couldn't get him off her mind. Thinking that he might be in greater financial stress than she, she slipped the bill into an envelope on which she quickly penned "Don't despair." She threw it out the window. The stranger below picked it up, read it, looked up, and smiled as he tipped his hat and went his way.

The next day she was about to leave the house when a knock came at the door. She found the same shabbily dressed man smiling as he handed her a roll of bills. When she asked what they were for, he replied:

"That's the sixty bucks you won, lady. *Don't Despair* paid five to one."

Deepening Your Roots

Luke 6:27 – 42; John 8:15; James 4:7 – 12

Branching Out

1. What's the nicest thing someone could do for you today? _____
   _____

2. Go do it for someone.

TOMORROW

I was driving up to Forest Home with easy-listening music crooning through the speaker. A quiet drive on a mellow Sunday afternoon. Then I saw something up ahead. Before I realized what it was, it flashed in my mind as something terribly wrong — out of place — distorted.

An overturned car — I could see it now. An ambulance screamed somewhere back. I felt like someone had pushed a fist into my stomach. Directing traffic around the accident, a highway patrolman briskly motioned on the crawling line of cars. I got too close of a look at the vehicle resting on its crumpled top. The scene hangs in my mind . . . the bystanders staring in open-mouthed disbelief . . . two men dragging limp bodies out of the wreckage onto the pavement. All of the passengers were either dead or terribly mutilated.

Such a warm, peaceful Sunday. The day was bright and filled with leisure hours. But for three people, that moment the world flipped — violently, crazily, fatally — upside down. What appeared to be another day of "fun-'n-games" became a day of infamous calamity. Naturally, I wondered if those victims knew our Lord — if they could smile at eternity. My pulse shot up so that I had to grip the wheel with both hands. Under my breath, I mumbled Proverbs 27:1:

> Do not boast about tomorrow, for you do not know what a day
> may bring forth.

James 4:13 – 14 was certainly written with that particular proverb in mind. I said it out loud — several times — as the traffic resumed speed and scattered heedless across the afternoon.

> Come now, you who say, "Today or tomorrow, we shall go to
> such and such a city, and spend a year there and engage in
> business and make a profit." Yet you do not know what your
> life will be like tomorrow. You are just a vapor that appears for
> a little while and then vanishes away.

Sit down for a moment, please. Find a quiet spot in your dwelling, just for sixty seconds. Think — just think about the two statements: ". . . you

do not know what your life will be like tomorrow . . ." and ". . . you do not know what a day may bring forth."

Man's knowledge seems impressive — awesome. We can split atoms, we can build skyscrapers, transplant kidneys, program computers, explore and explain outer space, and even unknot the problems of ecology. But when it comes to *tomorrow,* our knowledge plunges to zero. Whoever you are. You may be a Ph.D. from Yale, you may be a genius in your field with an I.Q. above 170, marvelously gifted and totally capable in any number of advanced, technological specialities — but you simply *do not know* what tomorrow will bring. Scientists may project, program, predict, deduct, deduce, and compute diagrams about the future. They're still only guessing. In algebraic terms, tomorrow remains factor X . . . a mystery. It cannot be explained. It defies all attempts to be exposed. It lies hidden in the depths of God's unfathomable, intricately interwoven plan. He has not been pleased to unveil it until this old earth spins sufficiently to see the dawn. And then . . . only one moment at a time.

Tomorrow. It may bring sickness, sorrow, or tragedy. It may announce an answer to your waiting prayer. It may introduce you to prosperity, the beginning of a friendship, a choice opportunity for sharing your Lord . . . or just another twenty-four hours of waiting, trusting, and claiming His presence. It may not even come! God may choose this very day to intervene and take you Home — either by death or by Rapture. We can speculate, we can dread, we can dream — but we do not know.

This sort of thinking leads to an inevitable question: Are you ready? "Ready for what?" you may ask. "Ready for *anything* " is my answer. Is your trust, your attitude of dependence sufficiently stable to sustain you *regardless?* Remember Job's avalanche? Should your Lord be pleased to turn you into a Job, would He still be your Treasure and your Triumph? Don't let the answer slip off your tongue too easily. Think about the implications of that question to your own life, health, job, and family. Should your Lord make you an Enoch, would you be reluctant to make that eternal journey?

Thank the Lord, it is His *love* that arranges our tomorrows . . . and we may be certain that whatever it brings, His love sent it our way. That is why I smile every time I read Romans 11:33. Let it bring a smile into your world.

> Oh, what a wonderful God we have! How great are his wisdom and knowledge and riches! How impossible it is for us to understand his decisions and his methods! (TLB).

Deepening Your Roots
Proverbs 16:1 – 9, 27:1; Luke 12:13 – 21

Branching Out

1. What plans do you have for tomorrow? Wait one day . . . then write in what actually took place.
2. On a calendar you use a lot, write one of the verses you read today and make an effort to incorporate it into your life.

෴ ෴ ෴

Growing Strong

I bet you're feeling good about yourself today. You should be if you took the week's assignments seriously. Hey, what was the most fun thing you did for a friend this week? Or, what did someone do for you?

_____

_____

_____

_____

ILLOGICAL LOGIC

The weather was bright and cheerful. The rays of a New Guinea sun burned down on a village normally occupied by the Tifalmin natives, but they were out in the field working on their farms and gathering firewood. It was a lazy Sunday afternoon. No one dreamed disaster was about to strike. Walt and Vonnie Steinkraus, a dedicated Wycliffe missionary couple, were at home resting alongside their daughters Kerry and Kathy.

At precisely 3:00 p.m., a freak of nature occurred. A huge section of the 300-foot mountain on the opposite side of the river from the Steinkraus's house suddenly broke loose. With a deafening roar and incredible force, a half-mile-wide, 100-foot-deep section plunged downward . . . scooping out sandbanks and crossing the river with lightning-like speed. It drove through the opposite bank and covered the village with rock, mud, and debris ten feet deep. The missionary family was buried in the landslide. Death was instantaneous. It's possible they never even heard a sound. Two eyewitnesses ran three miles to a mining camp and reported the scene. A Western Union telegram bore bleak news:

> MARCH 21/71 URGENT! WALT AND VONNIE STEINKRAUS AND CHILDREN BURIED IN VILLAGE BY LANDSLIDE SUNDAY 21ST. STOP. PLEASE NOTIFY NEXT OF KIN. STOP. VONNIE'S FATHER HAS HEART CONDITION.

The news stung deep. A numbing disbelief gripped relatives and friends across America. The Wycliffe family was stunned, even though many were seasoned veterans, tempered for years in the fires of hardship and affliction. How wrong it seemed . . . how unfair! *Why?* With a world full of reprobates and rebels, why a missionary family? With a thousand other vacant hillsides many miles from a living soul, why that mountain . . . at that time? With pockets of people all over the island not half as strategic as the Steinkraus couple, why them? Engaged in the painstaking process of translating the Bible into the Tifalmin tongue, Walt and Vonnie were taken before the project was complete.

Forgive the way this sounds, but God's heavenly plan doesn't always make earthly sense. Candidly, His logic seems a little weird at times.

Nobody likes to admit it verbally, but we all *think* it, right? His logic is illogical — to us, that is. Stop and think about that before you blindly toss it aside for fear of feeling like a heretic. What better answer do you have for those events in life that defy explanation?

- Like Job's boils, David's polygamy, the disciples' insensitivity.
- Or how about a knockout like Abigail getting stuck with a dummy like Nabal.
- How about the Lord's choice of Samson to judge the Jews.
- And the long period of time He let Saul harass David.
- We wonder about the trail of blood that consistently followed Paul.
- And the extent to which the wicked get away with murder.
- Why some babies are born healthy; others, deformed and damaged.
- Or — the family of six whose mother gets cancer.
- How about the number of religious charlatans that run free?
- And we can't forget the atrocities down through history:—like the senseless persecutions in the early centuries,—like the wholesale martyrdom of biblical reformers and saints,—like the brutal extermination of six million Jews.
- What about the endless theological debates among reliable scholars?
- The inequity of a precious child beaten by a drunken dad.
- The reason God leads you to move just about the time you get settled.

Don't you worry about such things? Not one is a nit-picking issue. Not one "makes sense." Try to square any one with *your* concept of logic and you wind up cross-eyed and tongue-tied.

Ready for another shocker? We're not supposed to have airtight answers! Why? Because our understanding is earthbound . . . human to the core . . . limited . . . finite. Our focus is from the ground up. Boxed in by the tight radius of *time* (as we measure it), multiplied by the circumference of *logic* (as we perceive it), we operate in a dimension totally unlike our Lord . . . who knows no such limitations. We see now. He sees forever. We judge on the basis of the temporal; He, on the basis of the eternal. We try to make each piece fit neatly into the next one as we put the puzzle of life together, naming it Equity or Fair. Not God. His logic is inscrutable, unsearchable, unfathomable. The Creator needs no creature to interpret His way. His reasons. His style. His vantage point is infinity. *"It is too high, I cannot attain it,"* admitted the psalmist.

And so, we *accept* rather than explain. We *trust* rather than try to make it all fit together so perfectly it squeaks. It helps to remember that each generation has only a few of the pieces, *none* of which may fit into one another. So stop trying to wrap everything in neat boxes.

Let's be illogical about this for a change. Otherwise, we try to play God's role. And most of us are fresh out of omniscience.

Deepening Your Roots
Isaiah 55:1 – 11; Psalm 73: 1; 2 Timothy 4:16 – 18

Branching Out

1. Write down something specific from your life that is hard to understand or that you question God about. Today, simply trust God with your "why" and allow Him to bring peace to your heart. _____

   _____

2. Name something in your life, or a part of your body, or in your surroundings, that cannot be changed. Now, answer this question: Have you accepted this unchangeable item even though you may not understand why God allowed it? If not, ask God to help you come to accept it, trust Him, and use it for His glory. _____

3. Name a person you know in a difficult situation who has chosen to trust God rather than question him. _____

THE STING OF PEARLS

Got your yellow pad and nickel pencil out? If not, just stop long enough to make a mental list of some of the things that irritate you. Here are a few suggestions that will get you started.

traffic jams
squeaking doors
interruptions
long lines
flat tires
deadlines
phone calls
doing dishes
being rushed
untrained pets
weeds
tight clothes
peeling onions

cold food
talkative people
incompetence
reminders
crying babies
balancing checkbooks
nosy neighbors
misplaced keys
mothers-in-law
late planes
stuck zippers
high prices

Any of those make you want to grind your teeth? Some of it sounds like today, doesn't it? It's easy to get the feeling that you can't win — no matter how hard you try. You start to entertain the thought I saw printed rather hurriedly on a small wooden plaque several weeks ago:

I am planning to have a nervous breakdown. I have earned it . . . I deserve it . . . I have worked hard for it . . . and nobody's going to keep me from having it!

If it weren't for irritations we'd be very patient, wouldn't we? We could wave calmly through life's placid sea and never encounter a ripple. Unfortunately, irritations comprise the major occupational hazard of the human race. One of these days it should dawn upon our minds that we'll never be completely free from irritations as long as we tread Planet Earth. Never. Upon arriving at such a profound conclusion, it would be wise to consider an alternative to losing our cool. The secret is *adjusting*.

Sure, that sounds simple. But it isn't. Several things tend to keep us on the ulcerated edge of irritability. If we lived in the zoo, the sign outside our cage might read: "Human Being — Creature of Habit." We tend to develop habit reactions, wrong though they may be. We are also usually in a hurry . . . inordinately wedded to the watch on our wrist. Furthermore, many of our expectations for the day are unrealistic. Echoing in our heads are the demanding voices of objectives that belong to a *week,* rather than a single day. All of this makes the needle on our inner pressure gauge whirl like Mario Andretti's tachometer. When you increase the heat to our highly pressurized system by a fiery irritation or two . . . or three . . . BOOM! Off goes the lid and out comes the steam.

It helps me if I remember that God is in charge of my day . . . not I. While He is pleased with the wise management of time and intelligent planning from day to day, He is mainly concerned with the development of inner character. He charts growth toward maturity, concerning Himself with the cultivation of priceless, attractive qualities that make us Christlike down deep within. One of His preferred methods of training us is through adjustment to irritation.

A perfect illustration?

The oyster and its pearl.

Pearls are the product of pain. For some unknown reason, the shell of the oyster gets pierced and an alien substance — a grain of sand — slips inside. On the entry of that foreign irritant, all the resources within the tiny, sensitive oyster rush to the spot and begin to release healing fluids that otherwise would have remained dormant. By and by the irritant is covered and the wound is healed — by a *pearl.* No other gem has so fascinating a history. It is the symbol of stress — a healed wound . . . a precious, tiny jewel conceived through irritation, born of adversity, nursed by adjustments. Had there been no wounding, no irritating interruption, there could have been no pearl. Some oysters are never wounded . . . and those who seek for gems toss them aside, fit only for stew.

No wonder our heavenly home has as its entrance *pearly* gates! Those who go through them need no explanation. They are the ones who have been wounded, bruised, and have responded to the sting of irritation with the pearl of adjustment.

J. B. Phillips must have realized this as he paraphrased James 1:2 – 4:

> When all kinds of trials crowd into your lives, my brothers, don't resent them as intruders, but welcome them as friends! Realize that they have come to test your endurance. But let the process go on until that endurance is fully developed, and you

will find you have become men (and women) of mature character. . . .

Deepening Your Roots
Daniel 6:1 – 28; Job 23:8 – 12

Branching Out

1. If you are a woman, wear pearl earrings, a ring, or a necklace today to remind yourself of the process we all go through and that it is possible to endure adversity and come out the winner. If you are a man, find some item that can help you remember today's thought.
2. Adjustment. When your first irritation of the day comes along, quickly tell yourself: "God is in control" and mentally make the pearl of adjustment.
3. Decide to let God be in control of your day. Have fun by writing down on a three-by-five card what happens in the next twenty-four hours. Review the card before you hit the sack.

ᴮITTERNESS

There is perhaps no more miserable existence on earth than that of a prisoner of war. The horror stories that emerge from P.O.W. hellholes around the world are enough to curl your hair.

During my training in the Marine Corps, our drill instructors did everything they could to break us, in hopes of preparing us for the possibility of enduring months — perhaps years — as prisoners behind enemy lines. No matter how intense the training may have been, however, it could not hold a candle to the actual terror of being there.

Regardless of the war or the enemy — Nazi Germany or Japan, North Korea or North Vietnam — the anguish was the same . . . deprivation, torture, starvation, loneliness, mistreatment, and boredom. All these things, mixed with a loss of health and hope, left some who were once strong and stable limp as a wimp and emotionally disabled.

Our hearts break every time we hear another tragic account from some who once stood tall in their uniforms but now stoop . . . and each time we see others occupying wheelchairs from which they will never escape.

As terrible as those memories and lingering agonies may be, there is another factor even more lamentable — the presence of bitterness. Many a man who was a victim of mistreatment in an enemy camp returned to the States liberated and free to start anew . . . yet, strangely, remains in prison. Though delivered from bondage and reunited with family and friends, some are still held captive by the bonds of bitterness. Bitterness seeps into the basement of our lives like run-off from a broken sewer pipe. Every form of ugliness begins to float to the surface of those murky waters: prejudice and profanity, suspicion and hate, cruelty and cynicism.

A change in location is no guarantee of a change in heart. Being released from external captors in no way means that one has automatically been released from internal corruption. There is no torment like the inner torment of bitterness, which is the by-product of an unforgiving spirit. It refuses to be soothed, it refuses to be healed, it refuses to forget. There is no prison more damaging than the bars of bitterness which will not let the battle end.

In the New Testament, every mention of bitterness comes from the same Greek root, *pic,* which means "to cut, to prick." The idea is a pricking or puncturing which is pungent and penetrating. We read in Luke 22:62 that Peter "wept bitterly." He wept because he was pricked in his conscience. He was "cut to the quick," we would say. In Acts 8:23, a man was said to have been "in the gall of bitterness" when he wanted to appear godly and spiritually powerful. He was simply a religious phony, bitter to the core.

Hebrews 12:15 states that a root of bitterness can spring up and cause trouble, causing many to be defiled. You cannot nurture the bitterness plant and at the same time keep it concealed. The bitter root bears bitter fruit. You may think you can hide it . . . live with it . . . "grin and bear it," but you cannot. Slowly, inexorably, that sharp, cutting edge of unforgiveness will work its way to the surface. The poison seedling will find insidious ways to cut into others. Ironically, the one who suffers most is the one who lashes out at those around him.

How can I make such a statement? Because of the parable Jesus presented in Matthew 18. Find a Bible and read verses 21 through 35. The context is "forgiveness." The main character is a man who refused to forgive a friend, even though he himself had recently been released from an enormous debt he had incurred. Because of his tacit refusal to forgive, this bitter man was "handed over to the torturers. . . ." And then Jesus adds the punch line:

> So shall my heavenly Father also do to you, if each of you does
> not forgive his brother from your heart (v. 35).

Did you hear what He said? He said that we who refuse to forgive — we who live in the gall of bitterness — will become victims of torture, meaning intense *inner* torment. If we nurture feelings of bitterness we are little better than inmates of an internal concentration camp. We lock ourselves in a lonely isolation chamber, walled in by our own refusal to forgive.

Please remember — Jesus was speaking to His *disciples,* not unbelievers. A Christian is a candidate for confinement — and unspeakable suffering — until he or she fully and completely forgives others . . . even when others are in the wrong.

I can now understand why Paul listed bitterness *first* when he said:

> Let all bitterness and wrath and anger and clamor and slander
> be put away from you, along with all malice. And be kind to

one another, tender-hearted, forgiving each other, just as God in Christ also has forgiven you (Ephesians 4:31 – 32).

For your sake, let me urge you to "put away all bitterness" now. There's no reason to stay in P.O.W. camp a minute longer. The escape route is clearly marked.

It leads to the cross . . . where the only One who had a right to be bitter wasn't.

Deepening Your Roots
Genesis 27:41 – 45; Matthew 18:21 – 35

Branching Out

1. Are you still bitter today over something that took place years ago? What is it?

_____

Are you ready to forgive that person (or maybe God)? Good!
2. Be quick to forgive someone today as you go about your work, chores at home, etc.
3. Ask a friend, or spouse, if he senses any bitterness present in you. If he says yes, deal with it today!

❧ ❧ ❧

Growing Strong

Ouch! Did I step on your toes this week or probe too deeply? Touch an area that brought conviction? Hey . . . that just means God is at work, causing growth. You've good reason to shout hurray! Go ahead. Shout. Then get a pen and complete this sentence for me: Getting rid of bitterness is like

_____

_____

_____

_____

STUMBLING

Nothing damages our dignity like stumbling!

I have seen people dressed to the hilt, stumble and fall flat on their faces as they were walking to church. I have witnessed serious and gifted soloists, stepping up to the pulpit with music in hand, stumble and fall as the sheets of music sailed like maple leaves in an October breeze. I've watched a sure and winning touchdown by a fleet split-end — nobody within fifteen yards — foiled by a stumble. I've looked on as brides and grooms stumbled in unison . . . as bandsmen stumbled in formation . . . as shoppers stumbled in stores . . . as rigid Marine officers stumbled while inspecting the troops . . . as elite, elegant ladies stumbled on stage . . . as emcees got tangled in mike wires and stumbled off stage . . . as cap and gown grads stumbled to their knees receiving their diplomas . . . and as an experienced, well-respected, eloquent speaker stumbled and fell just before he began to speak. I could never forget that one because in the fall he cut his lip and delivered his entire address while wiping the blood off his face!

And can't you remember when you have stumbled? Nothing is more humiliating or embarrassing than spilling our dignity as we fall flat on our pride. The first thing we do is take a quick look around to see who might have noticed. We long to become *invisible*. Some of my stumbling experiences make me shudder just to call them to mind.

But do you know something? Almost without exception the response of onlookers is sympathy . . . identification with the embarrassment . . . mutual ache . . . a deep sense of inner support. In fact, the immediate response is to help the stumbler back to his feet. I cannot remember a single occasion when anyone who stumbled was held down or stepped on by those nearby. I recall that there was instant concern for their hurt feelings and their physical welfare. I also recall that everyone who tripped got right back on his feet, shrugged off the momentary humiliation, and forged ahead. There's something to be learned, my friend, in all this business of stumbling.

In the penetrating letter of James, every verse is like a scalpel — cutting deep incisions in our conscience. Hidden within James 3:2 is something we often forget:

For we all stumble in many ways.

What's he saying? Nobody's perfect . . . to stumble is normal . . . a fact of life . . . an act that guarantees our humanness. He goes on to mention that we often stumble in what we *say.* When it comes to the tongue, we blow it! He says (in 2:10) that stumbling brings guilt . . . even if it is in one, small area. Isn't that the truth!

Perhaps you have *just* stumbled as you read this today. You feel guilty, you feel like a failure. You wish like crazy you had never opened your mouth . . . or done what you did . . . or responded like that. You're miserable, discouraged, and you'd like to hide, or better still — crawl off and die. Ridiculous! Get up out of that pool of self-pity, brush off the dirt with the promise of God's forgiveness — and move on!

Now I must add a word of realism. Instead of receiving the normal reaction of concern and support, you may find that some who saw you fall will want to hold you down or bad-mouth you because you slipped. Ignore them completely! They have forgotten that James 3:2 includes *them.* The only difference is that you didn't get to see them stumble. But they have, believe me, they have.

What all this adds up to is not difficult to discover:

> GOD WANTS TO USE YOU —
> STUMBLING AND ALL — BUT HE
> WON'T DO SO IF YOU REFUSE
> TO GET UP.

Stumblers who *give* up are a dime a dozen. In fact, they're useless. Stumblers who *get* up are rare. In fact, they're priceless.

Deepening Your Roots

Psalm 37:23 – 24; Hebrews 4:12 – 16

Branching Out

1. See someone stumble lately? How did you treat him? Talk or laugh about him? Remember James 2? How about empathizing with the person?

2. Keep track of people who stumble this week and note how you reacted to each one: _____

   _____

   _____

COMFORTING

*T*wo elementary-school boys were, for the first time in their lives, absolutely still. Deathly still. In separate pools of blood, each under a pale blanket, they awaited the arrival of the coroner. For them, school ended prematurely. With crushing authority, the grim reaper visited the vast metropolis of Los Angeles at the corner of Beach Boulevard and Rosecrans Avenue — unannounced and uninvited. In heavy traffic. In broad daylight. Death the Dictator came, saw, and conquered. He always does, which prompted George Bernard Shaw to write:

> The statistics on death are quite impressive. One out of one
> people die.

But what about those who *live on?* Those who try to pick up the jagged pieces? As I stood there beside my oldest son, fighting back tears, trying to swallow that knot in my throat, I kept thinking about two families that would never be the same. Two mothers and dads, especially. I could paint a portrait of the coming days: indescribable sorrow, disillusionment, sleepless nights, endless reminders, paralyzing anxiety, that unendurable sense of loss, that numbing mixture of anger, helplessness, denial, and confusion.

Let's pause here and pretend. Let's pretend you are the neighbor. One of those two grieving families lives next door. On an average Thursday afternoon, your phone rings . . . or a knock comes at the door. The information you hear stuns you. You're suddenly reeling, and you feel as if you're in a dream ("nightmare" might be a better word). Life screams to a halt. Thursday seems strangely sacred, almost eerie.

The grief of someone very near becomes so real you can taste it. The pain stabs deep and perhaps your first thought is, "Oh, how my heart goes out to_____!" Your second thought is, "What can I do to help? What would be the best expression of love, compassion, and sympathy?"

Suddenly, you're stuck. There's no set of rules to follow — no handbook for showing mercy. You hurriedly thumb through your Bible and find no sermon notes on "How to Sympathize." No, my friend, comfort for the sorrowing cannot be regulated and systematized. To go through

programmed motions with the grieving turns you into a good candidate for another "Job's counselor" . . . and none of us wants that title. What *can* you do? What *should* you do . . . or not do? What could be said that might be appreciated and appropriate?

Be real. As you reach out, admit your honest feelings to your friends. If the news stunned you, say so. If you suddenly feel tears coming, cry. If you are overwhelmed with pity and compassion, admit it. You may be a Christian with a firm hope in a life hereafter, but you're also human. Don't hide that. It may be through that gate a path of friendship will develop.

Be quiet. Your presence, not your words, will be most appreciated. The thick mantle of grief has fallen upon your friend, bringing dark, unexplainable sorrow. An abundance of words and attempts to instruct will only reveal an insensitive spirit to the grieving. The Joe Baylys, in the course of several years, lost three of their children. In his book, *The Last Thing We Talk About,* he shares his honest feelings when one of the children died:

> I was sitting, torn by grief. Someone came and talked to me of God's dealings, of why it happened, of hope beyond the grave. He talked constantly. He said things I knew were true.
>
> I was unmoved, except to wish he'd go away. He finally did.
>
> Another came and sat beside me. He didn't talk. He didn't ask me leading questions. He just sat beside me for an hour and more, listened when I said something, answered briefly, prayed simply, left.
>
> I was moved. I was comforted. I hated to see him go.

Be supportive. Those who comfort must have a tender heart of understanding. They don't come to quote verses or leave a stack of literature. They come simply to say they care. Nor do they attempt to erase today's hurt by emphasizing tomorrow's hope. They are committed to the support, the understanding of the grieving. Few things heal wounded spirits better than the balm of a supportive embrace.

> A little girl lost a playmate in death and one day reported to her family that she had gone to comfort the sorrowing mother. "What did you say?" asked her father. "Nothing," she replied, "I just climbed up on her lap and cried with her."

That's being supportive.

Be available. Everybody comes around the first day or two. But what about a month later? After the flowers? Or five months later? After the grass grows over the grave? Life, like the muddy Mississippi, keeps rolling along. Unfortunately, so do the memories of that little fella whose place at the supper table remains vacant. If ever the comforting hand of a friend is needed, it is then — when *other* kids are going swimming and snitching cookies and riding bikes. Be committed to comforting later on as well as now. Your appropriate suggestions that will help them break the spell of grief (C.S. Lewis wrote of "the laziness of grief") will help them begin again.

Like Jesus with the sisters of Lazarus in the crucible of grief, be real (He wept), be quiet (He took their angry rebukes), be supportive (He was deeply moved), be available (He stayed by their side). No big sermons, no leaflets, no attempts to correct their misunderstandings, not even a frown that suggested disapproval. He let grief run its course. Our Lord believed, as we should, that we are healed of grief only when we express it to the full.

Perhaps this explains why so many are grieving . . . and so few are comforting.

Deepening Your Roots
2 Samuel 1:17 – 27; John 11:17 – 44, 16:5 – 22

Branching Out

1. What is the one thing you can do for someone you know who is grieving?

   _____

   Do it.
2. Rather than sending a sympathy card or sending flowers to someone experiencing grief, do something different to show you care. For example, consider sending Christine Wyrtzen's album, *For Those Who Hurt,* or sending a book, or writing a letter about how much the person means to you, or sending a tea cup and saucer with a note saying, "I wish I could be there to care for you during your painful hours."
3. Embrace (hug) someone today and reassure him of your concern for him — regardless of whether he is experiencing grief or not.

CALL FOR HELP!

A PRAYER TO BE SAID
WHEN THE WORLD HAS GOTTEN YOU DOWN,
AND YOU FEEL ROTTEN,
AND YOU'RE TOO DOGGONE TIRED TO PRAY,
AND YOU'RE IN A BIG HURRY,
AND BESIDES, YOU'RE MAD AT EVERYBODY . . .
  help.

*T*here it was. One of those posters. Some are funny. Some are clever. Others beautiful. A few, thought-provoking. This one? Convicting. God really wanted me to get the message. He nudged me at a Christian conference center recently when I first read it in an administrator's office. A few weeks and many miles later He shot me the signal again — I practically ran into the same poster in a friend's office. Then just last week, while moving faster than a speeding bullet through a Portland publishing firm, I came face to face with it *again.* But this time the message broke through my defenses and wrestled me to the mat for the full count.

"My son, slow down. Ease back. Admit your needs."

Such good counsel. But so tough to carry out. Why is that? Why in the world is it such a struggle for us to cry out for assistance?

- Ants do it all the time and look at all *they* achieve.
- In my whole life I have never seen a football game won without substitutions.
- Even the finest of surgeons will arrange for help in extensive or delicate operations.
- Highway patrolmen travel in pairs.
- Through my whole career in the Marine Corps I was drilled to dig a foxhole for *two* in the event of battle.

Asking for help is smart. It's also the answer to fatigue and the "I'm dispensable" image. But something keeps us from this wise course of action, and that something is *pride.* Plain, stubborn unwillingness to admit need. The greatest battle many believers fight today is not with inefficiency, but with *super*efficiency. It's been bred into us by high-achieving parents, through years of high-pressure competition in school, and by that unyielding inner voice that keeps urging us to "Prove it to 'em! Show 'em you can do it without anyone's help!"

The result, painful though it is to admit, is a life-style of impatience. We become easily irritated — often angry. We work longer hours. Take less time off. Forget how to laugh. Cancel vacations. Allow longer and longer gaps between meaningful times in God's Word. Enjoy fewer and fewer moments in prayer and meditation. And all the while the specter of discouragement looms across our horizon like a dark storm front — threatening to choke out any remaining sunshine.

Say, my friend, it's time to declare it. You are not the Messiah of the twentieth century! There is no way you can keep pushing your life at that pace and expect to stay effective. Analyze yourself any way you please, you are H-U-M-A-N . . . nothing more. So? So slow down. So give your-self a break. So stop trying to cover all the bases and sell popcorn in the stands at the same time. So relax for a change!

Once you've put it in neutral, crack open your Bible to Exodus 18 and read aloud verses 18 – 27. It's the account of a visit Jethro made to the work place of his son-in-law. A fella by the name of Moses. Old Jethro frowned as he watched Moses flash from one need to another, from one person to another. From early morning until late at night the harried leader of the Israelites was neck-deep in decisions and activities. He must have looked very impressive — eating on the run, ripping from one end of camp to the other, planning appointments, meeting deadlines.

But Jethro wasn't impressed. "What is this thing that you are doing for the people?" he asked. Moses was somewhat defensive (most too-busy people are) as he attempted to justify his ridiculous schedule. Jethro didn't buy the story. Instead, he advised his son-in-law against trying to do everything alone. He reproved him with strong words:

> The thing that you are doing is not good. You will surely wear out. . . .

The Hebrew term means "to become old, exhausted." In three words, he told Moses to

CALL FOR HELP

The benefits of shifting and sharing the load? Read verses 22 – 23 for yourself. "It will be easier for you . . . you will be able to endure." That's interesting, isn't it? God wants our life-style to be easier than most of us realize. We seem to think it's more commendable and "spiritual" to have that tired-blood, overworked-underpaid, I've-really-got-it-tough look. You know, the martyr complex. That strained expression that conveys "I'm working so hard for Jesus" to the public. Maybe *they're* fooled, but He isn't. The truth of the matter is quite the contrary. That hurried, harried appearance usually means, "I'm too stubborn to slow down" or "I'm to insecure to say 'no'" or "I'm too proud to ask for help."

Since when is a bleeding ulcer a sign of spirituality? Or no time off and a seventy-hour week a mark of efficiency? When will we learn that efficiency is enhanced not by what we accomplish but more often by what we relinquish?

The world beginning to get you down? Feeling rotten? Too tired to pray . . . in too big a hurry? Ticked off at a lot of folks? Let me suggest one of the few four-letter words God loves to hear us shout when we're angry or discouraged:

Help!

Deepening Your Roots

Exodus 18:13 – 27; Nehemiah 2:11 – 18; Philippians 2:19 – 30, 4:2 – 3

Branching Out

1. Ask someone to help you today.
2. Next time someone yells for help, immediately stop what you are doing and assist the person. Don't ask them what's wrong. Go help!
3. *Before* someone asks you for help . . . offer it.

℗ ℗ ℗

Growing Strong

Putting others first. That's what this week was all about. Hey, isn't caring more exciting than dwelling upon yourself? I love it! And I love the thought that you're giving to others. Keep up the great attitude and superb actions. Now . . . who can you comfort today?

TROPHIES

*H*e was brilliant. Clearly a child prodigy . . . the pride of Salzburg . . . a performer *par excellence.*

At age five he wrote an advanced concerto for the harpsichord. Before he turned ten he had composed and published several violin sonatas and was playing from memory the best of Bach and Handel. Soon after his twelfth birthday he composed and conducted his own opera . . . and was awarded an honorary appointment as concertmaster with the Salzburg Symphony Orchestra. Before his brief life ended, he had written numerous operettas, cantatas, hymns, and oratorios, as well as forty-eight symphonies, forty-seven arias, duets, and quartets with orchestral accompaniment, and over a dozen operas. Some 600 works!

His official name was Johannes Chrysostomus Wolfgangus Amadeus Theophilus Mozart. With a handle like that, he *had* to be famous.

He was only thirty-five when he passed on. He was living in poverty and died in obscurity. His sick widow seemed indifferent to his burial. A few friends went as far as the church for his funeral but were deterred by a storm from going to the gravesite.

By the time anyone bothered to inquire, the location of his grave was impossible to identify. The unmarked grave of Mozart — perhaps the most gifted composer of all time — became lost forever. No shrine marks his resting place for music lovers to visit. No granite-engraved etchings for admirers to read. No place for candles to burn, flowers to embellish, tourists to gather. Mozart has joined the immortal, eternal ages — forever absent from sight. He is gone.

Or is he? Unlike Caesar, the good he did lives after him. The evil is interred with his bones. Only a handful of music buffs could begin to list three or four evils of that Austrian-born artist. Then what good lives on? *His unique contributions:* his style, his eminent innovations, that "Mozart touch." No other sound is like it. It is his, altogether. *A timeless trophy,* created by a genius, captured on the score, bringing warmth and delight to endless generations. In his music, Mozart lives on. Unexcelled.

Several years ago one of my children and I walked through a cemetery. We paused and read the stones. We knew none of the deceased. It was a nostalgic, gripping encounter. Hand in hand we walked and talked. Softly. Thoughtfully. It was as though we were on sacred soil. Time stopped at each marker. Quietness swept over us as we drove away. I shall not soon forget what I learned.

First, *life is brief.* Terribly brief. On every stone there is a little dash . . . a horizontal line . . . illustrating time. Mozart's stone (wherever it is) reads:

1756 – 1791

That's it. But if only that "dash" could speak! It'd teach us the next lesson.

Second, *opportunity is now.* Not later. *Now.* Your contribution, small though it may seem, is unique and altogether yours. Whatever it may be — it becomes that timeless trophy you invest daily. The ancient aphorism I heard as a boy occasionally haunts me:

> Four things come not back: the spoken word, the sped arrow, time past, the neglected opportunity.

Third, *death is sure.* You can't dodge it, save by the Rapture. It's coming, friend. And at that time, like Mozart, you may seem insignificant to others. Forgotten, even. The only thing that will live on will be your personal contributions, your unique investments during your lifetime. Not your name . . . or your grave . . . but your timeless trophy.

Okay, so you're not brilliant, a prodigy, a composer of symphonies. What are you? A mother of two, three kiddos? An executive, a salesman, a retired military officer, a student, a nurse, a divorcée, minister, teacher, widow, farmer? Your trophy is your *contribution* — whatever and wherever. Known or unknown. It's your investment, your gifted "touch," that will live on far beyond the grave. God displays these trophies forever.

It is said of Abel:

> . . . God testifying about his gifts . . . though he is dead, he still speaks (Hebrews 11:4b).

Such trophies never tarnish.

Deepening Your Roots

Ruth 2:1 – 12; Titus 2:7 – 8; Hebrews 11:1 – 40

Branching Out

1. What would you like your epitaph to say? _____
   _____

2. What would you like to receive a trophy for? _____
   _____

   Are you working toward receiving it?

3. Encourage someone today who seems to feel insignificant. Comment on the importance of who they are to you and to others.

FULFILLMENT

Al Weidman polishes Porsche wheels. It's his bag. And (best of all) he *loves* it! How'd he get into it? Well, he got fed up with the rat race.

For fifteen years he worked for an internationally-known corporation. He was a number, not a person, to the firm. Became the purchasing agent with a swell salary . . . but that was it. He drove fifty-five miles to work every day to a building with no windows and a job with no fulfillment. Monotony turned into misery . . . discouragement led to dread as Al saw less and less of his family and more and more of the freeway.

He and Susan and their four kids began to pray:

> Lord, something *has* to happen! Do something, anything. Change our lives. This is no way to live. Lord, take over.

He did. Al got laid off.

Sounds weird, but it was one of the happiest days of his life. The squirrel cage finally ground to a halt. The fifteen-year addiction was, at last, broken by God Himself. Great! Only one problem — what now? Well, faith suddenly moved from back-burner theory to front-burner reality. Talk about cold turkey! For the first time in their marriage, Al and Susan found themselves in the exciting spot of literally having to "trust in the Lord with all their hearts" rather than just memorizing it in a Bible study group. The result? *Fantastic!* Through an amazing chain of events that nobody but the Lord could weave together, the man who once did purchasing for a corporation (hating every minute of it) now does polishing for dealerships all over Southern California . . . and points beyond.

He's having the time of his life. Never before has he experienced such depths of delight. Is he making a living? More than he dreamed possible — but keep in mind, that's no longer his motivation. When the Lord took Al and Susan through the experiential operating room, it was for radical surgery. Life did a flip-flop. They determined their priorities would no longer be sacrificed on the altar of temporal values. When God got through with that couple, His blessings came up in spades. The differences now? Well, for openers, he no longer feels trapped, crushed beneath the load of so-called essentials. *He's free.* Freed from a slavery that at times seemed as brutal and demanding as a nineteenth-century plantation owner. But there's one thing better than that. *He's fulfilled.* Satisfied. He's found his niche. The dread is gone. Each new dawn brings a fresh delivery of anticipation.

Fulfillment has to be one of life's choicest gifts. A major building block toward authentic happiness. Solomon must have had it in mind when he wrote in Proverbs 13:19:

> Desire realized is sweet to the soul. . . .

Who can measure up to the pleasure of that scene? The longing of the heart — unrevealed and deep — leads to *dreams.* These dreams float as time passes, refusing to be sunk by the anchors of hindrance and hardship. They grow into *possibilities* kept alive by hope and determination. Vague possibilities lead to concrete *opportunities* that stir up the soul with gratifying, satisfying stimulation . . . which ultimately becomes actual *accomplishment,* the ace trump of fulfillment. And that is sweet, writes David's wisest son.

I agree with Longfellow:

> Tell me not, in mournful numbers,
> > Life is but an empty dream!
>
> Lives of great men all remind us
> > We can make our lives sublime,
> And, departing, leave behind us
> > Footprints on the sands of time.

Have you become a victim of routine? Beginning to think demoralizing thoughts like, "Aw, what's the use?" and "It isn't worth the effort"? Starting to sigh rather than smile . . . focusing on the hurdles rather than the tape at the end of the race? If so, you have a lot of company. Surrendering to despair is man's favorite pastime. God offers a better plan, but it takes effort to grab it and faith to claim it. Like Oscar Hammerstein put it:

> Climb every mountain, search high and low,
> > Follow every by-way, every path you know.
>
> Climb every mountain, ford every stream,
> > Follow every rainbow, 'til you find your dream.[9]

Please — take it from one who, years ago, almost stopped climbing and searching and following — stay at it! Climbing and dreaming sure beat a stale life without windows . . . and a cage without release.

Deepening Your Roots

Joshua 14:6 – 12; Nehemiah 1:1 – 11, 2:1 – 5

Branching Out

1. What are you climbing toward? _____
   Is it really what you want? _____
   If not, why not do what Al and Susan did: pray.
2. Read the book *With No Fear of Failure* if you need more encouragement or help in determining your "dream."
3. Write down three dreams you want to see happen to you in your lifetime:
   1. _____
   2. _____
   3. _____
   Start praying about these dreams and don't stop trusting God until all the "dreams" come true.

PROCRASTINATION

Allow me to introduce a professional thief.

Chances are you'd never pick this slick little guy out of a crowd, but many, over the years, have come to regard him as a formidable giant. Quick as a laser and silent as a moonbeam, he can pick any lock. Once inside, his winsome ways will captivate your attentions. You'll treat him like your best friend. But watch out. He'll strip you without a blink of remorse.

Master of clever logic that he is, the bandit will rearrange the facts just enough to gain your sympathies. When others call his character into question, you'll find yourself not only believing in him, but actually *quoting* and *defending* him. Too late, you'll see through his ruse and give him grudging credit as the shrewdest of all thieves. Some never come to such a realization at all. They stroll to their graves arm-in-arm with the very robber who has stolen away their lives.

His name? *Procrastination.* His speciality? Stealing time and incentive. Like the proverbial packrat, he makes off with priceless valuables, leaving cheap substitutes in their place: excuses, rationalizations, empty promises, embarrassment, and guilt. Like most crooks, this pro hits you when you're weak — the moment you relax your defenses. You wake up on a Saturday morning. It's been a beast of a week. Insistent voices of neglected tasks echo in your head and plead for attention. Suddenly your con-artist appears and begins to bargain with you. By sundown he's gone . . . and so is your day . . . and so is your hope.

You step on the bathroom scales and blink in disbelief. The dial tells you the truth — but the thief offers another interpretation. Stealing your surge of motivation, he whispers the magic word — *mañana* — and you reach for a donut to celebrate your philosophy:

Never do today what you can put off 'til tomorrow.

You face a crucial decision this afternoon. It's been building up for two weeks. You've ignored it, dodged it, postponed it — but you must not do so any longer. Today is "D" day. You've talked yourself into it. Thirty minutes before the deadline, the thief offers the perfect alibi and back on the shelf goes your decision, growing another day larger.

No piper was better paid. No liar was better respected. No bandit better rewarded. No giant better treated.

You name it — he comes out a winner every time even though he's a hard-core outlaw. He can outtalk any student when it comes to homework. He can outthink any executive when it comes to correspondence. He can outwork any homemaker when it comes to vacuuming or doing dishes. He can outlast any parent when it comes to discipline. He can outsmart any salesman when it comes to selling. He has one basic product and he centers all his energy toward that single goal: defeat. By the sheer genius of suggestion he becomes the epitome of what he destroys: success.

There once lived a politician named Felix. He was a governor during the first century. Before him stood a prisoner named Paul. On two separate occasions, Felix listened to Paul tell his story, presenting in simple terms the matter of faith in Jesus Christ. Felix heard every word but passed off the message with similar comments:

> When Lysias the commander comes down, I will decide your case (Acts 24:22).

> Go away for the present, and when I find time, I will summon you (Acts 24:25).

The governor heard Paul, but he listened to the thief. He intentionally put off the most significant moment of his life — a decision he will never forget. Never. Why? Because he listened to the wrong counsel. It was only a subtle suggestion. It wasn't a bold-face lie, like "There is no heaven," or, "There is no hell." It was simply, "There is no *hurry.*" Thereby the grim thief won another victory of defeat.

"How can *I* win?" you ask. What's the secret — the formula — for escaping this thief's intimidating web? How can I stop the giant from breaking and entering?

It's really very simple . . . so simple you won't believe it. All it takes is one word, perhaps the easiest word to utter in our language. Properly used, that single syllable carries more weight than a ton of good intentions. The thief cannot endure the sound of it. It sends him fleeing in frustration. If you use it often enough, he might get tired of hearing it — and start leaving you alone.

Curious? I'll make you a deal. I'll tell you the word if you'll promise to use it next time you're tempted to listen to the fast-talking embezzler. I have a warning, however. It may be easy to say — but it will require all the discipline you can muster to *mean* it. To implement it will demand, in fact, the power of God Himself.

The word is "Now."

Deepening Your Roots

Proverbs 14:23, 31:10 – 31; Ephesians 5:14 – 17

Branching Out

1. List two one-day projects you've put off doing:

   1. _____
   2. _____

   Choose one and get it done by tomorrow.
2. Don't take on any new project until you've completed those you've put off.
3. Write a letter today to someone you've been meaning to write to for months — maybe even years. Do it now.

ॐ ॐ ॐ

Growing Strong

Goodbye procrastination. Hello accomplishment. It's been a super week! Excited about what you got done? Me too. What pleases you the most as you think back over the tasks you finished?

_____

_____

_____

_____

IMPACTING LIVES

In his book, *A Thinking Man's Guide to Pro Football,* Paul Zimmerman quotes a physicist who had made an incredible discovery. The man had the facts to prove that when a 240-pound lineman (capable of running 100 yards in 11 seconds) collides with a 240-pound running back (capable of covering the same distance in 10 seconds), the resultant kinetic energy is "enough to move 66,000 pounds — or thirty-three tons — one inch."

That helps explain why some players stagger about the field mumbling to themselves after having their bell rung during a collision. The likelihood is that they have been hit on the helmet by a blow approaching 1,000 Gs. That means 1,000 times the force of gravity. Astronauts on takeoff experience approximately 10 Gs. Pilots tend to black out at about 20 Gs. A recent issue of *Sportsweek* magazine stated that "tests run on Detroit Lion's linebacker, Joe Schmidt, reportedly showed that he had to cope with blows which registered at 5,780 Gs." Small wonder that football, at various levels, kills twenty-eight players a year . . . or that half the veterans of pro ball will die before age fifty-eight . . . or that one survey revealed that each year thirty-two college and high school football players become paraplegics. The game has changed from merely a contact sport to a *collision* sport. With unbelievable force, athletes chosen for their abnormal size and remarkable speed, stun, cripple, and even kill each other upon impact.

That explains why Joe Namath admits that by the age of fifty he fully expects to have difficulty just putting one foot in front of the other . . . or why Merlin Olsen, scarcely forty years old, has severe, painful arthritis in both his knees. The human body was never designed by God to handle collisions of that magnitude, no matter how strong or coordinated or big it may be. We simply cannot take the physical impact.

What about spiritual impact? Well, that's a horse of a different wheelbase. It's doubtful that any impact, spiritually speaking, could ever be too great. In fact, the bigger the better. Most of us thrive on models that challenge our *status quo,* tough though they may be. It has always been so. Who can possibly gauge the impact an eighty-year-old Bedouin shepherd named Moses had on Egypt when he stood up against Pharaoh? Or how about Gideon when he successfully led that invasion with blown trumpets and broken pitchers and a stern battle cry? No one can measure the impact Elijah had on Ahab . . . or Nehemiah had on Tobiah . . . or Job had on Elihu . . . or John the Baptizer had on Israel . . . or Paul had on Agrippa . . . or Luther had on Rome . . . or Knox had on Bloody Mary . . . or all the God-appointed evangelists like Whitefield and Edwards and Wesley and Moody and Graham have had on England and America.

And how about *your* life? Who is it the Lord has used to model His message and challenge you to change, to shake off that tendency to settle for less than your full potential, to stretch and pursue and conquer new territory you once never dreamed possible? All of us can name at least one individual, can't we?

Here are four characteristics usually found in those who impact our lives:

1. *CONSISTENCY.* These folks are not restless flashes in the pan — here today, gone tomorrow. Neither are they given to fads and gimmicks. Those who impact lives stay at the task with reliable regularity. They seem unaffected by the fickle winds of change. They're *consistent.*

2. *AUTHENTICITY.* Probe all you wish, try all you like to find hypocritical flaws, and you search in vain. People who impact others are real to the core; no alloy covered over with a brittle layer of chrome, but solid, genuine stuff right down to the nubbies. They're *authentic.*

3. *UNSELFISHNESS.* Mustn't forget this one! Hands down it's there every time. Those who impact us the most watch out for themselves the least. They notice our needs and reach out to help, honestly concerned about our welfare. Their least-used words are "I," "me," "my," and "mine." They're *unselfish.*

4. *TIRELESSNESS.* With relentless determination they spend themselves. They refuse to quit. Possessing an enormous amount of enthusiasm for their labor, they press on regardless of the odds . . . virtually unconcerned with the obstacles. Actually, they are like pioneers — resilient and rugged. They're *tireless.*

Who impacts lives? Who is it God uses to collide with us so as to dent our frames and jolt our direction? The consistent, authentic, unselfish, tireless individuals who hate those words "let's just get by," and "it's too hard, let's just quit."

Chances are good that, without realizing it, you've been reading the profile of that single individual who has impacted your life more than any other person. And it's not some huge hulk who wore a helmet and shoulder pads, knocking people senseless. This person might even dislike football and wonder why in the world anybody would enjoy it.

Your mother. Don't forget to honor her on Mother's Day.

Deepening Your Roots

Exodus 1:15 – 22, 2:1 – 10; John 19:25 – 27

Branching Out

1. Besides sending your mother a card or flowers, write her a note and express to her something she has done for you in one of the four areas mentioned above. Be specific. Cite a certain time, place, statement, etc. She'll treasure this note.
2. Choose someone you could possibly care for or be a model to. Make it your prayer and effort in the next three months to work on this relationship.
3. Sacrifice. That's always part of being unselfish. Make a sacrifice today for someone else — but don't tell anyone you did so.
4. Adopt a mother. Find someone who can't be with her children today, or who is childless, and take her out to dinner. And if you're without a mother, adopt a substitute — maybe someone in a rest home, a widow in your church, etc.

LUXURIES

*E*very morning as I drive to my office I pass a sight that leaves me drooling. I mash my nose against the glass and stare as long as I possibly can before checking back into reality. The object of my glare is a sleek, shiny boat that sits neatly backed into a driveway. Its fiberglass, shallow hull is deep blue, and it, along with its tailored trailer, is spotless. The wrap-around windshield is trimmed in dazzling chrome, the engine sparkles in the light of dawn, the accessories and special appointments reveal quality and class. Only one thing is missing — ME. The boat has the wrong owner! My imagination has taken me to Catalina and back . . . I've pulled my family and a dozen others on water skis . . . in fantasy I've waxed it and pampered it, tinkered with its details, and traveled the highways a hundred times with it close behind.

Now maybe your thing isn't something that floats. Well, take your pick. When it comes to luxuries, Southern California will spoil you — and I mean *fast.* Yours might be a pool out back . . . or lovely furnishings in the den . . . or a new suit rather frequently . . . or something with four on the floor and mag wheels . . . an ancient piece of sculpture . . . a mountain cabin . . . a trip to Rome . . . an Omega watch . . . an original oil painting by one of the masters . . . some expensive set of books . . . a hand-carved desk at your office . . . sophisticated sound equipment . . . an exquisite gem or some super-expensive antique. Swell, so much for dreaming.

You're probably thinking, like Plato wrote in *The Republic,*

WEALTH IS THE PARENT OF LUXURY . . .

and since you haven't got the cash, you're silly to think about spawning such "children" of wealth. Perhaps you're reluctant to entertain *any* dreams since daily reality turns them into nightmares of unfulfilled desire. It is possible that you are even laboring under the whip of that eternal taskmaster, Fear, who buffets your fondest fantasy with three brutal blows from his lash — public criticism, personal guilt, and perverted humility.

Why not meet your secret longing head-on? Why not declare that it's there in your thoughts, waiting for an honest, wise, and intelligent response? I have a most interesting time asking Christians what they would really like to have — what they'd enjoy owning. I've had them look around like somebody would squeal on them . . . or squirm like a worm, feeling uneasy as they admit that down deep inside they actually cherish some specific, luxurious wish. They occasionally whisper it to me under their breath as if confessing some vice or awful crime. Nonsense!

Whoever started the rumor that possessing something expensive and luxurious was, in itself, suspect or sinful? Wasn't it Paul who openly declared that he had learned "how to enjoy prosperity . . . to be filled up . . . to have abundance . . ."? (Philippians 4:12, Berkeley). He didn't spend all his days in overalls eating crackers and beans, drinking river water, and living under some bridge. Somehow, sometimes he lived with expensive luxuries . . . and admitted that such things were enjoyed to the fullest. You'll never convince me that Paul always looked grubby or was uneasy when surrounded by the elite.

Now the only wrong in all this is when expensive and luxurious things possess *us*. On that axis, everything shifts. When that happens, the green ghost of greed invades our dwelling and haunts our once-contented mind . . . like the farmer Jesus mentioned in Luke 12:16 – 21, who substituted the material for the spiritual. That man, said Jesus, was an outright fool. To him, luxuries were *essential* to life . . . they were his *sole* means of happiness and security. He became occupied with the gift and failed to consult with or recognize the Giver.

Do you have some hidden hope which might be labeled a luxury? Here's my advice:

1. Admit it . . . don't ignore it.
2. Evaluate it . . . don't fear it.
3. Plan for it . . . don't grab it.
4. Enjoy it . . . don't worship it.

And the next time you see a bright blue boat with a wrap-around windshield and a "For Sale" sign on it, admire it . . . but don't buy it. It might be the one that belongs behind my car.

Deepening Your Roots

Genesis 33:1 – 9; 2 Corinthians 8:1 – 15; Philippians 4:10 – 13

Branching Out

1. Write down a "dream" you'd like to come true: _____
2. Give away something that constantly possesses you — like a box of choco-lates, or a gallon of ice cream, or some sports equipment. Do I dare mention your TV? Or let someone else use that boat or car for a weekend.

HOLDING THINGS LOOSELY

In her fine book, *Splinters in My Pride,* Marilee Zdenek reflects our deepest feelings. Those misty ones, hard to get a handle on. As the sights, sounds, and smells of different seasons began to create nostalgic itches inside me recently, she scratched one:

> It was hard to let you go:
> To watch womanhood reach out and snatch you
> Long before the mothering was done.
> But if God listened to mothers and gave in,
> Would the time for turning loose of daughters ever come?
> It was hard when you went away —
> For how was I to know
> The serendipity of letting go
> Would be seeing you come home again
> And meeting in a new way
> Woman to woman —
> Friend to friend.[10]

Letting go. Turning loose. Releasing the squeeze.

Being better at smothering than loving, we are blown away with the thought of relaxing our gargantuan grip. Because releasing introduces the terror of risk, the panic of losing control. The parting cannot happen without inward bleeding. The coward heart fears to surrender its prized toys. Even though it must say goodbye eventually.

Like releasing a dream; or allowing a child space to grow up; or letting a friend have the freedom to be and to do. What maturity that requires!

We are often hindered from giving up our treasures out of fear for their safety. But wait. Everything is safe which is committed to our God. In fact, nothing is really safe which is *not* so committed. No child. No job. No romance. No friend. No future. No dream.

Need some proof? Check out Abraham with his almost-adult son Isaac. Genesis 22. The old man's treasured delights rested in that boy. That relationship could well have bordered upon the perilous . . . if father would not come to grips with releasing son. But it was at that juncture that Jehovah-turned-pedagogue taught the patriarch a basic lesson in life.

> Take now your son, your only son, whom you love, Isaac, and go to the land of Moriah; and offer him there as a burnt offering . . . (Genesis 22:2).

It was time to turn him loose. Abraham might have started pleading or bargaining or manipulating, but that would not have caused the Almighty to choose an alternate course. No — Abraham had to open his hands and surrender on that ancient altar the one thing that eclipsed the Son from his heart. It hurt cruelly . . . beyond imagination. But it was effective.

The greater the possessiveness, the greater the pain. The old miser within us will never lie down quietly and die obediently to our whisper. He must be torn out like a cypress tap root. He must be extracted in agony and blood like a tooth from the jaw. And we will need to steel ourselves against his piteous begging, recognizing it as echoes from the hollow chamber of self-pity, one of the most hideous sins of the human heart.

What is it God wants me to do? To hold things loosely, that He might reign without a rival. With no threats to His throne. And with just enough splinters in my pride to keep my hands empty and my heart warm.

Deepening Your Roots
Genesis 22:1 – 18; Philippians 3:7 – 21

Branching Out

1. Look around your house and name someone or something that would be hard to give up or let go of: _____
   Release your grip by telling God He can have the person or the object.
2. Take the time you normally spend watching your favorite TV show and spend the minutes instead with your spouse, a child, or a friend.
3. Buy a book you really want to read, and then give it away without reading it yourself.

❧ ❧ ❧

Growing Strong

A tough week? Most weeks always include a few rough hours. And most contain some special moments. What's one from your week?

_____

_____

_____

MEDITATION

The lost art of the twentieth century is, in my opinion, meditation. We Americans are *masters* when it comes to activity . . . and entertainment . . . and planning . . . and preoccupation — but meditation? Forget it! Somehow we have the mistaken idea that meditation demands hours and hours, that it is the by-product of leisure (of which most of us have very little) and even laziness.

True meditation, however, is *not* daydreaming. It is *not* letting our minds drift here and there, thinking about nothing, and humming some religious melody with our eyes at half mast! Meditation is disciplined thought, forced on a single object or Scripture for a period of time. It is reflecting upon or pondering specific truths slowly, piece-by-piece . . . allowing our minds to dig deeply into a word, a phrase, an idea or principle from God's own Word. Meditation considers these things from every possible angle, with the purpose of getting insight, gaining practical benefit, and/or reaching some conclusion.

Meditation is not optional. The same Bible that commands us to "pray without ceasing," to "rejoice evermore," and "in everything give thanks" . . . also urges us to meditate. I find it interesting that this term appears no less than twenty times in the Word, with fourteen of those references occurring in the Psalms. In fact, the term only appears twice in all the New Testament — and in neither case is that the best translation. My point is this: meditation is essentially an Old Testament concept . . . and therefore understood from the viewpoint of its Hebrew origin.

Let me amplify. When you boil down the eighteen Old Testament verses that mention "meditate" or "meditation," you discover that they come from one of two Hebrew words. The first is the term HAG-GAH, and the second, SEE-AAGH. Both these terms are frequently translated "talk," "speak," and "utter." They both convey the idea of "musing" and "pondering" and, surprising though it may seem, both are terms used for voicing a complaint, or moaning during suffering. They also convey the idea of imagination. Broad terms, aren't they?

Summing up these findings, I suggest that our meditation is to be broad enough to include imagination as we ponder God's Word, and in keeping with the experiences and trials He brings our way. In other words, *we should link our lives with His Word in our times of meditation.*

Let me suggest five practical steps to follow in your development of this spiritual exercise. Let's use Proverbs 3:5 – 6 as our example:

1. *Emphasize different words and phrases.* In meditating on Proverbs 3:5 – 6, accent specific terms. "*Trust* in the Lord . . ." or "Trust in the Lord with *all* your heart." Think about *trusting* . . . and consider the vastness of that word *all.* When you read the warning ". . . do not lean on your *own* understanding," imagine the many ways you work things out for yourself.

2. *Paraphrase the verse. Make it personal.* Rethink and restate the verse using your words in the process. For example: "Lord, you are commanding me to turn my life over to you completely — to stop my habit of worrying and working things out my way, like I frequently do." Get the idea?

3. *Compare the verse with other Scripture.* Reflect on this in relation to two or three other passages. Weave them into your thoughts. How about Psalm 37:4 – 5 or Philippians 4:6 – 7 and 1 Peter 5:7? What an aid Scripture memory can be! It multiplies the value of meditation a hundredfold.

4. *Relate the verse to your present circumstance.* Let's suppose you are worried, you are restless and ill-at-ease within. You know it's wrong, but you can't seem to stop. You come across Proverbs 3:5 – 6, and decide to meditate on it. As you do, keep your problems in mind. Ask for insight from the Lord. List your worries one by one. Identify them. Look them over in the light of that passage. Tell Him your complaints as you meditate. Ask: "Am I ready to rely on God to take these things . . . or do I enjoy my worry?" Admit your weakness before Him.

5. *Use prayer as a follow-up.* Never fail to conclude with prayer. Ask Him to transfer your thoughts into your life. Thank Him in advance for the change He will bring.

> "This book . . . shall not depart from your mouth, but you shall meditate on it day and night, so that you may be careful to do according to all that is written in it . . ." (Joshua 1:8).

Deepening Your Roots

Joshua 1:6 – 8; Psalm 1:1 – 6, 119:97 – 104

Branching Out

1. List your worries: _____

   _____

   Now take point 4 above and do the steps I recommend.
2. Take five minutes of your lunch hour today and meditate on Proverbs 3:5 – 6.
3. Write out two verses you can meditate on this week.

FAMINE

The word hangs like an awful omen in our heads.

Mentally, we picture a brutal, grotesque image. Cow's hips protrude. Babies' eyes are hollow. Bloated stomachs growl angrily. Skin stretches across faces tight as a trampoline. The outline of the skull slowly emerges. Joints swell. Grim, despairing stares replace smiles. Hope is gone . . . life is reduced to a harsh existence as famine takes its toll. Those who have seen it cannot forget it. Those who haven't cannot imagine it.

We are told it is coming. "It's only a matter of time," declare the experts. There was a time when such predictions appeared only in science fiction books and novels, but no longer. Prophets of doom are now economists, university profs, and official spokesmen for our government, not to mention those authors who interpret our times as "threatening" or "terminal." Of greatest concern is the enormous population explosion that grips our globe. The statistics tell their own tale.

Our world reached the one billion mark by 1825. About one hundred years later we had doubled in population — *two* billion by 1925. By 1975 (only fifty years later) we doubled again — *four* billion. Should the trend continue we'll have *eight* billion by the year 2000 . . . and *sixteen* billion a short twelve years later, if that long! The supply of food required to feed eight or more billion people is unbelievable. Worse than that, it's unattainable in light of our current agricultural system. The gaunt shells of humanity that now populate East Africa will some future day cast their shadows on North America, we're told. One reputable authority predicts that there will come a time when the world's big cities will be living on bacon bits, fruit in a tube, recycled foods, protein pills and cakes, and reconstituted water.

For us who are so well fed, the idea of famine is foreign — almost a *fantasy*. It's something that plagues India or Biafra or China, never America! Fear of famine doesn't square with our "amber waves of grain," our "fruited plains," certainly not our streets lined with McDonalds, thirty-one flavors, and innumerable shops bulging with every conceivable type of food.

My first rude awakening to the reality of hunger occurred early in 1958 when our troop ship full of U.S. Marines pulled into the harbor of Yokohama, Japan. We were so thrilled to see land, having been at sea for seventeen days, we were initially unaware of the barges full of Japanese men and women that encircled our ship. I later discovered that this was a common occurrence. They had come to paint the ship while we were at the dock for several days. Their pay in return? The garbage from our tables! The thought stunned me.

There is another kind of famine equally tragic . . . but far more subtle. God spoke of it through the prophet Amos. Listen to his words:

> "The time is surely coming," says the Lord God, "when I will send a famine on the land — not a famine of bread or water, but of hearing the words of the Lord. Men will wander everywhere from sea to sea, seeking the Word of the Lord, searching, running here and going there, but will not find it (Amos 8:11 – 13, TLB).

We may find physical famine almost impossible to believe, but how about a *spiritual* famine? You don't have to wait until the year 2000 for that! Take a trip across these United States. Or pick a country — *any* country. Talk about a famine! It's easy to misread the words of Amos. He didn't predict a lack of churches or chapels or temples or tabernacles or seminars or sermons. He spoke of "a famine . . . of hearing the words of the Lord." Remember, a famine does not mean an absence of something . . . but a *shortage* of it . . . a scarcity that creates a scene of starvation.

In our enlightened, progressive, modern age, an ancient, dusty prophecy is fulfilled. Hearing the unadulterated truth of God is a rare experience. How easy to forget that! We have come upon hard times when those who declare and hear the Word of God are a novelty.

How easy to be spoiled . . . presumptuous . . . sassy . . . ungrateful . . . when our spiritual stomachs are full! Funny thing — those who are full usually want *more*. We belch out increased demands rather than humble gratitude to God for our horn o' plenty.

Tell me, when was the last time you thanked God for the sheer privilege of hearing more of His Word than you could ever digest? And when did you last share just a crumb from your table?

That's why there's a famine.

Deepening Your Roots

Nehemiah 8:1 – 12; Mark 12:41 – 44; Acts 13:44 – 48

Branching Out

1. Write a relief agency this week and request information on how you can care for someone in need.
2. Now, do you see a famine for the Word of God close to your home? How can you relieve *that* desperate need — in your family . . . across the street . . . at your church?

EXTERNALS AND INTERNALS

*H*oward Snyder ticks me off.

He also makes me think. I agree, and I disagree. I laugh, and I sigh. Part of me wants to slug him yet two minutes later embrace him. I shake my head at his extreme generalizations . . . and shortly thereafter nod in amazement at his acute evaluations, accurate to the nth degree.

No man deserves all those emotions! But Snyder yanks them out of me as I read (for the third time) his 1976 controversial volume, *The Problem of Wine Skins*. Tough book. And don't let the title throw you. It has little to do with literal wine and even *less* with leather wineskins. But it has a lot to do with the principles behind Jesus' words in Luke 5:37–38.

> No one puts new wine into old wineskins, for the new wine
> bursts the old skins, ruining the skins and spilling the wine.
> New wine must be put into new wineskins (TLB).

Let that soak in. Obviously our Lord is distinguishing there between things that are essential (the wine) and things that are useful but not primary (the skins). Who needs wineskins if there is no wine? Wine, you see, represents the basics, the changeless, timeless, everpotent, always-necessary message. The gospel. The Savior. The pristine truth of Scripture. And the wineskins? Clearly, they represent that which is secondary, subsidiary, manmade. Stuff like structure, traditions (now don't stop reading), and patterns of doing things which have grown up around and encased the "wine." Got the picture?

The wineskins are the point of contact between the wine and the world. And as the surrounding pressure mounts from society, the skins tend to cease being flexible. They are seldom replaced. They get thicker, hard, less elastic . . . and are ultimately unable to contain that volatile, vigorous vino within. They have reached the extreme of inflexibility. And, unfortunately, few indeed are those who can tolerate fresh, new, supple bags to contain the wine. We much prefer the old — even if it's brittle and leaks — rather than the new.

That was the rub in Jesus' day. He was too radical and fresh in His approach. He irritated the old guard. Frowning, they kept asking questions like:

> Why do Your disciples transgress the tradition of the elders? For they do not wash their hands when they eat bread (Matthew 15:2).

> Why do you eat and drink with the tax-gatherers and sinners? (Luke 5:30).

> Why are they [*the disciples*] doing what is not lawful on the Sabbath? (Mark 2:24).

I mean, "Shame on you, Jesus! If you're going to expect our respect, keep your hands off our wineskins!"

You see, they confused the external container with the internal treasure — even though the old Judaistic hand-me-downs were leaking badly.

Today we applaud His revolutionary determination. It was *that* quality which caused His contemporaries to mumble, "No man ever spoke as this Man does." But the barriers He scaled and the accusations He received increased the level of public anger to intense proportions. He wound up nailed to a cross, remember. And many returned to their old wineskins of religious tradition, thinking they were now safe from His words that had worried them for over three years.

But a remnant had tasted the wine. They had cultivated a new appetite. With new hearts they sang new songs. They preached a new hope from the new covenant. As new creations in Christ they offered "a new and living way" (Hebrews 10:20). Emerging from a cocoon of fear and intimidation, they flew free and bold. Willing to live in dens and caves of the earth, they swept the old world off its feet . . . "they turned it upside down," they literally "upset the world" (Acts 17:6).

That new breed of nontraditional thinkers emerged again in the sixteenth century. Unwilling to be crushed in the iron jaws of the papacy and all its trappings, they broke loose. Why? They despised traditional wineskins. They refused to clothe the resplendent riches of Christ in tacky religious rags. They chose to preserve the wine and replace the skins at the cost of being misunderstood. In their day they were quickly branded "heretics." Yet (strangely) today we extol them as courageous "reformers." It's amazing what a few hundred years will do to our perspective.

And what about *you?* Busy protecting and trying to preserve the wineskins? Working overtime carrying a torch of external tradition? Hey, I understand. I did that for almost twenty years of my Christian life. The wine got little of my attention as I patched up wineskins year after year. *What a waste!* Through a process of time and very painful events, I am breaking that nervous habit. The older I get, the less I care about the traditional skins and the more I crave the pure wine, the essentials, the external internals.

Thanks, Howard Snyder. I needed the reminder. But you still tick me off!

Deepening Your Roots
Luke 5:36 – 39; Galatians 2:6

Branching Out

1. Evaluate yourself and see if you can spot some traditionalism in your thinking or actions. If so, get bold and sever the old wineskin of traditionalism from your life.
2. Find a copy of Snyder's book at your local Christian bookstore. Allow him to challenge your thinking.

ॐ ॐ ॐ

Growing Strong

We talked serious business this week. Tough subjects. Convicting. But all are needed if we expect to grow strong. So, how have you been stretched in the past forty-eight hours?

_____

_____

_____

_____

SIMPLICITY

The scene was thick. The clouds were heavy and dark gray. The mood was tense. It was no time to take a walk in the park or stroll down Pennsylvania Avenue. The smell of death was in the air. A decision was essential. With paper and pen in hand, the lean, lank frame of a lonely man sat quietly at his desk. The dispatch he wrote was sent immediately. It shaped the destiny of a nation at war with itself.

It was a simple message ... a style altogether his. No ribbons of rhetoric were woven through the note. No satin frills, no enigmatic eloquence. It was plain, direct, brief, to the point. A bearded Army officer soon read it with a frown. It said:

April 7, 1865, 11 a.m.

Lieut. Gen. Grant,
  Gen. Sheridan says, "If the thing is pressed, I think that Lee will surrender."

Let the thing be pressed.
  A. Lincoln

Grant smiled in agreement. He did as he was ordered. Exactly two days later at Appomattox Court House, General Robert E. Lee surrendered. "The thing was pressed" and the war was ended.

SIMPLICITY. Profound, exacting, rare simplicity. Lincoln was a master of it. His words live on because of it. When assaulted by merciless critics, many expected a lengthy, complex defense of his actions. It never occurred. When questioned about his feelings, he answered, "I'm used to it." When asked if the end of the war or some governmental rehabilitation program might be the answer to America's needs, he admitted quite simply, "Human nature will not change." In response to a letter demanding the dismissal of the Postmaster General, he wrote, "Truth is generally the best vindication against slander." When encouraged to alter his convictions and push through a piece of defeated legislation by giving it another title, he reacted with typical simplicity, "If you call a tail a leg, how many legs has a dog? Five? No, calling a tail a leg don't *make* it a leg!"

SIMPLICITY. The difference between something being elegant or elaborate. The difference between class and common. Between just enough and too much. Between concentrated and diluted. Between communication and confusion.

Between:

> Hence from my sight — nor let me thus pollute mine eyes with looking on a wretch like thee, thou cause of my ills; I sicken at thy loathsome presence . . .

and:

> Scram!

SIMPLICITY. *Economy* of words mixed with *quality* of thought held together by *subtlety* of expression. Practicing a hard-to-define restraint so that some things are left for the listener or reader to conclude on his own. Clear and precise . . . yet not overdrawn. Charles Jehlinger, a former director of the American Academy of Dramatic Arts, used to instruct all apprentice actors with five words of advice:

> *Mean* more than you say.

It has been my observation that we Christians say all . . . too much, in fact. Instead of stopping with a concise statement of the forest — explicit and simple — we feel compelled to analyze, philosophize, scrutinize, and moralize over each individual tree . . . leaving the other person weary, unchallenged, confused, and (worst of all!) *bored.* Zealous to be ultra-accurate, we unload so much trivia the other person loses the thread of thought, not to mention his patience. Bewildered, he wades through the jungle of needless details, having lost his way, as well as his interest. Instead of being excited over the challenge to explore things on his own, lured by the anticipation of discovery, he gulps for air in the undertow caused by our endless waves of verbiage.

The longer I study Jesus' method of communicating, the more convinced I become that His genius rested in His ability to simplify and clarify issues that others confused and complicated. He used words anyone could understand . . . not just the initiated. He said just enough to inspire and motivate others to think on their own, to be inquisitive, to search further. And He punctuated His teaching with familiar, earthy, even humorous illustrations that riveted mental handles to abstract truths. Best of all

. . . He didn't try to impress people. All these things led others to seek His counsel and thrive on His instruction.

If He could summarize my thoughts for me today, I believe He would offer this advice:

- Make it clear.
  - Make it simple.
    - Emphasize the essentials.
      - Forget about impressing.
        - Leave some things unsaid.

We've got the greatest message on earth to declare. Most people have either never heard it or they've been confused because someone has complicated the issues. Jesus says, "If the thing is simplified, they will surrender."

Let the thing be simplified.

Deepening Your Roots
Job 16:3, 18:2; John 21:4 – 14

Branching Out

1. Check your speech. Do you use big words around people who do not have a large vocabulary? Work at speaking on their level.
2. Don't speak for five minutes today when around another group. Note here how you felt during those five minutes: _____
   _____
3. Read a letter or report you've written. Choose one paragraph from the letter and reduce it to one sentence.

KEEPING YOUR WORD

March 11, 1942, was a dark, desperate day at Corregidor. The Pacific theater of war was threatening and bleak. One island after another had been buffeted into submission. The enemy was now marching into the Philippines as confident and methodical as the star band in the Rose Bowl parade. Surrender was inevitable. The brilliant and bold soldier, Douglas MacArthur, had only three words for his comrades as he stepped into the escape boat destined for Australia:

I SHALL RETURN.

Upon arriving nine days later in the port of Adelaide, the sixty-two-year-old military statesman closed his remarks with the sentence:

I CAME THROUGH AND I SHALL RETURN.

A little over 2½ years later — October 20, 1944, to be exact — he stood once again on Philippine soil after landing safely at Leyte Island. This is what he said:

> This is the voice of freedom, General MacArthur speaking.
> People of the Philippines: I HAVE RETURNED!

MacArthur kept his word. His word was as good as his bond. Regardless of the odds against him, including the pressures and power of enemy strategy, he was bound and determined to make his promise good.

This rare breed of man is almost extinct. Whether an executive or an apprentice, a student or a teacher, a blue or white collar worker, a Christian or a pagan — rare indeed are those who keep their word. The prevalence of the problem has caused the coining of terms painfully familiar to us in our era: *credibility gap*. To say that something is "credible" is to say it is "capable of being believed, trustworthy." To refer to a "gap" in such suggests a "breach or a reason for doubt."

Jurors often have reason to doubt the testimony of a witness on the stand. Parents, likewise, have reason at times to doubt their children's word (and vice versa). Citizens frequently doubt the promises of politicians, and the credibility of an employee's word is questioned by the employer. Creditors can no longer believe a debtor's verbal promise to pay and many a mate has ample reason to doubt the word of his or her partner. This is a terrible dilemma! Precious few do what they *say* they will do without a reminder, a warning, or a threat. Unfortunately, this is true even among Christians.

Listen to what the Scriptures have to say about keeping your word:

> Therefore each of you must put off falsehood and speak truthfully to his neighbor . . . (Ephesians 4:25, NIV).

> And whatever you do, whether in word or deed, do it all in the name of the Lord Jesus . . . (Colossians 3:17, NIV).

> O Lord, who may abide in Thy tent? Who may dwell on Thy holy hill? He who walks with integrity . . . And speaks truth in his heart (Psalm 15:1 – 2).

> It is better not to vow than to make a vow and not fulfill it (Ecclesiastes 5:5, NIV).

> When a man . . . takes an oath to obligate himself by a pledge, he must not break his word but must do everything he said (Numbers 30:2, NIV).

Question: Judging yourself on this matter of keeping your word, are you bridging or widening the credibility gap? Are you encouraging or discouraging others? Let me help you answer that by using four familiar situations.

1. When you reply, "Yes, I'll pray for you" — do you?
2. When you tell someone they can depend on you to help them out — can they?
3. When you say you'll be there at such-and-such a time — are you?
4. When you obligate yourself to pay a debt on time — do you?

Granted, no one's perfect. But if you fail, do you own up to it? Do you quickly admit your failure to the person you promised and refuse to rationalize around it? If you do, you are *really* rare . . . but a person of genuine integrity. And one who is an encouragement and can encourage others.

Do you know something? I know another One who promised He would return. He, too, will keep His word. In fact, He's *never* broken one promise. There's no credibility gap with Him.

He will return!

Deepening Your Roots

1 Chronicles 17:16 – 27; 2 Chronicles 6:12 – 15; Psalm 145:13

Branching Out

1. What's a promise you made someone but have failed to keep? _____
   _____

   Go back and keep that promise this week, or let the person know the time and date you expect to fill that unfulfilled promise.
2. Make a promise to someone today . . . and fulfill it.
3. Find a promise in Scripture and write it down here. _____
   _____

   Claim it for yourself. Encourage yourself.

SURPRISES

The feelings are familiar. Mouth open. Eyes like saucers. Chill up the spine. Heart pounding in the throat. Momentary disbelief. We frown and attempt to piece the story together without a script or narrator. Sometimes alone, occasionally with others . . . then *boom!* "The flash of a mighty surprise" boggles the mind, leaving us somewhere between stunned and dumb with wonder. "Am I dreaming or is a miracle happening?" So it is with surprises.

O. Henry did it with his endings. World War II, with its beginning. Surprises start parties and they stop partnerships. They solve murders, they enhance birthdays and anniversaries, they embellish friendships. Kids at Christmas love 'em. Parents expect 'em. Coaches use 'em. Politicians diffuse 'em.

We like 'em and we hate 'em. Just a few one-liners illustrate both reactions.

"Dr. Brown would like to discuss your X-rays right away."

"Class, take out a clean piece of paper . . . it's pop quiz time."

"We've been on the wrong road for an hour. Here, look at the map."

"The alarm didn't go off. It's almost noon!"

"Hello . . . I'm calling from the bank regarding your checking account."

"Honey, the doctor heard *three* heartbeats today."

"The boss wants to see you. No need to take off your coat."

"Congratulations — you made the cheerleading squad."

"We are happy to inform you your manuscript has been accepted for publication."

"This is Officer Franklin. We have your son down at the station. He's under arrest."

"The tumor we suspected to be malignant is actually benign."

"It isn't a carburetor problem, ma'am. Your whole engine is shot!"

"Sweetie, that wasn't leftover stew. It was Alpo."

"Did you know the bathroom scales weigh twelve pounds *light?*"

"Mom . . . Dad . . . Byron wants to marry me!"

And on and on they go. The highs and lows of our lives are usually triggered by surprises. Within split seconds we are sobbing or laughing like crazy . . . staring in bewildered confusion or wishing we would wake up from a dream.

Ever stopped to trace the surprises through the Bible? That Book is *full* of them when you look at certain events through the eyes of people in that day. Like . . . when Adam and Eve stumbled upon Abel's fresh grave. When Enoch's footprints stopped abruptly. When Noah's neighbors first realized it was sprinkling. When aged Sarah said, *"Ze angel vasn't kidding, Abe!"* When Moses' ears heard words from a bush that wouldn't stop burning. When Pharaoh's wife screamed, *"He's dead! Our son is dead!"* When manna first fell from the sky. When water first ran from the rock. When Jericho's walls came tumbling down. When a ruddy runt named David whipped a rugged warrior named Goliath. When a judge named Samson said yes instead of no. When a prophet named Jonah said no instead of yes. When a woman from Samaria had a Jewish Stranger tell her all her secrets. When the disciples discovered that Judas was guilty. When the only perfect One who ever lived was nailed to a criminal's cross. When Mary saw Him through the fog that epochal Sunday morn.

And that's just a quick review of the snapshots. I mean, if we had time to enjoy the whole album, we'd be up 'til midnight. It's gasp-and-gulp city right up to the end.

And speaking of the end, that last page will be the *greatest* shock of all. Talk about "the flash of a mighty surprise!" How does "like a thief in the middle of the night" grab you? How about "in a moment . . . in the twinkling of an eye?" Gives me the willies just *writing* those words. Imagine all those open mouths, eyes like saucers, spine-tingling chills high up in the clouds!

Jesus' return will be the absolute greatest surprise. Well, maybe I had better not say *that*. The *greatest* surprise is that people like us will be included in the group, stunned and dumb with wonder. Let's face it, that won't be just a surprise or a dream. That'll be a flat-out miracle.

Deepening Your Roots

Genesis 17:15 – 17, 18:9 – 14; Joshua 6:1 – 22; 1 Corinthians 15:52 – 58

Branching Out

1. Plan and throw a surprise party for someone. Or kidnap a friend early Saturday morning and take him out for breakfast.
2. Ask God to surprise you in some creative way this week.

Growing Strong

Here's a surprise for you: Summer is here. Oh, I know it's not officially that season until June 21 . . . but I'm eager for some days of rest and relaxation. I suspect you are, too. So, no assignment or questions to answer today. Now, that's some surprise!

See you next week.

Summer

A Season of Rest

SUMMER

I can almost hear her singing it, can't you? Straight out of *Porgy and Bess* . . . the black lady rolls those big eyes and belts out:

> "Summertime and the livin' is easy, Fish are jumpin' and the cotton is high."

Makes us wanna git right down and run around the house barefoot, singin' that ole tune. We're talkin' cut-offs and tank tops, kite flyin', fun truckin', shaggin' flies, and *no school*. I mean, there ain't nothin' like those lazy, hazy days of summer, right? Makes no difference where we live, summer is easy livin'! From the windswept hills of Tennessee to the craggy shoreline of Oregon . . . from the surfers off Santa Barbara to the racers in Indianapolis . . . from the rugged Baja Peninsula to nostalgic Cape Cod . . . from muggy Houston to soggy Seattle, when it's summertime, it's vacation time. A long-awaited and much-needed season of relaxation and rest.

Speaking of rest, been doing much of it lately? Or is that resistance I'm feeling from you? If so, you're probably singing another song (it's usually in a minor key) with a hard-driving beat, a heavy rhythm, and lots of volume . . . sufficient to drown out all those comments from your family and a few close friends (and maybe your doctor?) urging you to add a little leisure to your life. Sure is easy to keep putting that off, isn't it? After all, there's a job to be done! *And* your to-do list isn't nearly accomplished. *And* you haven't reached your quota this month. *And* there are lots of folks depending on you. *And* if you plan to get ahead in this world, it's going to require a two-ended candle and a ton of energy. And . . . and . . . yes, I know, I know.

You want to know *how* I know? I hear those same messages inside my head. Being a high-achiever, work-ethic type myself, I've been beating that drum for almost half a century. "Be responsible!" "Press on!" "Make things happen!" "Work hard!" "Do it now!" If anybody understands, I do.

But I can no longer ignore the necessity of the summer season in my life . . . nor can you, friend. If God considered this planet needed several months of summer, it stands to reason that His people are equally in need of refreshment and rest. He even says so:

> There remains therefore a Sabbath rest for the people of God. For the one who has entered His rest has himself also rested from his works, as God did from His. Let us therefore be diligent to enter that rest . . . (Hebrews 4:9 – 11a).

Interesting (and convicting) command, isn't it? We are to be diligent to enter into rest. That doesn't mean a lazy, irresponsible life-style full of indolence and free of industry. No, this is first and foremost a *mental* rest, a quiet confidence in the living Lord. A refusal to churn, to fret, to strive. The summer season symbolizes all this and more, much more.

Perhaps the following "summer thoughts" will help you live a little easier and, who knows, you may even become easier to live *with!*

BUILDING MEMORIES

You guys go on without me. You'll have a great time — I'm sure of that. Sorry, family, but I have to work."

The place? Montgomery, Alabama.

The time? Several years ago.

The situation? A dad, who really loved his family and wanted them to enjoy a summer vacation, had to work. The press of business kept him tied to the office. But being committed to their happiness, he assured them of his desire that they take the trip and enjoy the fleeting summer days.

He helped them plan every day of the camping trip. They would load up the family station wagon, drive to California, camp up and down the coast, then travel back home together. Each day was carefully arranged — even the highways they would travel and the places they would stop. Dad knew their whole route, the time they would reach each state — planned almost to the hour — even when they would cross the Great Divide.

It's what he didn't tell them that made the difference.

The father took off work (he'd planned it all along) and arranged to have himself flown to an airport near where his family would be on that particular day of the trip. He had also arranged to have someone pick him up and drive him to a place where every car on that route had to pass. With a wide grin, he sat on his sleeping bag and waited for the arrival of that familiar station wagon packed full of kids and camping gear. When he spotted the station wagon, he stood up, stepped out onto the shoulder of the road, and stuck out his thumb.

Can you visualize it?

"Look! That guy looks just like . . . DAD!"

The family assumed he was a thousand miles away, sweating over a stack of papers. It's amazing they didn't drive off into a ditch or collapse from heart failure. Can you imagine the fun they had the rest of the way? And the memories they stored away in their mental scrapbook — could they ever be forgotten?

When later asked why he would go to all that trouble, the creative father replied, "Well . . . someday I'm going to be dead. When that happens, I want my kids and wife to say, 'You know, Dad was a lot of fun.'"[11]

Talk about a unique domestic game plan! What an outstanding model of a father who wants to be remembered for more than just the basics . . .

> ". . . turn out the lights." "Did you get the bed made?" "Get out there and cut the grass." "No, we can't. I gotta work." "How much does it cost?" "That's too much trouble, dear. Let's be practical." "Hold it down — I can't hear the news."

Oh, — but there's so much more in life! That beautiful music of living is composed, practiced, and perfected in the harmony of home. The freedom to laugh long and loudly . . . the encouragement to participate in creative activities . . . the spontaneity of relaxed relationships that plant memories and deepen our roots in the rich, rare soil of authentic happiness. Couldn't this be included in the "all things" Paul mentioned in Romans 8:32 and 1 Timothy 6:17? The apostle tells us that our God *"richly supplies us with all things to enjoy."*

We're missing it — God's best — if the fun memories are being eclipsed by the fierce ones. The world outside the family circle is dark enough. When the light goes out *within* the circle . . . how great is the darkness.

If life with mom and dad has become more of an endurance course than a refreshing catalyst, then your prime time project isn't too tough to identify. Too many of us are beginning to resemble stern-faced East German guards who once patrolled the wall rather than approachable, believable parents, building happy memories. And maybe even a few crazy ones, too. Don't worry, God can handle it. He's got a great sense of humor. He made *you,* didn't He?

I'd much rather my brood remember me as the dad who tossed their mother fully clothed into the swimming pool — and lived to tell the story — than as the preacher who frowned too much, yelled too loud, talked too long . . . and died too young.

Deepening Your Roots

1 Timothy 6:17; Luke 15:22 – 32; Psalm 145:3 – 7

Branching Out

1. Do something creative and special today with your family, a friend, or a co-worker, that is totally unexpected and will always bring back a fond, wonderful memory.
2. Bring your camera out of hiding and take some candid shots of someone you like. Get the film developed and create a mini-scrapbook for him.

LIVING IT UP

Pussy cat, pussy cat, where have you been?
I've been to London to look at the queen.
Pussy cat, pussy cat, what did you do there?
I frightened a little mouse under her chair.

Stupid cat. She had the chance of a lifetime. All of London stretched out before her. Westminster Abbey. The British Museum. Ten Downing Street. Trafalgar Square. The House of Parliament. The Marble Arch in Hyde Park. She could've heard the London Philharmonic or scrambled up an old wooden lamp post to watch the changing of the guard. I doubt that she even cared she was within walking distance of St. Paul's Cathedral. She probably didn't even realize it was the historic Thames rushing by beneath that big rusty bridge she scampered across chasing more mice.

After all, she didn't even scope out the queen as Her Majesty stood before her. Not this cat. She is such a mouseaholic, she can't stop the same old grind even when she's in London. What a bore!

Can you imagine the scene as her husband met her at the plane at L.A. International?

"Hi, Fluff. How was it? What did ya see? Tell me all about it."
"Well, Tom, it all started when I saw this little mouse under the queen's throne. From then on it was just like here. I chased mice all over London. Do you realize how many mice there are in that city?"
"You what? You mean to tell me you spent ten days in London and all you can say for it is this stuff about mice!"

There is an old Greek motto that says:

YOU WILL BREAK THE BOW IF YOU KEEP IT ALWAYS BENT.

Which, being translated loosely from the original, means, "There's more to being a cat than tracking mice." Or, "There's more to life than hard work." Loosening the strings on our bow means when we have some leisure, we live it up. We deliberately erase from our minds that we are a cop or an engineer or a lawyer or a preacher or a salesman or a prof. We back off the strings and blow it. We break the up-tight mold and do stuff that helps us stay sane. And fun to be with. And whole people. We consciously decide against playing everything safe . . . at least for a little while . . . as we gain some perspective that our rut normally keeps us from seeing.

Which means if we spend a week in Hawaii, we don't pinch pennies. We don't even talk about it. Or think about it. The same applies to an evening at a classy restaurant or a night at the Hollywood Bowl or a weekend at Aspen.

Or if we take a cruise, we don't focus on dieting. We refuse to be like the woman on the Titanic who, as she climbed into the lifeboat, facing an uncertain future, sobbed in anguish, "If I had known this was going to happen, I'd have had the chocolate mousse for dessert!"

Or if we go to the slopes, we don't chop firewood or change our oil or worry about the papers stacking up in our driveway. We get out there in all that snow and have fun! And when we are too dog-gone tired to take one more ride on the lift, we crawl back on the shuttle, slump down in the seat and laugh out loud.

Or if we shoot the rapids, we attack those babies! *Full bore!* We scream and spit and gag on a raft full of water as we forget about being responsible, sensible, professional, and proper. The aches and pains, we'll worry about later. Right now it's "let 'er rip!" That applies to an afternoon at Dodger Stadium or an evening with the Rams.

Maybe that's what Jim Elliot meant when he wrote, "Wherever you are, be all there. Live to the hilt every situation you believe to be the will of God." That's another way of putting the familiar line out of Paul's letter:

> And whatever you do in word or deed, do all in the name of
> the Lord Jesus, giving thanks through Him to God the Father
> (Colossians 3:17).

Ever followed that to its logical conclusion? Unless I miss the point entirely, it takes the galling guilt out of living it up. It means we are free to enjoy to full measure our leisure. Even if it is *really* expensive. Even if it is wild 'n wooly. Even if it is fattening or crazy or *completely* out of character.

But one word of advice . . . better keep it to yourself. A lot of folks never go anywhere without a thermometer, a raincoat, a full tank of gas, a gargle, a hot-water bottle, aspirin, a change of socks, plenty of hair spray, and a parachute. Oh, yeah, they're also the ones who keep asking, "What time is it?" And, "How much does this cost?" And, "Are you sure everybody will understand?"

They're the same ones who would commend Fluff for "behaving herself" in London.

Deepening Your Roots

Deuteronomy 6:1,2; 1 Chronicles 15:25 – 29, 29:6 – 28

Branching Out

1. Do something that is totally out of character for you, and causes others to laugh.
2. Blow it today! Be extravagant; don't pinch pennies. And don't you dare feel guilty about it afterwards.
3. Block out some leisure time on your calendar to ensure you'll take some days off for refreshment.

MAN'S QUEST

Greece said . . . Be wise, know yourself.
Rome said . . . Be strong, discipline yourself.
Judaism says . . . Be holy, conform yourself.
Epicureanism says . . . Be sensuous, enjoy yourself.
Education says . . . Be resourceful, expend yourself.
Psychology says . . . Be confident, fulfill yourself.
Materialism says . . . Be acquisitive, please yourself.
Pride says . . . Be superior, promote yourself.
Asceticism says . . . Be inferior, suppress yourself.
Diplomacy says . . . Be reasonable, control yourself.
Communism says . . . Be collective, secure yourself.
Humanism says . . . Be capable, trust yourself.
Philanthropy says . . . Be unselfish, give yourself.

And on and on and on goes the quest of man. No wonder people are confused! Pick any thought-dish from this smorgasbord of human philosophy, then digest it completely . . . and you will find yourself suffering from the worst case of indigestion imaginable. It may smell good and even satisfy your rhetorical palate during the time you are consuming it . . . but it will leave you hungry, uneasy, and searching for something else to satisfy.

Rollo May's words often interrupt my thinking as I ponder the plight of searching men and women today:

> It is an old and ironic habit of human beings to run faster when
> we have lost our way.

And so it is! Look across your office desk tomorrow and chances are you'll be observing a living example of someone still searching, still running to find inner satisfaction. Step out in front of your apartment or home tomorrow morning and look both ways . . . listen to the roar of automobiles . . . study the dwellings surrounding you. Those sights and sounds represent people who have, like Little Bo-Peep's sheep, "lost their way," and, tragedy upon tragedy — they don't know where to find it.

Many of them have tried hard to "be religious" or "live by the golden rule" or "tie a knot and hang on" or "be sincere," but they're still running blind and bored and baffled.

They are attempting to fill the inner vacuum with *everything but the only thing.* You name it, it's being tried. As Henry Thoreau declared:

> The mass of men lead lives of quiet desperation.

Robert Ingersol, the bold and brilliant agnostic, spent many years of his life opposing and attacking the Scriptures and Christ's claims. On his deathbed . . . at the end of his race, he uttered:

> Life is a narrow veil between the cold and barren peaks of two eternities. We strive in vain to look beyond the heights. We cry aloud, and the only answer is the echo of our wailing cry.

Ingersol's pursuit is best described in the bumper sticker I saw on my way to work:

DON'T FOLLOW ME . . . I'M LOST

Pontius Pilate, Judea's notorious governor, stood eyeball to eyeball with Jesus of Nazareth. In the judicial process of interrogation, he heard Christ refer to "everyone who is of the truth," to which Pilate replied, "What is truth?" That question hangs heavily on the thin wire of reason in many a mind this very hour. Pilate never waited for an answer. He whirled away in confused disgust. He should have stopped running and waited for the answer. Jesus could have told him that He alone had satisfying words of life . . . for He alone *is* "the way, the truth, and the life" (John 14:6).

Christianity is not a system of human philosophy nor a religious ritual nor a code of moral ethics — it is the impartation of divine life through Christ. Apart from the Way there is no going . . . apart from the Truth there is no knowing . . . apart from the Life there is no living.

God says . . . Be in Christ, rest yourself.

Deepening Your Roots

1 John 3:16 – 20; Matthew 11:25 – 30; Psalm 62:5 – 8, 91:1,2

Branching Out

1. Look at the pace of your life today. In a hurry? Rushing? Force yourself to take thirty minutes to relax; calm down and slowly do a task.
2. Decide from the list of philosophies which one you lean toward. Spot an area in your life where this philosophy is evident and replace it with God's perspective.
3. Discard an object in your house that is not in keeping with God's philosophy, or contends for time which might otherwise be spent in enjoying moments with God.

Growing Strong

Grab yourself a cup of coffee or cold drink and relax for a few minutes with me. Go ahead, prop those feet up and relax. It's break time and a chance to ponder about the week's happenings. What was the most relaxing event of the past seven days?

FATHERS

In an age of equal rights and equal time, it's only fair to give the dads equal attention. Over a month ago the moms were standing in the spotlight. Move over, ladies . . . make way for the men, in fact, a very select group of men — *fathers.* It's timely to do that since summer is the season for Father's Day.

As if you didn't know! Every store window, newspaper, and national magazine in America has been parading gift ideas before your eyes for the past thirty days. Families have been wondering whether to wrap us in robes, fill us with food, surprise us with skis, tickle us with tools, or just cover us with kisses. If I know dads, most of 'em are going to blush no matter what you do. They are so used to providing, receiving is kinda weird. Occasionally, it's downright embarrassing! Most dads are quick to say to their families (with pardonable pride):

Look — sit back and relax . . . and leave the striving to us!

Think about your father, okay? Meditate on what that one individual has contributed to you. Think about his influence over you, his investment in you, his insights to you. Study his face . . . the lines that are now indelibly etched on your mind. Listen again to the echo of his voice . . . that infectious laugh . . . those unique expressions that emerge through the miracle of memory. Feel his hand around yours . . . his strong, secure arm across your shoulders. That grip that once communicated a strange mixture of gentleness and determination . . . compassion and masculinity . . . "I understand" and "Now, straighten up!" Watch his walk. No other walk like his, is there? Those sure steps. That inimitable stride. Arms swinging and back arched just so.

Best of all, remember his exemplary character. The word is *integrity.* As you read this, pause and recall just one or two choice moments in your past when he stood alone . . . when he stood by you . . . in a time of storm. When he protected you from the bitter blast of life's harsh consequences. When he said, "Honey, I forgive you," instead of, "You ought to be ashamed!"

In the wake of such a legacy which time can never rob, give God thanks. That's all. Just thank the Giver of every good and perfect gift for

the meaningful marks your dad has branded on the core of your character
. . . the wholesome habits he has woven into the fabric of your flesh.
While meandering through this forest of nostalgia, stop at the great oak
named Proverbs and reflect upon the words the wise man carved into its
bark twenty-nine centuries ago:

> A righteous man walks in his integrity — How blessed are his
> sons [and daughters] after him.

Ah, how true!

Our Lord declares that you are the beneficiary in a perpetual, paternal
policy. For the balance of your life, you receive the dividends from your
father's wise and sacrificial investments in "integrity stock." Most of
those dividends were unknown and unclaimed until you were grown.
How many of us now find ourselves richly endowed!

He is not perfect. He would be the first to admit it. Nor is he infalli-
ble, much to his own dismay. Nor altogether fair . . . nor always right. But
there's one thing he is — always and altogether — *he is your dad* . . . the
only one you'll ever have. And quite frankly, there's only one thing he
needs on Father's Day — plain and simple — he needs to hear you say
four words:

> *Dad, I love you.*

That's the best gift you can give. If you give him your love, you can
keep all the other stuff. Come to think of it, it's the most important gift of
all.

Deepening Your Roots

Exodus 20:12; Ephesians 6:1 – 4; Hebrews 12:7 – 11; 1 Kings 2:1 – 4, 3:3 – 15

Branching Out

1. Write your dad a loving note and remind him of a special memory he has
   given you that shares how deep his love is for you.
2. Write down ten things about your dad that you can thank God for. Go ahead
   . . . thank God!
3. Rather than buying your dad a gift, make him something or do something special for him that he's always talked about doing, but never had time for. Build
   a memory together.

ANNIVERSARIES

I don't need to tell *you* what I think of marriage and the family. You who know me already know. If I'm ever guilty of grinding an axe, I suppose it would be the home . . . that place where life makes up its mind. No need to add to what you've heard from me over and over again — *or is there?* Maybe so.

There is a reason I am prompted to say more. I celebrated my twenty-fifth wedding anniversary a while ago. Seems incredible. I remember in my younger years looking upon those who celebrated their quarter-of-a-century anniversary as folks one hop away from a wheelchair. Amazing how time flies! About the time your face clears up, your mind gets fuzzy. Or at least a little *misty.* Why? I can think of four reasons.

MEMORIES. Those "watercolor memories," as Streisand sings it, have a way of washing across one's mind, like the surf upon the shore, when anniversaries come. Funny memories. Also painful ones. Yet all of them dripping with nostalgia. Like our honeymoon — a colossal comedy of errors. And our eighteen months of forced separation when we were 8000 miles apart, thanks to the military. Such lonely times. But so essential in our growing up and facing reality. My midstream switch in careers . . . back to school, that tiny apartment, those disciplined, mind-stretching hours poring over the books. The births of our four (plus the loss of two we never got to see) and those energy-draining years from diapers to kindergarten. Wow! How much we learned together . . . how deeply our roots grew together . . . how rugged and long were some of those roads we traveled together.

An anniversary says, "Don't ever forget the memories. They are imperishable."

CHANGES. You just don't live three-and-a-half decades with the same person without doing a flip-flop in several major areas of your life. I suppose the single most significant one with me is in the realm of sensitivity. I have learned to read between the lines, to hear feelings that are never spoken, to see anguish or anger, joy or jealousy, confusion or compassion in faces that communicate what the tongue may not declare. And what an authority I was thirty-five years ago! I had it all wired — but what a difference a wife and a pack of kids make! God has used them to temper my intensity. The change from an opinionated dogmatist to more of an openminded learner was really needed. And really overdue. That process, by the way, is still going on.

An anniversary says, "Be thankful for the changes. They are important."

DEPENDENCE. My marriage has taught me that I am neither all-sufficient nor totally self-sufficient. I *need* a wife. I need her support, her insight, her discernment, her counsel, her love, her presence, and her efficiency. She is not my crutch . . . but she is my God-given companion and partner, ever aware of my moods and my needs. She hears my secrets and keeps them well. She knows my faults and forgives them often. She feels my failures and apprehensions and encourages me through them. For ten full years Cynthia was unaware of the fact I needed her. I was one of those husbands who plowed through life like a freight train — bullish, intimidating, selfish, and on top. Finally, the cracks began to show. Couldn't hide 'em any longer. The Lord showed me the value of sharing my hurts and admitting my fears. Of saying things like, "I'm wrong . . . I'm really sorry." And even coming up front with my wife and declaring how very much I depend on her to help me hang in there.

An anniversary says, "You don't have to make it on your own. Your partner is irreplaceable."

DREAMS. One final thing is worth mentioning. Dreams are what you anticipate as a couple, then watch God pull off. Sometimes they are little things, like working in the garden together, dropping a few seeds and seeing the sprouts, then the fruit. Or praying together about one of the children . . . you know, asking God to grab his heart and soften his spirit. As that dream happens, you smile at each other. You understand. Occasionally, the dream is a big thing . . . calling for sustained sacrifice, mutually shared. Like getting through school. Or remodeling your home. Or getting out of debt. When the reality finally occurs, no words can describe the pleasure of the long embrace, that kiss of profound accomplishment.

An anniversary says, "Think of the dreams you have weathered together. They are intimate accomplishments."

Our silver anniversary was a beautiful combination of memories, changes, growing dependence, and dreams. They date back to June 18, 1955, when a couple of kids said, "I do" and committed themselves to each other for life . . . having no idea what threatening storms lay ahead of us or what unspeakable joys would weld us together. For life.

I am a grateful husband. May God be praised for the genius of marriage and the thrill of celebrating it annually with the one I love.

Deepening Your Roots
Book of Ruth; Hebrews 13:1 – 6

Branching Out

1. Name one way you've changed in the past twenty-five years. _____

   _____

   Ask someone the same question.
2. What is a memory for which you are thankful? Tell someone about it and why you're thankful.
3. Whether it's your anniversary or not, celebrate your marriage or a friendship by doing something special this evening. You don't have to be elaborate — but do something — even if it's popping popcorn together!

OVEREXPECTING

When you stop achieving long enough to think about it, our world is full of overexpecters. They are in every profession, most of the schools, many of the shops, and (dare I say it?) all the churches.

To the overexpecter, enough is never enough. There's always room for improvement, always an area or two that isn't quite up to snuff, always something to criticize. Always. The overexpecter uses words like "ought" and "should" and loves sentences that include "must" and "more." To them, "work harder" and "reach higher" are the rule rather than the exception. When you're around them you get the distinct impression that no matter how hard you've tried, you haven't measured up. And what's worse, *you never will.* Overexpecters don't say that, but the meaning oozes out of their frowns and glares. Sooner or later your motivation is sapped as demands and expectations replace excitement with guilt. The killer is that final moment when you realize you have become a weary slave of the impossible.

Fun fades. Laughter leaves. And what remains? This won't surprise anybody: The tyranny of the urgent. The uptight, the essential, the expected — *always* the expected. Which, being interpreted, means, "the making of a coronary."

It's like my friend Tim Hansel's 1973 journal entry:

> When laughter fades
>   the tendency toward self-absorption
>   squeezes the light to a pinpoint.
> Morning only intimidates you into another day
>   and creativity no longer has the energy to care.

Because nobody screws up enough courage to tell overexpecters where to get off, these things keep happening:

- The little child loses his love for art because he is told time and again to stop coloring outside the lines. Parents are often overexpecters.
- The wife erodes in her joy around the house because she never seems to please the man she married. Husbands are often overexpecters.

- The gifted and competent employee gets an ulcer because the boss finds it next to impossible to say two monosyllabic words, "good job." Employers are often overexpecters.
- The once-dedicated, motivated pastor in a small church finally decides to change careers because he realizes he will never please his people. Church members are often overexpecters.
- The high school athlete chooses to hang it up at midseason because he knows that no matter what, he'll never satisfy. Coaches are often overexpecters.
- And, yes, congregations get tired of being beaten and bruised with jabs, hooks, and uppercuts from pulpits. Preachers are often over-expecters.

So what's the answer? Obviously, it's not the opposite extreme. Few people who are healthy enjoy mediocrity. Life without challenge is about as exciting as watching shadows change on a sundial. No, I haven't got all the answers, but when I think over my own tendency toward overexpecting, six words help a lot. Honesty. Reality. Acceptance. Tolerance. Acknowledgement. Encouragement.

I frequently think of Jesus as the Model. He promised people "rest" if they would come to Him, not an endless list of unrealistic expectations. He even said His yoke would be "easy" and His burden "light." He *was something else*. Still is!

All of us high-achievers need big doses of the counsel that must have emerged out of a home-spun cocoon on some screened-in back porch south of the Mason-Dixon Line many years ago:

> When I works, I works hard;
> When I sits, I sits loose;
> When I thinks, I falls asleep.

Deepening Your Roots
Proverbs 11:7; Haggai 1:1 – 12; Luke 6:32 – 36; John 5:4 – 43

Branching Out

1. Name an area in which you expect too much of yourself: _____

   _____

   Now, allow yourself a more realistic expectation: _____

   _____

2. Fill in the blanks:
   I expect my spouse (friend) to _____
   I expect my pastor to _____
   I expect my boss to _____
   Next time they don't meet up to your expectations ask yourself if you're over-demanding.
3. What's something others expect from you that is a "fair" expectation which you should meet, but usually don't: _____

   _____

   Work this week on fulfilling that expectation.

~~ ~~ ~~

Growing Strong

Man, I can't wait to hear how you "celebrated" this week with your mate or a good friend. I bet you came up with a creative idea that made popping popcorn seem dull. So, what did you do?

_____

_____

_____

_____

IN THE SHADE OF A JUNIPER

A major portion of our eye troubles could probably be diagnosed "ingrownius eyeballitus." Ingrown eyeballs. It strikes us all. In both dramatic and subtle ways, the stubborn enemy of our souls urges us to look ever inward instead of outward and upward. He whispers little nothings in our ears. He reminds us of how unappreciated and ill-treated we are . . . how important yet overlooked . . . how gifted yet ignored . . . how capable yet unrecognized . . . how bright yet eclipsed.

This clever adversary slips into the office of the faithful worker who has been bypassed, unpromoted. Looking up from his cluttered desk, the worker's mind is suddenly swamped with the silt of self-pity. Slipping down the hall and into the sick-room of the sufferer, the enemy pauses long enough to announce: "You've been forgotten. No one cares about you — not really. Out of sight, out of mind." Kneeling behind the bench warmer he whispers, "Face it, man, first string is out of reach. You'll never make it." To the unemployed he says, "No chance!" To the divorced he says, "No place!" To the bereaved he says, "No hope!" To the struggling he says, "No way!"

The most damaging impact of self-pity is its ultimate end. Cuddle and nurse it as an infant and you'll have on your hands in a brief period of time a beast, a monster, a raging, coarse brute that will spread the poison of bitterness and paranoia throughout your system. A frown will soon replace your smile. A pungent criticism will replace a pleasant, "I understand." Suspicion and resentment will submerge your selfish island like a tidal wave. You will soon discover that the sea of self-pity has brought with it prickly urchins of doubt, despair, and even the desire to die.

An exaggeration? A wild imagination? If you think so, sit with me beneath the shade of a juniper tree located at 19 First Kings, the address of a prophet named Elijah. The leather-girded prophet had just finished mopping up a victory over Ahab and his Baal-worshiping cronies. God stamped His approval upon Elijah in such a way that all Israel realized he was God's mouthpiece. At this point Jezebel, Ahab's spouse (he was her mouse), declared and predicted Elijah's death within twenty-four hours. Surely the seasoned prophet had faced criticism before. He lived with bad press and constant threats — all prophets do. That's par for the course! But this threat somehow found its mark in the chink of his armor.

Elijah ran for his life. Finally, ninety miles later, he collapsed beneath a juniper tree. Overwhelmed with self-pity, the prophet whined, "I've had enough . . . take away my life. I've got to die sometime, and it might as well be now."

Later on he admitted:

> I have worked very hard for the Lord God of the heavens; but the people of Israel have broken their covenant with you and torn down your altars and killed your prophets, and only I am left; and now they are trying to kill me, too (1 Kings 19:10, TLB).

There you have it. Self-pity in the raw. Elijah's eyes were so ingrown he saw two of everything — except God. He felt unloved, cast off, and out of it. Most of all, he believed his situation so isolated him that he only was left. Nobody else was near and in the prophet's mind that included God. Self-pity is the smog that pollutes and obscures the light of the Son. The more you're out in it, the deeper it hurts. The more your eyes shed tears, the greater the sting of loneliness.

But God didn't rebuke His man. He didn't club him nor did He strike him dead. Instead, He encouraged him to take a long rest and enjoy a catered meal or two. Jehovah helped Elijah get his eyes off himself and his situation. Gently, He prodded the prophet to focus anew on his God. A little later, the Lord gave him a close friend named Elisha with whom he might share his life and his load.

Feeling sorry for yourself today? Caught in that ancient "sin-drome" of self-pity? Why not try God's remedy: A good, well-deserved mental rest where you stop trying to work things out *yourself* . . . a decent, well-balanced diet . . . a long, well-needed look at your Savior in His Word . . . topped off with some quality time with a friend.

You will be amazed at the outcome. You may even discover that what you thought was approaching blindness was only an advanced case of ingrown eyeballs.

Deepening Your Roots
Proverbs 4:20 – 27; Luke 11:33 – 36; John 9:1 – 41; 2 Corinthians 4:16 – 18

Branching Out
1. Eat well-balanced meals today (not junk food), plus take time to read and think and allow God to refresh your spirit.
2. Are you getting a case of "ingrown eyeballs"? Call a friend for some fresh perspective.

INSIGHT

Are you ready for a surprise? You blink twenty-five times every minute. Each blink takes you about one-fifth of a second. Therefore, if you take a ten-hour automobile trip, averaging forty miles per hour, you will drive twenty miles with your eyes *closed.*

I know a fact far more surprising than that. Some people go through *life* with their eyes closed. They look but don't really "see" . . . they observe the surface but omit the underneath . . . they focus on images but not issues . . . vision is present but perception is absent. If life were a painting, they would see colors but no genius in the strokes of the brush. If it were a journey, they would notice a road but no majestic, awesome scenery. If it were a meal, they would eat and drink but overlook the exquisite beauty of the china and the delicate touch of wine in the sauce. If it were a poem, they would read print on the page but miss altogether the passion of the poet. Remove insight and you suddenly reduce life to *existence* with frequent flashes of boredom and indifference.

Those without insight dwell mainly in the realm of the obvious . . . the expected . . . the essentials. The dimensions that interest them are length and width, not depth. Please understand, I do not mean to be critical of those who *cannot* go deeper . . . but of those who can but *will not.* I'm not pointing my finger at inability but rather refusal.

As a concrete illustration, take the boatload of disciples in Mark, chapter 6. Immediately after Jesus had miraculously fed thousands of people with a few loaves and fish, He sent His men away in a boat as He slipped off to a quiet place on the mountain to pray. A storm later broke upon the sea and they were filled with panic. He came to their rescue shortly thereafter and calmed the sea as He stilled the wind and assured them there was no reason to be afraid. Mark makes a comment worth remembering:

> . . . they were greatly astonished, for they had not gained any insight from the incident of the loaves, but their heart was hardened (vv. 51b – 52).

It wasn't that they were unable to understand. They didn't want to understand! William Barclay of Glasgow says, "Their minds were obtuse." That was the root problem. Those men were insensitive, dull, blunt-brained. They weren't ding-a-lings by nature, but by choice — and therein rested not the tragedy but the blame! They didn't need Jesus' pity as much as they deserved a rebuke. By then they had been sufficiently exposed to their miracle-working Master to respond with keen insight to their circumstances. Had they applied what they observed earlier that day when the thousands were fed, their response to the storm would have been insightful.

Hebrews 5 is addressed to similar disciples today. Hours upon hours have been logged under the teaching of the Word, and opportunities to use those truths have been legion. But what does this passage say? It says some have become "dull of hearing" — thick, lazy, sluggish, lacking insight. Maturity — the result of mixing insight with practice — is rare today . . . and so the discernment between good and evil, brought on by "trained senses," is frequently conspicuous by its absence.

What are a few practical rewards? Parents with insight usually raise kids that are secure, fulfilled, relaxed, free to forge out ideas and to think. Single adults with insight won't feel they *must* marry — the sooner the better. Teachers with insight create an atmosphere conducive to learning. Bosses with insight develop employees and remain sensitive to surrounding needs. Students with insight learn far more than the required subject — they indeed glean an education.

I challenge you: Open your eyes! Think! Apply! Dig! Listen! There's a lot of difference between necessary blinking and unnecessary blindness.

Deepening Your Roots

Mark 6:45 – 56; Luke 24:36 – 45; Colossians 3:2; Hebrews 5:1 – 14;
1 Peter 1:13 – 15; 1 Kings 4:29

Branching Out

1. Next time you're forced to think, don't back off. Dig in. Interact. Think! Write down what you learned. _____

2. Rather than just read today's Scripture, study it. Ponder over each verse. Write down a new insight: _____

APPRAISING LIFE

It's been awhile since you took stock of where you're going, hasn't it? And how about an evaluation of the kids? Or your marriage? Or your own future? You know what I mean, trimming off the fat of lazy thinking and taking a lean, hard look at the years remaining.

As I write these words, I'm looking ahead to my sixtieth birthday. If Christ doesn't return (and I don't die in the meantime), I figure I've got about ten, maybe fifteen remaining years of effective service.

How old are you? How many years lie between now and when you turn sixty-five or seventy? It's high time you came to terms with your future, isn't it?

And if that doesn't grab you, consider your *family* in the next decade. In only ten years Cynthia and I will have a son forty-three, a daughter forty-one, another daughter thirty-seven, and our "baby" will be thirty-four! Seems impossible. Especially since I can remember when our place resembled a cross between Grand Central Station, the Indianapolis 500, and the San Diego Zoo. But, as the old newsreel says, "Time marches on."

Occasions set aside for evaluation and regrouping are needed. Even the sports world has its time out and seventh-inning stretch and pit stop and half time, so why shouldn't we? Force yourself to pull off the road, put your pace into neutral, and ask some hard questions. Here are a few worth personal consideration:

1. Am I really happy, genuinely challenged and fulfilled in life?

2. In light of eternity, am I making a consistent investment for God's glory and His cause?

3. Is the direction my life is now taking leading me toward a satisfying and meaningful future?

4. Can I honestly say that I am in the nucleus of God's will for me?

And for the kids:

1. Am I spending sufficient time with the children so that they know I love and accept them and care very much about their future?

2. Am I communicating life goals, a proper value system, a standard of moral purity, a drive for excellence, and commitment to loyalty, integrity, generosity, and honesty to my children? Do they really *know* how I feel about these things?

3. Are they aware that they are worthwhile and valuable? Are they growing up to be positive, confident, secure, highly esteemed young men and women?

4. When they leave the nest, will they be able to stand alone?

Please read General Douglas MacArthur's prayer for his son. Read the words slowly, deliberately, and — if possible — aloud.

> Build me a son, O Lord, who will be strong enough to know when he is weak, and brave enough to face himself when he is afraid; one who will be proud and unbending in honest defeat, and humble and gentle in victory.
>
> Build me a son whose wishbone will not be where his backbone should be; a son who will know Thee and that to know himself is the foundation stone of knowledge.
>
> Lead him, I pray, not in the path of ease and comfort, but under the stress and spur of difficulties and challenge. Here let him learn to stand up in the storm; here let him learn compassion for those who fail.
>
> Build me a son whose heart will be clean, whose goal will be high; a son who will master himself before he seeks to master other men; one who will learn to laugh, yet never forget how to weep; one who will reach into the future, yet never forget the past.
>
> And after all these things are his, add, I pray, enough of a sense of humor, so that he may always be serious, yet never take himself too seriously. Give him humility, so that he may always remember the simplicity of greatness, the open mind of true wisdom, the meekness of true strength.
>
> Then I, his father, will dare to whisper, "I have not lived in vain."

For what are you asking the Lord on behalf of your life and your children? I challenge you, stop long enough to think it over. And don't just think, get alone and *write down* your thoughts, your dreams, your aspirations. Refuse to let tonight's television programs or some insignificant activity interrupt this necessary discipline. If you put it off, you may lose the urgency you sense right now.

> Home is a lot of things . . . but mainly it is the place where life makes up its mind.

Solomon, the wise, offers solid counsel:

> Remember also your Creator . . . before the evil days come and the years draw near when you will say, "I have no delight in them"; . . . Remember Him before . . . the spirit will return to God who gave it (Ecclesiastes 12:1, 6 – 7).

By doing these things — and following through with the necessary changes that will enable you to accomplish your plans — you will get back on target. And best of all, you will be able to say, "I have not lived in vain."

Deepening Your Roots

Ecclesiastes 12:1 – 14; Proverbs 30:7 – 9; 2 Corinthians 5:6 – 10; Philippians 3:4; 1 Peter 1:3 – 9

Branching Out

1. How many, and what people, do you think will be living with you in ten years?
2. Tonight answer the question: "What are you asking the Lord on behalf of your life?" Write your answer here: _____
   _____
3. Determine two new life goals and write them here:
   1. _____
   2. _____

᮫ ᮫ ᮫

Growing Strong

Two weeks ago we were talking about "celebration" and "popcorn." This week we zeroed in on serious matters. Striking a balance between the two is essential, so I'm glad we've taken the time to look both ways before heading down the center.

But for today, let's be serious one more time and have you make some remarks about the summer ahead. What's one thing you want God to do in your life by September 1?

_____

_____

_____

_____

ACTING MEDIUM

The children worked long and hard on their own little cardboard shack. It was to be a special spot — a clubhouse — where they could meet in solemn assembly or just laugh, play games, and fool around. As they thought long and hard about their rules, they came up with three rather perceptive ones:

1. Nobody act big.
2. Nobody act small.
3. Everybody act medium.[12]

Not bad theology!
In different words, God says the very same thing:

> . . . give preference to one another in honor (Romans 12:10).

> . . . whoever wishes to become great among you shall be your servant, and whoever wishes to be first among you shall be your slave (Matthew 20:26 – 27).

> Let another praise you, and not your own mouth; a stranger, and not your own lips (Proverbs 27:2).

Just "act medium." Believable, honest, human, thoughtful, and down-to-earth. Regardless of your elevated position or high pile of honors or row of degrees or endless list of achievements, just stay real. Work hard at counteracting the celebrity syndrome. Junk any idea that you deserve some kind of pat on the back or wristwatch for a job well done. Who did you do it for, anyway? If you did it for God, He has an infinite number of unseen ways to reward you. If you did it for man, no wonder you're clawing for glory!

But it's so subtle. So easy to draw out that praise for yourself, isn't it? Especially around the house when you do a few extras.

A certain firm has made headlines out of deflating overblown egos. Its well-trained employees accept contracts to squash juicy pies into the faces of pompous individuals. In its first few months, over sixty hits were made at $35 per splash! All on disbelieving, immaculately dressed, prim-and-proper victims.

Imagine this scene: A dignified, well-tailored executive vice president waits for the elevator to open on the eighteenth floor. As he steps out, a stranger whips a pie out of a cardboard box and splosh! Giving the pie a professional twist, the hitman jumps into the elevator headed for the main floor. There stands Vice President Shmotz . . . his once-spotless suit, matching vest, and tie now dripping with lemon meringue goo and crust.

An employee of the pie-tossing company said, "A pie in the face brings a man's dignity down to where it should be and puts the big guys on the same level with everyone else."[13]

Even Biola College weathered the recent pie-throwing rage. No one was safe from the meringue gang — neither the professors nor even the school's great-hearted president who took it on the chin like a champ. I'd hate to think how many college presidents would have responded with their super-guarded, highly polished egos smeared with bright gold pumpkin pie and whipping cream. I wonder how many would "act medium."

Again what was it the Son of David said?

Let another praise you . . . and not your own lips.

Meaning what? Meaning no self-reference to some enviable accomplishment. Meaning no desire to manipulate and manufacture praise. Meaning authentic surprise when applauded. Genuine, rare humility — regardless.

One final warning. Don't try to fake it. False humility stinks worse than raw conceit. The answer is not in trying to *appear* worthless and "wormy" but in consistently taking notice of others' achievements, recognizing others' skill and contributions . . . and saying so.

Got the rules memorized? "Nobody act big. Nobody act small. Everybody act medium." Such good advice from a clubhouse full of kids, who, by the way, are pretty good at practicing what they preach.

And they also laugh out loud when you get a pie in the kisser. Believe me, I know.

Deepening Your Roots
1 Peter 5:5, 6; Matthew 20:20 – 28

Branching Out

1. Try not to use the word "I" today. Everytime you hear it roll off your lips, chalk up 10¢. At the end of the day give the loot to your kids or to a friend.
2. Don't praise yourself or ask for commendation (i.e., How did I do?).

A Rare and Remarkable Virtue

Perhaps you've uttered the American's Prayer at some anxious moment recently:

Lord, give me patience . . . and I want it *right now!*

This rare and remarkable virtue is within the *and-so-forth* section in Galatians chapter 5. You know how we quote that passage . . . "the fruit of the Spirit is love, joy, peace, *and-so-forth*." That lazy habit has caused a very important series of virtues to become forgotten. Allow me to quote Galatians 5:22 – 23 — in full.

But the fruit of the Spirit is love, joy, peace, patience, kindness, goodness, faithfulness, gentleness, self-control; against such things there is no law.

Notice, please, the fourth on the list. Patience. The original Greek term unloads a lot of meaning upon us. MAKROTHUMIA is the term, and it's a compound word. MAKROS means "long or far," and THUMOS means "hot, anger, or wrath." Putting it together, we come up with "long-anger." You've heard the English expression "short-tempered"? Well, I suppose we could coin an expression for patience — *long-tempered* — and not miss the accurate meaning very far.

Generally speaking, the Greek word is not used of patience in regard to things or events, but of patience in regard to *people.* Chrysostom defined MAKROTHUMIA as the spirit which could take revenge if it liked, but utterly refuses to do so. I find that this characteristic is a needed quality for the pastor of a flock. Listen to the Lord's counsel to me as a Christian minister:

. . . giving no cause for offense in anything, in order that the ministry be not discredited, but in everything commending ourselves as servants of God, in much endurance . . . in purity, in knowledge, in *patience,* in kindness . . . (2 Corinthians 6:3 – 4, 6).

If one attempts to lead a congregation without this Spirit-given virtue, he is driven to frustration, irritability, and severity. His pulpit becomes an avenue of anger, his preaching a diatribe of demands, and his person insulting and intolerant as Diotrephes of old. No, God encourages me and my ilk to be "long-tempered."

But there is more. This beautiful characteristic of Christ is equally important among all Christians . . . and that includes *you,* my friend. Without it, you cannot walk in a manner worthy of your calling (Ephesians 4:2; Colossians 3:12). And — you are to demonstrate it before *everyone* (1 Thessalonians 5:14). That includes children, spouses, employers, neighbors, slow drivers, people who make mistakes, senior citizens, and God! In fact, patience is a by-product of love (1 Corinthians 13:4).

If you and I were asked to name an example of this enviable quality, Job would be our man. Now I am of the opinion that he didn't sit down one day and make up his mind to be a patient person. Surely he never tried to bargain with God for that virtue. In fact, the term doesn't even appear in the entire book of Job — check for yourself. James 5:11, however, makes a remark about the "endurance of Job" and we know from that comment that he was one who was patient.

How did Job become a patient person? The secret is found in the original term in James 5:11, rendered "endurance." It is HUPOMONE, meaning "to abide under." Job rested and endured under the load of suffering. He determined that he would "abide under" the blast furnace of affliction regardless of its heat. The result was patience. As the slag of self-will, phony pride, stubbornness, and resentment floated to the top under the heat of heartache, grief, pain, and sorrow, patience formed — like the purifying process of raw gold. That explains why Paul says that trials and tribulations bring about patience and perseverance within us (Romans 5:3 – 4).

Deepening Your Roots

James 5:7 – 11; Romans 5:1 – 5; Galatians 5:19 – 24

Branching Out

1. What's happening in your life right now that's trying your patience? _____

   _____

   Rather than get angry, do what Job did: abide under it.
2. Think of someone you admire for their patient spirit. Ask the person for advice and how he has developed that long-tempered ability.

TAKE TIME TO BE TENDER

Back when I was a kid I got a bellyache that wouldn't go away. It hurt so bad I couldn't stand up straight, or sit down without increasing the pain. Finally, my folks hauled me over to a big house in west Houston where a doctor lived. He had turned the back section into his office and clinic.

It was a hot, muggy afternoon. I was scared.

The doc decided I needed a quick exam — but he really felt I was suffering from an attack of appendicitis. He had whispered that with certainty under his breath to my mom. I remember the fear that gripped me when I pictured myself having to go to a big, white-brick hospital, be put to sleep, get cut on, then endure having those stitches jerked out.

Looking back, however, I really believe that "quick exam" hurt worse than the surgery the next day. The guy was rough, I mean really rough. He poked and thumped and pulled and pushed at me like I was Raggedy Andy. I was already in pain, but when old Dr. Vice Grip got through, I felt like I had been his personal punching bag. To him, I was nothing more than a ten-year-old specimen of humanity. Male, blond, slight build, ninety-nine-degree temperature, with undetermined abdominal pain — and nauseated.

Never once do I recall his looking at me, listening to me, talking with me, or encouraging me in any way. Although young, I distinctly remember feeling like I bored the man — like case No. 13 that day, appendectomy No. 796 for him in his practice. And if the truth were known, an irritating interruption in his plans for nine holes later that afternoon.

Granted, a ten-year-old with a bellyache is not the greatest challenge for a seasoned physician to face . . . but his insensitivity left a lasting impression. His lack of tender caring canceled out the significance of all those neatly framed diplomas, achievements, and awards plastered across the wall. He may have been bright . . . but he was even *more* brutal.

At that painful, terrifying moment of my life, I needed more than credentials. Even as a little kid I needed compassion. A touch of kindness. A gentle, considerate, soft-spoken word of assurance. Something to cushion the blows of the man's cut-and-dried verdict, "This boy needs surgery — meet me at Memorial at five o'clock today." Over and out.

Looking back over thirty-five years, I've learned a valuable lesson: When people are hurting, they need more than an accurate analysis and diagnosis. More than professional advice. More, much more, than a stern, firm turn of a verbal wrench that cinches everything down tight.

Attorneys, doctors, counselors, physical therapists, dentists, fellow ministers, nurses, teachers, disciplers, parents, hear ye, *hear ye!* Fragile and delicate are the feelings of most who seek our help. They need to sense we are there because we care . . . not just because it's our job. Truth and tact make great bedfellows.

Sound too liberal? Weak? Would it help if you could see that some-one like the Apostle Paul embraced this philosophy? He did. Although a brilliant and disciplined man, he was tender.

> You know we never used flattery, nor did we put on a mask to cover up greed — God is our witness. We were not looking for praise from men, not from you or anyone else.
>
> As apostles of Christ we could have been a burden to you, but we were gentle among you, like a mother caring for her lit-tle children. We loved you so much that we were delighted to share with you not only the gospel of God but our lives as well, because you had become so dear to us (1 Thessalonians 2:5–8, NIV).

Someday we shall all be at the receiving end — you can count on it. We shall be the ones in need of affirmation, encouragement, a gentle touch of tenderness. It's like the time-worn counsel of the good doctor Thomas Sydenham, the "English Hippocrates" (1624 – 1689). Addressing himself to the professionals of his day, Dr. Sydenham wrote:

> It becomes every person who purposes to give himself to the care of others, seriously to consider the four following things: First, that he must one day give an account to the Supreme Judge of all the lives entrusted to his care. Second, that all his skill and knowledge and energy, as they have been given him by God, so they should be exercized for His glory and the good of mankind, and not for mere gain or ambition. Third, and not more beautifully than truly, let him reflect that he has undertaken the care of no mean creature; for, in order that he may estimate the value, the greatness of the human race, the only begotten Son of God became Himself a man, and thus ennobled it with His divine dignity, and far more than

this, died to redeem it. And fourth, that the doctor being himself a mortal human being, should be diligent and tender in relieving his suffering patients, inasmuch as he himself must one day be a like sufferer.

And that applies to ten-year-olds with a bellyache, eighty-year-olds with a backache, anybody with a headache . . . and everybody with a heartache.

Deepening Your Roots
Acts 24:23; Luke 10:25 – 37; Genesis 47:11 – 12

Branching Out

1. Find someone who's sick in bed, or in the hospital, and do some gentle caring toward him.
2. Search out and find a young child who is ill and give him some TLC.
3. When you send in that payment to your doctor or dentist, include a note of encouragement or an item that would communicate you care about his health and well-being.

Growing Strong

Giving to others isn't easy, is it? It's much easier to disregard the little nudges inside your heart and head that say, "give that person some help." Much easier to be selfish, act as if we don't see the need, play detour, or deaf. Oh . . . but when we do care life seems so much more worthwhile. Say . . . did anybody come to your rescue this week? Did you care for anybody? If not, before the day is over, set aside your shy or selfish self and do something for another. Then come back and tell me what you did. Make it a worthwhile day.

RISKING LIBERTY

*T*here is something all of us want to be, need to be, and ought to be, but only a few really are. A very small percentage of those in God's family can honestly and boldly declare, "I am _____." Even though we think it's good and we say it's right. Even though we love its benefits and we defend its value. Though it's ours to claim, we don't. Though it's available to enjoy, we won't. It is biblically supported, theologically sound, commanded by God, and desired by man . . . but rare is the Christian who fully enters into it with enthusiasm.

What is it? *Freedom,* that's what. All of us want to be free, need to be free, ought to be free. But wait, does God really say it's OK? You decide.

> It was for freedom that Christ set us free; therefore keep standing firm and do not be subject again to a yoke of slavery (Galatians 5:1).

> For you were called to freedom, brethren (Galatians 5:13a).

> . . . and you shall know the truth, and the truth shall make you free. . . . If therefore the Son shall make you free, you shall be free indeed (John 8:32, 36).

> Now the Lord is the Spirit; and where the Spirit of the Lord is, there is liberty (2 Corinthians 3:17).

There's more, much more. In fact, there is an entire letter in the New Testament devoted to this one subject. It's Galatians, a book of the Bible someone dubbed the "magna carta of Christian liberty." Good description. Sit down and read it soon. It is designed to set you free. It is so potent it says that those who choose to remain enslaved have (get this) "fallen from grace" (Galatians 5:4b). Wow!

Liberty and slavery, you see, are absolutely incompatible. Opposites. One is out in the open, the other behind bars.

But let's not tiptoe around with peripheral problems. Let's come to terms with our struggle with liberty. It's the *risk* involved. Misuse is another way to put it. You can hardly abuse slavery, but you certainly can liberty. Many do. Which brings up the basic questions: "With such a potential for misuse, is it really wise to teach Christians that they are free? Is it safe to tear up the man-made lists and let out the rope? Isn't it risky to promote liberty, living by grace, being free to become who we really are?

Safe? No. Risky? You'd better believe it.

The risk of liberty is that some people are bound to misuse it. And because of that, most choose the safe option and say little about freedom other than shouting, "Don't turn it into license!" Now listen — there is *always* the danger that some will do the wrong thing, the destructive thing, the sinful thing. It's like letting our teenagers go. Tossing them the keys is a risk. Every time. But the alternative is not a valid option. No kid ever grew up to become responsible and mature without Mom and Dad encouraging the freedom to grow.

It is, admittedly, a difficult thing to do, but preserving and promoting the freedom of the individual believer to be responsible, to make decisions, to determine choices (even wrong ones occasionally), and to live with the consequences of his actions is the key to developing a "liberty mentality" rather than an enslaved captive. We must, I repeat, we *must* encourage maturity with our brothers and sisters in the family of God. Since Christ has set us free, we dare not imprison them behind the legalistic bars of our own opinions, traditions, or personal preferences.

I've read that the life cycle of a silkworm from egg to worm to moth includes the state at which the worm spins about itself a remarkable cocoon. This little sack is composed of 400 to 800 yards of silk fiber which seals it from the inside as it waits for metamorphosis. At the completion of the cycle, the adult moth will break the cocoon, tearing apart the fine silk cords that bind it, and fly free. But the silkworm farmer does not allow most to become adults. At a key point in the cycle, he steams the cocoons to keep the moths inside from maturing. If he didn't do this, they would go free, leaving a trail of broken threads which are useless to the exploiters. If they were allowed to mature and escape, by the way, the reproductive moth would lay up to 350 eggs. But they are not allowed to do so . . .

Could it be that many immature, caged Christians are kept from maturing because their ecclesiastical "captors" cannot fulfill selfish purposes in free people? Who wants their secure — though immature — traditions left behind in shambles? And we can't forget the hassle, either.

Teaching people how to fly takes a lot more time and trouble than just allowing them to crawl.

A room full of moths is certainly a bigger challenge than a box full of worms.

Deepening Your Roots

1 Corinthians 9:19; 2 Corinthians 3:1 – 18

Branching Out

1. How would you fill in the blank: "I am _____
_____."

2. What keeps you from being free? _____
_____

   Tackle one of your infringements and claim the truth: I am FREE in Christ.

3. Do you keep others from being free? Are you afraid to allow your spouse, friend, or children to make mistakes? Decide who you have the most difficulty setting free and make an effort to let them go it alone this week without your protective hand or thoughts. If they should fail, be the first to encourage them, not gloat over their mistake or say, "I told you so."

COMPROMISE AND CONSEQUENCE

I don't know anyone who would like to build a summer home at the base of Mt. St. Helens. Not many would stand in line to buy real estate in Venice. It would be tough trying to get campers to pitch their tents where Big Foot had been spotted.

No family I know is interested in vacationing in a houseboat twenty feet above Niagara Falls. Or swimming in the Amazon near a school of piranhas. Or taking an evening stroll through Harlem. Or building a new home that straddles the San Andreas fault.

There's not a dad in America who'd let his daughter date a convicted murderer . . . or encourage his boy to wash windows at San Quentin.

I mean, some things make no sense at all. Like lighting a match to see if your gas tank is empty. Or stroking a rhino to see if he's tame. Man, that's lethal! They've got a name for nuts who try such stunts. Victims. Or (if they live to tell the story) just plain *stupid.*

And yet there's a strange species of Christian running loose today who flirts with risks far greater than any of the above. That's right. And they will do so with such a calm face you'd swear they had ice water in their veins. You could never guess by a glance they are balancing on the thin edge of disaster. Without a pole. And without a net.

Who are they? They are the ones who rewrite the Bible to accommodate their life-style. We've all met them. From the skin out they have all the appearance of Your Basic Believer, but down inside, operation rationalization transpires daily. They are experts at rephrasing or explaining away the painful truth of the text.

How do they think? Well, it's not very complicated. Whenever they run across Scripture verses or principles that attack their position, they alter them to accommodate their practice. That way, two things occur:

1. All desires (no matter how wrong) are fulfilled.
2. All guilt (no matter how justified) is erased.

That way everybody can do his own thing and nobody has any reason to question anybody's action. If he does, call him a legalist and plow right on. Oh yeah, you've gotta talk a lot about grace, too. That helps to spook the bunch who would otherwise criticize.

What are some examples? Just look around and listen. Here is a sampling of accommodating theology:

- God wants me to be happy. I can't be happy married to her. So I'm leaving . . . and I know He'll understand.
- There was a time when this might have been considered immoral. But not today. The Lord gave me this desire and wants me to enjoy it.
- Look, nobody's perfect. So I got in deeper than I planned. Sure, it's a little shady, but what's grace all about, anyway?
- Me? Ask His forgiveness? That's ridiculous. My relationship with God is much deeper than shallow techniques like that.
- Hey, if it feels good, have at it! Life's too short to sweat the small stuff. We're not under law, you know.
- So what if a little hanky-panky . . . a little fun 'n games goes on? What's life about without some spice and risk? All those 'thou shalt nots' are unrealistic.

If that's true . . . if that's right, then what in the world does it mean to be *holy?*

> As obedient children, do not be conformed to the former lusts which were yours in your ignorance, but like the Holy One who called you, be holy yourselves also in all your behavior; because it is written, "You shall be holy, for I am holy" (1 Peter 1:14–16).

Or *pure?*

> For this is the will of God, your sanctification; that is, that you abstain from sexual immorality . . . abstain from every form of evil (1 Thessalonians 4:3, 5:22).

Or *under grace?*

> What then? Shall we sin because we are not under law but under grace? May it never be! (Romans 6:15).

Or *undefiled?*

> Let marriage be held in honor among all, and let the marriage be undefiled; for fornicators and adulterers God will judge (Hebrews 13:4).

The simple fact is this: We reap *precisely* what we sow. If we sow a life-style that is more comfortable or easier or even happier — but is in direct disobedience to God's revealed Word — we ultimately reap *disaster.*

> Do not be deceived, God is not mocked; for whatever a man sows, this he will also reap. For the one who sows to his own flesh shall from the flesh reap corruption . . . (Galatians 6:7–8a).

It may not come soon . . . but it will come. And when it does, no one will have to explain what it means to be holy, pure, under grace, or undefiled. When the bills come due, the wages of willful sin are paid in full. God may seem slow, but He doesn't compromise with consequences.

Deepening Your Roots

Leviticus 18:1 – 30; Galatians 3:1 – 14; Ephesians 5:1 – 11; 1 Thessalonians 4:1 – 7

Branching Out

1. Confide in a Christian friend you trust and ask him to help you overcome a sin you keep repeating.
2. Memorize a verse from Scripture that will help you choose right the next time you're confronted with a temptation or want to rationalize.
3. Get serious. Ask God to help you overcome an area of your life you know isn't godly. If you're not ready to ask God for help, then ask Him to help you become convicted about it.

WORM THEOLOGY

*E*ver get a song on your mind? Sure, it happens to everyone. It can drive you crazy . . . like a silly commercial jingle. The Madison Avenue guy makes them that way — so they'll stick like cockleburs to a spaniel's ear. Sometimes, however, the melody on the brain is a welcome one. Like a solid, old hymn that keeps us company during a lonely afternoon.

It happened to me last week. Isaac Watts struck again. One of his best (he wrote over 600!) lingered in my head for more than an hour before I actually formed the words with my mouth. Suddenly, I found myself listening to what Watts wrote over two centuries ago:

> Alas! and did my Savior bleed?
>   And did my Sovereign die?
> Would He devote that sacred head
>   For such a worm as I?

I frowned as that last line faded away. "A worm"? Does God see people as "worms"? When Christ died did He "devote that sacred head" for *worms?* Now, obviously, Watts wanted to portray a vivid illustration of sinful mankind — lost, undeserving, spiritually worthless, wicked within. Dipping his brush in Job 25 and Isaiah 41, the hymnist painted such a picture, using the very term Scripture uses — *worm.* He was biblical and therefore justified in his choice of terms for the text. Frankly, we were worm-like when our righteous God found us — lowly, wandering, dirty, unattractive, grubby creatures.

But that doesn't mean we work hard at making ourselves into worms now. *A child of God is not a worm.* If God had wanted you to be a worm, He could have very easily made you one! He's very good at worms, you know. There's an infinite variety of the wriggly creatures. When Watts wrote of worms, he was merely using a word picture. Many others, however, have framed it as a model to follow, calling it humility. This "worm theology" creates enormous problems.

It wears many faces — all sad. It crawls out from between the mattress and the springs in the morning, telling itself, "I'm nothing. I'm a worm. Woe, woe. I can't do anything and even if I appear to be doing something, it's not really me. Woe! I must annihilate self-respect . . . crucify all motivation and ambition. If any good accidentally leaks out, I must quickly hide it or categorically deny I had anything to do with it. How could *I* accomplish anything of value? I mean, who am I? I'm a worm. Good for nothing except crawling very slowly, drowning in mud puddles, or getting stepped on. Woe, woe, woe."

There's one main problem with this sort of thinking — *it's phony.* No matter how diligently we labor to appear genuinely humble, it amounts to nothing more than trying to look good in another way. Self-made worms carry around little signs you have to squint at to read:

> I bet I'm twice as humble as you.

And therein lies the ugly sin: PRIDE.

Heretical though it may sound, no one who actually hates himself can adequately share the love of Christ. Our Lord taught that we were to love our neighbors *as* we love ourselves. Think that over. If we don't properly love ourselves, where does that leave our neighbors? I have yet to witness an effective, happy, fulfilled Christian whose image of himself was poor . . . who *really* believed he was a worm.

Have you taken time this week to consider before your Lord and His Word who you really are? It's impossible to imagine that one who is adopted into God's family, accepted in the Beloved, a recipient of the riches of Christ, called to be His ambassador, and the object of infinite grace, mercy, love, and peace, ought to slither around like a nightcrawler. If you ask me, *that's* heresy!

Sinful? Oh yes. Undeserving? Absolutely. Imperfect? Who isn't? Selfish? Indeed! Wrong? More often than not.

But a *worm?* Useless? Unimportant? Spineless? Meaningless? No, not that. God declared us righteous. He lifted us out of the miry clay and set us upon a rock. He invites us to approach Him with boldness. And He means it!

> No condemnation now I dread;
> Jesus, and all in Him is mine!
> Alive in Him, my living Head,
> And clothed in righteousness Divine.
> Bold, I approach the eternal throne,
> And claim the crown, through Christ my own.

Now *there's* a song to get stuck in your mind.

Deepening Your Roots

Job 25:1 – 5; Psalm 8:1 – 9; Isaiah 41:14 – 16; Romans 3:21 – 26; Hebrews 4:16

Branching Out

1. Do something for yourself today that brings you happiness. As you do it, remind yourself that "you're important, too!"
2. Do something for your neighbor that you would like your neighbor to do for you.
3. Memorize a song you sing at church. Let it get stuck in your mind.

ᔥ ᔥ ᔥ

Growing Strong

You should be at, near, or just beyond the halfway point in this book and your year. If you've read the articles, dug deeper into the Scriptures, and attempted on occasion to branch out, you're to be commended. You're a "gold star" pupil! I hope you're liking the book, but better yet, I hope you're growing and becoming stronger. Share with me one way this book has helped you grow in the past six months:

_____

_____

_____

_____

FAILURES

Snake River Canyon coiled up, rattled its tail, and sank its fangs into its would-be captor. On a sultry Sunday afternoon its 1,700-foot jaws yawned wide as it swallowed a strange-tasting capsule prescribed for it by Dr. Robert C. Truax, the scientist-designer of *Sky Cycle X-2*. Starring in the show was a guy some people tagged Captain Marvel, who looked more like Billy Batson unable to remember the magic word. But before we label him a showman . . . or a show-off . . . I suggest we consider the outcome of this showdown.

Any third grader could have told you the vaunted skycycle leap across the canyon was a triple-A flop — a classic fizzle. The skycycle gave up in mid-air; the driver floated to safety beneath a nylon cloud. But you won't find him sitting long-faced in a dark corner today. Most people send an ambulance and a wrecker to mop up their mistakes. He could have sent a Brink's armored car. As bystanders shouted "Rip off!" he was thinking about write-offs. Anyone who can walk away from a failure with a smile, a bulging rear pocket, and his pride still intact has to have *something* going for him. The real six-million dollar man, if you can believe it, is a two-wheeled wonder named Evel Knievel. Nobody — but *nobody* in the long history of sports ever came off a more abysmal failure better than he. The remains of Dr. Truax's flopcycle littered the canyon, but the man who took off like a bird made out like a banker.

When you stop and think it over, there's an abiding truth in that Idaho extravaganza all of us ought to capture and cultivate. It's much greater than money and far deeper than a canyon jump. There's a philosophy of life here I'm now convinced is worth one's pursuit. Here it is:

> THE PERSON WHO SUCCEEDS IS NOT THE ONE
> WHO HOLDS BACK, FEARING FAILURE, NOR
> THE ONE WHO NEVER FAILS . . . BUT RATHER
> THE ONE WHO MOVES ON IN SPITE OF FAILURE .

As Lowell wrote:

> Not failure, but low aim, is crime.

As Teddy Roosevelt believed:

> Far better it is to dare mighty things, to win glorious triumphs, even though checkered by failure, than to take rank with those poor spirits who neither enjoy much nor suffer much because they live in the gray twilight that knows neither victory nor defeat.

Give me a "skycycle" and a 108-foot take-off ramp with all its risks any day — before you sentence me to the path of predictability between the stone walls of routine and fear. God asks that we believe Him *regardless* of the risks — in spite of the danger — ignoring the odds. The ancient city of Jericho was defeated because Joshua and his troops defied the "normal procedure" of battle . . . never once fearing failure. The Gentiles heard of Christ Jesus because Paul and a few companions kept getting back up after being knocked down. Peter's two letters are in the Book because he refused to live in the shadow of his bad track record.

Great accomplishments are often attempted but only occasionally reached. What is interesting (and encouraging) is that those who reach them are usually those who missed many times before. Failures, you see, are only temporary tests to prepare us for permanent triumphs.

Whoever you are today — listen to me! Sitting there licking your wounds will only result in a bitter aftertaste. Sighs and tears and thoughts of quitting are understandable for the moment but *inexcusable* for the future. Get up and get on with it!

And if you're looking for an absolute guarantee against future failures, I know of only one — death.

Deepening Your Roots
Joshua 6:1 – 27; 1 Samuel 17:1 – 50; 1 Chronicles 11:15 – 19

Branching Out
1. Start doing something that you've put off because of the risk of failure.
2. Make a meal tonight using two new recipes. Take the risk.
3. Go to a local ice cream parlor and try a flavor you've never had.

THE BROKEN WING

*I*t is quite probable that someone reading my words this moment is fighting an inner battle with a ghost from the past. The skeleton in one of yesterday's closets is beginning to rattle louder and louder. Putting adhesive tape around the closet and moving the bureau in front of the door does little to muffle the clattering bones. You wonder, possibly, "Who knows?" You think, probably, "I've had it . . . can't win . . . party's over."

The anchor that tumbled off your boat is dragging and snagging on the bottom. Guilt and anxiety have come aboard, pointing out the great dark hulks of shipwrecks below. They busy themselves drilling worry-holes in your hull and you are beginning to sink. Down in the hold, you can hear them chant an old lie as they work: "The bird with the broken pinion never soared as high again. . . ."

Allow me to present a case in opposition to these destructive and inaccurate accusers. It may be true that you've done or experienced things which would embarrass you if they became public knowledge. You may have committed a terrible and tragic sin that was never traced back to you. You may have a criminal record or a moral charge or a domestic conflict that, to this moment, is private information. You may wrestle with a past that has been fractured and wounded by a mental or emotional breakdown. Futile attempts at suicide may add to the previous scar tissue and increase your fear of being labeled "sick" or "nervous." It is possible that you live with memories, covered now by the sands of time, of an illicit relationship or a financial failure or a terrible habit or a divorce or a scandalous involvement. You feel that any one of these things might mar or cripple your reputation if the dirty details ever spilled on the table of gluttonous gossipers.

But wait a minute. Before you surrender your case as hopeless, consider the liberating evidence offered in the Bible. Take an honest look at men and women whom God used *in spite* of their past! *Abraham,* founder of Israel and tagged "the friend of God," was once a worshiper of idols. *Joseph* had a prison record but later became prime minister of Egypt. *Moses* was a murderer, but later became the one who delivered his nation from the slavery of Pharaoh. *Jephthah* was an illegitimate child who ran around with a tough bunch of hoods before he was chosen by God to become His personal representative. *Rahab* was a harlot in the streets of Jericho but was later used in such a mighty way that God enlisted her among the members of His hall of fame in Hebrews 11.

Still unconvinced? There's more. *Eli* and *Samuel* were both poor, inconsistent fathers, but proved to be strong men in God's hand regardless. *Jonah* and *John Mark* were missionaries who ran away from hardship like cowards but were ever-so-profitable later on. *Peter* openly denied the Lord and cursed Him, only to return and become God's choicest spokesman among the early years of the infant church. *Paul* was so hard and vicious in his early life the disciples and apostles refused to believe he'd actually become a Christian . . . but you know how greatly God used him. We could go on and on. The files of heaven are filled with stories of redeemed, refitted renegades and rebels.

How magnificent is grace! How malignant is guilt! How sweet are the promises! How sour is the past! How precious and broad is God's love! How petty and narrow are man's limitations! How refreshing is the Lord! How rigid is the legalist!

There is not a single saint who sits in a single church free from a few things he or she is ashamed of — not one of us! The one who thinks otherwise is worse than all the rest combined. In plain, garden-variety English, we were all taken from the same dunghill. And so we all fight the same fight with the filth of the flesh regardless of how loudly we sing, how piously we pray, or how sweetly we say hello.

Mark it — when God forgives, He forgets. He is not only willing but pleased to use any vessel — just as long as it is clean *today*. It may be cracked or chipped. It may be worn or it may have never been used before. You can count on this — the past ended one second ago. From this point onward, you can be clean, filled with His Spirit, and used in many different ways for His honor. God's glorious grace says: "Throw guilt and anxiety overboard . . . draw the anchor . . . trim the sails . . . man the rudder . . . a strong gale is coming!"

Deepening Your Roots

Daniel 9:4 – 19; Luke 7:36 – 48; Acts 10:34 – 43

Branching Out

1. In celebration of God's forgivenesses towards you, be the first to forget and forgive an action your spouse or friend did to you.
2. Look through your garage and try to come up with an old clay pot that has a crack or two in it. Set it on the kitchen counter or in a place where you'll see it often. Leave it there for a week and let it remind you of the fact that God delights in using us, His vessels, no matter how "weak" we are.

SEARCHING FOR SHELTER

*D*iscouragement.

Where does it come from?

Sometimes it feels like a dry, barren wind off a lonely desert. And something inside us begins to wilt.

At other times it feels like chilling mist. Seeping through our pores, it numbs the spirit and fogs the path before us.

What is it about discouragement that strips our lives of joy and leaves us feeling vulnerable and exposed?

I don't know all the reasons. I don't even know most of the reasons. But I do know *one* of the reasons: We don't have a refuge. Shelters are hard to come by these days . . . you know, people who care enough to listen. Who are good at keeping secrets. And we all need harbors to pull into when we feel weather-worn and blasted by the storm.

I have an old Marine buddy who became a Christian several years after he was discharged from the Corps. When news of his conversion reached me, I was pleasantly surprised. He was one of those guys you'd never picture as being interested in spiritual things. He cursed loudly, drank heavily, fought hard, chased women, loved weapons, and hated chapel service. *He was a great marine.* But God? They weren't on speaking terms when I bumped around with him.

Then one day we ran into each other. As the conversation turned to his salvation, he frowned, put his hand on my shoulder, and admitted:

"Chuck, the only thing I miss is that old fellowship all the guys in our outfit used to have down at the slop shoot (Greek for tavern on base). Man, we'd sit around, laugh, tell stories, drink a few beers, and really let our hair down. It was great! I just haven't found anything to take the place of that great time we used to enjoy. I ain't got nobody to admit my faults to . . . to have 'em put their arms around me and tell me I'm still okay."

My stomach churned. Not because I was shocked, but because I had to agree. The man needed a refuge . . . someone to hear him out. The incident reminded me of something I read several months ago:

> The neighborhood bar is possibly the best counterfeit there
> is to the fellowship Christ wants to give His church. It's an
> imitation, dispensing liquor instead of grace, escape rather

than reality, but it is a permissive, accepting, and inclusive fellowship. It is unshockable. It is democratic. You can tell people secrets and they usually don't tell others or even want to. The bar flourishes not because most people are alcoholics, but because God has put into the human heart the desire to know and be known, to love and be loved, and so many seek a counterfeit at the price of a few beers.

With all my heart I believe that Christ wants His church to be . . . a fellowship where people can come in and say, "I'm sunk!" "I've had it!"[14]

Let me get painfully specific. Where do *you* turn when the bottom drops out of *your* life? Or when you face an issue that is embarrassing . . . maybe even scandalous. Like:

- You just discovered your son is a practicing homosexual.
- Your mate is talking separation or divorce.
- Your daughter has run away . . . for the fourth time . . . and you're afraid she's pregnant.
- You've lost your job. It's your own fault.
- Financially, you've blown it.
- Your parent is an alcoholic.
- Your wife is having an affair.
- You flunked your entrance exam or you messed up the interview.
- You're in jail because you broke the law.

What do you need when circumstances puncture your fragile dikes and threaten to engulf your life with pain and confusion?

You need a shelter. A listener. Someone who understands.

But to whom do you turn when there's no one to tell your troubles to? Where do you find encouragement?

Without preaching, I'd like to call to your attention a man who turned to the living Lord and found in Him a place to rest and repair. His name? David. Cornered, bruised by adversity, and struggling with a low self-esteem, he wrote these words in his journal of woes:

> In you, O LORD, I have taken refuge;
> let me never be put to shame;
> deliver me in your righteousness.
> Turn your ear to me,
> come quickly to my rescue;

be my rock of refuge,
a strong fortress to save me
(Psalm 31:1 – 2, NIV).

Failing in strength and wounded in spirit, David cries out his need for a "refuge." The Hebrew term speaks of a protective place, a place of safety, security, secrecy. He tells the Lord that He—Jehovah God—became his refuge. In Him the troubled man found encouragement.

Now the question: Why do we need a refuge? As I read on through this psalm, I find three reasons unfolding:

First, because we are in distress and sorrow accompanies us.

Be merciful to me, O LORD, for I am in distress;
my eyes grow weak with sorrow,
my soul and my body with grief.
My life is consumed by anguish
(vv. 9 – 10a, NIV).

Eyes get red from weeping. The heavy weights of sorrow press down. Depression, that serpent of despair, slithers silently through the soul's back door.

Depression is

Debilitating, defeating,
Deepening gloom.

Trudging wearily through
The grocery store,
Unable to make a simple choice,
Or to count out correct change.

Surveying an unbelievably messy house,
Piles of laundry,
Work undone, and not being
Able to lift a finger.
Doubting that God cares,
Doubting in my prayers,
Doubting He's even there.

Sitting, staring wild-eyed into space,
Desperately wanting out of the human race.[15]

Heavy! But that's why we need a refuge.

Second, because we are sinful and guilt accuses us.

> My strength fails because of my guilt and my bones grow
> weak (v. 10b, NIV).

There is shame between these lines.

Embarrassment. "It's my fault." What tough words to choke out! "I'm to blame."

An old British minister says it all when he writes:

> This is the bitterest of all—to know that suffering need not
> have been; that it is the harvest of one's own sowing; that the
> vulture which feeds on the vitals is a nestling of one's own
> rearing. Ah me! This is pain![16]

Harried and haunted by self-inflicted sorrow, we desperately search for a place to hide. But perhaps the most devastating blow of all is dealt by others.

Third, because we are surrounded by adversaries and misunderstanding assaults us.

> Because of all my enemies, I am the utter contempt of my
>   neighbors;
> I am a dread to my friends—
>   those who see me on the street flee from me.
> I am forgotten by them as though I were dead;
>   I have become like broken pottery.
> For I hear the slander of many;
>   there is terror on every side;
> they conspire against me
>   and plot to take my life (vv. 11 – 13, NIV).

See how the hurting is handled?

"Utter contempt . . . a dread . . . those who see me flee from me . . . I am forgotten . . . I hear slander . . . there is terror . . . they conspire against me. . . ." Sound like a page out of your journal?

Tortured by the whisperings of others, we feel like a wounded, bleeding mouse in the paws of a hungry cat. The thought of what people are saying is more than we can bear. Gossip (even its name hisses) gives the final shove as we strive for balance at the ragged edge of despair.

Discouraged people don't need critics. They hurt enough already. They don't need more guilt or piled-on distress. They need encouragement. They need a refuge.

A place to hide and heal.

A willing, caring, available someone. A confidant and comrade-at-arms. Can't find one? Why not share David's shelter? The One he called My Strength, Mighty Rock, Fortress, Stronghold, and High Tower.

David's Refuge *never* failed. Not even once. And he never regretted the times he dropped his heavy load and ran for cover.

Neither will you.

Deepening Your Roots
Psalm 18:1 – 3, 16 – 19, 32:6 – 7, 71:1 – 3

Branching Out

1. When you hear of, or are with, someone who has failed, don't criticize — be a refuge. Be forgiving and loving by listening to him and holding him with your arms of comfort.
2. Don't whisper gossip today about anyone! And don't listen to someone else's gossip either!
3. When you hear of the difficulty or failure of someone else, don't stay away. Keep being a friend and find a way to be a refuge to the person.

❧ ❧ ❧

Growing Strong

Speaking of failures . . . did you blow it this week? So did I! Satan smiles smugly when we get discouraged and throw in the towel. Let's not give him that satisfaction. Knowing how our enemy hates love and forgiveness, let's give those very things to ourselves and others . . . starting today. Report back to me at the end of the day how you're doing.

MANIPULATION

When C. S. Lewis was a student at Oxford, he made a number of friends, some of whom became lifelong companions. Several in that close circle went off to become authors, like Lewis himself. Over the years, they loved to get together to talk and read to each other in their works in progress. These sessions never failed to hone and shape their thinking. Among the group were Nevill Coghill and Owen Barfield, men who were cultivating the literary craft . . . but in no way as prolific or as profound as their friend. Lewis's reputation soon eclipsed them all. The ink flowed from his pen much more rapidly than theirs, and at increasingly shorter intervals, old Clive Stapes was producing meaningful materials for the world to read. This could have driven a wedge between them, but he didn't let that happen.

The more popular scholar seemed to appreciate more than ever his long-standing friends. Not once did they sense that Lewis desired to control them. Barfield once admitted:

> I never recall a single remark, a single word or silence, a single look . . . which would go to suggest that he felt his opinion was entitled to more respect than that of old friends. I wonder how many famous men there have been of whom this could truthfully be said.

An absence of manipulation. No interest in pushing for his own way or putting down others, or in using his role or record of achievement as a subtle yet forceful lever.

Manipulation is the attempt to control, obligate, or take advantage of others by unfair or insidious means. It is practiced by insecure people who are attempting to look superior by making others squirm. Oh, it isn't usually done in a bold, up-front manner, but rather indirectly, obliquely. By little hints. Or well-timed comments. Or facial expressions.

The *Take-Charge Manipulator* is one type. This is the individual who has to come out smarter or stronger than you in order to be happy with you around. To see if you fit into this category, answer the following questions:

1. Do I drop hints that signal I know more about what's being discussed than those in charge?

2. Do I enjoy correcting factual errors in conversation?

3. Do I control an argument, looking for ways to show that the other person is at fault?

4. Do I make others feel guilty when I want a certain action?

The *Poor-Me Manipulator* is the opposite extreme. This individual attempts to get his or her way by appearing weak. After all, who can hit you while you're down and helpless? These people "clutch" at you, using sighs, tears, sickness, even depression to gain control and get their way. They love the role of victim, which seldom fails to arouse sympathy. Wives and husbands are great at this. So are kids! We can appear so needy, so ill . . . until we see it's not working. Then it's amazing how much energy we can muster as anger replaces weakness.

The *I-Must-Be-Needed Manipulator* is yet another type. This person is not so much one to clutch and cling, but rather to cultivate an obligation. The mother (or mother-in-law) with grown children has to deal with this, especially if she isn't employed, gets her housework done by 9:00 a.m., and is bored. Her phone rings and it's a married daughter who shares a problem she is struggling with. Mama is in her car and on her way over before the gal on the other end of the line has hung up. She steps in and gets things rolling (just like the old days!) without even being invited. Let her daughter get a little resentful and the poor-me syndrome gets set in motion, like fast . . . "Well, how ungrateful can you be, young lady!" With a slam she stomps out like a little girl who had her doll snatched away.

Manipulation is an infantile technique and yet it is practiced mainly by adults. No profession is immune. Pastors can easily resort to it, using the Bible as their defense. Physicians can rely on it as well, practicing behind the cover of the untouchable brotherhood. So can attorneys who know how to read "legalese" and secretly enjoy the power of intimidation. Or the teacher who possesses the ultimate lever — *the grade book.*

Once again our Example stands tall. Although deity in flesh, not once did He take unfair advantage of finite men and women who spent time with Him. Although Himself omniscient, He gave others room to learn, to express themselves . . . even when they were dead wrong and He could have silenced them. Never once did our Lord maneuver simply to gain the upper hand or to come out smelling like a rose. With wisdom He held His power in check and yet on those few occasions when He did release it, the purpose was to glorify God, never to manipulate man.

Paul picked up the same style from his Master. Why, he had sufficient authority to get what he wanted without even saying "please." A snap of his fingers would have brought food to his table or put shekels in his pocket. No way! He simply refused to throw his apostolic weight around.

> Never once did we try to win you with flattery, as you very well know, and God knows we were not just pretending to be your friends so that you would give us money! As for praise, we have never asked for it from you or anyone else, although as apostles of Christ we certainly had a right to some honor from you (1 Thessalonians 2:5 – 6, TLB).

If you are in a position of authority, no matter how small or how large, the temptation to manipulate will never go away. You may have the authority to claim certain honors ... to call attention to your right to be listened to. You may even be encouraged to do so by well-meaning devotees who want to see you get ahead. Don't yield. Resist at all cost.

If C. S. Lewis could restrain with all his brilliance, popularity, and record of achievements, so can we. There's a word for those who shun this counsel and push people around to get their way.

Lonely.

Deepening Your Roots
Genesis 27:1 – 35; Luke 4:1 – 12; 1 Thessalonians 2:1 – 16

Branching Out

1. Next time you sense someone manipulating you, graciously confront the person with how you feel. Learn from the experience by storing in your mind how being manipulated made you feel.
2. Give someone a note before your next business meeting, or family gathering, and ask the individual to observe you, watching for any manipulative comments or actions.

DISORIENTATION

Right now I'm looking at a cartoon that portrays a disheveled, stubble-faced, pajama-clad man who has evidently just thrown back the covers of his bed and put his warm feet on the cold floor. "On Monday mornings," he mumbles, "I don't know if I'm alive or on tape."

Now there's a guy I can identify with! Reminds me of the story President Harry Truman enjoyed telling. A man was hit on the head at work. The blow was so severe he was knocked unconscious for an extended period of time. His family, convinced he was dead, called the funeral home and asked the local undertaker to pick him up at the hospital, which he did. Early the following morning this dear man suddenly awoke and sat straight up in the casket. Confused, he blinked several times and looked around, trying to put the whole thing together. He thought:

> *"If I'm alive, what in the world am I doing in this soft, satin-filled box? And if I'm dead, why do I have to go to the bathroom?"*

Disorientation is the pits. When you travel a lot (like airline personnel) you have to deal with it. When you fight deadlines as days run into nights (like tax consultants and publishing editors) you have to work out ways to cope with it. When you are confined to tight places or inescapable spaces (like astronauts or prisoners or victims of confining illnesses) — again, that old bug-a-boo is there ready to bite, leaving you in the wake of depression or one of its emotional relatives.

I find it also happens after extremely busy times in my life. While the dust is flying and activities are happening and decisions are occurring and plans are unfolding, we sorta tie a knot and hang on. We keep thinking that soon it will be over and things will return to normal. But "normal," when it finally happens, seems strange, almost unmanageable. This is never more emphatic than when people "retire" from their occupations which have kept them in touch and needed all their adult lives. Abruptly — after a brief flurry of farewells, thank-yous, nice words, and a gold watch — that individual feels put out to pasture. Out of touch. No longer needed. Life is strangely reduced to fading memories, an abstruse existence sandwiched between the foggy feelings of uselessness and loss of identity.

I watched my own father cave in after he retired, as disorientation replaced definitive living. His sense of humor soon lost its keen edge. His once-adventurous spirit turned to restlessness. He talked less, he traveled less, and, what's worse — he *thought* less. Not because he was without money or without health . . . but because he was without purpose. And without close friends. And without the plant superintendent giving him a to-do list every day as he showed up (always forty-five minutes early). No longer was there a shop whistle at quitting time or the grinding sounds of a turret lathe as dark-blue chips of steel screamed while being stripped away. Now all was quiet. Desperately quiet. Maddeningly quiet. Not even television could fill the void. And it wasn't twelve months before the thief of senility began to steal away the man's drive. Oh, he lived many, many years beyond sixty-five. But most of those years, I'm saddened to say, were marked by tragic disorientation.

Why bother you with all this? Why worry about such a distant dilemma in this day of circus-like atmosphere and a schedule that would fatigue a rhino? Well, as Solomon once said,

> . . . Because childhood and the prime of life are fleeting (Ecclesiastes 11:10).

And because there may be a time when

> . . . the years draw near when you will say, "I have no delight in them" (Ecclesiastes 12:1).

You see, there's nothing in the Bible that says none of that will happen before you "retire." Monday morning blues are not restricted to folks in Leisure World. Disorientation is not a cloud that floats only over Sun City. Nor is it limited to Vietnam vets or inmates at a camp in Siberia.

Wanna fight it? Make and cultivate a few very close friends. Stay in touch with people. Give of yourself. Read widely. Exercise regularly and strenuously. Turn the TV off. Fight the rut of routine. Leave time for leisure. Have more fun. Take up a hobby or pastime that gets you outdoors. Don't let your occupation enslave you. Eat less. Laugh more. Quit fussing. Encourage at least one person every day. Stop living for money. Plant a garden. Replace fake plants with real ones in your home. Trust

God for something that seems impossible. Loosen up your intensity. Stop taking yourself (and your kids) so seriously. Start today.

Yesterday was Monday. I went sailing with a friend. It was great therapy out on the blue Pacific. Today is Tuesday. I'm looking forward to Wednesday and Thursday and even Friday because I pulled out all the stops on Monday. I may even preach better on Sunday because I sailed last Monday . . . but I wouldn't bet on it.

On Monday I was live, but everything on Sunday is taped.

Deepening Your Roots

Numbers 8:20 – 25; 1 Kings 2:1 – 11; Luke 19:11 – 26

Branching Out

1. Do something this week that you've never done before. Write what you did here: _____
2. Encourage one person every day this week. Record the names.

   1. _____
   2. _____
   3. _____
   4. _____
   5. _____
   6. _____
   7. _____

RELAYING THE TRUTH

*I*t was late afternoon when the boat's engine sputtered, stalled, and refused to restart. Gallons of water surged into the craft as it pitched on sickening, six-foot swells. The five Jaegers had done all they knew to do, but it wasn't enough. An exciting fishing trip was now a thing of horror. They were going under.

Grim-faced, George Jaeger, his three sons, and his elderly father methodically tightened the buckles on their life jackets, tied themselves together with a rope, and slipped silently into a black and boiling Atlantic.

George glanced at his watch as the boat finally disappeared — 6:30 p.m. Very little was said. It grew dark. First one boy and then another swallowed too much salt water, gagged, and strangled on the brine as they fought to keep their heads up. The helpless father heard his sons, one by one, then his dad, choke and drown. But George couldn't surrender. After eight nightmarish hours, he staggered onto the shore, still pulling the rope that bound him to the bodies of the other four. Pause to try and imagine the sight!

"I realized they were all dead — my three boys and my father — but I guess I didn't want to accept it, so I kept swimming all night long," he later told reporters. "My youngest boy, Clifford, was the first to go. I had always taught our children not to fear death because it was being with Jesus Christ." Before Cliff died, his dad heard him say, "I'd rather be with Jesus than go on fighting."

In that vivid Atlantic memory, George Jaeger had a chance to witness the impact of his fifteen years as a father. The boys died quietly, with courage and dignity. Up to the very last minute, one by one they modeled the truth passed on by their father: When under pressure, stay calm . . . think . . . even if death is near, keep under control. So they did and so they died. When the ultimate test was administered in an angry sea, they handed in perfect scores.

In her bestseller, *What Is a Family?*, Edith Schaeffer devotes her longest chapter to the idea that a family is a *perpetual relay of truth*. A place where principles are hammered and honed on the anvil of everyday living. Where character traits are sculptured under the watchful eyes of moms and dads. Where steel-strong fibers are woven into the fabric of inner constitution.

The relay place. A race with a hundred batons.

- *Determination.* "Stick with it, regardless."
- *Honesty.* "Speak and live the truth — always."
- *Responsibility.* "Be dependable, be trustworthy."
- *Thoughtfulness.* "Think of others before yourself."
- *Confidentiality.* "Don't tell secrets. Seal your lips."
- *Punctuality.* "Be on time."
- *Self-control.* "When under stress, stay calm."
- *Patience.* "Fight irritability. Be willing to wait."
- *Purity.* "Reject anything that lowers your standards."
- *Compassion.* "When another hurts, feel it with him."
- *Diligence.* "Work hard. Tough it out."

And how is this done? Over the long haul, believe me. This race is not a sprint, it's a marathon. There are no fifty-yard-dash courses on character building. Relays require right timing and smooth hand-offs — practiced around the track hour after hour when nobody is looking. And where is this practice track? Where is this place where rough edges cannot remain hidden, must not be left untouched? Inside your own front door. The *home* is God's built-in training facility.

That's why He urged all the dads in Moses' day to relay the truth:

> . . . and you shall teach them diligently to your sons and shall talk of them when you sit in your house and when you walk by the way and when you lie down and when you rise up (Deuteronomy 6:7).

That's the plan — the inimitable strategy which makes winners out of runners. Relay the truth — diligently, consistently. One final warning, however. If you determine to make this your goal, you'll have to outdistance two relentless foes: slow starts and sloppy handoffs. Keep in mind, moms and dads, you really don't have forever. Negligence will catch you from behind and beat you in the stretch if you let up. And don't think your kids will let you get away with faking it, either.

I read about a salesman who knocked on the door of a rundown apartment house in a low-rent district. The mother didn't want to talk to the guy, so she told her little boy to tell him she couldn't come to the door because she was in the bathtub. Her son answered the door this way: "We ain't got no bathtub, but Mom told me to tell you she's in it."

Furthermore, it won't work for you to play catch-up by dumping a truckload of truth once or twice a year. The secret of good parenting is consistency. Never forget that.

Got the game plan, now? Stay at it, day in and day out. And make sure your handoffs are crisp and sharp throughout this race against time. Relays are won or lost at that critical moment when a young hand reaches back and gropes for the baton.

Ask George Jaeger.

Deepening Your Roots
Deuteronomy 6:4 – 9; Luke 2:21 – 51

Branching Out

1. Talk to at least one of your children or a friend about death.
2. Ask your kids, or a friend you respect, to name one way you are inconsistent. Don't defend yourself. Rather, accept their observation as truth and work on changing it.
3. Pick an activity and do it at the exact same time for five days in a row. Evaluate your consistency, or inconsistency.

ঝ ঝ ঝ

Growing Strong

Aren't kids great? Our four children have taught me so much. What did you learn from yours (or a friend's) this week?

_____

_____

_____

_____

GOD'S CONTROL

*T*he bitter news of Dawson Trotman's drowning swept like cold wind across Schroon Lake to the shoreline. Eyewitnesses tell of the profound anxiety, the tears, the helpless disbelief in the faces of those who now looked out across the deep blue water. Everyone's face except one — Lila Trotman. Dawson's widow. As she suddenly walked upon the scene a close friend shouted, "Oh, Lila . . . he's gone. Dawson's gone!" To that she replied in calm assurance the words of Psalm 115:3:

> But our God is in the heavens;
> He does whatever He pleases.

All of the anguish, the sudden loneliness that normally consumes and cripples those who survive did not invade that woman's heart. Instead, she leaned hard upon her sovereign Lord.

As you read these words . . . does that seem strange to you? Does it seem unusual to refer to a tragic death as being God's pleasure? Honestly now, do you think God's control over us is total . . . or partial? Let's allow His Word to speak on this deep subject:

> Thou hast enclosed me behind and before,
> And laid Thy hand upon me.
> Thine eyes have seen my unformed substance;
> And in Thy book they were all written,
> The days that were ordained for me,
> When as yet there was not one of them
> (Psalm 139:5, 16).

> Woe to the one who quarrels with his Maker —
> An earthenware vessel among the vessels of earth!
> Will the clay say to the potter, "What are you doing?"
> (Isaiah 45:9).

> . . . I am God, and there is no other;
> I am God, and there is no one like Me . . .
> Saying, "My purpose will be established,
> And I will accomplish all My good pleasure"
> (Isaiah 46:9 – 10).

> . . . He does according to His will in the host of heaven
> And among the inhabitants of earth;

292

And no one can ward off His hand
Or say to Him, "What has Thou done?"
(Daniel 4:35).

There are more. Patiently, repeatedly, in a dozen different ways the Word makes the point. Accept it or not, God's calling the shots. He's running the show. Either He's in *full* control or He's off His throne. It's as foolish to say He's "almost sovereign" as it would be to say I'm "almost married" or Kennedy was "almost president" or the surgeon's gloves are "almost sterile."

If you're trying to grasp all the ramifications of this great truth . . . don't. You can't anyway. Feverishly toiling to unravel all the knots can turn you into a fanatical freak . . . it will push you to the edge of your mental capacity . . . it will result in endless hours of theological hairsplitting. The finite can *never* plumb the depths of the infinite . . . so don't waste your time trying.

It was a glorious day when I was liberated from the concentration camp of fear . . . the fear of saying, "I don't understand the reasons why, but I accept God's hand in what has happened." It was a *greater* day when I realized that nobody expected me to have all the answers . . . least of all God! If I could figure it all out, I'd qualify as His adviser, and Scripture makes it clear He doesn't need my puny counsel. He wants my unreserved love, my unqualified devotion, my undaunted trust — not my unenlightened analysis of His ways.

One of the marks of spiritual maturity is the quiet confidence that God is in control . . . without the need to understand why He does what He does. Lila Trotman bore such a mark as she faced the ways of God that were "unsearchable . . . and unfathomable."

What marks *your* life?

Deepening Your Roots
Isaiah 45:5 – 9, 46:8 – 11; Daniel 5:18 – 21

Branching Out

1. Do you remember an event or struggle during the past year when you decided to trust God? Are you glad you did? Why? _____
2. Ask God to reveal (sometime during the day) an area you're controlling that needs to be turned over to Him.

VERY THIN WIRES

I recall a phrase from one of Alexander Whyte's works. It came to mind early this morning. The old biographer wrote of our tendency

". . . to hang very heavy weights on very thin wires."

We really do.

We hang the very heavy weight of our happiness on the very thin wire of our health. High-risk investment! People I know who have that wide, vertical, zipper-like scar down the middle of their chests are living proof that we all are only a pulse beat this side away from that side. Something as tiny as a blood clot, smaller, much smaller than a pea, if lodged in the wrong place, can suddenly turn our speech to a slur and reduce our steps to a shuffle . . . if that.

Two doors away from our home an entire family has been transformed from a life of activity, laughter, and hope to a quiet, introspective group of serious-looking, almost-out-of-touch people. Their only son — a brilliant, alive, bright collegian with a "sky's the limit" promising future — had a head-on collision with a semi.

Snap went the wire. Totaled car. Almost totaled driver. Toppled family. The boy, quasi-conscious, hardly resembles the young man who used to catch my passes on Thanksgiving afternoon and light fireworks with our Curt every Fourth of July. He may never walk again. Or talk. Or think clearly. Swiftly, silently, like a deep river, life moves right on as that family now turns in every night with a sigh. Health is a very thin wire, unable to support our happiness.

We hang the very heavy weight of our peace on the very thin wire of our possessions. We know better, but we still do it. Materialistic to the core, we convince ourselves that life *does* consist in the abundance of things we possess . . . that contentment is *not* limited to food and clothing . . . that the birds of the air and the lilies of the field don't know what they're missing without all those creature comforts.

Enter brushland fires on the furious wings of Santa Ana winds. Exit southern California homes and appliances and furniture and beds to sleep in and cars to drive and peace. *Snap goes the wire* when something as heavy as peace is so inseparably linked to something as thin as our possessions.

We're only asking for trouble when we lead ourselves to believe that our internal agitation will subside once we get that place in the mountains or a quaint condo at the beach or a little larger boat or a little better job or a microwave for Christmas or a second TV or stereo upstairs or an original oil in the living room or a Shop Smith in the garage or . . . or . . . or. . . . It's not that owning any of that stuff is wrong — you know that — but when it's pursued in hopes of acquiring peace in the package, no way!

We also hang the very heavy weight of our security on the very thin wire of our savings. Solomon was right, as usual:

> Cast but a glance at riches, and they are gone, For they will surely sprout wings And fly off to the sky like an eagle (Proverbs 23:5, NIV).

That's part of the syndrome Haggai the prophet describes:

> You earn wages, only to put them in a purse with holes in it (Haggai 1:6).

Yussif, the Terrible Turk, needed that reminder two generations ago. He was a 350-pound wrestler who won it all in Europe before coming to America to grab more glory. Yussif challenged Strangler Lewis, our 200-pound champion grappler. The Turk tossed the Strangler around like a teddy bear and won. The new world champ picked up what he loved the most — money — 5,000 dollars of it, which he demanded in U.S. gold. He crammed it into the money belt he wore around his huge circumference before setting sail back to Europe on the *S.S. Burgoyne*.

Many miles at sea, the ship began to sink. Yussif went over the side with his bulging belt full of gold still strapped around his enormous frame. The added weight was too much for even the Terrible Turk to stay afloat. Before the lifeboats could reach him, he plunged straight to the bottom of the Atlantic like an oversize iron cannon . . . never to be seen again. *Snap went the thin wire* of the Turk's savings . . . and all hope of his security. That true story illustrates these immortal words:

> Riches profit not in the day of wrath . . . (Proverbs 11:4).

Whyte was right. The very thin wires of physical health, material possessions, and financial savings are no match for eternal heavyweights like lasting happiness, deep peace, and personal security.

Only one Person can step into a life
and give it happiness even when health fails . . .
and give it peace even when possessions fade . . .
and give it security when savings fly away.

You can have it all — everything — on the wire called Jesus Christ.
That wire will *never* snap. Not for a lifetime. Not for eternity.

Deepening Your Roots

Luke 16:1 – 15; 2 Corinthians 12:14; 1 Timothy 6:3 – 10;
1 Peter 5:1 – 9; 1 John 3:16 – 18

Branching Out

1. Look around your home and ask yourself, "Is there anything I can't live without?" If it possesses you, get rid of it!
2. Be generous. Test your back pocket. Be an anonymous giver today and send some money to a friend or enemy! Or, buy a sack of groceries for a family in need. But give it incognito.
3. Start a bank account and distribute all monies to those in need.

"FINAL DESCENT...
COMMENCE PRAYER"

The following incident took place in 1968 on an airliner bound for New York. It was a routine flight, and normally a boring affair. The kind of flights I like — uneventful. But this one proved to be otherwise.

Descending to the destination, the pilot realized the landing gear refused to engage. He worked the controls back and forth, trying again and again to make the gear lock down into place. No success. He then asked the control tower for instructions as he circled the landing field. Responding to the crisis, airport personnel sprayed the runway with foam as fire trucks and other emergency vehicles moved into position. Disaster was only minutes away.

The passengers, meanwhile, were told of each maneuver in that calm, cheery voice pilots manage to use at times like this. Flight attendants glided about the cabin with an air of cool reserve. Passengers were told to place their heads between their knees and grab their ankles just before impact. It was one of those I-can't-believe-this-is-happening-to-me experiences. There were tears, no doubt, and a few screams of despair. The landing was now seconds away.

Suddenly the pilot announced over the intercom:

> We are beginning our final descent. At this moment, in accordance with International Aviation Codes established at Geneva, it is my obligation to inform you that if you believe in God you should commence prayer.

I'm happy to report that the belly landing occurred without a hitch. No one was injured and, aside from some rather extensive damage to the plane, the airline hardly remembered the incident. In fact, a relative of one of the passengers called the airline the very next day and asked about the prayer rule the pilot had quoted. No one volunteered any information on the subject. Back to that cool reserve, it was simply, "No comment."

Amazing. The only thing that brought out into the open a deep-down "secret rule" was crisis. Pushed to the brink, back to the wall, right up to the wire, all escape routes closed . . . only then does our society crack open a hint of recognition that God just might be there and — "if you believe . . . you should commence prayer."

Reminds me of a dialogue I watched on the tube several years ago. The guy being interviewed had "come back alive" from Mount St. Helens with pictures *and sound track* of his own personal nightmare. A reporter for a local television station, he was in close proximity to the crater when the mountain suddenly rumbled to life, spewing steam and ash miles into the air. The reporter literally ran for his life. With camera rolling and the mike on. The pictures were, of course, blurred and murky, but his voice was something else. Periodically, he'd click on his gear.

He admitted after all this was played on the talk show that he only vaguely recalled saying many of those things. It was eerie, almost too personal to be disclosed. He breathed deeply, sobbed several times, panted, and spoke directly to God. No formality, no clichés — just the despairing cry of a creature in a crisis. Things like, "Oh, God, oh, my God . . . help! Help!! . . . Oh, Lord God, get me through. God, I need you, please help me; I don't know where I am" — more sobbing, more rapid breathing, spitting, gagging, coughing, panting — "It's so hot, so dark, help me, God! Please, please, please, please . . . oh, God!"

There's nothing to compare with crisis when it comes to finding out the otherwise hidden truth of the soul. Any soul. We may mask it, ignore it, pass it off with cool sophistication and intellectual denial . . . but take away the cushion of comfort, remove the shield of safety, interject the threat of death without the presence of people to take the panic out of the moment, and it's fairly certain most in the ranks of humanity "commence prayer."

David certainly did. When in "the slimy pit . . . the mud and the mire," he testifies that Jehovah heard his cry (Psalm 40:1 – 2). So did Paul and Silas in that ancient Philippian prison when all seemed hopeless (Acts 16:25 – 26). It was from "the deep" Jonah cried for help . . . choking on salt water and engulfed by the Mediterranean currents, the prodigal prophet called out in his distress (Jonah 2:1 – 4). Old King Nebuchadnezzar did, too, fresh off a siege of insanity when he had lost his reason and lived like a wild beast in the open field. That former mental patient "raised his eyes toward heaven" and poured out the feelings of his soul to the Lord God, the very One the king had denied in earlier years (Daniel 4:29 – 37).

Crisis crushes. And in crushing, it often refines and purifies. You may be discouraged today because the crushing has not yet led to a surrender. I've stood beside too many of the dying, ministered to too many of the broken and bruised to believe that crushing is an end in itself. Unfortunately, however, it usually takes the brutal blows of affliction to soften and penetrate hard hearts. Even though such blows often seem unfair.

Remember Alexander Solzhenitsyn's admission:

> It was only when I lay there on rotting prison straw that I sensed within myself the first stirring of Good. Gradually, it was disclosed to me that the line separating good and evil passes, not through states, nor between classes, nor between political parties either, but right through all human hearts. So, bless you, prison, for having been my life.[17]

Those words provide a perfect illustration of the psalmist's instruction:

> Before I was afflicted I went astray, but now I obey your word.
> It was good for me to be afflicted so that I might learn your decrees
> (Psalm 119:67, 71, NIV).

After crises crush sufficiently, God steps in to comfort and teach.

Feel headed for a crash? Engulfed in crisis? Tune in the calm voice of your Pilot.

He knows precisely what He is doing. And belly-landings don't frighten Him one bit.

Deepening Your Roots

Jonah 2:1 – 7; Luke 6:12; Philippians 4:6, 7; 1 Peter 3:12

Branching Out

1. What's one lesson you've learned out of a crisis you've faced in the last six months? _____

2. Offer to pray for someone who is in the midst of a crisis. If possible, pray *with* the person. It will encourage him!
3. Try to comfort someone without giving advice. Just be there!

Growing Strong

Generosity, I find, is like a rare gem. Not many of us possess it. Oh, but when it is seen it sparkles! What admiration it brings from onlookers. Are you sparkling today? Or have you misplaced the gem called generosity? Give me your opinion:

_____

_____

_____

_____

RESTRAINT

Yesterday, I got drunk.

Now wait a minute! Before you pick up your phone and notify six of your closest friends, let me explain. I was the victim of a dentist's drill. As he was about to do his thing on my ivories, he inserted eighty milligrams of *Nembutol* into my innocent bloodstream . . . resulting thereafter in a flow of words and actions that were *anything* but innocent, I am told. I have been informed that a tape recording was made which probably would call into question my ordination as well as cause my old Marine Corps drill instructor to blush. I am sure that the entire dental office — that motley group of rascals — has sufficient information to blackmail me. But they are sworn to secrecy. I hope.

My neighbors probably raised some eyebrows when my dear wife helped me out of the car and I staggered to the door, singing loudly. She informed me that I saw a mosquito and took a rather exaggerated swing at it. That led to a few other verbal expressions totally unlike a man of the cloth. When I awoke on the patio three hours later, my children were still giggling and snickering over my irresponsible homecoming. They also are sworn to secrecy. *They better be!*

Isn't it amazing what happens when the clamps of restraint are loosened? In some cases it's unbelievable! I would never, under normal conditions, declare: "Dentistry is a rip off!" But I did yesterday. Right in front of my dentist and his drill team. I would not say to a young lady, "You talk too much — get out!" But that's exactly what I said to one of his capable assistants.

Thanks to *Nembutol,* I became an open book with no secret sections or hidden chapters containing guarded, private feelings and thoughts. For several unrestrained hours, my emotions ran rampant, and there's no way to recover the damage or remove the raw facts from that page of my life.

Of course, I was under the influence of a pain-killing drug, so I'm automatically excused, or so they assure me. Because of the circumstances, it's nothing more than a funny, harmless episode that makes us chuckle.

But that isn't always so.

The removal of restraint is usually neither excusable nor amusing. In fact, restraining ourselves is so important that God lists it as a fruit of the Spirit in Galatians 5:22 – 23. *Self-control,* another word for restraint, is honored by the Lord as the "anchor virtue" on His relay team that runs life's race for His glory. Many other voices are saying, "Let it all hang out" and "tell it like it is" and "hold nothing back" and "be open . . . express your feelings without restraint!" It's easy to buy that kind of advice. But when I go to my Bible, I find contrary counsel being marketed.

When we are angered, God instructs us to restrain ourselves. For proof, ponder Proverbs 14:29, 15:1, and 29:11, along with Ephesians 4:26 – 27. He further tells us not even to associate with one given to anger (Proverbs 22:24 – 25) or place him into leadership in the church (1 Timothy 3:2 – 3).

When we are tempted, He admonishes us to say no to lust and restrain our carnal nature (1 Corinthians 9:26 – 27; 2 Timothy 2:22).

When we are prompted to talk too much, He says, "Hold it! Better keep that to yourself!" (Proverbs 17:28; Job 13:5; Ephesians 4:29). Restraint of the tongue is a mark of wisdom. It is a slippery eel in need of being in check between our cheeks.

When food is stacked before us, God is pleased when we restrain ourselves from gluttony (Proverbs 23:1 – 2; 1 Corinthians 10:31 – 32). Being fat is often a telltale sign that control is lacking.

When money is to be earned, spent, saved, or invested, the use of restraint is the order of the day (Matthew 6:19 – 21; Luke 14:28 – 30; Romans 13:7 – 8).

Removing restraint from your life may seem like an exciting adventure, but it inevitably leads to tragedy. It's a lot like removing the brakes from your car. That may be daring and filled with thrills for awhile, but injury is certain. Take away the brakes and your life, like your car, is transformed into an unguided missile — destined for disaster.

Let's all learn a lesson from my extra-curricular escapades this week.

> When medicine is needed
> To dull the pain you're in,
> Your actions may be silly
> Yet they really are not "sin."
> But when you willfully lose control
> And set restraint aside,
> Your actions then are sinful
> And pain is multiplied.

Deepening Your Roots

Proverbs 17:14, 28; 22:24 – 25; 29:11; Ephesians 4:26 – 27; 2 Timothy 2:22

Branching Out

1. Take one of these (food, tongue, money, or TV) and put a restraint on it by doing one of the following today: a) Eat *no* sweets; b) Don't say one critical remark; c) Don't spend any money in twenty-four hours; or d) Don't turn on the TV.
2. Play detective or researcher and find out what a "restraining order" means in our legal system.
3. You're bound to get angry this week. When you do, put a restraint on your tongue and mind; don't say a word and don't allow your mind to think critically of another.

MODELING GOD'S MESSAGE

*H*osea started a scandal in the parsonage. Why? Hold onto your hat — he married a prostitute. Talk about gossip! His name became a byword for "fool." Respect for him dropped to *zero.* His reputation was suddenly null and void. "Small wonder he is listed first among the *minor* prophets," some sneer . . . "He must have been some kind of a nut."

No. Wrong again, O critic. Hands down, Hosea was one of the most patient, tender, and loving of all the ancient prophets. Obedient to the core. Faithful to the end. "Then why in the world would a man such as he fall for a woman such as she?" Keep holding onto your hat—*God told him to!* That's right. God chose Hosea to model his message before all Israel, like a neon sign alongside the freeway. Like bold headlines in the *Times.* Of course, they didn't know it at first.

Barmaids giggled and merchants snickered as wedding bells rang across the valley. "Hey, did you hear the latest? Gomer got married—she got herself a preacher!" How humiliating it must have been. Everywhere they went on their honeymoon, she saw familiar faces. Insulting insinuations were uttered in smothered tones. Hosea must have bit his tongue until it bled. His marriage was an act of love . . . but to the public it was a joke. Before God, he stood justified and obedient. Before man, undiscerning and idiotic.

He must have replayed his memory hundreds of times, remembering God's directive:

> "Go, take to yourself a wife of harlotry and have children of harlotry . . ." (Hosea 1:2).

That's exactly what happened. She gave birth to a daughter and two sons while Hosea's wife—each was illegitimate—before she left home and went back into the streets. Hosea's wound was scarcely healed before he heard God's voice thundering from the heavens telling him to go out, find her, and bring her back into his home with the family. He did. For a couple of dollars and several bushels of barley *he bought her from others' arms* and claimed her as his own. Stretch your imagination and try to picture the love and dedication it took for Hosea to carry out God's instructions. The Living Bible paraphrases the statement:

"Go and get your wife again and bring her back to you and love her, even though she loves adultery" (Hosea 3:1).

Not another soul in Israel heard the voice. Only Hosea. Therefore, rumors turned into ridicule as his fellow Jews watched with open mouths as he stooped down and lovingly carried her home. Little did the people realize they were observing a *living object lesson*—a divine pantomime — designed by God to illustrate the truth of their own lives.

From the fourth chapter to the end of his journal (once Hosea had their attention), he exhorted them to listen . . . to hear . . . to return. Fifteen times he shouted, "RETURN!" but they never did. Even though he modeled the message as no other man on earth would be asked to do, they ignored his cries. He told them the truth: "*You* are the harlot! *You* have left Jehovah's love. *You* have resisted His affection and denied your marriage. He continues to call you His own . . . but *you* refuse to return. He loves you still. Return!" They didn't. And three tragic years later Israel crumbled in the hands of Assyria.

Having a tough time modeling God's message? Feel unappreciated? Misunderstood? A little foolish? Ridiculed? So it goes, pilgrim. Rose gardens and pillow fights went out with the flood. These are rugged days. Without much padding in the seats or protection from the wind. It takes two things to keep from folding in the stretch: a tough hide and a tender heart. Hosea had both. And the scars to prove it. He died rejected and ignored.

So did Christ . . . until the resurrection.

Deepening Your Roots
Hosea 1:1 – 11, 3:1 – 5, 6:1; Acts 20:20 – 21; Luke 15:8 – 10, 11:32

Branching Out
1. Pray each day this week for someone you know who refuses to return to God.
2. Find a phrase or verse in the book of Hosea that motivates you to remain faithful to God. Write the verse down and tape it to the inside of one of your kitchen cupboards that you open often, or the dashboard of your car.

COMPARISON

*I*f I may select a well-known phrase from the cobwebs of the fourteenth century and wipe away the dust to garner your attention, it is:

COMPARISONS ARE ODIOUS.

Odious . . . disgusting, detestable. If you want to be a miserable mortal, then compare. You compare when you place someone beside someone else for the purpose of emphasizing the differences or showing the likenesses. This applies to places and things as well as people. We can become so proficient at this activity that we sustain our addiction through an unconscious force of habit. Inadvertently, the wheels of our thinking slide over into the ruts of this odious mindset. Comparison appears in at least two patterns.

Pattern one: We compare ourselves with others. You can imagine the results already. Either you are prompted to feel smug and proud because your strengths outweigh his weaknesses . . . or, more often, you begin to feel threatened, inferior, and blue because you fail to measure up. Striving to emulate a self-imposed standard, you begin to slide from the pleasant plateau of the *real you* to the sinking sands of *I don't know who*. This sometimes leads to extreme role-playing where you try every way to adapt and alter your portrait to fit into someone else's frame. In simpler terms, you've pawned your real personality for a phony disguise. That's odious! Paul penned similar sentiments to a church that had become known for its comparison cliques:

> We do not dare to classify or compare ourselves with those who commend themselves. When they measure themselves and compare themselves with themselves, they are not wise (2 Corinthians 10:12, NIV).

The very next verse tells us, "Our goal is to measure up to God's plan *for us* " (TLB). Not for someone else, but for you, personally. God's great desire for us is that we fulfill His plan for us in our *own* lives. In His way — His timing.

Pattern two: We compare others with others. This is worse than unfair, it's stupid. And often cruel. Children suffer most from well-meaning adults who catalog one child's talents in front of another child in some misbegotten effort at motivation. "Look at your sister Debbie. If she can get an A in math, so can you." Or, "See how easily Jimmy learned to swim? Why are you so afraid?" That sort of comparison is toxic — poisoning a child's self-image and smothering the very motivation the parent was seeking to kindle.

But children aren't the only victims. People compare preachers and teachers, church philosophies and orders of service, soloists and song leaders, personalities and prayers, wives and mothers, families and friends, homes and cars, salaries and jobs, scholarship and salesmanship, husbands and fathers, weights and worries, luxuries and limitations, pain and pleasure. That's odious! Why not accept people and places and things *exactly as they are?* Isn't that true maturity? Why not accept and adjust to differences as quickly and enthusiastically as God forgives our wrong and stands behind our efforts to try, try again? When love flows, acceptance grows.

Do you know what it is that kicks the slats out from under yesterday's routine and challenges us to rise and shine on today's menu of hours and minutes? It's *variety*. It's not the similarity of days that brings fresh motivation and stimulates enthusiasm — it's the lack of such, the varied *differences* that keep our attitudes positive and pleasing. To try to compare one day with another, then complain because today wasn't at all like yesterday, would be sheer folly and foolishness. The same principle applies to people.

Now listen very carefully: God, our wise and creative Maker, has been pleased to make everyone different and no one perfect. The sooner we appreciate and accept that fact, the deeper we will appreciate and accept one another, just as our Designer planned us. Actually, there is only one thing that would be worse than constant comparison, and that is if everyone were just alike.

Can you think of anything more odious?

Deepening Your Roots
2 Corinthians 10:1 – 18; Galatians:1 – 5; James 2:1 – 12

Branching Out

1. Identify a person you often compare yourself to: _____

_____

Is there a special way you try to act, or mimic, or dress like that person? If so, work on eliminating that action, etc. Return to the *real* you.

2. List three trademarks you like about yourself that others cannot copy (for example, your smile).

   1. _____

   2. _____

   3. _____

3. Who are you trying to change? _____

_____

How about letting God have that responsibility this week while you concentrate on accepting, encouraging, and loving that person?

Growing Strong

You may be feeling down today, wondering if you're really growing at all, or maybe questioning your value as a person. You are valuable! And you are growing! You just can't see it. But God promises He's at work inside you, causing you to grow. Maybe if we turn back some pages in this book and return to an earlier season we'll be able to catch a glimpse of some changes. Turn to page 74, glance over ten or more pages, and check back in with me to let me know if you now see an area where you've grown.

_____

_____

_____

_____

Choosing Your Words

A good scriptural basis for the time I invest each week in my writing ministry would be Ecclesiastes 12:9 – 11. It says:

> In addition to being a wise man, the Preacher also taught the people knowledge; and he pondered, searched out and arranged many proverbs. The Preacher sought to find delightful words and to write words of truth correctly. The words of wise men are like goads, and masters of these collections are like well-driven nails. . . .

It is encouraging to see that Solomon didn't just dump a load of verbiage on the page. He "pondered," he "searched out," he "arranged" his thoughts in the teaching of knowledge. He also "sought to find delightful words" so as to write truth correctly, using *just* the right terms.

One of our church members recently said to me, "You know, I not only appreciate truth, I also appreciate the turn of a phrase." We all do! Our eyes get weary of grinding through the same old verbal ruts. They dance with delight upon some vivid vocabulary excursion provided through the reading gate, along the picturesque path of well-chosen words. Shakespeare's coined phrase, "the mind's eye," tells us that he enjoyed walking the path as well as leading his readers down it.

But it was Bacon who said it best:

> Reading maketh a full man;
> Speaking, a ready man;
> Writing, an exact man.

When confused or uncertain, it often helps to do your thinking with pen and pad. Exercising the exacting discipline of squeezing thoughts through the fingertips (reducing elusive, shadowy ideas to "well-driven nails" on paper) is good for our minds. This enables us to become clear thinkers who communicate in concrete, well-arranged "goads" that puncture the thick clouds of sloppy thinking.

I chuckled as I read the following statements. They are literal sentences taken from actual letters received by public welfare departments. The use of wrong words or phrases illustrates the opposite of what I've been trying to say.

"I cannot get sick pay. I have six children. Can you tell me why?"

"I am glad to report that my husband who was reported missing is dead."

"I am very much annoyed to find that you have branded my boy illiterate, as this is a dirty lie. I was married a week before he was born."

"Mrs. Jones has not had any clothes for a year and has been visited by the clergy regularly."

J. B. Phillips, author of the modern English paraphrase of the New Testament, expresses in a nutshell all I am saying:

> . . . if . . . words are to enter men's hearts and bear fruit, they must be the right words shaped cunningly to pass men's defenses and explode silently and effectually within their minds.

To speak or write of Christ in a dull, boring manner is the greatest of all insults. Maybe this explains why so many missionary letters are quietly ignored and unread . . . or why so many attempts to share our faith are unsuccessful . . . or why so many discipline problems occur in Sunday school classes.

Let's get serious about removing the yawn on the other fella's face . . . especially you who are communicating about Christ. It's really true: A mist in the pulpit *does* create a fog in the pew.

Deepening Your Roots

Proverbs 22:17 – 21; 1 Corinthians 2:4, 6 – 13; 2 Timothy 3:16 – 17, 4:1 – 5

Branching Out

1. Read something and circle three words you don't know the meaning of. Write those words and their definitions here:

   1. _____

   2. _____

   3. _____

2. Start reading a book that is more difficult than anything you've ever read.

NIT-PICKING

Two congregations of differing denominations were located only a few blocks from each other in a small community. They thought it might be better if they would merge and become one united body, larger and more effective, rather than two struggling churches. Good idea ... but both were too petty to pull it off. The problem? They couldn't agree on how they would recite the Lord's Prayer. One group wanted "forgive us our trespasses" while the others demanded "forgive us our debts." So the newspaper reported that one church went back to its trespasses while the other returned to its debts!

I read last week of two unmarried sisters who lived together. Because of a slight disagreement over an insignificant issue, they stopped speaking to each other. Unable and unwilling to move out of their small house, they continued to use the same rooms, eat at the same table (separately), and sleep in the same bedroom. Without one word. A chalk line divided the sleeping area into two halves, separating a doorway and fireplace. Each could come and go, cook and eat, sew and read without crossing over into her sister's domain. Through the night each could hear the breathing of the foe ... but because neither was willing to take the first step to reconciliation and forgiveness, they coexisted for *years* in grinding silence.

Such silly skirmishes would be hilarious if they weren't so prevalent — and damaging. It's one thing to stand firm in major issues clearly set forth in Scriptures. It's another thing to pick fights over jots and tittles. I never cease to be amazed at how petty we Christians can be over things that really don't amount to a hill of beans in the final analysis. But there we stand, ramrod rigid, nose to nose, as if heaven were holding its breath. Or to use Dean Rusk's phrase, "We negotiate eyeball to eyeball, and each side is afraid to blink."

> Believe as I believe — no more, no less;
> That I am right (and no one else) confess.
> Feel as I feel, think only as I think;
> Eat what I eat, and drink but what I drink.
> Look as I look, do always as I do;
> And then — and only then — I'll fellowship with you.

So wrote the captain of the nit-picking brigade.

While I was ministering at a Bible conference last summer I tightened my belt, rolled up my pants, and waded into this touchy subject. Afterwards I was concerned to hear from many in attendance that they had similar convictions but didn't feel free to say so since their pastors kept fanning personal flames and picking scabs off old sores. Preachers can be awfully small! Taking pot shots in sermons when we know nobody can answer back. Shooting jabs and pounding the pulpit on minor matters that make our adversary yawn and smile. Instead of equipping and edifying the saints with solid, well-documented, carefully applied truth from the Book that exalts Christ, many would rather promote an exclusive emphasis that is divisive, argumentative, and blindly opinionated.

One lady at the conference informed me that she and her family had vacationed in Michigan and had seen the name of a church they would never forget:

THE ORIGINAL CHURCH OF GOD, NUMBER TWO.

Some things make the Lord smile. That kind of thing must make Him nauseated!

The greater lights of the Protestant Reformation were, of course, Tyndale, Luther, Calvin, Zwingli, Savonarola, Knox, and a half dozen other grand men of God. But one man who never got much press (but deserved much praise) was Philipp Melanchthon, a brilliant yet calm theologian who was Martin Luther's chief associate in leading the Reformation. In a day of major, far-reaching battles and fiery assaults from one man to another, this gentleman summed it up in a superb axiom:

> In essentials, unity; in nonessentials, liberty; in all things, charity.

In nonessentials, *liberty.* Remember that! Like cosmetics, guitars, kind of clothing, choice of car, expression of worship, entertainment preference, Sunday activities, style of music, philosophy of raising kids, cultural tastes, holiday traditions, luxury items, and scores of other such things. They supply fodder for nit-picking gossips. But in light of eternity—who cares? Not one is in the "essential" category.

How broad was Christ! On one occasion His twelve nailed a guy for casting out demons in the name of Jesus . . . *"because he was not following us"* (Mark 9:38). The Lord braced them for doing that. He wanted them to get rid of any idea that they had a monopoly on miracles. He wouldn't tolerate their bigoted spirit. Our Savior *never* nit-picked.

As long as our knowledge is imperfect and our preferences vary and our opinions differ, let's leave a lot of room in areas that don't really matter. Diversity and variety provide the Body with a beautiful blend of balance . . . but a squint-eyed, severe spirit is a killer, strangling its victims with a noose of caustic criticism.

Just how much freedom do you really allow others to enjoy? Believe me, that's not a nit-picking question.

Deepening Your Roots
Mark 9:38 – 41; Acts 11:1 – 18; 1 Corinthians 9:1 – 18

Branching Out

1. Write down two actions a friend of yours does that "bother" you.

    1. _____
    2. _____

    Decide whether or not these actions are "essentials" or "nonessentials." If they are nonessentials, then determine to allow the person the freedom to be himself.

2. Name three things or issues you are adamantly for or against:

    1. _____
    2. _____
    3. _____

    Now, do you give others the liberty to take an opposing view or do you insist they believe as you?

Staying Alert

Your mind is a muscle. It needs to be stretched to stay sharp. It needs to be prodded and pushed to perform. Let it get idle and lazy on you, and that muscle will become a pitiful mass of flab in an incredibly brief period of time.

How can you stretch your mind? What are some good mental exercises that will keep the cobwebs away? I offer three suggestions:

READ. You may be too crippled and too poor to travel — but between the covers of a book are ideas and insights that await the joy of discovery. William Tyndale was up in years when he was imprisoned. Shortly before his martyrdom he wrote to the governor asking for:

> . . . a warmer cap, a candle, a piece of cloth to patch my leggings. . . . but above all, I beseech and entreat your clemency to . . . permit me to have my Hebrew Bible, Hebrew Grammar, and Hebrew Dictionary, that I may spend time . . . in study.[18]

The powers of your perception will be magnified through reading. Read wisely. Read widely. Read slowly. Scan. Read history as well as current events . . . magazines and periodicals as well as classics and poetry . . . biographies and novels as well as the daily news and devotionals.

Don't have much time? Neither did John Wesley. But his passion for reading was so severe he made it a part of his schedule — he read mostly *on horseback.* He rode between fifty and ninety miles a day with the book propped up in his saddle . . . and got through *thousands* of volumes during his lifetime. Knowing that reading attacks thickness of thought, Wesley told many a younger minister either to read — or get out of the ministry.

TALK. Conversation adds the oil needed to keep our mental machinery running smoothly. The give-and-take involved in rap sessions, the question-answer dialogue connected to discussion, provides the grinding wheel needed to keep us keen.

Far too much of our talk is surface jargon . . . shallow, predictable, obvious, pointless. Talk is too valuable to waste. Leave the discussion of people and weather to the newscasters! Delve into issues, ideas, controversial subjects, things that really matter. Ask and answer "why" and "how" . . . rather than "what" and "when." Probe. Question. Socrates was considered wise — not because he knew all the answers, but because he knew how to ask the right questions. Few experiences are more stimulating than eyeball-to-eyeball, soul-to-soul talks that force us to *think* and *reason* through specifics. For the sheer excitement of learning, talk!

WRITE. Thoughts disentangle themselves over the lips . . . and through the fingertips. How true! The old gray matter increases its creases when you put it down on paper. Start a journal. A journal isn't a diary. It's more. A journal doesn't record what you do — it records what you *think*. It spells out your ideas, your feelings, your struggles, your discoveries, your dreams. In short, it helps you articulate *who you are.*

Who knows? Your memoirs might make the bestseller list in the year 2000. And speaking of that, why not try writing an article for your favorite magazine? Editors are on a constant safari for rare species like you.

Deepening Your Roots

1 Kings 4:29 – 34; Proverbs 2:1 – 10, 4:5 – 7; Isaiah 26:3; Romans 8:5 – 11, 12:2

Branching Out

1. Read a book *this week!* Make it a fun challenge by setting up five goals while reading. Here are some ideas: a) read one chapter out loud to someone; b) read one chapter in the tub; c) read one chapter in bed; d) read one chapter at lunch; e) read one chapter at a park.
2. Draw up three questions that ask why and how.

   1. _____
   2. _____
   3. _____

   Now, go and find someone to talk to using these questions.

ベ ベ ベ

Growing Strong

I'll bet your mind is alive and active today! Reading always gets those mental juices flowin' for me. How about you? What good book did you devour this week? _____

THE CASE AGAINST VANILLA

I cannot imagine anything more boring and less desirable than being poured into the mold of predictability as I grow older. Few things interest me less than the routine, the norm, the expected, the status quo. Call it the rebel in me, but I simply cannot bear plain vanilla when life offers so many other colorful and stimulating flavors. A fresh run at life by an untried route will get my vote every time — in spite of the risk. Stay open-minded for a moment and I'll try to show you why.

John Gardner once pointed out that by their mid-thirties, most people have stopped acquiring new skills and new attitudes in any aspect of their lives. Does that jolt you? Stop and think, you who are over thirty. How long has it been since *you* acquired a new skill? How many brand-new attitudes have you adopted — personal, political, social, spiritual, financial — since you turned thirty?

Let's probe a little deeper. Do you drive to work the same way every morning? Are you compelled to approach a problem the identical way every time? Does a maverick (even *wild*) idea challenge you or cause you to retreat into the security of your shell? Have you lost that enthusiastic zest for discovery and adventure?

Say, you're older than you thought. You're older than you ought! God has arranged an "abundant life" for you, but it's slipping past. You're fast becoming addicted to the narcotic of predictability . . . and the longer you persist, the greater will be the pain of withdrawal.

Living and learning are linked; so are existing and expiring. Each day delivers a totally new set of circumstances and experiences. The same hours and minutes which capture the wonder of a child may deepen the rut of an adult.

Ever watched a preschooler's approach to life? His constant curiosity and probing inquisitiveness make every day completely fresh and exciting. To him, learning is natural; to the adult, it's a nuisance.

"Well," you rationalize, "I'm just too set. That's the way I am . . . you can't change me." *Who* can't change you? *God?* Like Israel of old, this sort of thinking puts limits on the Lord, discounting His power and denying His presence. Settling down to the hum-drum, bland diet of tasteless existence is a sure invitation for slackness and indolence to invade and plague your dwelling.

"So how do I break out?" you ask. "I guess I could row to Hawaii in a four-foot dinghy or schedule a February vacation in Iceland . . . maybe the family could tackle Everest this summer. . . ."

Unnecessary! Life abounds with everyday problems needing transformation into creative projects. Try taking life by the throat and achieve mastery over a few things that have haunted and harassed you long enough. Or — how about a course at a nearby school this fall . . . or a serious study of some subject all on your own. Why not broaden yourself in some *new* way to the greater glory of God?

Remember our old friend, Caleb? He was eighty-five and still growing when he gripped an uncertain future and put the torch to the bridges behind him. At a time when the ease and comfort of retirement seemed predictable, he fearlessly faced the invincible giants of the mountain. Read Joshua 14 again. There was no dust on that fella. Every new sunrise introduced another reminder that his body and rocking chair weren't made for each other. While his peers were yawning, Caleb was yearning.

Every one of us was poured into a mold . . . but some are "moldier" than others. If you are determined and work quickly, you can keep the concrete of predictability from setting rock-hard up to your ears. Then again, if the risks and potential dangers of sailing your ship in the vast oceans of uncertainty make you seasick, you'd better anchor yourself near the shallow shore of security. Concrete sinks fast, you know.

Deepening Your Roots
Genesis 12:1 – 8; Joshua 14:1 – 15; Luke 6:27 – 28

Branching Out
1. It's time to acquire a new skill . . . so sign up today to take a class, or to play a new sport, or to finally learn how to drive, etc.
2. Break the routine. Go to a restaurant, or a grocery store, or library, etc., that you've never been to.
3. Buy a book on a topic you're interested in but have never pursued. Read it!

RATIONALIZATION

There I stood, the helpless victim of incredible pressure. The scene? (Immediately you'll understand my plight.) A used car lot. A fast-talking salesman. Begging kids. The hour was late. You know, the whole bit. To top it all off, there sat the cutest little Volkswagen you can imagine. Bright red. And a *convertible!* What could I do but at least slip behind the wheel and see how it "fit." That did it. We *had* to take a drive, even if it was absolutely out of the question that we'd ever buy the thing. Top down, cool breeze blowing by, quiet engine, KBIG music flowing out of dual speakers, quick acceleration, only 4500 miles. Wow!

Suddenly, I came back to reality. "This thing is a teenager's car," I could hear my conscience say. "How undignified can you get, Swindoll?" thumped its index finger on my chest. "Pretty undignified," I snapped back. I mean, if one of my associate pastors can whip around town on his Honda 360 . . . why in the world should I drive a black, four-door Rambler sedan? And, furthermore, this thing's a collector's item — and my wife's crazy about it — and it gets great gas mileage — and it looks so lonely and unloved in the car lot — and I can always drive the station-wagon when I have a funeral — and — and — and.

Well, it's mine. Correction, it's *ours.* Rationalization and I bought it. And I'm still trying to believe it! Frankly, my biggest job is convincing folks that it's not my oldest son's car. I'm happy to lease it to him for a night or two (another rationalization); but make no mistake about it, Curt's dad owns it, not Curt!

All this has made me do a lot of thinking about our tendency to rationalize, which the dictionary defines as "providing plausible but untrue reasons for conduct." In other words, it's what we do when we substitute false explanations for true reasons . . . when we cloud our actual motives with a smoke screen of nice-sounding excuses. One of the reasons we do this is to dull the pain of reality. Another reason we do it is to quiet the sounds of guilt, that dragon whose deep bass voice is always ready to blast us with its deafening roar. Often we employ it to justify ourselves in the eyes of others.

Sometimes rationalization causes people to gloss over obvious sin. Aaron used it when his brother, Moses, faced him with his sin of fashioning a molten calf before the Israelites and encouraging them to worship it.

Covered with gold dust, Aaron rationalized with wide eyes by saying, "You know the people yourself, that they are prone to evil. For they said to me, 'Make a god for us who will go before us. . . .' And I said to them, 'Whoever has any gold, let them tear it off.' So they gave it to me, and I threw it into the fire, and out came this calf" (Exodus 32:22 – 24).

Amazing! He was just an innocent bystander whose heart was as pure as the driven snow. After dumping in a few golden earrings and necklaces, out jumped this engraved calf! It was those wicked people . . . not him. Not on your life.

The Bible is replete with similar accounts. And so is life. How much better it is to call a spade a spade. Instead of thinking of spiritual-sounding excuses or scriptural phrases that ease the conscience, let's come up front and just tell the truth . . . even though you can't make it sound "biblical." Along with being Christians, we are also quite human, remember.

If you own something really nice, don't try to hide it or diminish it because it has the appearance you fudged on your tithe. For goodness sake, enjoy it! You're unwise to *flaunt* it, but to attach some super-spiritual rationalization to it is totally unnecessary. And don't be afraid some missionary might find out. You'd be surprised how downright human and realistic most missionaries are!

So here's the principle: If you're wrong in what you're doing, stop. No rationalization will make it right. If you're right, relax. Rationalization will only confuse the issue. The main thing is that you please the Lord with a clear conscience.

And that truth applies whether you drive a red VW convertible, a black Rambler, or a gold Continental (you lucky dog).

Deepening Your Roots

Genesis 20:1 – 6; Exodus 32:1 – 24; Acts 4:32 – 37, 5:1 – 4, 24:10 – 16;
Hebrews 13:15 – 18; 2 Timothy 1:3; 1 Peter 3:13 – 17

Branching Out

1. What did you rationalize in the last twenty-four hours? _____

   _____
   Admit it to someone else.
2. Did you "rationalize" when you bought your car? _____
   How? _____
3. On your next big decision write down your pro/con reasons and then ask someone if they see any "rationalizing" in your thinking and choice.

LONG WINDS, DEEP ROOTS

Mrs. Moses' cookbook surely had a special section on "A Thousand and One Ways to Fix Manna." Unless I miss my guess, she had tried them all . . . *ninety-nine times*. What potatoes are to Idaho, pineapples are to Hawaii, wheat to Kansas, and crab gumbo to New Orleans, manna was to the wandering Hebrews for forty weary years (Exodus 16:35). They boiled it, baked it, broiled it, barbecued it, breaded it, and buttered it. They ate it cold, hot, raw, cooked, sliced for sandwiches, baked in pies, and sprinkled on their cereal. You name it — they tried it.

When everyone came in to eat, they didn't ask, *"What's for supper?"* but, *"How'd you fix it?"* Mealtime was about as exciting as watching paint dry or listening to the minutes of last year's meeting. The most familiar sound around the table was not slurping or smacking. It was *gagging*. Oh, how they hated it. Numbers 11 tells us they actually lost their appetite because they were sick of all that manna. Everyone remembered the fish, cucumbers, leeks, onions, garlic, and melons back in Egypt — and you've got to be pretty miserable to dream of a combination plate like that.

Hold on here! Let's fine-tune that picture. A closer look at the circumstances paints a different scene altogether. Let me explain. These people didn't have to work for their food or clothing . . . not one day for forty years! Every morning, instead of going out to get the newspaper like you and I do, they gathered up the day's groceries — delivered to their front door. For forty years! There was no inflation, no sales tax, and no long lines at the checkout counter. Just a constant, daily supply of nourishing food. As a matter of fact, God called it *food from heaven . . . the bread of angels* (Psalm 78:24 – 25).

Accompanying this morning miracle was the faithful cloud by day and the comforting fire by night which gave them visible assurance of God's presence and protection. When thirst came, He quenched it with water that flowed from rocks like rivers. Those people enjoyed a perpetual catering service without cost, limit, labor, or hassle. All they had to do was show up, look up, eat up, and clean up. Yet for all of this, they came to the place where they resented heavenly-cooked angels' bread. Already having much, they now wanted more. Having plenty, they now wanted variety. Having tired of manna, they now wanted meat.

Exodus 16:4 provides additional insight often overlooked:

> ... the LORD said to Moses, "Behold, I will rain bread from heaven ... and the people shall go out and gather a day's portion every day, that I may test them. ..."

Look carefully at the last five words. The manna was more than it appeared to be — basically it was a *test.* It was God's examination, carefully planned, wisely implemented, and administered on a daily basis (note in the verse especially the phrase *every day*). God custom-designed the diet to be a day-after-day, week-after-week test of their obedience, their patience, and their determination to persevere in spite of the monotony of the manna. The exam results came back with a big red "F" across the front.

When I was only a boy, the Swindolls occasionally enjoyed a family reunion at my grandfather's bay cottage near the Gulf in deep south Texas. Since the crowds were so large, we'd hire the same man each time to help with the cooking. His name was *Coats.* His skin was as black as a cast-iron skillet and his quick smile and quaint comments are a lasting memory to me. I remember standing near Coats one evening at sunset, watching him smear the sauce on the chunks of beef cooking slowly over a pit of coals. He was telling me about his life, which had been etched with trouble and tragedy. He rubbed his big, leathery hand through my white hair as he knelt down to my height and said:

> Little Charles — the hardest thing about life is that it's so daily.

A simple way to say it, but what could be more true? *Life is so daily.* The tests that come like a flash and last no longer than a dash seldom do more than bring a brief crash. But the marathons — the relentless, incessant, persistent, continual tests that won't go away — ah, these are the ones that bruise but build character. Since virtue is not hereditary, God dispenses His test of manna to each saint in each generation, watching to see if there will be a heavenly appetite to accept a heavenly food.

If finding God's way in the suddenness of storms makes our faith grow broad, then trusting God's wisdom in the "dailyness" of living makes it grow deep. And strong.

Whatever may be your circumstances — however long it may have lasted — wherever you may be today, I bring this reminder: The stronger the winds, the deeper the roots, and the longer the winds . . . the more beautiful the tree.

Deepening Your Roots

Exodus 16:1 – 36; Isaiah 40:21 – 31; Matthew 13:1 – 29; Ephesians 3:14 – 21

Branching Out

1. Try eating tuna, eggs, cottage cheese, or chicken for three meals in a row to sense how the Israelites felt eating manna over and over.
2. Supply food for someone this week either by delivering a meal, sack of groceries, or treating him to dinner. Tell the person about this assignment and something you learned from today's "Deepening Your Roots" study.
3. Instead of griping or complaining about that boring job or a chore (e.g., picking up after your kids for the nth time, or taking out the trash again), do it with a thankful heart. Be glad you have that job, those kids, strength, etc.

ॐ ॐ ॐ

Growing Strong

Been counting your blessings (especially at mealtimes) since being reminded about "manna"? Me too. Let's continue . . . Count out ten more of your blessings in the space below:

_____

_____

_____

_____

_____

_____

_____

_____

_____

TAKING TIME

*E*ight words are brashly smeared across the dashboard of the speedboat
tied up at Gulf Shores, Alabama. They reflect the flash and flair of its
owner whose fast life was often publicized in sporting news across
America. In the off-season, the left-handed speedster in the Gulf of
Mexico resembled a shiftless, beachcombing drifter with his stubble
beard, disheveled hair, and darting eyes rather than one of the highest-
paid quarterbacks in Oakland Raider history. If his profession didn't fit
his looks, his nickname certainly did. *SNAKE.* As swift and sneaky in a
swamp as he was on the field, Ken Stabler knows one speed . . . full throttle.

So we shouldn't be surprised to read the saucy sign on his dashboard
that warns all passengers:

GET IN, SIT DOWN, SHUT UP, HANG ON.

If you plan to ride with Snake Stabler, be ready for one sustained roar
during the trip. Somehow there's this itch inside him that isn't scratched,
apart from the scream of an engine and the blur of salt water waves rushing beneath to the tune of 80+ miles per hour. Once you get in and sit
down, you have the distinct feeling that shutting up and hanging on come
naturally. Once you've committed yourself to such an accelerated velocity, nothing short of survival really matters.

All that's OK if survival is the only thing that matters. If, however, the
things that make life rich and meaningful to us (and those traveling with
us) involve more than survival, then speed is an awfully thin wire to hang
from. In other words, if we really want some things to count, if we genuinely desire some depth to emerge, some impact to be made, some profound and enduring investment to cast a comforting shadow across
another's life (your child, a friend, whomever), it is essential that we slow
down . . . at times, stop completely. And think. Now . . . not later. Don't
you dare put this off another day!

My oldest son and I were lingering in a local gift shop some time ago.
Our eyes fell upon a row of large posters that were framed and stacked
together. We laughed at some nutty ones, we studied some serious ones

. . . but one stood alone as our favorite. When Curt found it, he said nothing at first, then moments later he whispered quietly, "Wow, Dad, that's good!" It was a picture of a misty morning on a calm lake. In a little skiff were a father and his son looking at the two corks floating at the ends of their fishing lines. The sun was tipping its hat over the mountains in the distance. Stretching across the scene was peace, refreshment, easygoing small talk. Two wistful words beneath the border appropriately released the message:

TAKE TIME

In my younger years I was irritated with the well-worn tune attached to the old-fashioned sounding words of William Longstaff:

Take time to be holy,
Speak oft with thy Lord;
Take time to be holy,
The world rushes on. . . .

Thirty-five years, four children, many miles and mistakes later, those words make a lot of sense. They are like the psalmist's plea in Psalm 46:10:

CEASE STRIVING AND KNOW THAT I AM GOD. . . .

Or our Lord's counsel in Matthew 11:28:

COME TO ME . . . I WILL GIVE YOU REST.

Eight calm words from David. Eight restful words from Jesus, who never *rushed* anywhere! How unlike those eight panic words from the speedboat!

Deepening Your Roots
John 2:1 – 12, 7:1 – 9, 10:40 – 11:23

Branching Out

1. Don't rush through any task today. Take your time.
2. Force yourself to not use the car today. Instead, walk to work (if possible), or to school, or to the store.
3. Rather than rush through dinner tonight, make everyone stay at the table an extra fifteen minutes. Relax together and talk about something you're looking forward to seeing or doing.

OF ROOTS AND WINGS

"Grab here, *amigo*." I grabbed.

"Hold tight, *por favor*." I held on.

"When you come back toward shore and I blow whistle, you pull cord *pronto!*"

Within seconds I was airborne. A loud "whoosh," a long, strong jerk, and I was 300 feet or so above the picturesque beach at Puerto Vallarta. You guessed it . . . my first try at parasailing. Four-and-a-half minutes of indescribable ecstasy sandwiched between a few seconds of sheer panic. Talk about fun!

Above me was the bluest, clearest sky you could imagine. Behind me was a full-blown, dazzling red and white parachute. Down in front, attached to my harness and a long yellow rope, was a speed boat at full throttle. Below, the turquoise sea, various sailing vessels, a long row of hotels, sun bathers the size of ants, and one beautiful lady wondering if she would soon be a widow.

The wind whipped through my hair and tore at my swimsuit. But the sensation of flying in silence with nothing surrounding me besides a few nylon straps was absolutely breathtaking. The spectacular view plus the enjoyable feelings of soaring like a seagull introduced me to an adventurous freedom rarely encountered by earth dwellers.

I must confess, for those few minutes I lost all concern for things that otherwise occupy my attention. Self-consciousness vanished. Worries fled away. Demands and deadlines were forgotten, strangely erased by the swishing sound of the wind. *It was glorious!* I don't believe that as an adult I've ever felt quite so free, so unencumbered, so completely removed from others' expectations and my own responsibilities.

Such are the benefits of leisure. True, authentic, carefree relaxation. The kind Jesus had in mind when He encouraged His twelve to come apart and rest awhile. How easy to forget the necessity of recreation . . . how quick we are to discount its value! In our neurotic drive for more, more, more, we ignore how uncreative and boring we become. All roots and no wings has the makings of Dullsville, U.S.A. Life closes in and takes the shape of a chore instead of a challenge. Fun and laughter, originally designed by God to remove the friction of monotony from the machinery of existence, begin to be viewed as enemies instead of friends.

Intensity, that ugly yet persuasive twin of hurry, convinces us we haven't the right to relax . . . we must not take time for leisure . \ . we can't afford such rootless, risky luxury. Its message is loud, logical, sensible, strong, and *wrong*.

We *do* need relief. We *must* discover ways to loosen the strings periodically and fly. To quote the venerable prophet, Vance Havner, "If we don't come apart, we *will* come apart."

Find what brings you relief and take time to soar!

A motorcycle ride along quiet trails.
An afternoon of sailing.
A mountain to climb.
A weekend on the slopes.
A journey of some significant distance on a bike.
A long run on a longer beach.
A leisurely river ride in a rubber raft.

Isn't it time to think seriously about that trip you've talked about for so long? Or that fishing expedition? Or that weekend camp-out with your good friends? Try some winged adventure that turns you on and expands your world and frees your mind and calms your nerves. Don't wait! Quit worrying about the risk or complaining about the cost. We keep coming back to those two essentials — roots and wings — but it's my observation that most of us are long on the former and short on the latter.

Take it from a rookie parasailer . . . go for it! Stop thinking "*mañana*." Grab here. Hold on tight, *amigo*.

Deepening Your Roots

Proverbs 11:24; Acts 3:17 – 19; 1 Corinthians 16:17, 18; Philemon 20 – 21

Branching Out

1. Take time out sometime today and do one of the following: go watch some airplanes take off or land; eat lunch alone outside and in a new location; go fly a kite; go fishing; go sailing; go skate boarding; ride a kid's bike; or take a nap in the park.
2. Have you ever been camping with your family? Plan a trip this month. If you don't have the equipment, borrow it. Enjoy flexing your wings a little, my friend.

OPERATION RELAXATION

Some days start right, others end right. This one did both, for a change. During the daylight hours things fell into place and as the evening approached, it got better! As I planned, I got home before Monday Night Football. The smell of homemade clam chowder was lingering inside the front door. After hugging the kids and kissing the cook, I settled into my favorite chair . . . loosened my tie, and kicked off my shoes. Detecting a new aroma, our miniature schnauzer, Heidi, moved across the room.

Upstairs, our two youngest were fiddling around with a rabbit, two hamsters, and a guinea pig — the protesting squeals of man and beast wafting down the stairwell. Our older daughter (finally off the phone) was out front enjoying the companionship of a neighbor gal . . . and a couple of guys, if I'm not mistaken. Curt was on the floor in his room strumming out a few chords on his steel strings — singing "Raindrops Keep Fallin' on My Head" as a lazy California sun was saying goodbye for the day. In between chopped onions and diced potatoes, Cynthia had doubled over with laughter as she tried to finish a chapter of Erma Bombeck's, *The Grass Is Always Greener Over the Septic Tank.*

No amount of money could buy the feeling that swept over me — incredible contentment . . . an inner sense of fulfillment . . . a surge of release and relief as the noise and pace of the world were strangely muffled by the sounds and smells of home. The comfortable fingers of nostalgia wrapped themselves around me and warmed me within.

Although my "to do" list was mostly "yet to be done," the day was over. Tomorrow would usher in its own set of needs and responsibilities, but that was tomorrow. We all enjoyed supper (at half time, of course), then knocked out the cleanup in exactly five minutes . . . a new Swindoll world record . . . as we moved faster than six speeding bullets, laughing like mad.

What therapy! How essential! And yet, how seldom families really relax. It's almost as though we're afraid to shift into neutral and let the motor idle. With a drive that borders near the neurotic, wc Americans hit the floor running at 6:00 a.m., then drop, exhausted, at 12:00 midnight . . .

scarcely able to remember what transpired during that eighteen-hour episode of relentless actions and words. If God is going to get our attention, He'd better plan on (1) making an appointment, (2) taking a number, or (3) pulling us over with a flashing blue light on the freeway—otherwise, forget it! Strange, isn't it, that we place such a high priority on achievement we actually feel guilty when we accomplish nothing over a period of several hours. Such an experience requires justification when others ask, "What did you do last night?"

I visited a small town during a recent trip through central Oregon. It was one of those places that was so relaxed I found myself getting antsy. Life moves along there about the speed of a glacier. You know . . . the type of town where people gather to watch hub caps rust. I asked my friend:

"How do you stand it? Doesn't the slow pace drive you crazy?"

He responded with a smile. "Well, it took us about eight months to unwind. You gotta *learn* how to relax, Chuck. It isn't something that you do automatically. Now, we love it."

I've thought a lot about that. Relaxing isn't automatic. It's a skill that must be learned . . . cultivated. And since most of us don't live in a sleepy little town, here are a few suggestions to help you develop a workable plan.

1. Block out several evenings each month on your calendar. Make special plans to do *nothing*—except something you (or your family) would enjoy.

2. Loosen up the tight wires of your life by not taking yourself so seriously . . . nor your job. Sure, some things *are* terribly serious — but not everything. The old Greek motto is still true: "You will break the bow if you keep it always bent."

3. Look for times during each day when something humorous or unusual makes laughter appropriate . . . then laugh out loud! That helps flush out the nervous system. Solomon tells us this is good medicine.

4. When you relax, *really relax* . . . blow it . . . enjoy the leisure . . . let out all the stops . . . ignore what some narrow-minded, squint-eyed critic might think or say. For sure, you'll get flak from those who burn out.

I'm of the opinion that a relaxed, easygoing Christian is miles more attractive and effective than the rigid, uptight brother who squeaks when he walks and whines when he talks.

Deepening Your Roots

2 Samuel 16:13 – 14; Psalm 23:1 – 3

Branching Out

1. Do one of the suggestions above.
2. Go out for clam chowder and have fun. (*No* serious talking allowed. Only laughter).
3. Have everyone in the family secretly write down a thing to do (that doesn't cost anything). Put all the ideas in a box or hat and one of you draw one card. You must do whatever the person requests.

ॐ ॐ ॐ

Growing Strong

I hate to break the news, but those hazy, lazy days of summer are coming to an end. At least for *Growing Strong in the Seasons of Life*. It's been a relaxing three months! How about you? Did you ease up, include a few more refreshment breaks, and stay cooler this year? Hope so. Now it's time to usher in autumn, that colorful season that brings with it a flood of memories. Speaking of memories, what's your favorite one of this summer?

_____

_____

_____

_____

Autumn

A Season of Reflection

AUTUMN

*O*f all the seasons, autumn is my favorite. There's a feel about it, a distinct and undeniable aura that surrounds it. Being a football freak, I naturally would favor autumn. But of course it's much deeper than that.

Those leaves are part of it. What color, what artistry! Crisp, frosty mornings also help. What a refreshing change from oppressively hot afternoons and sweltering nights! Then there is a helpful return to routine as school starts. And along comes Thanksgiving, a nostalgic reminder that God has indeed "shed His grace on thee." The firewood is cut. The pumpkins are getting bigger. Our hearts are overflowing.

Let's think of autumn as a season of reflection. Time to gain new perspective. To stroll along the back roads of our minds. To think about what. And where. And why. Such visits through the museum of memory never fail to assist us in evaluating the way we were and establishing the way we want to be. This implies change, another reason autumn seems to represent a season of reflection. It's during this season the foliage changes. And the weather changes. And the time changes. Birds make their annual journey southward. Squirrels finish storing their nuts. Salmon start their phenomenal swim back to their spawning grounds. And many of the larger animals take their final stretch before curling up for a long winter's nap. With incredible consistency, all these creatures in the natural world act out their individual pageants without external instruction or some script to follow.

Quietly, without flare or fanfare, God graciously moves upon our lives, taking us from summer to autumn, a season when He mysteriously writes His agenda on the tablets of our hearts. Patiently He waits for change to begin. Without exception, it does. And we reflect on that as well.

Has autumn arrived in your life? Think before you answer. Close your eyes for a minute or so and consider what God has been doing deep within your heart.

Allow me to remind you of something you may have forgotten. It's a quotation from the New Testament:

> . . . God Who began the good work within you will keep right on helping you grow in His grace until His work within you is finally finished on that day when Jesus Christ returns (Philippians 1:6, TLB).

At the root of God's agenda is this promise. Think of it as a guarantee. The One who started "the good work within you" won't leave the task unfinished. At the end of the course, God won't get an "incomplete." For sure, He won't fail! Remember, it takes four seasons to make a year.

The autumn season of your life may be uncomfortable. Unemployment might be your lot. Or a broken romance. Perhaps you are grieving over a recent loss. Maybe you're lonely. Or hungry. Or cold. You feel anxious about those ugly clouds on the horizon that indicate an ominous tomorrow. The winds of adversity are picking up and you feel afraid.

Remember a comment I shared with you back at the beginning when you began reading this book?

"The roots grow deep when the winds are strong."

If autumn, the season of reflection, has come, expect your roots to deepen. Count on it. Yet, be assured of this, the Lord God *specializes* in roots. He plans to deepen you and strengthen you. But He won't overdo it. He is sovereignly and compassionately at work. We are more impressed with the fruit. Not God — He's watching over the roots. We like the product, He emphasizes the process. And painful though it may be, "He who began . . . will keep right on . . . until His work . . . is finished." So we can boldly declare, "Come wind, come weather, *welcome autumn!*"

If you have entered this season, may these "autumn thoughts" encourage and strengthen you.

DOING VS. BEING

My high school graduating class had its fortieth anniversary reunion some time ago. I'm sure they had a ball. A *blast* would better describe it, knowing that crowd. You gotta understand the east side of Houston back in the 1950s to have some idea of that explosive student body . . . a couple of thousand strong and a lot of 'em mean as a junkyard dog with a nail in his paw. Knife fights in the boys' washroom were almost as commonplace as fireworks in assembly, racial slurs in the hall, and beat-up Harley Davidsons in the alley.

Since I wasn't able to attend the reunion, I decided to blow the dust off my yearbook and stroll down nostalgia lane. Faces aroused smiles and stories as one memory after another washed over me. Funny, I remembered a project we seniors were given before the yearbook went to press back in '52. We were asked to think about the next twenty years and answer, "What do I want to do?" The plan was to record our dreams and goals in the yearbook, then evaluate them when we met again at each subsequent reunion . . . you know, sort of a decade-by-decade checkup. Some of the goals are not fitting to repeat, but some are both interesting and revealing.

Several said: "Make a million bucks."
Others:

- "Win all-American honors and play professional football."
- "Be the concertmaster of a symphony orchestra."
- "Own my own race car and win the Indy 500."
- "Rob Chase Manhattan Bank and escape to Fiji."
- "Finish medical school and have a practice in Honolulu."
- "Marry a rich movie star and live in Beverly Hills."
- "Become the world heavyweight boxing champion."
- "Sing at the Metropolitan Opera."
- "Make a living writing short stories, plays, and novels."
- "Travel abroad as a news correspondent."
- "Live fast, die young, and leave a good-looking corpse."

All sorts of goals. Some admirable, some questionable, some crazy, a few stupid.

Without wanting to sound needlessly critical, as I look back over three decades, I think we were asked to answer the wrong question. What we want to *do* is not nearly as important as what we want to *be*. And the longer I live the more significant that becomes. It's possible to do lots of things yet be *zilch* as a person.

Doing is usually connected with a vocation or career, *how we make a living*. Being is much deeper. It relates to character, who we are, and *how we make a life*. Doing is tied in closely with activity, accomplishments, and tangible things — like salary, prestige, involvements, roles, and trophies. Being, on the other hand, has more to do with intangibles, the kind of people we become down inside, much of which can't be measured by objective yardsticks and impressive awards. But of the two, *being* will ultimately outdistance *doing* every time. It may take half a lifetime to perfect . . . but hands down, it's far more valuable. And lasting. And inspiring.

Remember those familiar words from Colossians 3? Twice we read, *"Whatsoever you do . . . whatever you do . . ."* (vv. 17, 23). It's almost as if the Lord is saying, "Makes no difference what it is, *whatever* you do . . ." But then He immediately addresses things that have to do with *being*. Like being thankful, being considerate, being obedient, being sincere, being diligent. Same pattern — God emphasizes being more than doing.

So then, are you giving thought these days to things that count? I hope so. Goal-setting and achieving are important, especially if we are in need of being motivated. Moving in the right direction is a great way to break the mold of mediocrity. It's helpful to ask, "What do I want to *do?*"

But while you're at it, take a deeper look inside. Ask yourself the harder question, "What do I want to *be?*" Then listen to your heart . . . your inner spirit. True treasures will emerge. Pick one or two to start with. Don't tell anybody, just concentrate some time and attention on that particular target. Watch God work. It will amaze you how He arranges circumstances so that the very target you and He decided on will begin to take shape within you. Sometimes it will be painful; other times, sheer joy. It won't happen overnight, but that's a major difference between doing and being. One may take only twenty years; the other, the better part of your lifetime.

One can be recorded in a yearbook and is easily forgotten; but the other requires a lifebook, which is on display forever.

Deepening Your Roots

Ecclesiastes 2:11, 4:4; 1 Thessalonians 5:16

Branching Out

1. Look through your old high school yearbook. Think back to what you thought you'd be doing today.
2. What do you want to be? _____

   _____

   (This is between you and God, so don't tell anyone.)
3. Evaluate whether your lifestyle emphasizes "doing" more than "being." If the answer is yes, seek to eliminate a "doing" to allow more time to develop the "being" part of you.

THE FINAL PRIORITY

Somebody copied the following paraphrase from a well-worn carbon in the billfold of a thirty-year veteran missionary. With her husband, she was on her way to another tour of duty at Khartoum, Sudan. No one seems to know who authored it, but whoever it was captured the essence of the greatest essay on love ever written.

If I have the language ever so perfectly and speak like a pundit, and have not the love that grips the heart, I am nothing. If I have decorations and diplomas and am proficient in up-to-date methods and have not the touch of understanding love, I am nothing.

If I am able to worst my opponents in argument so as to make fools of them, and have not the wooing note, I am nothing. If I have all faith and great ideals and magnificent plans and wonderful visions, and have not the love that sweats and bleeds and weeps and prays and pleads, I am nothing.

If I surrender all prospects, and leaving home and friends and comforts, give myself to the showy sacrifice of a missionary career, and turn sour and selfish amid the daily annoyances and personal slights of a missionary life, and though I give my body to be consumed in the heat and sweat and mildew of India, and have not the love that yields its rights, its coveted leisure, its pet plans, I am nothing, *nothing*. Virtue has ceased to go out of me.

If I can heal all manner of sickness and disease, but wound hearts and hurt feelings for want of love that is kind, I am nothing. If I write books and publish articles that set the world agape and fail to transcribe the word of the cross in the language of love, I am nothing. Worse, I may be competent, busy, fussy, punctilious, and well-equipped, but like the church at Laodicea — nauseating to Christ.

How about you and me committing ourselves to a life like this . . . a life that amounts to something . . . rather than nothing.

Each new day God brings our way is a fresh opportunity.

Deepening Your Roots

Matthew 12:33 – 37; John 17:20 – 26; 1 John 4:7 – 21

Branching Out

1. Love a missionary today by either writing him a letter, buying him a gift, sending a care package, calling long distance, etc.
2. Lift out a phrase from today's reading that convicted you and work at improving that attitude or action. Don't forget to seek God's assistance.
3. Complete the following to fit your particular vocation. If I am able to _____

   _____

   but have not _____

   _____

   then I am nothing more than _____

   _____

A Rabbit on the Swim Team

The Springfield, Oregon, Public Schools Newsletter published an article that caught my eye some time ago. As I read it, it struck me that I was reading a parable of familiar frustration in the Christian home and Body of Christ today.

> Once upon a time, the animals decided they should do something meaningful to meet the problems of the new world. So they organized a school.
>
> They adopted an activity curriculum of running, climbing, swimming and flying. To make it easier to administer the curriculum, all the animals took all the subjects.
>
> The *duck* was excellent in swimming; in fact, better than his instructor. But he made only passing grades in flying, and was very poor in running. Since he was slow in running, he had to drop swimming and stay after school to practice running. This caused his web feet to be badly worn, so that he was only average in swimming. But average was quite acceptable, so nobody worried about that — except the duck.
>
> The *rabbit* started at the top of his class in running, but developed a nervous twitch in his leg muscles because of so much make-up work in swimming.
>
> The *squirrel* was excellent in climbing, but he encountered constant frustration in flying class because his teacher made him start from the ground up instead of from the treetop down. He developed "charlie horses" from overexertion, and so only got a C in climbing and a D in running.
>
> The *eagle* was a problem child and was severely disciplined for being a non-conformist. In climbing classes he beat all the others to the top of the tree, but insisted on using his own way to get there . . .

The obvious moral of the story is a simple one — each creature has its own set of capabilities in which it will naturally excel — unless it is expected or forced to fill a mold that doesn't fit. When that happens, frustration, discouragement, and even guilt bring overall mediocrity or complete defeat. A duck is a duck — and *only* a duck. It is built to swim, not to run or fly and certainly not to climb. A squirrel is a squirrel — and *only* that. To move it out of its forte, climbing, and then expect it to swim or fly will drive a squirrel nuts. Eagles are beautiful creatures in the air but not in a foot race. The rabbit will win every time unless, of course, the eagle gets hungry.

What is true of creatures in the forest is true of Christians in the family; both the family of believers and that family under your roof. God has not made us all the same. He never intended to. It was He who planned and designed the differences, unique capabilities, and variations in the Body. So concerned was He that we realize this, He spelled it out several times in His final will and testament. Please take the time to read the thirty-one verses of 1 Corinthians 12 *slowly* and *aloud*.

Let's summarize some of these compelling truths:

God has placed you in His family and given you a certain mixture that makes you unique. No mixture is insignificant!

That mix pleases Him completely. Nobody else is exactly like you. That should bring you pleasure, too.

When you operate in the realm of capabilities, you will excel, the whole Body will benefit, and you will experience incredible satisfaction.

When others operate in their realm, balance, unity, and health automatically occur in the Body. But when you compare . . . or force . . . or entertain expectations that are beyond your or others' God-given capabilities, mediocrity or frustration or phoniness or total defeat is predictable.

If God made you a duck saint — you're a duck, friend. Swim like mad, but don't get bent out of shape because you wobble when you run or flap instead of fly. Furthermore, if you're an eagle saint, stop expecting squirrel saints to soar, or rabbit saints to build the same kind of nests you do.

I'll let you in on my own experience — the trap I fell into years ago. Having been exposed to a few of the "greats" in various churches and an outstanding seminary, I (like some of the other guys in the class) tried to be like *them*. You know, think like, sound like, look like. For over ten years in the ministry I — a rabbit — worked hard at swimming like a duck or flying like an eagle. I was a frustrated composite creature . . . like that weird beast in the second chapter of Daniel. And my feet of clay were slowly crumbling beneath me. It was awful! The worst part of all, what little bit of originality or creativity I had was being consumed in that false role I was forcing. One day my insightful and caring wife asked me, "Why not just be *you?* Why try to be like anybody else?" Well, friends and neighbors, this rabbit quit the swim team and gave up flying lessons and stopped trying to climb. Talk about relief! And best of all, I learned it was OK to be me . . . and let my family members be themselves. Originality and creativity flowed anew!

So relax. Enjoy your spiritual species. Cultivate your own capabilities. Your own style. Appreciate the members of your family or your fellowship for who they are, even though their outlook or style may be miles different from yours. Rabbits don't fly. Eagles don't swim. Ducks look funny trying to climb. Squirrels don't have feathers.

Stop comparing. Enjoy being you! There's plenty of room in the forest.

Deepening Your Roots

Song of Solomon 6:9; Isaiah 40:25 – 26, 46:5 – 9; 1 Corinthians 12:1 – 31

Branching Out

1. Identify one thing/action you are involved in that is forcing you to be something you're not: _____
   If possible, remove yourself from that activity and see if you sense relief.
2. When you compare yourself with others, what do you generally find you don't match up to? _____
   Now evaluate whether that's due to your trying to be something that simply is not you, or ever will be . . . and accept that.
3. Look at your friendships and determine if you're pressuring anyone to conform to your standards or skills. If so, back off, let the person be himself, and do something to encourage him to be himself.

❦ ❦ ❦

Growing Strong

Doing some inner housekeeping is good, isn't it? Especially in this season of change. If you've struggled through some personal character battles this week, I congratulate you. But here's a caution. Concentrating on yourself too much can open the door to discouragement. Now's a good moment to focus on the One who is sufficient for your every need.

SELF-PRAISE

"Self-praise," says an ancient adage, "smells bad." In other words, *it stinks up the works.*

Regardless of how we prepare it, garnish it with little extras, slice and serve it up on our finest silver piece, the odor remains. No amount of seasoning can eliminate the offensive smell. Unlike a good wife, age only makes it worse. It is much like the poisoned rat in the wall — if it isn't removed the stench becomes increasingly unbearable. Leave it untouched and within a span of time it will taint and defile everything that comes near it.

I got nauseated last week. It wasn't from something I ate ... but from *someone I met.* My out-of-town travels resulted in a short-term liberal arts education of self-praise to teach me some things I hope I never fully forget. This individual is a widely traveled, well-educated, much-experienced Christian in his fifties. He is engaged in a ministry that touches many lives. He is fundamental in faith, biblical in belief, and evangelical in emphasis. For a number of years he has held a respected position that carries with it a good deal of responsibility and a great deal of time logged in the limelight. Such credentials deserve a measure of respect like the rank on the shoulders of a military officer or the rows of medals on his chest. Both merit a salute in spite of the man inside the uniform. In no way do I wish to diminish the significance of his position nor his record of achievement. But my point is this — he *knew* better ... he had the ability to correct himself ... but he chose to be, quite frankly, a pompous preacher!

You got the distinct impression that when the two of you were together, the more important one was not you. Little mistakes irked him. Slight omissions irritated him. The attitude of a servant was conspicuous by its absence. It was highly important to him that everyone knew who he was, where he'd been, how he'd done, and what he thought. While everyone else much preferred to be on a first-name basis (rather that "Reverend" or "Minister") he demanded, "Call *me* Doctor ..." His voice had a professional tone. As humorous things occurred, he found no reason to smile ... and as the group got closer and closer in spirit, he became increasingly more threatened. I confess that I was tempted to short-sheet him one night — or to order a Schlitz in his name and have it brought up to his room — or to ask the desk clerk to give him a call about 2:30 a.m. and yell, "Okay, buddy, out of the sack, rise and shine!" But I didn't. Now I almost wish I had. Just for the fun of watching the guy squirm!

Now let's get back to the basics. God says he *hates* "haughty eyes" (Proverbs 6:17). He calls a proud heart "sin" (Proverbs 21:4). He says if praise is going to be directed your way, "Let another praise you, and not your own mouth" (Proverbs 27:2). He drives home the message in Galatians 6:3:

> . . . if anyone thinks he is something when he is nothing, he deceives himself.

There is no greater deception than *self*-deception. It is a tragic trap laid for everyone, but especially vulnerable are those who have achieved . . . and start reading their own clippings the next morning.

Here's my advice. Three of the lessons I've learned since my encounter last week with Doctor Hot Shot are:

1. Get a good education — but *get over it*. Dig in and pay the price for solid, challenging years in school, and apply your education with all your ability, but *please* spare others from the tiring reminders of how honored they should feel in your presence.

2. Reach the maximum of your potential — but *don't talk about it*. Keep uppermost in your mind the plain truth about yourself . . . you have to put your pants on one leg at a time just like everybody else.

3. Walk devotedly with God — but *don't try to look like it*. If you are genuinely God's man or woman, others will know it.

Deepening Your Roots

Proverbs 21:4; Luke 18:9 – 14; John 12:42 – 43; Galatians 6:12 – 14

Branching Out

1. I dare you to remove all those diplomas from the wall in your office — or any object that promotes you and your achievements.
2. Check your "pride quotient" by listening and counting how many times you talk about yourself today. Whenever you hear the word "I" it's a clue you're patting yourself on the back.
3. Don't tell anyone about what *you* did this week that would indicate you've got a handle on your spiritual life. In other words, take on point three above.

MONUMENTS

Not far from Lincoln, Kansas, stands a strange group of gravestones. A guy named Davis, a farmer and self-made man, had them erected. He began as a lowly hired hand and by sheer determination and frugality he managed to amass a considerable fortune in his lifetime. In the process, however, the farmer did not make many friends. Nor was he close to his wife's family, since they thought she had married beneath her dignity. Embittered, he vowed never to leave his in-laws a thin dime.

When his wife died, Davis erected an elaborate statue in her memory. He hired a sculptor to design a monument which showed both her and him at opposite ends of a love seat. He was so pleased with the result that he commissioned another statue — this time of himself, kneeling at her grave, placing a wreath on it. That impressed him so greatly that he planned a third monument, this time of his wife kneeling at *his* future gravesite, depositing a wreath. He had the sculptor add a pair of wings on her back, since she was no longer alive, giving her the appearance of an angel. One idea led to another until he'd spent no less than a quarter million dollars on the monuments to himself and his wife!

Whenever someone from the town would suggest he might be interested in a community project (a hospital, a park and swimming pool for the children, a municipal building, etc.), the old miser would frown, set his jaw, and shout back, "What's this town ever done for me? I don't owe this town nothin'!"

After using up all his resources on stone statues and selfish pursuits, John Davis died at 92, a grim-faced resident of the poorhouse. But the monuments ... it's strange.... Each one is slowly sinking into the Kansas soil, fast becoming victims of time, vandalism, and neglect. Monuments of spite. Sad reminders of a self-centered, unsympathetic life. There is a certain poetic justice in the fact that within a few years, they will all be gone.

Oh, by the way, very few people attended Mr. Davis's funeral. It is reported that only one person seemed genuinely moved by any sense of personal loss. He was Horace England ... the tombstone salesman.[19]

Before we're too severe with the late Mr. Davis, let's take an honest look at the monuments being erected today — some of which are no less revealing, if not quite so obvious. A close investigation will reveal at least four:

- FORTUNE
- FAME
- POWER
- PLEASURE

Much the same as the Davis gravestone, these monuments are built in clusters, making them appear formidable . . . and acceptable. As the idols in ancient Athens, our society is saturated with them.

FORTUNE. How neatly it fits our times! Its inscription at the base is bold: "Get rich." The statuesque figures in the monument are impressive: a hard-working young executive; a clever, diligent businessman unwilling to admit to the greed behind his long hours and relentless drive.

FAME. Another monument tailor-made for Century Twenty. It reads: "Be famous." All its figures are bowing in worship to the popularity cult, eagerly anticipating the day when their desire to be known, seen, quoted, applauded, and exalted will be satisfied. Young and old surround the scene.

POWER. Etched in the flesh of this human edifice are the words: "Take control." These figures are capitalizing on every opportunity to seize the reins of authority and race to the top . . . regardless. "Look out for number one!"

PLEASURE. The fourth monument is perhaps the most familiar of all. Its message, echoed countless times in the media, is straightforward: "Indulge yourself." If it looks good, enjoy it! If it tastes good, drink it! If it feels good, do it! Like the line out of the Academy Award winning song "You Light Up My Life" that says:

> It can't be wrong
> If it feels so right . . .

Conspicuous by its absence is the forgotten philosophy of Jesus Christ. He's the One who taught the truth about being eternally rich through giving rather than getting. About serving others rather than leaving footprints on their backs in the race for the farthest star. About surrendering rights rather than clamoring for more control. About limiting your liberty out of love and saying no when the flesh pleads for yes. You know — the whole package wrapped up in one simple statement . . .

> . . . seek first His kingdom, and His righteousness; and all these things shall be added to you (Matthew 6:33).

No elaborate set of statues. No sculptures done in marble — not even an epitaph for the world to read. And when He died, few cared because few understood. They were too busy building their own monuments.

We still are.

Deepening Your Roots

Proverbs 11:7, 16; 28:28; Ecclesiastes 5:10 – 20; 1 Corinthians 4:18 – 21

Branching Out

1. Do something that shows you're not seeking control at home or on the job.
2. What keeps you from "seeking first the kingdom of God"?

CRACKS IN THE WALL

The longer I live the less I *know* for sure.

That sounds like 50% heresy ... but it's 100% honesty. In my younger years I had a lot more answers than I do now. Things were absolutely black and white, right or wrong, yes or no, in or out, but a lot of that is beginning to change. The more I travel and read and wrestle and think the less simplistic things seem.

I now find myself uncomfortable with sweeping generalities ... with neat little categories and well-defined classifications.

Take people, for example. They cannot be squeezed into pigeon holes. People and situations are far more complex than most of us are willing to admit.

- Not all Episcopalians are liberal.
- Not all athletes are thickheaded.
- Not all Republicans are Christian good guys.
- Not all collegians are rebels.
- Not all artists are kooks.
- Not all movies are questionable.
- Not all questions are answerable.
- Not all verses are clear.
- Not all problems are easily solved.
- Not all deaths are explainable.

Maybe the list comes as a jolt. Great! Jolts are fine if they make you think. We evangelicals are good at building rigid walls out of dogmatic stones ... cemented together by the mortar of tradition. We erect these walls in systematic circles — then place within each our over-simplified, ultra-inflexible "position." Within each fortress we build human machines that are programmed not to think but to say the "right" things and respond the "right" way at any given moment. Our self-concept remains undisturbed and secure since no challenging force is ever allowed over the walls. Occasionally, however, a strange thing happens — a little restlessness springs up *within* the walls. A few ideas are challenged. Questions are entertained. Alternative options are then released. Talk about threat! Suddenly our superprotected, cliché-ridden answers don't cut it. Our over-simplified package offers no solution. The stones start to shift as the mortar cracks.

Two common reactions are available to us. *One:* We can maintain the status quo "position" and patch the wall by resisting change with rigidity. *Two:* We can openly admit *"I do not know,"* as the wall crumbles. Then we can do some new thinking by facing the facts as they actually are. The first approach is the most popular. We are masters at rationalizing around our inflexible behavior. We imply that change always represents a departure from the truth of Scripture.

Now some changes *do* pull us away from Scripture. They must definitely be avoided. But let's be absolutely certain that we are standing on scriptural rock, not traditional sand. We have a changeless message — Jesus Christ — but He must be proclaimed in a changing, challenging era. Such calls for a breakdown of stone walls and a breakthrough of fresh, keen thinking based on scriptural insights. No longer can we offer tired, trite statements that are as stiff and tasteless as last year's gum beneath the pew. The thinking person deserves an intelligent, sensible answer. He is weary of oversimplified bromides mouthed by insensitive robots within the walls.

Perhaps by now my words sound closer to 90% heresy. All I ask is that you examine *your* life. Socrates once said,

> The unexamined life is not worth living.

If you've stopped thinking and started going through unexamined motions, you've really stopped living and started existing.

That kind of "life" isn't much fun, nor very rewarding. I'd call it about 100% heresy . . . and only 50% honesty.

Deepening Your Roots
Matthew 15:1 – 9; Mark 7:1 – 13; Colossians 2:8 – 23

Branching Out

1. If you're the type who has a comment or opinion on everything, sometime today respond to a person by replying: "I don't know."
2. What's something you're resistant to? _____

_____

Is it a black and white issue that Scripture gives a clear-cut answer on, or is it an issue based solely upon tradition?

ᘓ ᘓ ᘓ

Growing Strong

Come across a big crack in your wall this week that was hard to admit was a part of you? I understand. It's not fun looking at flaws. But better to find them now and do something about them than carry them with you throughout life. Right?

Would you do me a favor? Stop right now and thank God for that flaw, and that He is able to help you overcome or remove it from your life. Then tell me something positive about yourself.

_____

_____

_____

_____

TIME

We set our clocks back one hour last Saturday night.

Every time I mess around with that spring-up, fall-back routine, I smile. It always reminds me of the backwoods lady in Louisiana who wrote the government one summer complaining about this new-fangled plan called daylight savings time. She argued, "That extra hour of sunshine done burnt up all my tomater plants."

It is rather remarkable how much difference one hour makes, even when you don't raise tomaters. It hits me abruptly when I look out my window in the late afternoon, expecting to see a mellow golden glow at dusk, but finding, instead, everything black. The opposite occurs at dawn. It will take all of us several days to become accustomed to the switch. Funny, we'd never notice it if it were a gradual thing, like only a couple minutes a week. But it's sudden. Out of the blue we're a full hour into brighter mornings and darker evenings now that fall has fallen.

Time continues to be one of those intriguing subjects to me. On some occasions it seems so elusive, so slippery. Whoosh, there goes a week . . . *a month!* Yet there are other segments of time that pass with the speed of a glacier. And have you noticed how stubborn and uncooperative time is? When you want time to zip on by, it drags. Then, when you want it to slow down to a crawl, it's tomorrow already.

Another thing: Time may be a great healer, but it's a rotten beautician. It's also terribly relative. Two weeks on a vacation, for example, is never the same as two weeks on a diet, is it? Also . . . some folks can stay longer in an hour than others can in a week. And have you noticed how quickly deadlines arrive, even though you try to push them away? On the contrary, isn't it amazing how slowly habits are broken, even though you desire to conquer them immediately?

And in every one of those situations, each hour had exactly sixty minutes — no more, no less.

I've just about come full circle with this time business. God alone is its Master . . . not us. He is the only One who "changes the times and the seasons" (Daniel 2:21). I especially like the way David put it:

But as for me, I trust in Thee, O LORD, I say,
"Thou art my God."
My times are in Thy hand . . . (Psalm 31:14 – 15a).

Makes good sense. Since He has an "appointed time for everything . . . for every event under heaven — " (Ecclesiastes 3:1), an ideal method of time management is T-R-U-S-T, putting the pressure it brings back into His hand. That certainly beats the alternative! If you really mean it when you say, "Thou art my God . . ." then hand over to Him the things He alone can master. We could call it Operation Entrust.

- Is time dragging?   TRUST
- Are deadlines arriving?   TRUST
- Those habits lingering?   TRUST
- That diet getting old?   TRUST
- Unwanted guests staying?   TRUST
- Beginning to look (and feel) older? TRUST
- Prayers aren't being answered?   TRUST
- Recovery taking longer?   TRUST
- Employment lacking challenge?   TRUST
- Finances fading fast?   TRUST
- Promotion more remote?   TRUST
- Romance not blossoming?   TRUST
- Decisions getting complicated?   TRUST
- Dreams becoming distant?   TRUST
- School less satisfying?   TRUST
- Feeling unappreciated? Used?   TRUST
- Dreading winter?   TRUST

Maybe it will help to read again the psalmist's lines:

I say, "Thou art my God." My times are in Thy hand.

Want a practical suggestion? Cement those twelve words into the creases of your memory. Then, each morning for the rest of this month, right after you plant your feet beside your bed, look out the window and repeat those words out loud. Quietly, yet with feeling. If you want to get downright fanatical about it, you can even add on a prayer like:

Today, Lord, each hour is yours . . . not mine.
Whatever happens, I trust You completely.

But don't get too carried away with this predawn project. Enough is enough. Too much early morning devotion could make you miss breakfast and late for work. Several days like that back-to-back and you wouldn't have to sweat the time. In fact, you'd have all the time you needed without the hassle of employment!

Come to think of it, you could even get into raising tomaters . . . uh, if that extra hour of sun don't burn 'em up.

Deepening Your Roots
Psalm 40:1 – 4, 130:5 – 6; Proverbs 20:22; Daniel 2:19 – 23; Hebrews 6:13 – 15

Branching Out
1. What's something you feel pressured about? _____

   _____

   Are you trusting God with it? How about talking to Him right now about the pressure you're feeling.
2. Memorize, "I say, 'Thou art my God.' My times are in Thy hands." (Psalm 31:14 – 15a) and quote it each morning.
3. Name an area of your life that's hard to entrust to God: _____

   _____

   Trust Him with it today, tomorrow, and however long it takes for you to sense His — not your — control of it.

THE PLUG-IN DRUG

A fascinating experiment on addiction was reported in an issue of *Good Housekeeping* magazine.[20] Not drug addition. Not alcohol addiction. Not tobacco or candy addiction. It was on television addiction.

A Detroit newspaper made an offer to 120 families in the city. The families were promised $500 each if they would agree not to watch TV for one month. That's right — 500 bucks if they'd keep the tube turned off for just thirty days. Guess how many turned down the offer.

Ninety-three.

Of the twenty-seven families that said yes, five were studied and reported on in the magazine article. Right away you realize it was quite an adjustment for them. Each family had been watching television from 40 to 70 hours a week . . . that's between 5.7 and 10 hours *a day*. Think of it! Every day of every week the monotonous sounds and electronic pictures were a continual part of those households — year in and year out.

Serious pains accompanied the sudden, cold-turkey withdrawal from the plug-in drug. Remarkable things occurred, some almost bizarre. Like the lady who started talking to the cat or the couple who *stopped* talking to each other altogether!

But some good things also occurred. Books were pulled off the shelf, dusty from neglect, and read. Families played games, listened to the radio, and enjoyed playing records together. In one family two young kids spent some time practicing how to spell their names and addresses!

Miracles of miracles, several actually reported the younger kids took their baths at night without throwing a fit. And *some* (better sit down) willingly practiced their piano lessons.

The results? Well, the "no TV month" families finally had to admit four facts:

1. Their family members were brought closer together.
2. More eyeball-to-eyeball time between parents and children took place.
3. There was a marked increase in patience between family members.
4. Creativity was enhanced.

I would love to report otherwise . . . but I must be honest rather than wishful and add that television eventually won out once again. All five families returned to their addiction for nearly the same number of hours as before. *Some more.*

It's not the TV that disturbs me. No, it's just another gadget that can be used and enjoyed on occasion. It's the abuse that bothers me — the paralyzing addiction that stifles human creativity and cripples personal relationships. I agree with the comment made in the *Christian Medical Society Journal* :

> The primary danger of the television screen lies not so much in the behavior it produces as the behavior it prevents.[21]

Turning on the television set can turn off the process that transforms children into people . . . and paralyzed viewers into thinking, caring persons. That's why the nine-year-old in San Francisco was overheard saying:

> "I'd lot rather watch TV than play outside 'cause it's boring outside. They always have the same rides, like swings and things."[22]

One reputable authority declares that children raised on television come to adulthood with no evident signs of decline in overall intelligence. There is apparently no huge brain drain, but there are a few peculiarities that concern the pros in this field.

- Increased communication in a near nonverbal speech ("like man . . . uh . . . you know . . . uh . . .").
- Much less spontaneity and fewer imaginative concepts coming from young adults.
- An intense, almost irrational, dependence on music with a heavy beat as their only art form.
- The ever-present drug scene.
- Greater interest in passive experiences than those requiring mental interaction and active involvement.

Since television sets sit in ninety-seven percent of American homes (more homes have TV than indoor plumbing), these problems aren't decreasing.

Hey, let's do something about this, folks! It's a tough, uphill battle, but it *isn't* insurmountable. Coming off the addiction is always hard. It actually boils down to the correct use of two of the smallest things in your house, the on-off knob on your set and the simple yet powerful word *No.*

Now, don't look around for much support. You'll have to hammer out your own philosophy. One that fits you and your family. But, for sure, do something soon. Let's take seriously these words:

> Fix your thoughts on what is true and good and right. Think about things that are pure and lovely, and dwell on the fine, good things in others. [— Paul, to twentieth-century Christians] (Philippians 4:8, TLB)

Believe me, the ultimate benefits you'll enjoy will be worth much more than $500 and they will certainly last a lot longer.

For a change, unplug the plug-in drug.

Deepening Your Roots
Psalm 25:15; Ezekiel 20:21 – 31; 1 John 2:15 – 17

Branching Out

1. I challenge you to turn your TV off for one entire week and fill those free hours with at least one good book, listening to some new music, playing a game, taking a walk, visiting with someone you've not seen in over three months.
2. For every hour of TV you watch, spend the same amount of time reading a book.

PLEASE BE CAREFUL

The package arrived safely. Somebody was thoughtful to remember to stick an important reminder on it when it was mailed. Oh, it had a few scuff marks and a bent corner or two, but by and large, nothing was damaged. Actually, it wasn't that expensive . . . just a photo of my family sandwiched between two flats of cardboard.

Just a picture of six people with the same last name, four of whom were delivered by God into our home between 1961 and 1970. The reminder on the package jumped out at me:

FRAGILE: HANDLE WITH CARE

We've tried to do that. Like all other parents, there have been times of exasperation and exhaustion, frustration and failure, but deep down inside we have tried not to forget just how fragile these individually prepared arrows in our quiver really are.

Their mother and I realized this anew recently as we gulped and groaned our way through a televised presentation on child abuse. We choked back the tears as we heard and watched two hours of grim realism, more shocking and depressing than any make-believe horror movie director could ever devise. You better sit down before you read these factual statistics. Take a deep breath.

- Two hundred thousand children are physically abused each year.
- Of those, between 60,000 and 100,000 are *sexually* abused.
- Fifteen to twenty percent of American families abuse their children.
- Two-thirds of all child abuse occurs with children under four years of age . . . one-third are *under six months.*
- The number one killer of children under five years of age is child abuse.
- Four thousand children die annually because of child abuse. It is estimated that, including the *unreported* abuses, the number could be as high as 50,000.
- Child-abusers are found in every category of our society. No social or economic or religious types are excluded.

No, most child-abusers are not mentally deficient. Only ten percent are classified "mentally disturbed." The rest are people who appear to be very normal; they just "cannot cope." Maybe *you're* in the ninety-percent category. You can get help through counselors and public agencies. Please do. You'll be treated with professional and personal care, I am told. For the sake of your child, please do.

But maybe all you need is a little encouragement, a few well-worded reminders to "handle with care" those little people who may seem to be anything but fragile. I think if we would let them talk, here's what they would say:

- My hands are small; please don't expect perfection whenever I make my bed, draw a picture, or throw a ball. My legs are short; please slow down so I can keep up with you.
- My eyes have not seen the world as yours have; please let me explore safely. Don't restrict me unnecessarily.
- Housework will always be there. I'm only little for a short time — please take time to explain things to me about this wonderful world, and do so willingly.
- My feelings are tender; please be sensitive to my needs. Don't nag me all day long . . . treat me as you would like to be treated.
- I am a special gift from God; please treasure me as God intended you to do, holding me accountable for my actions, giving me guidelines to live by, and disciplining me in a loving manner.
- I need your encouragement to grow. Please go easy on the criticism; remember you can criticize the things I do without criticizing me.
- Please give me the freedom to make decisions concerning myself. Permit me to fail, so that I can learn from my mistakes. Then someday I'll be prepared to make the kind of decisions life requires of me.
- Please don't do things over for me. Somehow that makes me feel that my efforts didn't quite measure up to your expectations. I know it's hard, but please don't try to compare me with my brother or my sister.
- Please don't be afraid to leave for a weekend together. Kids need vacations from parents, just as parents need vacations from kids. Besides, it's a great way to show us kids that your marriage is very special.[23]

Because they are fragile, handling children with care is essential. You'll be glad you did when all you have is an old photo and the memory of a package God delivered into your care many, many years ago.

Deepening Your Roots

1 Kings 3:16 – 27; Psalm 127:1 – 5; Proverbs 17:6; Luke 18:15 – 17

Branching Out

1. Set aside one hour a day this week and play with your children. Do whatever *they* desire to do. Let them tell/show you what fun is all about.
2. Do something special with each of your (or a friend's) children this week. Don't do it as a group; give each one a special time to be alone with you.
3. Take a picture of your (or a friend's) children this week and when developed frame it. Write on the back of the photo: Fragile — Handle with Care.

❧ ❧ ❧

Growing Strong

I can't help believing you are a different person today. That is, if you took on one or more of the Branching Out assignments this week. You're bound to be pleased with yourself if you did, and have at least three new things to share. OK, share something with me:

_____

_____

_____

_____

℞ESENTMENT

*L*eonard Holt was a paragon of respectability. He was a middle-aged, hard-working lab technician who had worked at the same Pennsylvania paper mill for nineteen years. Having been a Boy Scout leader, an affectionate father, a member of the local fire brigade, and a regular churchgoer, he was admired as a model in his community. Until . . .

. . . that image exploded in a well-planned hour of bloodshed one brisk October morning. Holt decided to mount a one-man revolt against the world he inwardly resented. A proficient marksman, he stuffed two pistols into his coat pockets — a .45 automatic and a Smith and Wesson .38 — before he drove his station wagon to the mill. Parking quietly, he gripped a gun in each fist, then slowly stalked into the shop. He started shooting with such calculated frenzy that it resembled a scene out of "Gunsmoke." He filled several of his fellow workmen with two and three bullets apiece, firing more than thirty shots in all . . . deliberately killing some of the men he had known for over fifteen years. When a posse was formed to capture the man, they found him standing in his doorway, snarling defiantly:

"Come and get me, you _____ ;
I'm not taking any more of your _____ ."

Total bewilderment swept over the neighborhood. Puzzled policemen and friends finally discovered a tenuous chain of logic behind his brief reign of terror. Down deep within the heart and soul of Leonard Holt rumbled intense resentment. The man who had appeared like a monk on the outside was seething with murderous hatred within. A subsequent investigation led officials to numerous discoveries yielding such evidence. Several of the victims had been promoted over him while he remained in the same position. More than one in his car pool had quit riding with him due to his reckless driving. A neighbor had been threatened, then struck by Holt after an argument over a fallen tree. The man was *brimming* with resentful rage that could be held in check no longer.

Beneath his picture in *Time* magazine, the caption told the truth:

RESPONSIBLE, RESPECTABLE — AND RESENTFUL.

So it is with resentment. Allowed to fester through neglect, the toxic fumes of hatred foam to a boil within the steamroom of the soul. Pressure mounts to a maddening magnitude. By then it's only a matter of time. The damage is always tragic, often irreparable:

- a battered child
- a crime of passion
- ugly, caustic words
- loss of a job
- a runaway
- a bad record
- domestic disharmony
- a ruined testimony

None of this is new. Solomon described the problem long ago:

> Pretty words may hide a wicked heart, just as a pretty glaze covers a common clay pot.
> A man with hate in his heart may sound pleasant enough, but don't believe him; for he is cursing you in his heart. Though he pretends to be so kind, his hatred will finally come to light for all to see (Proverbs 26:23 – 26, TLB).

The answer to resentment isn't complicated, it's just painful. It requires *honesty.* You must first admit it's there. It then requires *humility.* You must confess it before the One who died for such sins. It may even be necessary for you to make it right with those you have offended out of resentful bitterness. Finally, it requires *vulnerability* — a willingness to keep that tendency submissive to God's regular reproof, and a genuinely teachable, unguarded attitude.

Nobody ever dreamed Leonard Holt had a problem with resentment. And nobody dreams *you* do either.

Not yet . . .

Deepening Your Roots

2 Timothy 2:24; Hebrews 12:14, 15; James 3:14 – 16; 1 John 2:9 – 11

Branching Out

1. Be honest. What's a resentment you harbor inside yourself? _____
   _____

2. Talk to a fellow worker, a friend, or your spouse and quietly probe to see if there is any problem between the two of you.

3. Would people be surprised if they knew your inner thoughts? _____
   Are some of those thoughts "resentment"?

HEALTH

*T*o set the record straight, I am neither a doctor nor the son of a doctor, and since I may *sound* like a doctor, you must not be misled. What I have to share comes not from intensive medical training but from extensive practical thinking. Because I am not qualified to write a prescription, hoping you'll take the medicine, I will write a philosophy, hoping you'll take the message.

Frank Burgess, the American humorist, told the truth when he said,

"Our bodies are apt to be our autobiographies."

Arthur Schopenhauer, the astute German philosopher, put it another way:

The greatest mistake a man can make is to sacrifice health for any other advantage.

Health is the thing that makes you feel that *now* is the best time of the year. Next to having a good conscience, health is to be valued most. But it isn't! Of all the good and perfect gifts God grants us, it is the least recognized. We either ignore it (like a bad habit) or we take advantage of it (like a good wife). Health is the stepchild of our lives. Mistreated and misunderstood, it exists without encouragement and serves us without reward. Occasionally, it is like the timid student in school who raises her hand for help but finds the teacher too busy to notice or too demanding to care. But there are also times when health loses its cool and refuses to stay silent any longer. Its frustrations reach such a fevered pitch that it screams for our attention . . . and it gets it!

Many of us are notoriously negligent when it comes to maintaining good health. Take *rest,* for example. Written across our minds is the statement made famous by some so-called dedicated saint:

"I'd rather burn out than rust out!"

What kind of a choice is that? Either way, you're "out." That's like saying, "I'd rather die while skiing than while sleeping." Whichever the choice, you're a cold corpse. Good health depends upon proper rest. Compromising here is just plain carnal! It is no better than gossip or stealing or murder. Rest can be as spiritual as hours in prayer—*maybe more.*

Take *food,* for another example. Your body and mine cannot be better than the food used each day to nourish, strengthen, and rebuild them—no matter how much we love the Lord! God never intended that we function on a constant diet of imitation or refined foods, devoid of nutrition and inundated with preservatives . . . raised in fields polluted with insecticides and other poisons. You may be a Bible teacher, gifted, and in great demand — but if you cram only junk down the throat, your health will go down the tube. Good food (and the right amount) can be as spiritual as teaching the truth — *sometimes more.*

Exercise is yet another example. No amount of witnessing or worship can substitute for regular physical exercise. Every cell and organ of the old "bod" tends to increase in efficiency through exercise. Vigorous exercise stimulates the mind, the blood, the muscles, the senses. It even affects our worries by flushing them out as we perspire in recreation and an active change of pace. It's no surprise to me that the very first preparation suggested by Dr. Laurence J. Peter on "How to make things go right" is: REVITALIZE YOUR BODY. Exercise can be as spiritual as attending a church service—*perhaps more.*

Three questions: How are we to glorify God? Where is the temple of the Holy Spirit? What is to be presented to the Lord as a living sacrifice?

One answer: The body. Let's not think that loud prayers and lengthy Bible studies and lovely church services will cause God to smile at lousy health habits.

Keep your balance. It's a long drop from the thin wire of fanaticism to the hard floor of realism . . . and the sudden stop never helps anybody.

Deepening Your Roots

Proverbs 23:23 and 21; Daniel 1:8 – 16; 1 Corinthians 6:12 – 19

Branching Out

1. If you are overweight and unable to shake off those pounds, then seek help — even if it costs. Or, if you've been putting off dropping those excess pounds, decide today to lose _____ (amount) by _____ , and do it!

2. Choose three items from the list below and stop eating them for one month. See if you feel better by that time. Absolutely no cheating. Reward yourself in thirty days if you did this assignment.

chocolate	coffee
ice cream	cake
candy	cookies
pop	pie

3. Take up some sport or exercise program and do it consistently (three to five times a week) for one month. Write down how you feel today and then how you feel in one month.

ISOLATION AND INVOLVEMENT

*E*levators are weird places, aren't they? Especially crowded ones.

You're crammed in close with folks you've never met, so you try really hard not to touch them. And nobody talks, either. The one thing you may hear is an occasional "Out, please" or "Oh, I'm sorry" as somebody clumsily steps on someone's toe. You don't look at anyone; in fact, you don't look anywhere but up, watching those dumb numbers go on and off. Strange. People who are all about the same height and speak the same language are suddenly as silent as a roomful of nuns when they occupy common space.

It's almost as if there's an official sign that reads:

NO TALKING, NO SMILING, NO TOUCHING, AND NO EYE CONTACT ALLOWED WITHOUT WRITTEN CONSENT OF THE MANAGEMENT. NO EXCEPTIONS!!

Years ago I was speaking on the campus of the University of Oklahoma. After the meeting, a crazy group of three or four guys invited me to have a Coke with them. Since we were several floors up in the student center, we decided to take the elevator down. As the door slid open, the thing was full of people who gave us that hey-you-guys-aren't-gonna-try-to-get-in-are-you? look. But we did, naturally. I was last. There wasn't even room to turn around. I felt the door close against my back as everyone stared in my direction. I smiled big and said loudly, "You might have wondered why we called this meeting today!" The place broke open with laughter. It was the most amazing thing to watch . . . people actually *talking,* actually *relating* to each other . . . on an elevator.

I've been thinking lately that an elevator is a microcosm of our world today: a large, impersonal institution where anonymity, isolation, and independence are the uniform of the day. A basic quality of our healthy social lives is being diluted, distorted, and demeaned by the "elevator mentality." We are way out of balance in the area of relating to people.

One published report by Ralph Larkin, a sociologist, on the crises facing suburban youth, underscores several aspects of this new malaise of the spirit. Many children of American affluence are depicted as passively accepting a way of life they view as empty and meaningless. A syndrome is now set in motion that includes "a low threshold of boredom, a constricted expression of emotions, and an apparent absence of joy in anything that is not immediately consumable."[24] Makes sense when you observe the significant role now played by music, drugs, booze, sex and status-symbol possessions. Take away rock concerts and sports events and you seldom witness much display of strong emotion.

Exit: Involvement and motivation. Enter: Indifference, noncommitment, disengagement, no sharing or caring . . . meals eaten with hi-fi headsets turned up loud, even separate bedrooms, each with a personal telephone, TV and turntable, private toilet, and an it's-none-of-your-business attitude. No hassles . . . no conflicts . . . no accountability. No need to share. Or reach out. Or give a rip. Just watch the numbers and look at nobody.

Dr. Philip Zimbardo, a professor of psychology at Stanford and author of one of the most widely used textbooks in the field, addresses this issue in a *Psychology Today* article entitled "The Age of Indifference." He pulls no punches as he writes:

> I know of no more potent killer than isolation. There is no more destructive influence on physical and mental health than the isolation of you from me and of us from them. It has been shown to be a central agent in the etiology of depression, paranoia, schizophrenia, rape, suicide, mass murder . . .

And then he adds:

> The devil's strategy for our times is to trivialize human existence in a number of ways: by isolating us from one another while creating the delusion that the reasons are time pressures, work demands, or anxieties created by economic uncertainty; by fostering narcissism and the fierce competition to be No. 1 . . .[25]

Ouch!

We must come to terms with all this. We must come down hard on it . . . the need is *urgent!*

Our Savior modeled the answer perfectly. He didn't just preach it. He cared. He listened. He served. He reached out. He supported. He affirmed and encouraged. He stayed in touch. He walked with people . . . never took the elevator.

The only escape from indifference is to think of people as our most cherished resource. We need to work hard at re-establishing family fun, meaningful mealtimes, people involvement, evenings *without* the television blaring, nonsuperficial conversations, times when we genuinely get involved with folks in need—not *just* pray for them.

Stop the elevator. I want to get off.

<u>Deepening</u> <u>Your</u> <u>Roots</u>

Proverbs 18:1; Mark 2:13 – 17; Luke 14:12 – 23;
Acts 2:43 – 47; 6:1 – 4; Revelation 19:7 – 9

<u>Branching</u> <u>Out</u>

1. Next time you're on an elevator, break the ice and talk to a stranger.
2. Set aside an evening this week when you either invite someone over, or take the initiative and visit someone who you know tends to stay at home and away from people.
3. Decide on something you normally always do "alone" (eat lunch by yourself, grocery shop, take a walk, etc.) and find someone to join you.

෴ ෴ ෴

<u>Growing Strong</u>

I'm either your hero or your enemy today, depending on how you handled this week's three touchy subjects: overweight, resentment, and isolation. For you who made progress this week in one of these areas, tell me what provoked you to change your old patterns or habits: _____

_____

_____

And for you who feel like you regressed, tell me what's keeping you from forging ahead: _____

_____

_____

_____

"THE OPRA AIN'T OVER"

*T*he words were painted in bright red on a banner hung over the wall near the forty-yard line of Texas Stadium, home of the Dallas Cowboys football team, on Sunday afternoon.

The guys in silver and blue were struggling to stay in the race for the playoffs. So a dyed-in-the-wool Cowboy fan decided he would offer some back-home encouragement straight out of his country-western repertoire. He scratched around his garage on Saturday and found some paint, a big brush, and a ruler . . . then splashed those words on a king-sized bed sheet for all America to read:

THE OPRA AIN'T OVER 'TIL THE FAT LADY SINGS.

It was his way of saying, "We're hanging in there. Don't count us out. We have three games left before anybody can say for sure . . . so we're not givin' up! The opra ain't over."

Sure is easy to jump to conclusions, isn't it? People who study trends make it their business to manufacture out of their imaginations the proposed (and "inevitable") end result. Pollsters do that, too. After a sampling of three percent of our country, vast and stunning stats are predicted. Our worry increases. We are all informed that so-and-so will, *for sure,* wind up doing such-and-such. At times it's downright scary. And discouraging.

Every once in a while it's helpful to remember times when those folks wound up with egg on their faces. Much to our amazement, the incredible often happens.

- Like when Wellington whipped Napoleon
- Or Truman beat Dewey
- And Washington won in the Rose Bowl
- Like the time the earthquake didn't hit
- And England *didn't* surrender
- And *Star Wars* didn't grab a fistful of Academy Awards
- And Hitler *wasn't* the anti-Christ
- And the communists *didn't* take over America by 1980

- And Muhammad Ali *could* get beaten
- And a nation *could* continue on through the disillusionments of Vietnam, White House and senatorial scandals, assassination attempts, energy crises, nuclear mishaps, and economic recessions.

Yes, at many a turn we have all been tempted to jump to so-called "obvious" conclusions, only to be surprised by a strange curve thrown our way. God is good at that. When He does, it really encourages His people. Can you recall a few biblical examples?

- A wiry teenager, armed with only a sling and a stone, whipped a giant over nine feet tall. Nobody would've predicted that.
- With an Egyptian army fast approaching and no possible way to escape, all looked bleak. But not so! Against nature and reversing the pull of gravity, a sea opened up and allowed the Hebrews to walk across.
- And how about the vast, "indestructible" wall around Jericho? Who would've imagined?
- Or that dead-end street at Golgotha miraculously opening back up at an empty tomb three days later?
- Or a handful of very human disciples turning the world upside down?

Anybody — and I mean anybody — who would have been near enough to have witnessed any one of those predicaments would certainly have said, "Curtains . . . the opra is over!"

A lot of you who read this page are backed up against a set of circumstances that seem to spell T-H-E E-N-D. All looks almost hopeless. Pretty well finished. Apparently over. Maybe you need to read that again, underlining those words:

seem to . . . almost . . . pretty well . . . apparently.

Your adversary would love for you to assume the worst. He'd enjoy seeing you heave a sigh and resign yourself to depressed feelings that accompany defeat, failure, maximum resentment, and minimum faith. After all, it's fairly obvious you're through. Well . . . since when has "fairly obvious" drawn the curtain on the last act? It's been my experience that when God is involved, *anything* can happen. The One who directed that stone in between Goliath's eyes and split the Red Sea down the middle and leveled that wall around Jericho and brought His Son back from beyond takes a delight in mixing up the odds as He alters the obvious and bypasses the inevitable.

The blind songwriter, Fanny Crosby, put it another way:

Chords that were broken will vibrate once more.

In other words, don't manufacture conclusions. Don't even think in terms of "this is the way things will turn out." Be open. Stay that way. God has a beautiful way of bringing good vibrations out of broken chords. When the Lord is in it, anything is possible. In His performances there are dozens of "fat ladies" waiting to sing the finale.

The opra ain't over.

Deepening Your Roots
James 4:13 – 17; Proverbs 19:21; Matthew 19:26;
Genesis 15:2 – 4, 16:1 – 4, 21:1 – 7

Branching Out

1. What's something you've jumped to conclusions on? _____
   _____

2. Write down how you think your day will turn out: _____
   _____

   At today's end, note what really took place: _____
   _____

3. What's a circumstance you're facing that appears to spell THE END? Pray about it now and ask God to teach you in this situation the principle from today's thought.

PRESUMPTION

There is a very delicate line between faith and presumption. On the surface both appear daring, courageous, and impressive. Underneath, however, one is met with God's approval while the other incites His wrath and prompts His judgment.

Let's think about this word, presumption, for a few moments. Actually, it is a combination of two English terms: *pre* meaning "in front of, before, ahead" and *assume* meaning "to take upon oneself, to take over." Mixing that together we come up with the idea of running ahead and taking over, the act of taking something beforehand. Webster suggests that when one presumes, one "takes upon oneself without leave or warrant," one "goes beyond what is right or proper, overstepping due bounds, taking unwarranted liberties."

Excerpts from the following newspaper article regarding a church service in Newport, Tennessee, illustrates presumption:

TWO PREACHERS DIE IN TEST OF FAITH

Two . . . preachers who had survived the bites of poisonous snakes tested their faith with strychnine and died . . . a few hours after drinking the poison . . .

Cocke County officers said copper-heads and rattlesnakes were handled at the mountain sect's religious service Saturday night.

After the snakes had been handled, Mr. Williams and Mr. Pack drank the strychnine as a further test of their faith.

Both preachers had survived snakebites at previous religious services.

I must confess that upon reading that article, I immediately took issue with the repeated statement that this was a "test of their faith." No, in my opinion, that wasn't faith, it *was* presumption. They took upon themselves certain liberties that were unwarranted . . . they overstepped their proper bounds . . . they therefore incurred God's judgment, not His favor. As the congregation was oohing and ahhing, God's heart was breaking. Their act was a circus-like display of the flesh designed to attract attention. The shadow of the Almighty did not rest upon it. As with Saul, who flaunted his role and presumed upon the priesthood (1 Samuel 13), death finally came and censured the arrogant act. Leprosy fell upon Uzziah for a similar deed according to 2 Chronicles 26:16 – 21 (please read).

Not all presumptuous acts are as notorious as these I have mentioned. Sometimes when we are determined to have our own way — especially when we are restless, tired of waiting, anxious for action — we run ahead and then salve our conscience by calling our decision "faith." I believe that this is what David had in mind when he wrote Psalm 19:12 – 13:

> Who can discern his errors? Acquit me of hidden faults. Also keep back Thy servant from presumptuous sins; Let them not rule over me . . .

Because we are not aware of our "hidden faults," we need divine assistance and acquittal. We are prone to rush on, refusing to be patient and to quietly wait for God's time. This tendency toward "presumptuous sins" is ever with us. David asked that God might keep him back — hold him, restrain him — from presumptuous sins. He added, "Let them not rule over me." That seems to suggest that presumption can dominate a person's life. Once we fall into the habit, we can presume upon God without even realizing we are doing so. We can believe in our hearts that our actions are humble steps of faith when all the while they are as presumptuous as handling snakes and drinking poison, though not nearly so sensational.

Admittedly, it is often difficult to know the difference between faith and presumption. That is all the more reason to pray as David prayed, "Keep back Thy servant . . ." How pleasing it must be to God to hear us genuinely say, "Hold me back . . . I'm willing to wait . . . I want *Your* will most of all, my Father."

Are you waiting for His leading today? Good for you! If the light is red or even yellow, you're wise to let Him hold you back. When it turns green, you'll know it. Don't race your motor while you're waiting. You'll burn up all your fuel . . . and you might slip across that delicate line. God's moving-violation fines are quite expensive. Ask the congregation in Newport, Tennessee.

<u>Deepening</u> <u>Your</u> <u>Roots</u>

Numbers 14:41 – 45; 1 Corinthians 10:9 – 11; 2 Chronicles 26:16 – 21

<u>Branching</u> <u>Out</u>

1. In the habit of rushing ahead of God? Name one area or thing you're not willing to wait on God for: _____

   _____

   Now, be like David and ask God to hold you back and keep you from moving ahead of Him.
2. Force yourself to wait an extra twenty-four hours before making a decision today that you felt must be decided on by this afternoon or evening.
3. Name a matter that you tend to deal with in your own way and time: _____

   _____

   How about letting God in on the situation?

DESIGNER-LABEL PLANET

With the help of a telescope or a microscope we are ushered immediately into a world of incredible, infinite design. Take your choice: planets or paramecia . . . astronomy or biology . . . "the infinite meadows of heaven" (Longfellow) or the diminutive microbes of earth — and sheer, unemotional intelligence will *force* you to mumble to yourself, "Behind all this was more than chance. This design is the result of a designer!" His name? God, the Creator.

To deny that these worlds beyond the lens are the results of God's design is to defy all mathematical calculations of chance. Let me prove that by borrowing the following illustration from a noted scientist and former president of the New York Academy of Sciences, Dr. A. Cressy Morrison. Suppose I would take ten pennies and mark them from 1 to 10 and give them to you to put into your pocket. I'd ask you to give them a good shake, then I'd say, "I'm going to reach into your pocket and draw out penny number 1." My chance of doing this would be 1 in 10 . . . and you would be surprised if I accomplished it. Now, let's go further. I would put number 1 back into your pocket, have you shake them again, and I'd say, "I will now draw out number 2." My chances are much slimmer — 1 in 100. If I were to draw out number 3 in the same way, the chance would be 1 in 1000. If I draw out each number in order, following the identical process, the ultimate chance factor would reach the unbelievable figure of 1 chance in 10 billion!

If I performed that act before your eyes you would probably say, "The game is fixed." That's exactly what I am saying about the galaxies and the germs — and, more important, your life and mine on this earth. The arrangement *is* fixed . . . there is a Designer — God — and He is not silent. As a matter of fact, He declares His presence twenty-four hours a day. How? Listen to Psalm 19:1 – 4 (TLB):

> The heavens are telling the glory of God; they are a marvelous display of His craftsmanship. Day and night they keep on telling about God. Without a sound or word, silent in the skies,

their message reaches out to all the world. The sun lives in the heavens where God placed it. . . .

Let's think about that. Let's remind ourselves of a few fundamental, proven facts of science we learned in high school. It is amazing how they dovetail with Psalm 19.

1. Temperature. The sun is 12,000 degrees Fahrenheit. All of earth's heat is from the sun. We are 93 million miles away — just the right distance, I might add. If the earth's temperature were an *average* of 50 degrees hotter or colder, all life on this planet would cease to exist. Why is the sun 12,000 degrees hot? Why not 1200 degrees . . . or 120,000 . . . or 24,000? Why was the earth fixed at *exactly* the right distance away so that we could have a pleasant 70 degrees temperature this morning? Why not twice as far, twice as close . . . or 1000 times as far? Answer: because all life would perish. Was this delicately chosen to meet the requirements of the living cell . . . or by chance?

2. Rotation. This planet rotates 365 times each year as it passes around the sun. Suppose it rotated 36 times instead? Well, our days and nights would be ten times as long — we'd be terribly hot on one side and unbearably cold on the other . . . and life would begin to disappear. By chance?

3. Air. Let's limit our thoughts to one element of air — oxygen. This ingredient constitutes about 21 percent of our atmosphere. Why 21 percent? Why not 4 percent or 10 percent . . . or, for that matter, *50 percent?* Well, if 50 percent, the first time someone lit a match we'd *all* be on fire. Is 21 percent by chance?

What's my point? This planet was designed by God so that it would support one thing: life. Without life, earth would be another planetary wasteland. It would be like a wedding without a bride . . . a car without gears and wheels. Why life? Because only through life can matter understand God and glorify its Maker! Only through faith in the Lord Jesus Christ can the designed know and glorify the Designer.

Deepening Your Roots
Psalm 33:6 – 22; 65; 104

Branching Out
1. Look in the newspaper or a magazine and find some other scientific data which could also illustrate today's thought.

2. Watch an educational TV program today that teaches you something new about science.

∾ ∾ ∾

Growing Strong

How's your world? Feeling insignificant? Lost among the masses? Forgotten? I feel that way, too, some days. It happens every time I look at life from my vantage point, rather than God's. How's your perspective today? Are you leaning on God and asking Him to give you His outlook? Tell me about it. _____

_____

_____

_____

GROWING OLD

Growing old, like taxes, is a fact we all must face. Now, you're not going to get me to declare when growing *up* stops and growing *old* starts — not on your life! But there are some signs we can read along life's journey that suggest we are entering the transition (how's that for diplomacy?).

Physically, the aging "bod" puts on the brakes. You begin to huff and puff when you used to rip and zip. You prefer to sit more than stand . . . to watch more than do . . . to forget your birthday rather than remember it! *Mentally,* the aging brain longs for relief. You can't remember like you used to, and you don't respond like you ought to. You start thinking more about yesterday and tomorrow and less about today. *Emotionally,* you undergo strange fears and feelings you once swore would "never occur in me," such as:

- Being negative, critical, and downright ornery at times.
- Being reluctant to let those who are younger carry more responsibility.
- Feeling unwanted and "in the way."
- Preoccupied with "what if" rather frequently.
- Feeling guilty over previous mistakes and wrong decisions.
- Feeling forgotten, unloved, lonely, and passed by.
- Threatened by sounds, speed, financial uncertainty, and disease.
- Resisting the need to adjust and adapt.

All this — and there is much more — is worsened by the memory of those days when you once were so very efficient, capable, needed, and fulfilled. As you look into the mirror, you're forced to admit that the fingers of age have begun to scratch their marks upon your house of clay . . . and it's hard to believe your twilight years could be of any worth.

How wrong! How terribly wrong! How destructive such thoughts can be! How quickly such thinking can sentence you to the prison cell of self-pity, surrounded by the four bleak walls of doubt, depression, uselessness, and grief.

God's patriarchs have always been among His choicest possessions. Abraham was far more effective once he grew old and mellow. Moses wasn't used with any measure of success until he turned eighty. Caleb was eighty-five when he began to enjoy God's best goals. Samuel was old, old when the God of Israel led him to establish the "school of the prophets," an institution that had a lasting influence for spirituality and godliness in the centuries to come. And who could deny the way God used Paul during his last days on his knees, writing words of encouragement in letters we cherish today!

No one fails to see that growing old has its difficulties and heartaches. It does, indeed. But to see only the hot sands of your desert experience and miss the lovely oases here and there (though they may be few) is to turn the latter part of your journey through life into an arid, tasteless endurance which makes everyone miserable.

Please don't forget — God has decided to let you live this long. Your old age is not a mistake . . . nor an oversight . . . nor an afterthought. Isn't it about time you cooled your tongue and softened your smile with a refreshing drink from the water of God's oasis? You've been thirsty a long, long time.

Deepening Your Roots
Proverbs 16:31; Psalm 92:14; Isaiah 46:4; Titus 2:2 – 3

Branching Out

1. Spend time with an elderly person and find out some of his fondest memories, and in what ways God has used him, or he hopes God will use him.
2. Begin praying about your future, that you will be a faithful and valuable vessel.
3. Ask this question of three elderly people whom you consider to be godly: What would you do over or do differently to develop a closer relationship with God? Heed their words.

REALITY

I arrived at my office unusually early this morning. Things were quiet, the sky was heavy and overcast, a normal California fall morning. My mind was on my schedule as I fumbled with the keys. In standard Swindoll fashion I pushed the door wide open in a hurry — only to be stopped dead in my tracks. A chill went up my back as I peered into the spooky study. The light switch is across the room, so I stood there at the door staring at the most startling reminder of reality imaginable! In the middle of the floor, sitting on rollers, was a *casket* . . . with a wilted spray of flowers on top alongside a picture of ME! Now, my friend, if you want to know how to awaken someone from early morning slumber, *this routine will surely do it!* I suppose I stood there five minutes without moving a muscle as I blinked and gathered my senses. I checked my watch and was pleased to see the second hand still moving. All my reflexes responded correctly and my breath still brought a patch of fog to the mirror. "Praise God," I thought, "I'm still here."

But the fact is, I won't always be. That's reality. The practical joker taught me an unforgettable lesson. Some future day, some quiet, heavily overcast morning, the sun will rise again on this earth, but that day I will be gone . . . absent from this body. Dust will settle on these books I love . . . another will have the keys I now carry . . . and answer this phone . . . and fill this room with his voice and laughter and tears. That's reality. Painful and difficult as it may be to tolerate such thoughts — that's fact, that's real!

It was in 1935 that Thomas Stearns Eliot wrote:

Human kind cannot bear very much reality.

Thirty years later the old British poet and his loved ones were forced to bear it. He stopped writing . . . and breathing.

Reality, though difficult, is dependable. It always keeps its word, though its word may be hard to bear.

I would much prefer to live my life on the sharp, cutting edge of reality than dreaming on the soft, phony mattress of fantasy. Reality is the tempered poker that keeps the fires alive . . . it's the spark that prompts the engine to keep running . . . the hard set of facts that refuses to let feeling overrule logic. It's reality that forces every Alice out of her Wonderland and into God's wonderful plan. Its undaunted determination has pulled many a wanderer, lost in the maze of meanderings, back to the real world of right and wrong, the false and the true. Reality, I remind you, is the world from which most every emotionally — and mentally — disturbed patient has escaped — and the point to which they must return before health is restored. Hard as it may be to bear, it brings a practical security second to none. It is, unquestionably, the healthiest place on earth.

It was Jesus' realistic view of the Pharisees that exposed the sackcloth of hypocrisy beneath their religious robes (Matthew 23). It was His realistic attitude toward the devil that resulted in Satan's departing from Him (Matthew 4:1 – 11). It was reality that enabled Him to perform spiritual heart surgery on the woman at the well (John 4) . . . and to stand uncondemningly beside the adulteress (John 8) . . . and to pray as He did the night of His arrest (John 17). Reality, in fact, was part of His motive in bearing the cross for you and me.

While our entire world is sinking in the quagmire of human opinions, theories, philosophies, and dreams, our Lord invites us to stand firmly on the rock of reality. And what does the realistic mind-set include? Well, these are eternally etched in the granite of God's Book. They include such things as:

- Man is a depraved sinner, terribly in need.
- Our only hope is in Jesus Christ — His death and resurrection.
- Receiving Him brings instant forgiveness and eternal grace.
- Death is certain but not the end.
- Heaven is a real place.
- So is hell.
- We cannot escape standing before Him.
- The time to prepare is NOW.

Some quiet, heavily overcast morning you and I will be *forced* to face reality. The second hand on our inner watch will suddenly stop. Time will be no more. At that moment — even before your casket is ordered — your passport will be clutched in your hand. What will it read? "REDEEMED" or "CONDEMNED"? Face it, man — that's reality! And *that day* it won't be a joke. That day you won't be reading this — you'll be experiencing *that.*

Deepening Your Roots

Job 19:25 – 27; 1 Corinthians 15:1 – 58; Colossians 2:17

Branching Out

1. Write down on a 3×5 card the list from today's article (things included in the granite of God's Book — Man is a depraved sinner . . ., Our only hope . . ., etc.). Put this card by your phone to read often this week and to remind you of the reality of God's words.
2. Play detective this week as you're viewing the tube: watch for one very realistic commercial, and one that's totally *un*realistic.

LIFELINES

I'm writing these words on my forty-second birthday.

No big deal . . . just another stabbing realization that I'm not getting any younger. I know that because the cake won't hold all the candles. Even if it could the frosting would melt before I'd be able to blow all of them out. My kind and thoughtful secretary reminded me of another approach I could take. She gave me a birthday card showing an old guy standing beside a cake *covered* with candles. On the front it reads:

Don't feel you're getting old if you can't blow out all the candles . . .

And inside:

. . . just BEAT 'em out with your cane.

Children are about as encouraging. In all seriousness my youngest asked me recently if they had *catsup* when I was a boy. I tried not to look offended — he could have asked if they had the wheel. But I was pleased to inform him that we not only had catsup . . . but also electricity, talking movies, the radio, cars, and indoor plumbing. He seemed amazed as he gave me that you-gotta-be-kidding look, then turned and walked away. I suddenly felt the need to lie down and take a nap.

But birthdays are milestones . . . significant points in the passing of time . . . specific yet mute reminders that more sand has passed through the hour glass. They do, however, give us a handle on the measurement of time which, when you boil it down into minutes, really moves along at a pretty good clip. There are 60 of them every hour . . . 1,440 every day . . . over 10 thousand of them each week . . . about 525 thousand per year. As of today — I've experienced over 22 million of them. Talk about feeling old!

But they pass so quietly, so consistently, they fool you. That's part of the reason C. S. Lewis used to say:

The safest road to hell is the gradual one — the gentle slope, soft underfoot, without sudden turnings, without milestones, without signposts. The long, dull, monotonous years of middle-aged prosperity or adversity are excellent campaigning weather for the devil.

We mark our calendars with *deadlines* — dates that set limits for the completion of objectives and projects. To ignore those deadlines brings consequences. To live without deadlines is to live an inefficient, unorganized life, drifting with the breeze of impulse on the fickle wave of moods. We set deadlines because they help us accomplish the essentials . . . they discipline our use of time . . . they measure the length of our leash on the clothesline of demands.

God, however, brings about birthdays . . . not as deadlines but *lifelines.* He builds them into our calendar once every year to enable us to make an annual appraisal, not only of our length of life but our depth. Not simply to tell us we're growing older . . . but to help us determine if we are also growing deeper. These lifelines are not like that insurance policy you invested in last year. There's no automatic promise of annual renewal. Obviously, if God has given you another year to live for Him, He has some things in mind . . . He has some very special plans to pull off through your life. Surely it includes more than existing 1,440 minutes a day!

The psalmist gives us the perfect prayer to pray every year our lifeline rolls around.

> So teach us to number our days, that we may present to Thee
> a heart of wisdom (Psalm 90:12).

Now let me caution you. Don't expect wisdom to come into your life like great chunks of rock on a conveyor belt. It isn't like that. It's not splashy and bold . . . nor is it dispensed like a prescription across a counter. Wisdom comes privately from God as a by-product of right decisions, godly reactions, and the application of scriptural principles to daily circumstances. Wisdom comes, for example, not from seeking after a ministry . . . but more from anticipating the fruit of a disciplined life.

Not from trying to do great things for God . . . but more from being faithful to the small, obscure tasks few people ever see.

Stop and reflect. Are you just growing *old* . . . or are you also growing *up?* As you "number your days" do you count just years — the grinding measurement of minutes — or can you find marks of wisdom . . . character traits that were not there when you were younger?

Take a look. You really don't have a lot longer, you know. As a matter of fact, one of these years your lifeline will be God's deadline.

Deepening Your Roots

Proverbs 4:1 – 19; Job 12:10 – 13; Proverbs 16:31

Branching Out

1. List ten ways you've grown deeper in the last decade.

    1. _____

    2. _____

    3. _____

    4. _____

    5. _____

    6. _____

    7. _____

    8. _____

    9. _____

   10. _____

2. Identify three areas of your life that you'd like to see changed in the coming decade: _____

_____

Choose the most important to you. Decide on three things you could do to make your wish come true: _____

_____

Begin doing one of those today.

                          ❧ ❧ ❧

Growing Strong

You enjoyed your week, didn't you? I'll bet that's due to your conversations with some older people who probably gave you a laugh or two and several thoughts to ponder. I'd like to hear about your time. Quote me something from one of your dialogues with one of these mature saints:

_____

_____

_____

_____

ADVERSITY AND PROSPERITY

There are two extreme tests that disturb our balance in life. Each has its own set of problems. On one side is *adversity*. Solomon realized this when he wrote:

> If you faint in the day of adversity, your strength is small (Proverbs 24:10, RSV).

The *Good News Bible* paraphrases that verse:

> If you are weak in a crisis, you are weak indeed.

Adversity is a good test of our resiliency, our ability to cope, to stand back up, to recover from misfortune. Adversity is a painful pedagogue.

On the other side is *prosperity*. In all honesty, it's a tougher test than adversity. The Scottish essayist and historian, Thomas Carlyle, agreed when he said:

> Adversity is sometimes hard upon a man; but for one man who can stand prosperity, there are a hundred that will stand adversity.[26]

Precious few are those who can live in the lap of luxury . . . who can keep their moral, spiritual, and financial equilibrium . . . while balancing on the elevated tightrope of success. It's ironic that most of us can handle a sudden demotion much better than a sizable promotion.

Why?

Well, it really isn't too difficult to explain. When adversity strikes, life becomes rather simple. Our need is to survive. But when prosperity occurs, life gets complicated. And our needs are numerous, often extremely complex. Invariably, our integrity is put to the test. And there is about one in a hundred who can dance to the tune of success without paying the piper named Compromise.

Now, before we get too carried away, let's understand that being successful isn't necessarily wrong. Being promoted, being elevated to a place of prominence can come from God Himself.

> For not from the east, nor from the west,
> nor from the desert comes exaltation;

But God is the judge;
He puts down one, and exalts another (Psalm 75:6–7).

Asaph, the guy who wrote those words, was correct. It is the Lord's sovereign right to demote as well as to promote . . . and we seldom know why He chooses whom. Any biblical proof that some have been snatched from obscurity and exalted to prosperity without losing their integrity? Any examples of prosperous people who kept their balance while walking on the wire? Sure, several of them.

- Daniel was lifted from a lowly peon in a boot camp at Babylon to a national commander in charge of one-third of the kingdom (Daniel 6:1–2).
- Amos was promoted from a fig-picker in Tekoa, nothing more than an ancient sharecropper, to the prophet of God at Bethel, the royal residence of the king (Amos 7:14–15).
- Job was a rancher in Uz when God prospered him and granted him financial independence (Job 1:1–5).
- And not one of the three lost his integrity in the process.

But the classic example is David, according to the last three verses of Psalm 78:

He also chose David His servant, and took him from the sheepfolds; from the care of the ewes with suckling lambs He brought him, to shepherd Jacob His people, and Israel His inheritance. So he shepherded them according to the integrity of his heart, and guided them with his skillful hands.

As Jehovah scanned the Judean landscape in search of Saul's successor, He found a youth in his mid-teens who possessed a unique combination:

the humility of a servant, the heart of a shepherd, the hands of skill.

And by his thirtieth birthday, Jesse's youngest held the premier office in his nation. King. At his fingertips was a vast treasury, unlimited privileges, and enormous power.

And how did he handle such prosperity? Read that final verse again. He shepherded the nation "according to integrity." He was Carlyle's "one in a hundred."

Are *you?*

If so, when you give your word, you do it. Exactly as you said you would. Because integrity means you are verbally trustworthy. Furthermore, when the bills come due, you pay them. Because integrity means you are financially dependable. Also, when you're tempted to mess around with an illicit sexual affair, you resist. Because integrity means you are morally pure. You don't fudge because you're able to cover your tracks. Neither do you fake it because you're now a big shot. Being successful doesn't give anybody the right to call wrong right. Or the OK to say something's OK if it isn't OK.

Adversity or prosperity, both are tough tests on our balance. To stay balanced through adversity, resiliency is required. But to stay balanced through prosperity—ah, that demands *integrity.* The swift wind of compromise is a lot more devastating than the sudden jolt of misfortune.

That's why walking on a wire is harder than standing up in a storm. Height has a strange way of disturbing our balance.

Deepening Your Roots
Micah 6:8; Daniel 1:1 – 21; Proverbs 22:1

Branching Out

1. Quick — jot down the names of six people whom you deem successful: ___

   _____
   _____
   _____
   _____

   Put a word by each name that describes how that person handles his success. After you've done that, note your impressions or perhaps a lesson you can learn from your own evaluation. _____

2. Rate your success quotient_____—what's more important:
   • your level of success or your walk with God?
   • your staying successful or your keeping happy?
   • your retaining a position or your respect?
   Dialogue with a friend on how you answered these questions.

3. Ask someone if he thinks you're successful. Note his response and your reaction to his comments.

UNAMBITIOUS LEADERSHIP

*L*et's take a look at the important balance between natural and spiritual leadership. A leader, obviously, must have some God-given natural qualities that cause others to respond to his or her *influence.* At the same time, the *Christian* leader must possess a marked degree of Spirit-directed, humble devotion to the Lord Jesus Christ . . . lest he fall into the category of a self-appointed, ambitious creature who simply loves the spotlight. It is upon this point I want to camp for a few minutes.

Dr. A. W. Tozer wrote:

> A true and safe leader is likely to be one who has no desire to lead, but is forced into a position of leadership by the inward pressure of the Holy Spirit and the press of the external situation. Such were Moses and David and the Old Testament prophets. I think there was hardly a great leader from Paul to the present day but was drafted by the Holy Spirit for the task, and commissioned by the Lord of the Church to fill a position he had little heart for. I believe it might be accepted as a fairly reliable rule of thumb that the man who is ambitious to lead is disqualified as a leader.

Spiritual leaders, you see, are not made by majority vote or ecclesiastical decisions, by conferences or synods. Only God can make them!

> For not from the east, nor from the west,
> nor from the desert comes exaltation;
> But God is the judge;
> He puts down one, and exalts another (Psalm 75: 7).

This means, then, that God makes it *His* responsibility to prepare, nurture, train, and promote certain people to places of leadership. That's *His* business, not ours. Listen to Jeremiah 45:5:

> But you, are you seeking great things for yourself? Do not seek them. . . .

May those words never be forgotten. We live in a do-it-yourself era. We are programmed to think in terms of promotion, advertisement, public image, and appeal. Such things commercialize the ministry and smack of side-show tactics . . . or, to use Paul's words:

> . . . walking in craftiness . . . adulterating the Word of God . . . preaching ourselves . . .

Do I address one who is gifted, capable, qualified to lead, but God has not yet promoted you? Let me warn you of the danger of *selfish ambition.* Quietly and in subtle ways you can manipulate others to notice you, to be impressed with you. The cheap narcotic of ambition can deaden the pain of your inner conscience . . . but you can ride the crest of your self-made fame just so long. In the end, alas, it stings like a serpent.

Solomon's words fit well:

> For the ways of a man are before the eyes of the LORD, And He watches all his paths. His own iniquities will capture the wicked, And he will be held with the cords of his sin (Proverbs 5:21–22).

Let me end on a positive note. God knows what He's about. If He has you sidelined, out of the action for awhile, He knows what He's doing. You just stay faithful . . . stay flexible . . . stay available . . . stay humble, like David with his sheep (even *after* he had been anointed king!). Learn your lessons well in the schoolroom of obscurity. God is preparing you as His chosen arrow. As yet your shaft is hidden in His quiver, in the shadows . . . but at the precise moment at which it will tell with the greatest effect, He will reach for you and launch you to that place of His appointment.

Deepening Your Roots
Joshua 1:1 – 5; Proverbs 25:6 – 7; Luke 14:1 – 11

Branching Out

1. Are you in a leadership position? Did you get there by your own efforts or do you sense God's intervention and appointing you to such a role? (Be honest!) I challenge you each morning to get down on your knees and seek God's power to keep you a loving, humble, and effective leader (or parent) — for *His* glory, not yours.
2. Seeking a promotion or working on climbing the ladder to success? Why not let God decide when and how you should be exalted. *Quietly* trust Him with your job or career.
3. Not sure what you should be doing with your life? Do what David did: Stay put, work hard, take time for God, and leave your future with Him.

ℙHARISAISM

Jesus opened a five-gallon can of worms the day He preached His sermon on the mount. There wasn't a Pharisee within gunshot range who wouldn't have given his last denarius to see Him strung up by sundown. Did they hate Him! They hated Him because He refused to let them get away with their phony religious drool and their super-spiritual ooze that was polluting the public.

The Messiah unsheathed His sharp sword of truth the day He ascended the mountain. When He came down that evening, it was dripping with the blood of hypocrites. If ever an individual exposed pride, Jesus did that day. His words bit into their hides like harpoons into whale blubber. Never in their notorious, smug careers had they been pierced with such deadly accuracy. Like bloated beasts of the deep they floated to the surface for all to see.

If there was one thing Jesus despised, it was the very thing every Pharisee majored in at seminary: showing off, or, to cushion it a bit, self-righteousness. They were the Holy Joes of Palestine, the first to enlist undiscerning recruits into the Royal Order of Back-Stabbers. They were past-masters in the practice of put-down prayers, and spent their days working on ways to impress others with their somber expression and monotonous, dismal drone. Worst of all, by sowing the seeds of legalistic thorns and nurturing them into forbidding vines of religious intolerance, the Pharisees prevented honest seekers from approaching their God.

Even today, the bite of legalism spreads a paralyzing venom into the Body of Christ. Its poison blinds our eyes, dulls our edge, and arouses pride in our hearts. Soon our love is eclipsed as it turns into a mental clipboard with a long checklist, a thick filter requiring others to measure up before we move in. The joy of friendship is fractured by a judgmental attitude and a critical look. It seems stupid to me that fellowship must be limited to the narrow ranks of predictable personalities clad in "acceptable" attire. The short haircut, clean-shaven, tailored suit look (with matching vest and tie, of course) seem essential in many circles. Just because I prefer a certain style or attire doesn't mean that it's best or that it's for everyone. Nor does it mean that the opposite is any *less* pleasing to God.

Our problem is a gross intolerance of those who don't fit *our* mold — an attitude which reveals itself in the stoic stare or a caustic comment. Such legalistic and prejudiced reactions will thin the ranks of the local church faster than fire in the basement or flu in the pew. If you question that, take a serious look at the Galatians letter. Paul's pen flowed with heated ink as he rebuked them for "deserting" Christ (1:6), "nullifying the grace of God" (2:21), becoming "bewitched" by legalism (3:1), and desiring "to be enslaved" by this crippling disease (4:9).

Sure . . . there are limits to our freedom. Grace *does not* condone license. Love has its biblical restrictions. The opposite of legalism is not "do as you please." But listen! The limitations are far broader than most of us realize. I can't believe, for example, that the only music God smiles on is highbrow or hymns. Why not country-folk or Dixieland as well? Nor do I believe the necessary garment for entering the Veil is a suit and tie. Why won't cutoffs or jeans and Hang Ten tee-shirts do just as well? Shocked? Let's remember who it is that becomes wrought-up over outward appearances. Certainly not God!

> . . . God sees not as man sees, for man looks at the outward appearance, but the LORD looks at the heart (1 Samuel 16:7b).

And who can prove that the only voice God will bless is the ordained minister on Sunday? How about the salesman Tuesday afternoon or the high school teacher Friday morning?

It is helpful to remember that our Lord reserved His strongest and longest sermon not for struggling sinners, discouraged disciples, or even prosperous people, but for hypocrites, glory hogs, legalists—the present-day Pharisees.

The message on the mountain delivered that afternoon centuries ago echoes down the canyons of time with pristine force and clarity.

Listen to Matthew 6:1:

> Beware of practicing your righteousness before men to be noticed by them . . .

In other words, stop showing off! Stop looking down your nose at others who don't fill your preconceived mold. Stop displaying your own goodness. Stop calling attention to your righteousness. Stop lusting to be noticed. Implied in this is the warning to beware of those who refuse to stop such behavior. And then, to blaze that warning into their memories, He went on to give three specific examples of how people show off their own righteousness so that others might ooh and aah over them.

Matthew 6:2 talks about "when you give alms" or when you are involved in acts of charity assisting others in need. He says don't "sound a trumpet" when you do this. Keep it quiet . . . even a secret (6:4). Don't scream for attention like Tarzan swinging through the jungle. Stay out of the picture, remain anonymous. Don't expect to have your name plastered all over the place. Pharisees *love* to show off their gifts to others. They *love* to be made over. They *love* to remind others who did this and that, or gave such and such to so and so. Jesus says: Don't show off when you use your money to help somebody out.

Matthew 6:5 talks about what to do "when you pray." He warns us against being supplicational showoffs who love to stand in prominent places and mouth meaningless mush in order to be seen and heard. Pharisees love syrupy words and sugar-crusted platitudes. They've got the technique for sounding high-and-holy down pat. Everything they say in their prayers causes listeners to think that this pious soul resides in heaven and was tutored at the feet of Michael the archangel and King James V. You're confident that they haven't had a dirty thought in the past eighteen years . . . but you're also quietly aware that there's a huge chasm between what is coming out of the showoff's mouth and where your head is right then. Jesus says: Don't show off when you talk with your Father.

Matthew 6:16 talks about what to do "when you fast." Now that's the time the showoff really hits his stride. He works overtime trying to appear humble and sad, hoping to look hungry and exhausted like some freak who just finished crossing the Sahara that afternoon. "Do not be as the hypocrites!" Christ commands. Instead, we ought to look and sound fresh, clean, and completely natural. Why? Because that's *real* — that's *genuine* — that's what He promises He will *reward*. Jesus says: Don't show off when you miss a couple or three meals.

Let's face it. Jesus spoke with jabbing, harsh words concerning the Pharisees. When it came to narrow legalism or self-righteous showing off, our Lord pulled no punches. He found it to be the only way to deal with those people who hung around the place of worship disdaining and despising other people. No less than seven times He pronounced "Woe to you" — because that's the only language a Pharisee understands, unfortunately.

Two final comments:

First . . . if you tend toward Pharisaism in any form, *stop it!* If you are the type of person who tries to bully others and look down at others (all the while thinking how impressed God must be to have you on His team) you are a twentieth-century Pharisee. And frankly, that includes some who wear longer hair and prefer a guitar to a pipe organ. Pharisees can also delight in looking "cool."

Second . . . if a modern-day Pharisee tries to control your life, *stop him! Stop her!* Remind the religious phony that the splinter within your eye is between you and your Lord, and to pay attention to the tree trunk in his own eye. Chances are, however, that once an individual is infected, he will go right on nit-picking and self-praising for the rest of his shallow life, choked by the thorns of his own conceit. Pharisees, remember, are terribly hard of listening.

Deepening Your Roots
Proverbs 30:12; Matthew 7:1–5, 23:1–26

Branching Out

1. Pray with a child and speak his language. Learn from the child the wonder he has of life and the freedom and honesty with his words and thoughts. Try talking to God in that same way.
2. Go without a meal someday soon and use your lunch or dinner time to talk to and enjoy God. Don't tell anyone what you plan to do, or what you did.

෴ ෴ ෴

Growing Strong

Let's take a break today and do some reflecting. After all, this is autumn! OK, think back to your childhood and to a moment in time when you were very happy. Note your memory here: _____

_____

_____

Now, do one of the following: go create that same or similar memory for another child, or get a friend and go create another happy moment to reflect upon in years to come. Put away your leadership objectives for the day and be a kid again!

FEAR

We were rapidly descending through a night of thick fog at 200 miles per hour, but the seasoned pilot of the twin-engine Aero Commander was loving every dip, roll, and lurch. At one point he looked over at me, smiled, and exclaimed, "Hey, Chuck, isn't this great?" I didn't answer. As the lonely plane knifed through the overcast pre-dawn sky, I was reviewing every Bible verse I'd ever known and re-confessing every wrong I'd ever done. It was like hurtling 200 miles an hour down the Santa Ana Freeway with a white bedsheet wrapped across the windshield and your radio turned up just beneath the threshold of audible pain.

I couldn't believe my companion-in-flight. He was whistling and humming like it was all a bike ride through the park. His passenger, however, had ten fingernails imbedded in the cushion. I stared longingly for something — *anything* — through the blanket of white surrounding us. Our flight record may have indicated two passengers on that eerie Monday morning, but I can vouch for at least three. An unyielding creature called Fear and I shared the same seat.

Drifting in through cracks in the floorboards or filtering down like a chilling mist, the fog called Fear whispers omens of the unknown and the unseen. Surrounding individuals with its blinding, billowy robe, the creature hisses, "What if . . . what if?" One blast of its awful breath transforms saints into atheists, reversing a person's entire mind-set. Its bite releases a paralyzing venom in its victim, and it isn't long before doubt begins to dull the vision. To one who falls prey to this attack, the creature displays no mercy. As we fall, it steps on our face with the weight of a Sherman tank . . . and laughs at our crippled condition as it prepares for another assault.

Fear. Ever met this beast? Sure you have. It creeps into your cockpit by a dozen different doors. Fear of failure. Fear of crowds. Fear of disease. Fear of rejection. Fear of unemployment. Fear of what others are saying about you. Fear of moving away. Fear of height or depth or distance or death. Fear of being yourself. Fear of buying. Fear of selling. Fear of financial reversal. Fear of war. Fear of the dark. Fear of being alone.

Lurking in the shadows around every imaginable corner, it threatens to poison your inner peace and outward poise. Bully that it is, the creature relies on scare tactics and surprise attacks. It watches for your vulnerable moment, then picks the lock that safeguards your security. Once inside, it strikes quickly to transform spiritual muscle into mental mush. The prognosis for recovery is neither bright nor cheery.

David's twenty-seventh psalm, however, is known to contain an unusually effective antitoxin. With broad, bold strokes, the monarch of Israel pens a prescription guaranteed to infuse iron into our bones. He meets Fear face-to-face at the door of his dwelling with two questions:

Whom shall I dread?
Whom shall I fear?

He slams the door in Fear's face with the declaration:

My heart will not fear . . . in spite of this I shall be confident (v. 3).

He then whistles and hums to himself as he walks back into the family room, kitchen, office, or bedroom, reminding himself of the daily dosage required to counteract Fear's repeated attacks:

PRAYER: I have asked from the Lord (v. 4).
VISION: I behold the beauty of the Lord (v. 4).
GOD'S WORD: I meditate in His temple (v. 4).
GOD'S PROTECTION: In the day of trouble He will conceal me/ hide me/lift me (v. 5).
MOMENT-BY-MOMENT WORSHIP: I will sing (v. 6).
REST: I had believed . . . wait for the Lord (vv. 13 – 14).
DETERMINATION: Let your heart take courage (v. 14).

Oh, how I needed this prescription in that dark cockpit as we dropped thousands of feet through the fog. Could it be that a cold overcast obscures your horizons right now? Tell you what — let's share the same seat and relax for a change. God's never missed the runway through all the centuries of fearful fog. But you might fasten your seat belt, friend. It could get a little rough before we land.

Deepening Your Roots
Psalm 27; 2 Timothy 1:7; Isaiah 51:12 – 16

Branching Out

1. State three fears you have: _____
   _____
   _____

   Choose one and read some other material that could help reduce some of that fear. And slam the door in Fear's face by claiming God's protection as David did.

2. Take another of your fears from the above list: _____
   Decide what would be the worst that could happen if the fear were real: ___
   _____

   How is God bigger than the fear? _____
   _____

COURAGE

Miss Hurricane Carla was a flirt.

She winked at Galveston, whistled at Palacios, waved at Corpus Christi, waltzed with Port Lavaca, and walked away with Rockport, Aransas Pass, and half of Matagorda Island. Her previous escort warned us that she was a wicked woman . . . but few fishermen believed those rumors that blew in from the fickle waters of the gulf. Not only was she wicked, she was expensive and *mean.* That mid-September date many years ago cost us 400 million dollars . . . and forty lives.

One of my closest friends lived through that ordeal. He spent two terrible days and sleepless nights in his attic, surrounded by rattlesnakes, water moccasins, and other sassy visitors who had been flushed out of their habitat. Does he have the stories to tell! I would compare his courage—and the courage of hundreds like him who endured the dangers of Carla's rage—to anyone who has courted one of death's sisters and lived to describe the romance.

COURAGE. It has several names: bravery, valor, fearlessness, audacity, chivalry, heroism, confidence, nerve . . . and a few *nicknames:* guts, grit, gristle, backbone, pluck, spunk.

But whatever the name, it's never met its match. The heights of the Himalayas only encourage it. The depths of the Caribbean merely excite it. The sounds of war stimulate it. The difficulty of a job motivates it. The demands of competition inspire it. Criticism challenges it . . . adventure arouses it . . . danger incites it . . . threats quicken it.

COURAGE. That's another word for inner strength, presence of mind against odds, determination to hang in there, to venture, persevere, withstand hardship. It's got *keeping* power. It's what kept the pioneers rolling forward in those covered wagons in spite of the elements and mountains and flaming arrows. It's what makes the amputee reject pity and continue to take life by the throat. It's what forces every married couple having trouble *never* to say, "Let's terminate." It's what encourages the divorcée to face tomorrow. It's what keeps the young mother with the kids in spite of a personal energy crisis. It's what keeps a nation free in spite of attacks. As Thomas Jefferson wrote in his letter to William Stevens Smith:

> The tree of liberty must be refreshed from time to time with the blood of patriots and tyrants. It is its natural manure.

COURAGE. David had it when he grabbed his sling in the Valley of Elah. Daniel demonstrated it when he refused to worship Nebuchadnezzar's statue in Babylon. Elijah evidenced it when he faced the prophets of Baal on Carmel. Job showed it when he was covered with boils and surrounded by misunderstanding. Moses used it when he stood against Pharaoh and refused to be intimidated. The fact is, *it's impossible to live victoriously for Christ without courage.* That's why God's thrice-spoken command to Joshua is as timeless as it is true:

Be strong and courageous! (Joshua 1:6,7,9).

Are you? Honestly now—are you? Or are you quick to quit . . . ready to run when the heat rises?

Let it be remembered that real courage is not limited to the battlefield or the Indianapolis 500 or bravely catching a thief in your house. The *real* tests of courage are much broader . . . much deeper . . . much quieter. They are the *inner* tests, like remaining faithful when nobody's looking . . . like enduring pain when the room is empty . . . like standing alone when you're misunderstood.

You will never be asked to share your attic with a rattler. But every day, in some way, your courage will be tested. Your tests may not be as exciting as a beachhead landing or sailing around Cape Horn or a space walk. It may be as simple as saying no, as uneventful as facing a pile of dirty laundry, or as unknown as a struggle within yourself between right and wrong. God's medal-of-honor winners are made in secret because their most courageous acts occur down deep inside . . . away from the hurricane of public opinion . . . up in the attic, hidden from public knowledge.

Deepening Your Roots
Daniel 3; Hebrews 13:6; Proverbs 29:25

Branching Out

1. We've all been brave at some point in time — whether we were recognized for it or not. What's a courageous act you've done? _____

2. What's something you can be courageous about today? _____

SONGLESS SAINTS

I was on a scriptural safari. Prowling through the Ephesian letter, I was tracking an elusive, totally unrelated verse when God's sharp sword flashed, suddenly slicing me to the core.

> . . . speaking to one another in psalms and hymns and spiritual songs, singing and making melody with your heart to the Lord (Ephesians 5:19).

Everyone knows Ephesians 5:18, where we are told to "be filled with the Spirit" . . . but have you ever noticed that verse 18 ends with a comma, not a period? The next verse describes the very first result of being under the Spirit's control . . . *we sing!* We make melody with our hearts. We communicate His presence within us by presenting our own, individual concert of sacred music to Him.

Let's take it another step. The church building is not once referred to in Ephesians 5. I mention that because we Christians have so centralized our singing that we seldom engage in it once we drive away from the building with stained glass and an organ. Stop and think. Did you sing on the way *home* from church last Sunday? How about Monday, when you drove to work . . . or around the supper table . . . or Tuesday as you dressed for the day? Chances are, you didn't even sing before or after you spent some time with the Lord *any* day last week.

Why? The Spirit-filled saint is a song-filled saint! Animals can't sing. Neither can pews or pulpits or Bibles or buildings. Only you. And your melody is broadcast right into heaven—live—where God's antenna is always receptive . . . where the soothing strains of your song are always appreciated.

Believe me, if Martin Luther lived today, he'd be heartsick. That rugged warrior of the faith had two basic objectives when he fired the reformation cannon into the sixteenth-century wall of spiritual ignorance. First, he wanted to give the people a Bible they could read on their own, and second, to give them a hymnal so they could sing on their own. The Bible we have, and its words we read. The hymnal we have, but where, oh, where has the melody gone? Mr. Songless Saint is about as acquainted with his hymnal as his six-year-old daughter is with the Dow Jones averages. Christians know more verses by heart from Ecclesiastes and Ezekiel than from the well-worn hymnal they use over 100 times a year! We simply do not sing as often as we ought, and therein lies the blame and the shame.

Allow me to offer a few corrective suggestions:

Whenever and wherever you sing, concentrate on the words. If it helps, close your eyes. Let yourself get so lost in the accompanying melody that you momentarily forget where you are and what others might think. Frankly, I find it impossible to praise my Lord in song at the same time I feel self-conscious.

Make a concentrated effort to add one or two songs to your day. Remind yourself periodically of the words of a chorus or hymn you love and add them to your driving schedule or soap-and-shower time.

Sing often with a friend or members of your family. It helps melt down all sorts of invisible barriers. Singing before grace at mealtime in the evening is *so* enjoyable, but I warn you, you may become addicted.

Blow the dust off your record player and put on some beautiful music in the house. The family atmosphere will change for the better if you do this occasionally. And don't forget to sing along, adding your own harmony and "special effects."

Never mind how beautiful or pitiful you may sound. Sing loud enough to drown out those defeating thoughts that normally clamor for attention. Release yourself from that cage of introspective reluctance — SING OUT! You are not auditioning for the choir, you're making melody with your heart.

If you listen closely when you're through, you may hear the hosts of heaven shouting for joy. Then again, it might be your neighbor . . . screaming for relief.

Deepening Your Roots

1 Chronicles 16:7 – 36; Psalm 30:9, 100:2, 149:1 – 5; Luke 19:40

Branching Out

1. Sing a song in place of saying grace today.
2. Turn on the stereo, choose a record, play it . . . and sing along with the music.
3. Take a walk or drive by yourself, and as you go create your own music and song for God. He'll love it.

Growing Strong

Still singing? Good. Keep it up. The world needs to hear and see more happy people. And are you still growing? Super. Keep at it. The world needs more men and women who seriously care about their life with Christ. By the way . . . how do you feel the world sees you? Happy? Christ-like? _____

_____

_____

_____

Back to the Basics

The late football strategist, Vince Lombardi, was a fanatic about fundamentals. Those who played under his leadership often spoke of his intensity, his drive, his endless enthusiasm for the guts of the game. Time and again he would come back to the basic techniques of blocking and tackling. On one occasion his team, the Green Bay Packers, lost to an inferior squad. It was bad enough to lose . . . but to lose to *that* team was absolutely inexcusable. Coach Lombardi called a practice the very next morning. The men sat silently, looking more like whipped puppies than a team of champions. They had no idea what to expect from the man they feared the most.

Gritting his teeth and staring holes through one athlete after another, Lombardi began:

"Ok, we go back to the basics this morning. . . ."

Holding a football high enough for all to see, he continued to yell:

". . . gentlemen, *this is a football!* "

How basic can you get? He's got guys sitting there who have been playing on gridirons for fifteen to twenty years . . . who know offensive and defensive plays better than they know their kids' names . . . and he introduces them to a football! That's like saying, "Maestro, this is a baton." Or, "Librarian, this is a book." Or, "Marine, this is a rifle." Or, "Mother, this is a skillet." Talk about the obvious!

Why in the world would a seasoned coach talk to professional athletes like that? Apparently it worked, for no one else ever led his team to three consecutive world championships. But—*how?* Lombardi operated on a simple philosophy. He believed that excellence could be best achieved by perfecting the basics of the sport. Razzle-dazzle, crowd-pleasing, risk-taking plays would fill a stadium (for a while) and even win some games (occasionally), but in the final analysis the consistent winners would be the teams that played smart, heads-up, hard-nose football. His strategy? Know your position. Learn how to do it right. Then do it with all your might! That simple plan put Green Bay, Wisconsin, on the map. Before

Lombardi's advent, it was a frozen whistle stop between Oshkosh and Iceland.

What works in the game of football works in the church as well. But in the ranks of Christendom, it's easy to get a little confused. Change that: a *lot* confused. When you say "church" today, it's like ordering a malt . . . you've got thirty-one flavors to choose from. You can select wheeler-dealers, snake handlers, positive thinkers, or self realizers. Rock bands with colored lights, hooded "priests" with bloody knives, shaved heads with pretty flowers, and screaming showmen with healing lines are also available. If that doesn't satisfy, search for your favorite "ism" and it's sure to turn up: humanism, liberalism, extreme Calvinism, political activism, anticommunism, supernatural spiritism, or fighting fundamentalism.

But wait! What are the absolute basics of "the church"? What is the foundational task of a biblically oriented local assembly? Filtering out everything that isn't essential, what's left? Let's listen to the Coach. He tells us we have *four* major priorities if we're going to call ourselves a church:

> teaching . . . fellowship . . . breaking bread . . . prayer (Acts 2:42).

To these four we are to "continually devote ourselves." Solid, balanced, "winning" churches keep at the task of perfecting those basics. These form the *what* aspect of the church.

The *how* is equally important. Again, the Coach addresses the team. He declares that the church getting the job done is engaged in:

> . . . equipping the saints for the work of service, to the building up of the body . . . (Ephesians 4:12).

"Hey, that's easy," you say. "How simple can you get?" you ask. Are you ready for a shocker? The toughest job you can imagine is maintaining these basic assignments. Most people have no idea how easy it would be to leave the essentials and get involved in other activities.

Believe me—there is a steady stream of requests from good, wholesome, helpful sources to use the pulpit as a platform for their cause. I repeat—good and wholesome things, but not essential . . . not directly related to our basic purpose: the interpretation, the exposition, the application of Holy Scripture . . . with relevance, enthusiasm, clarity, and conviction. First and foremost, that is what a pulpit ministry is all about.

But churches like that are so rare across our land, it makes you want to stand up and say:

"Ladies and gentlemen, *this* is a *Bible!* "

Deepening Your Roots

Acts 2:42–47; Ephesians 4:12–16, 2:19 – 22

Branching Out

1. While you're in church this Sunday make sure you do the four basics: take in some teaching; talk to at least three other people; participate in communion; and pray.
2. Make arrangements to have lunch after church next week with a friend. Include in your dinner talk two positive or important truths you learned from the message or gained by being among other Christians.

BUSYNESS

*R*un, saint, run!
Appointments, activities, assignments . . . run!
Demands, decisions, deadlines . . . run!
Schedules, services, seminars . . . run!
Plans, programs, people . . .
Stop!

Step aside and sit down. Let your motor idle down for a minute and think for a change. Think about your pace . . . your busyness. How did you get trapped in that squirrel cage? What is it down inside your boiler room that keeps pouring the coal on your fire? Caught your breath yet? Take a glance back over your shoulder, say, three or four months. Could you list anything significant accomplished? How about feelings of fulfillment — very many? Probably not, if you're honest.

There's a man in Oklahoma City named James Sullivan who knows how you feel. Back in the 1960s he blew his town wide open developing the largest Young Life Club in the nation. And that's not all he blew wide open. Along the way, he managed to sacrifice his health and his family. Blazing along the success track, Sullivan became a difficult man to keep up with, let alone live with. His wife, Carolyn, was getting tired. So were his children, who seldom saw their father. When they did, he was irritable. Although he never realized it at the time, Sullivan's full-throttle lifestyle was actually an escape technique. Listen to his admission in his book, *The Frog Who Never Became a Prince:*

> I was a man who existed in a shell . . . guilt, resentment, and
> hatred welled up within me. The resulting hard feelings I
> developed became almost insurmountable.

What happened? Wasn't this guy a Christian, working for Jesus, spreading the Gospel, reaching the youth? Yes, indeed. But Sullivan substituted activity for living, busyness for meaningful priorities. One Thanksgiving Carolyn asked him a question as he was racing out the door to speak at some camp. "Do you know, or do you even care, that from the

middle of September until today, you have not been home *one* night?"
Not long after that, she broke emotionally. He contemplated suicide.

STINGING WORDS—BUT TRUE. SOUND FAMILIAR? HERE'S
WHY:

Busyness rapes relationships. It substitutes shallow frenzy for deep
friendship. It promises satisfying dreams but delivers hollow nightmares.
It feeds the ego but starves the inner man. It fills a calendar but fractures
a family. It cultivates a program but plows under priorities.

Many a church boasts about its active program: "Something every
night of the week for everybody." What a shame! With good intentions
the local assembly can *create* the very atmosphere it was designed to
curb. The One who instructed us to "be still and know that I am God"
must hurt when He witnesses our frantic, compulsive, agitated motions.
In place of a quiet, responsive spirit we offer Him an inner washing
machine — churning with anxiety, clogged with too much activity, and
spilling over with resentment and impatience. Sometimes He must watch
our convulsions with a heavy sigh.

My mentor was wise. He once declared:

> Much of our activity these days is nothing more than a cheap
> anesthetic to deaden the pain of an empty life.

SEARCHING WORDS—BUT TRUE. WANT TO CHANGE?
HERE'S HOW:

First, *admit it.* You are too busy. Say it to yourself . . . your family . . .
your friends. Openly and willingly *acknowledge* that what you are doing
is wrong and something must be done—now. I did that recently and,
through tears, my family and I cleared some bridges the thorns of neglect
had overgrown.

Second, *stop it.* Starting today, refuse every possible activity which
isn't absolutely necessary. Sound ruthless? So is the clock. So is your
health. Start saying no. Practice saying it aloud a few times—form the letters in your mouth. The phonetic structure of this two-letter word really
isn't all that difficult. If feasible, resign from a committee or two . . . or
three or four. Quit feeling so important. They'll get somebody else. Or
maybe they'll wise up and adopt a better plan.

Third, *maintain it.* It's easy to start fast and fade quickly. Discuss with
your family some ways of investing time with *them*—without the TV . . .
without apologies for playing and laughing and doing nutty, fun things
. . . without gobs of money having to be spent to "entertain" you.

Fourth, *share it.* It won't be very long before you begin gleaning the benefits of putting first things first. Tell others. Infect them with some germs of your excitement. Believe me, there are a lot of activity-addicts within the fellowship of faith who'd love to stop running . . . if they only knew how.

Ask James Sullivan. His nickname is "Frog." By the time he got kissed, it was almost too late.

Almost.

Deepening Your Roots
Psalm 127; Ecclesiastes 2:22–26; Matthew 6:25–34

Branching Out

1. Talk to a friend or your family (spouse *and* children) and ask them this question: Am I too busy, rushing about, involved in too many activities? If they say, "yeah," then talk further on what you should eliminate from your life. Then do it!

2. Go back to a friend you've offended by never writing, visiting with, etc. Apologize and let him know you're trying to give people more of a priority in life than projects or activities.

SPIRITUAL LEADERSHIP

*L*eadership is *influence*. To the extent we influence others, we lead them. Lord Montgomery implied this when he wrote . . .

> Leadership is the capacity and will to rally men and women to a common purpose, and the character which inspires confidence.

We could name many great people who did just that, whether they were military personnel, athletic coaches, political figures, business executives, salesmen, or spiritual statesmen. *Influence* best describes the effect of their lives.

If I were asked to name some of the standard qualities or characteristics usually found among natural-born leaders, I would list:

Enthusiasm	Optimism
Persistence	Ambition
Competitiveness	Knowledge
Insight	Inquisitiveness
Independence	Friendliness
Adventurousness	Security
Decisiveness	Integrity
Flexibility	Discipline
Sense of Humor	Creativity
Practicality	Poise
Aggressiveness	

None can deny that these are standard qualities found in "natural" leaders. But *my* question is: Are these qualities necessary in "spiritual" leaders, too? Before you answer too quickly, I would refer you to some biblical leaders who would've done rather poorly on a "natural" leadership test. The incredible thing is that God picked people whom we would have overlooked!

How about withdrawn, insecure, fearful, doubting Moses? (Read Exodus 3:10–4:14.) Or the uncultured, negative, ill-prepared, unwanted, dogmatic, clumsy fig-picker Amos? (Get acquainted with him in Amos 7:10–17.) And we dare not forget impulsive, short-sighted, boastful Peter, who frequently suffered from foot-in-mouth disease!

I am not suggesting these men did not have any natural traits of leadership—but rather that they broke the mold of what we generally classify as "a model leader." God's remnant of leaders is often a ragged lot . . . frequently made up of fresh-thinking, non-conforming, even weird-looking characters who desperately love the Lord Jesus Christ and are remarkably available to Him and His will. These people (and you may be one!) possess the basic ingredients of faith, vision, teachability, determination, and love—and they are involved in changing the world.

When I read that God is searching this planet for men and women (please stop and read 2 Chronicles 16:9a and Ezekiel 22:30), I do not find that He has a structured, well-defined frame into which they must fit. In fact, some of those God used most effectively were made up of the strangest mixture you could imagine. If you doubt this, check out that rough gang of 400 indebted unorganized malcontents that surrounded David in the *cave of Adullam* (1 Samuel 22:1–2). I find myself extraordinarily challenged to trace these men through the balance of David's life, and discover that these became his elite, courageous band of fighting men—heroes, if you please—from whom a number of leaders emerged.

I believe you anticipate my point. Let's be as open and flexible and tolerant as God is! Perhaps *you* don't fit the mold. Maybe you don't embrace the party-line system, so you're beginning to think "I'm not useful to God—I'll never be a leader in the ranks of Christianity." Take heart, discouraged believer! I rather suspect that others of you are about to write off your maverick *kids*. Listen, they may be right on target. God may have a distinct, unique role of leadership just for that youngster of yours. Hang in there, parents! These young people may look and sound strange to some adults . . . but I'm not about to sigh and ask why. For all we know, God is on the verge of doing something great through their leadership.

Let me assure you—if all adults had written off a young, repulsive, aggressive, strong-willed teenager forty years ago . . . the book you hold in your hands would have never existed.

Deepening Your Roots
Exodus 3:10–4:14; Amos 7:10–17; 2 Chronicles 16:9a; Ezekiel 22:30

Branching Out
1. Name someone you know who is in a leadership position: _____

Now, name a weakness he has as a leader:_____
_____
Pray for that person and ask that God would be strong where he is weak.

2. Are you a leader? If so, ask God how you could improve in your leadership skills: _____
_____
(Note an area you think God is zeroing in on.)

3. Afraid of leadership? Feel totally inadequate to lead? That's OK. But check your heart and make sure you are open and willing to allow God to use you as a leader if that's His pleasure. Remember Moses!

℞ ℞ ℞

Growing Strong

All right, friend, it's time for a checkup. The moment when we test those muscles of yours and find out if you're growing strong. Ready? All you have to do is answer these few questions:

	Yes	No
1. Did you do three or more Branching Outs this week?	☐	☐
2. Can you recall any verses you were to memorize this year?	☐	☐
3. Have you learned three new truths about God in the past six months?	☐	☐
4. Can you name three or more ways you've become more Christ-like?	☐	☐
5. Are you more in love with God today than when you began reading this book and His Word?	☐	☐

A FIRE FOR COLD HEARTS

It happened in a large, seventy-five-year-old stone house on the west side of Houston. A massive stairway led up to several bedrooms. The den down below was done in rough-hewn boards with soft leather chairs and a couple of matching sofas. The wet bar had been converted into a small library, including a shelf of tape recordings and a multiple-speaker sound system. The ideal place to spend a weekend . . . unfortunately, my wife and I were there just for the evening.

The smell of char-broiled T-bones drifted through the rooms. The ladies laughed in the kitchen as they fussed around with ranch-style baked beans, a variety of salads, and homemade pies. Everybody knew everybody. An easy, relaxing atmosphere made you want to kick off your shoes and run your fingers over the thick, black hair of the sleeping Labrador retriever sprawled across the hearth of a crackling fireplace.

The host, a lifelong Christian friend, leaned his broad shoulders against the mantle as he told of the bass that got away last week. While the guys chided him loudly for exaggerating ("it had to weigh ten to twelve pounds!"), my eyes ran a horizontal path across the carved message on the mantle. The room was too dark to read what it said from where I sat. I was intrigued and strangely drawn from my overstuffed chair to get a closer look.

I ran my fingers along the outline of each letter as my lips silently formed the words:

IF YOUR HEART IS COLD MY FIRE CANNOT WARM IT.

"Hmmmm," I thought, "how true."

Fireplaces don't warm hearts. Neither does fine furniture nor a four-car garage nor a full stomach nor a job with a six-figure salary. No, a cold heart can be warmed only by the fire of the living God.

I settled back down, stayed quiet, and mused over those thoughts. I even prayed as I stared into the fire:

"Lord, keep my heart warm. Stop me when I rev my motor and get to moving too fast toward stuff I think will make me happy.

Guard me from this stupid tendency to substitute things for You."

The dinner bell broke the spell. I stood up with all the men and we strolled toward the patio. I took a quick glance to remind myself of the words on the mantle one more time. The logs were now burned down to embers, and in the glow I remembered:

IF YOUR HEART IS COLD MY FIRE CANNOT WARM IT.

I thanked God for His fire that has never burned down.

That memorable scenario happened over thirty years ago. My heart has, since then, occasionally cooled off. Today, however, it is warm because He never left me when I was cold.

Deepening Your Roots

Deuteronomy 8:11–14; Matthew 24:12; Revelation 2:4–5

Branching Out

1. How would you rate the temperature of your heart?
   — hot; excited about God   — semi-warm
   — burning zeal   — lukewarm
   — very warm   — cold
   — warm   — icy
2. Ask God to rekindle the flame by bringing you a friend to pray with daily.
3. Build a fire tonight, roast marshmallows or pop corn in the fireplace, and talk with whoever is present (maybe just God) about the need to always stay close to Him. If you don't have a fireplace, visit a friend's house who has one, or drop in on a restaurant you know that keeps the wood burning.

BIBLICAL ILLITERACY

Standing ankle deep in snow, I copied the following inscription from the main wall near the old iron gate that leads to the campus of Harvard University:

> After God had carried us safe to New England and we had builded our houses, provided necessaries for our livelihood, reared convenient places for God's worship and settled the civil government, one of the next things we longed for and looked after was to advance learning and perpetuate it to posterity, dreading to leave an illiterate ministry to the churches when our present ministers lie in the dust.

No, you didn't make a mistake in your reading. The oldest institution of higher learning in our nation, founded just sixteen years after the Pilgrims landed at Plymouth, was established for the stated purpose of perpetuating an educated, well-trained body of godly men who would proclaim God's Word with intelligence, conviction, and authority. This was carried out until European liberalism, with its subtle narcotic of humanism and socialism, paralyzed the nerve centers of theological thought in our great land. Putting it bluntly, when the storm troopers of that damnable heresy captured the flag of biblical Christianity, all the forces of hell broke loose! It is safe to say that since that time, Mr. and Mrs. American Christian have been gasping for fresh, clean air beneath the suffocating blanket of sterile religion, Bible-less preaching, and lukewarm formalities like Laodicea of old. Except for a few, isolated islands of virility and hope, the tide has risen sharply and swept away the landmarks of genuine, Century One Christianity.

But all is not lost, believe me. We have the challenge and opportunity of standing erect against the tide of biblical illiteracy. We can face the flood without fear . . . *if* we continue to grow in grace and knowledge of our Lord and Savior (2 Peter 3:18). God has promised that we shall be blessed and protected *if* we will equip ourselves for the battle. But wait. . . . Look back at those "ifs." . . . If we grow . . . if we equip ourselves. *Are you?* Peel off that old mask and stare at yourself. Are YOU REALLY GROWING, spiritually? Are your spiritual muscles getting developed—I mean *really* getting developed? Are you drinking at the well of living water *daily* . . . or at least on a regular basis, *on your own?*

Is your faith claiming specific objectives . . . or just collecting dust? How are your quiet times with the Lord—are they meaningful or miserable, are they fresh or forced?

How about my suggesting a biblical project for the next few months before you settle down for a long winter's nap? Pick one of the following for yourself and refuse to quit until it's completed . . . or create one of your own.

- Read the entire book of James aloud each week from now until New Year's Day. (Or choose your own—preferably a short one.)
- Make a list of the arguments you hear from others most often *against* becoming a Christian. Then search the Scriptures for specific passages that give you insight and answers. (Read 1 Peter 3:14–15 first.)
- Commit to memory an entire chapter of one of your favorite Bible books . . . like Matthew 6 or John 15 or Romans 8 (or 12) or 1 Corinthians 13 or James 3 or 1 John 1. Do this by the end of the year.
- Find a biblical passage on prayer. Go to it every day with at least six of your most crucial needs. Leave room on the right side of your list to record the time and way God answered your requests. Do not stop until you are confident you should.

I cannot guarantee instant growth . . . nor can I promise that this will be easy. But after all, good soldiers of the cross have victory in mind, not luxury (please read 2 Timothy 2:1–4). And if I read my American history book correctly, I don't recall much being accomplished, spiritually or otherwise, without sacrifice and hardship. Resisting the tide is always hard work.

Brace up, island-dweller. When the battle's done and the victory's won, we will have plenty of time to take it easy and soak up the Son—an eternity, in fact.

Deepening Your Roots
2 Timothy 2:1–4; 1 Peter 2:2–3; Revelation 3:15, 16

Branching Out
1. Do two of the assignments in the article.
2. Visit a Christian bookstore and purchase a book that addresses an issue you're struggling with or need to be informed about. Read it!

TAKING GOD SERIOUSLY

Comic caveman "B.C." leans on one of the strip's ever-present boulders. The rock is inscribed "Trivia Test," and B.C. is administering the exam to one of his deadpan prehistoric buddies.

"Here's one from the Bible," he says. "What were the last words uttered by Lot's wife?"

Without a moment's hesitation his skin-clad friend replies: *"The heck with your fanatical beliefs, I'm going to take one last look!"*

She may not have said it, but that's what she was thinking—*or worse.*

The sordid account of Sodomite lifestyle is graphically portrayed in Genesis 19. And it's anything but funny. The place was shot through with open and shameless perversions. According to verse 4, these were practiced by

> . . . both young and old, all the people from every quarter.

The vile city of Sodom would've made New York's sleazy Forty-second Street look like a bike ride along old Cape Cod. It was gross. Absolutely and completely degenerate. Over-populated with disgustingly wicked weirdos—professionals in the world of porno . . . the original nest of homosexuals. Not pathetic sickies but willfully debased sinners who regularly practiced indecent and degrading acts on one another. In God's evaluation

> . . . their sin is exceedingly grave (Genesis 18:20b).

For some strange reason, Lot was drawn to Sodom. He and his family lived among these people and, no doubt, became accustomed to their ways, possibly viewing the perversions as acceptable.

Then God stepped in. Jealous for Lot's deliverance, He clearly announced the evacuation plan:

> Escape for your life! Do not look behind you, and do not stay anywhere in the valley; escape to the mountains, lest you be swept away (Genesis 19:17).

What a gracious act! The Lord cared enough for Lot and his family to map out a plan that would lead to safety. Nothing complicated. No riddles. Just "run for your life — don't look back; don't stop until you're in the mountains."

Behind this serious warning, a severe extermination plot was unfolding. Doomsday was approaching. The worst holocaust in the history of ancient civilization.

> Then the LORD rained on Sodom and Gomorrah brimstone and fire from the LORD out of heaven, and He overthrew those cities and all the valley, and all the inhabitants of the cities, and what grew on the ground (Genesis 19:24–25).

I can almost feel the heat on my face as I read those words. The corrupt cities sank slowly as the waters of the Dead Sea bubbled over them and their charred inhabitants.

And Lot? Well, he was running for his life, with his two daughters nearby. The family was saved! No, not all the family. Mrs. Lot didn't make it. Apparently, she couldn't bring herself to believe God meant what He said.

It's interesting how Scripture records her demise:

> But his wife, from behind him, looked back; and she became a pillar of salt (Genesis 19:26).

QUESTION: Why was she "behind him"? Who knows for sure? I'd suggest she was still attached to that lifestyle. She willfully refused to cut off her emotional ties. All this business of running away and not looking back was awfully extreme, terribly unrealistic. To quote the caveman:

> *"The heck with your fanatical beliefs, I'm going to take one last look!"*

The bottom line of Mrs. Lot's philosophy could have been etched on her salt-block tombstone:

THERE'S NO NEED TO TAKE GOD SERIOUSLY.

I know of no philosophy more popular today. It's the reason we're caught these days in the do-your-own-thing *sin*drome. What a subtle web the spider of self has woven! Millions are stuck—and instead of screaming, "I'm caught!" they shout, with a smile, "I'm free!"

If you don't take God seriously, then there's no need to take your marriage seriously . . . or the rearing of children . . . or such character traits as submission, faithfulness, sexual purity, humility, repentance, and honesty.

Take a long lick of salt this evening.

It stings, doesn't it?

Deepening Your Roots

Genesis 19:1–28; Jeremiah 6:13–19; Luke 17:20–33

Branching Out

1. Go to your kitchen, pull out the box of salt and sprinkle some in the palm of your hand. Now, take one long lick. Then come back and describe your reaction: _____

_____

2. What are some things in your life that God has asked you to leave behind?

_____

Evaluate whether or not you've actually left these things behind, or if you keep "looking back." Purpose in your heart not to be like Mrs. Lot.

❧ ❧ ❧

Growing Strong

Don't look back! Look ahead.

OK, let's do. And why not have some fun while we're at it, right? So . . . looking down the road a ways, tell me what you hope to be doing ten years from now: _____

_____

_____

and what inner Christ-like quality you hope will be most evident in your life: _____

_____

_____

NOSTALGIA

Glen Campbell, with that guitar of his slung over his shoulder, has an uncanny ability to resurrect memories in the tender spots of my deepdown soul. His "Galveston" and "Gentle on My Mind" transport me to the dusty back roads of my memory as people and places step out of the shadows and visit with me for a brief moment or two. Crazy, isn't it? Almost weird! Suddenly, without announcement, nostalgia sweeps over me and I am trapped in its sticky web for an exhilarating experience that's always too brief to satisfy . . . too vivid to ignore . . . too deep to describe . . . too personal to share.

Nostalgia. That abnormal yearning within us to step into the time tunnel and recover the irrecoverable. That wistful dream, that sentimental journey taken within the mind—always traveled alone and therefore seldom discussed. Here's where it sometimes starts:

- A barefoot walk along a sandy beach.
- A quiet visit to the place you were raised.
- Listening to a rippling brook running alone over the rocks through a forest of autumn leaves.
- Singing the song of your *alma mater.*
- Looking over childhood photos in the family album.
- Watching your now-grown "child" leave home.
- Standing silently beside the grave of a close personal friend or relative.
- The smell and sounds of a warm fireplace.
- An old letter, bruised with age, signed by one who loved you.
- Climbing to the top of a wind-swept hill.
- Getting alone—all alone—and reading aloud.
- Christmas Eve, late at night.
- Certain poems . . . certain melodies.
- Weddings . . . graduations . . . diplomas.
- Snow . . . sleds . . . toboggans.
- Saying goodbye.

Ah, yes . . . you've been there. I can tell by that smile that you're trying to hide.

The holiday season brings it back with a special surge of poignancy. The smells from the kitchen, my loving wife, the laughter of the kids, the memories of home and family, the inexpressible gratitude to God for my home . . . my country . . . and my Savior . . . all converge upon me that one day as nostalgia's net tightens around me and holds me close within its imaginary ropes of security.

I have often wondered how Jesus must have entertained nostalgic feelings as He visited this planet He originally created. How moving is that passage which reads: *He came to His own* . . . (John 1:11). You see, when Jesus came as a man, He lived and walked among familiar territory. He was no stranger to this old earth . . . it was "to His own things" (literally) He returned — and my, how nostalgic the journey must have been for Him at times! Because He was not wanted, He was driven to a life of silence, solitude, and simplicity. The mountains and the sea became His habitat. It was there he communed best with His Father, and it was there He trained His band of followers. Is it any wonder that the hills and the water still hold the mysteries of nostalgia and mediation?

Take a drive and get alone sometime this week — even if it's for only an hour. In the stillness of your surroundings, give nostalgia the go-ahead signal. Let it run free . . . release your grip and see where it takes you. That's one of my treasured pastimes during the holidays, and I want you to enjoy it with me.

If we meet together on the back roads of our memory, I will be so pleased—and I promise not to tell a soul. I'm good at keeping nostalgic secrets.

Deepening Your Roots

Matthew 26:6–13; Luke 22:7–19; 1 Thessalonians 3:6–13

Branching Out

1. Take a drive alone.
2. Recount a special holiday from your past and write someone else you shared it with why it brings back such fond memories. Pass on a bit of nostalgia.
3. Get the family album out of that box of ol' pictures hidden away and enjoy an evening of nostalgia.

GRACE REVISITED

Most of us did not learn to pray in church.

And we weren't taught it in school, or even in pajamas beside our bed at night. If the truth were know, we've done more praying around the kitchen table than anywhere else on earth. From our earliest years we've been programmed: If you don't pray, you don't eat. It started with Pablum in the high chair, and it continues through porterhouse at the restaurant. Right? Like passing the salt or doing the dishes, a meal is incomplete without it.

Our first impressions of communicating with the Almighty were formed in the high chair with cereal and pudding smeared all over our faces. We peeked and gurgled while everybody else sat silent and still. We then learned to fold our hands and close our eyes. Soon we picked up the cue to add our own "Amen" (which usually followed ". . . in Jesus' name"). Then came the day we soloed. We mumbled, looked around, got mixed up, then quickly closed with a relieved "Amen!" as we searched Mom and Dad's faces for approval.

Then we went through three very definite stages over the next eight to ten years of grace — stages that are common in most Christian families. Stage one . . . *snickering*. For some strange reason, prayer before the meal became the "comedy hour" when I was growing up. In spite of parental frowns and glares, threats and thrashings . . . my sister and I could *not* keep from laughing. I remember one time we giggled so long and so loud that our mother finally joined in. My older brother was praying (he usually remembered every missionary from Alaska to Zurich) and purposely refused to quit. He finished by praying for the *three of us*.

Stage two . . . *doubting*. This is a cynical cycle, a tough one to endure. We start questioning the habit—the custom. With an air of pseudo-sophistication, we think:

"What does it matter if I *don't* say grace?"

"This is a ritual—it serves no purpose—God knows I'm grateful."

Junior high years abound with these maverick thoughts. The whole scene of bowing heads and closing eyes and saying "religious words" suddenly seems childish . . . needless.

Stage three . . . *preaching.* This one is difficult to handle because it usually comes from well-meaning lips. Out of sincerity and a desire to prompt obedience, we use the time in prayer as an avenue to rebuke a family member or (very subtly) reinforce our own piety. Parents can easily fall into this manipulative technique, since it's impossible to be interrupted in prayer. The temptations of taking to the platform before our captive audience seem irresistible.

After passing through these stages, however, we begin to realize how good it is to cultivate this healthy habit. "Asking the blessing" is a sweet, much-needed, refreshing pause during hectic days. But since it occurs so often, the easiest trap to fall into is sameness. The perfunctory uttering of meaningless, repetitious clichés that become boring *even to God.* Our Lord Jesus thundered warning after warning against the empty verbosity which characterized the Pharisees.

Without claiming to have all the answers, I offer several suggestions a family can build on together.

1. *Think before you pray.* What's on the table? Call the food and drink by name. "Thank you, Lord, for the hot chicken-and-rice casserole in front of us. Thanks for the cold lemonade . . ." What kind of day are you facing—or have you faced? Pray with those things in mind. Draw your prayer out of real life. Don't lapse into mechanical mutterings or convenient religious jargon. You're not just "saying a blessing," you're talking to your God!

2. *Involve others in prayer.* Try some sentence prayers around the table. Ask the family for requests.

3. *Sing your table blessing.* Try it a few times. After the family has recovered from the shock of shattering the norm, it might catch on. The Doxology, a familiar hymn, or a chorus of worship works great . . . and offers a change of pace. Holding hands can be meaningful.

4. *Keep it brief, please.* There's nothing like watching a thick film form over the gravy while you plow through all five stanzas of Wesley's "And Can It Be?" Remember what the blessing is all about—a pause to praise our faithful Provider—a moment of focus on the Giver of every good gift. You don't have to pray around the world three times or highlight every relative between the poles and all the ships at sea. God's watching the heart, not totaling up the verbiage.

5. *Occasionally pray after the meal.* When the mood is loose or the meal is served in "shifts" or picnic-style settings, be flexible. An attitude

of worship is occasionally much easier when the hunger pangs have eased up.

Is your prayer time at the table losing its punch? Here's a way to find out. When the meal is over and you get up to do the dishes, ask if anyone remembers what was prayed for. If they do, great. If they don't, sit back down at the table and ask why. You've got a lot more to be concerned about than a stack of dishes.

Deepening Your Roots
Psalm 104:10–15, 104:27–35, 107:1–9, 22; Acts 27:35

Branching Out

1. Try one of the suggestions from today's reading.
2. Take a lesson from at least three kids this week by listening to their prayers at mealtime. Be as fresh and honest as they are when praying before you dig in to eat.
3. Take a survey of ten people (or listen in on people praying at meal time) and inquire as to their prayers at mealtime. Are they always the same?

THANKSGIVING

I've got a love affair going with Thanksgiving. It has been going on for over fifty years, as far back as I can remember. Hands down, it's my favorite holiday of all.

Here's why.

First of all, it seems to blend together all we Americans hold precious and dear—without the sham and plastic mask of commercialism. Shopping centers jump from Halloween to Christmas. It's spooks to Santa . . . pumpkins to presents . . . orange and black to red and green. It's doubtful that any of us has ever seen (or *will* ever see) a Pilgrim hype. Just can't be done. Except for grocery stores, merchants are mute when Thanksgiving rolls around.

Second, it highlights the home and family. Thanksgiving is synonymous with stuff that can be found only at home—the warmth of a fireplace, early morning fussing around in the kitchen, kids and grandkids, long distance phone calls, family reunions, singing around the piano, holding hands and praying before that special meal, the Cowboys versus somebody (they always beat) on the tube, a touch football game in the street or backyard, friends dropping by, pumpkin pie, homemade rolls, and six million calories.

It is a time of quiet reflection upon the past and an annual reminder that God has, again, been ever so faithful. The solid and simple things of life are brought into clear focus, so much so that everything else fades into insignificance.

Thanksgiving is good for our roots . . . it deepens them and strengthens them and thickens them . . . making our trunks and limbs more secure in spite of the threatening gale of our times. The meal, the memories, the music Thanksgiving brings have a way of blocking out the gaunt giant of selfishness and ushering in the sincere spirit of gratitude, love, and genuine joy.

Third, it drips with national nostalgia. For me, even more so than the Fourth of July. *That* holiday reminds us of a battle we won, giving us independence. This one takes us back to a simple slice of life over 350 years ago when our forefathers and foremothers realized their *depen*dence on each other to survive. With Thanksgiving comes a surge of renewed patriotism, a quiet inner peace that whispers, *"I am proud to be an American."*

I recall, as a little barefoot boy with a cowlick of snow-white hair on my forehead, standing erect in my classroom and repeating the "Pledge of Allegiance" one Thanksgiving season. Our nation was at war and times were hard. My teacher had lost her husband on the bloodwashed shores of Normandy. As we later bowed our heads for prayer she wept aloud. I did too. All the class joined in. She stumbled through one of the most moving expressions of gratitude and praise that ever emerged from a soul plunged in pain. At that time in my young life, I fell strangely in love with Thanksgiving. Lost in sympathy and a boy's pity for his teacher, I walked home very slowly that afternoon. Although only a child, I had profound feelings of gratitude for my country . . . my friends . . . my school . . . my church . . . my family. I swore before God that I would fight to the end to keep this land free from foes who would want to take away America's distinctives and the joys of living in this good land. I have never forgotten my childhood promise. I never shall.

Thanksgiving puts steel into our patriotic veins. It reminds us of our great heritage. It carries us back with numbing nostalgia to that first dreadful winter at Plymouth where less than half the handful of people survived. It speaks in clear, crisp tones of forgotten terms, like: integrity . . . bravery . . . respect . . . faith . . . vigilance . . . dignity . . . honor . . . freedom . . . discipline . . . sacrifice . . . godliness.

Its historic halls echo with the voices of Washington, Franklin, Jefferson, Adams, Henry, Lincoln, Lee, and Jackson who challenge us to trim off the fat of indolence, compromise, passivity, and the stigma of strife. It gives a depth of relevance and meaning to the nineteenth-century words of Katharine Lee Bates:

> O beautiful for spacious skies,
>   For amber waves of grain,
> For purple mountain majesties
>   Above the fruited plain!
>
> O beautiful for patriot dream
>   That sees beyond the years
> Thine alabaster cites gleam
>   Undimmed by human tears!
>
> America! America!
>   God shed His grace on thee
> And crown thy good with brotherhood
>   From sea to shining sea!

Nostalgia washes over me as I take a walk in the woods and reflect on those brave men and women whose bodies lie beneath white crosses—veterans who fought and died that I might live and be free—and as I consider those statesmen who hammered out our laws on the anvil of wisdom, compassion, and human dignity. People who cared about the future of this grand land, not just their own comforts. Visionaries. Tough-minded, clear-thinking, sacrificial souls who did more than talk about integrity. They modeled it.

Fourth and finally, it turns our heads upward. Just the word "Thanksgiving" prompts the spirit of humility. Genuine gratitude to God for His mercy, His abundance, His protection, His smile of favor. At this holiday, as at no other, we count our blessings and we run out of time before we exhaust the list. And best of all, life simplifies itself. At Thanksgiving we come back to the soil and the sun and the rain which combine their efforts to produce the miracle of life, resulting in food for our stomachs and shelter for our bodies . . . direct gifts from our God of grace. From the annals of our rich heritage, there has been preserved this announcement which was made 381 years ago. It says it all:

TO ALL YE PILGRIMS

Inasmuch as the great Father has given us this year an abundant harvest of Indian corn, wheat, beans, squashes, and garden vegetables, and has made the forests to abound with game and the sea with fish and clams, and inasmuch as He has protected us from the ravages of the savages, has spared us from pestilence and disease, has granted us freedom to worship God according to the dictates of our own conscience; now, I, your magistrate, do proclaim that all ye Pilgrims, with your wives and little ones, do gather at ye meeting house, on ye hill, between the hours of 9 and 12 in the day time, on Thursday, November ye 29th of the year of our Lord one thousand six hundred and twenty-three, and the third year since ye Pilgrims landed on ye Pilgrim Rock, there to listen to ye pastor, and render thanksgiving to ye Almighty God for all His blessings.

— William Bradford Governor of Plymouth Colony,
1623

Deepening Your Roots

Exodus 12; Psalm 35:18; 66:1–9; 67

Branching Out

1. Say the pledge of allegiance some time during Thanksgiving Day or sing "God Bless America" or our national anthem.
2. Have each person (following the meal) state something about the person on their right for which they are thankful.

❧ ❧ ❧

Growing Strong

If I timed it right, *Thanksgiving* was a part of your week. Mine too. Now that it's behind us, let's jot down the most encouraging words said to us that day, or the most touching moment of the whole day. You go first . . . _____

_____

_____

_____

GENTLENESS

*T*ough and tender.

That's the combination every woman wants in a man. A balanced blend, an essential mixture of strong stability *plus* consideration, tact, understanding, and compassion. A better word is *gentleness* . . . but for some peculiar reason, that idea seems alien to the masculine temperament.

Observe the media-myth man. The man portrayed on the tube is rugged, hairy, built like a linebacker, drives a slick sports car, and walks with a swagger. In the beer ads he's all out for grabbing the gusto. With women he is a conqueror . . . fast and furious. In business he's "bullish." Even with a razor or hair dryer he's cocky, superconfident. If you don't believe it, ask *him*. The media-myth is, basically, *tough*. Spanish-speaking people would say he is known for his *machismo*. To the majority of young men—that's their hero, their masculine model.

Now let's understand something. A man *ought* to be a man! Few things are more repulsive than a man who carries himself like a woman . . . or wears stuff that suggests femininity. And we are living in an era when the roles are definitely eroding. I heard about a preacher who was conducting a wedding ceremony for a couple like this — both bride and groom having the same length hair and dressed in similar attire. Confused over their identity, he closed the ceremony with:

Would one of you kiss the bride?

The right kind of toughness-strength of character—ought to mark the man of today . . . but not only that. Tenderness—gentleness—is equally important.

God considers it so important He places it on the list of nine qualities He feels should mark the life of His children:

> But the fruit of the Spirit is love, joy, peace, patience, kindness, goodness, faithfulness, gentleness, self-control; against such things there is no law (Galatians 5:22–23).

There it is . . . number eight. The Greek word translated "gentleness" is *prautes,* and it brims with meaning. In secular writings, the Greeks used it when referring to people or things that demonstrated a certain soothing quality—like an ointment that took the sting out of a burn. They also used this word to describe the right atmosphere which should prevail during a question-answer period in a classroom; the idea of discussing things without losing one's temper or becoming strongly defensive.

And think about this one. *Prautes* described the controlled conduct of one who had the power to act otherwise. Like a king who chose to be gracious instead of a tyrant. Like a military commander who patiently trained an awkward squad of soldiers. Plato called *prautes* "the cement of society" as he used this word in the sense of politeness, courtesy, and kindness.

Gentleness has *three close traveling companions* in the New Testament:

1. It keeps company with agape-love (1 Corinthians 4:21).
2. It is a friend of meekness (2 Corinthians 10:1).
3. It is attached to humility (Ephesians 4:2).

Similarly, according to the New Testament, gentleness is the proper attitude when faced with *three difficult assignments:*

1. When faced with the need to exercise discipline in the Body of Christ (Galatians 6:1).
2. When faced with personal opposition (2 Timothy 2:25).
3. When faced with the truth of God's Word—being open and teachable (James 1:21).

Remember, our goal is balance . . . always balance. Not either-or, but both-and. Not just *tough*. That alone makes a man cold, distant, intolerant, unbearable. But tough *and* tender . . . gentle, thoughtful, teachable, considerate.

Both.

Like Christ.

Deepening Your Roots

Isaiah 40:11; 1 Corinthians 4:21; Ephesians 4:2; 1 Peter 3:8–12

Branching Out

1. What's a way you can show tenderness to another?_____

    _____

    Put your answer to work today. Be tender!
2. Exhibit gentleness in some way today by not losing your temper or becoming defensive.
3. Look for an incident today in which a person displayed a tender spirit. Compliment that person for his right attitude, words, or action.

One Long Extended Gift

Although it may be a little ahead of schedule, it's not too early to give some things away this Christmas. Not just on Christmas Day, but during the days leading up to December 25. We could call these daily gifts "our Christmas projects." Maybe one per day from now 'til then. Here are thirty-two suggestions. Take your choice.

- Mend a quarrel.
- Seek out a forgotten friend.
- Dismiss suspicion.
- Write a long-overdue love note.
- Hug someone tightly and whisper, "I love you so."
- Forgive an enemy.
- Be gentle and patient with an angry person.
- Express appreciation.
- Gladden the heart of a child.
- Find the time to keep a promise.
- Make or bake something for someone else. Anonymously.
- Release a grudge.
- Listen.
- Speak kindly to a stranger.
- Enter into another's sorrow.
- Smile. Laugh a little. Laugh a little more.
- Take a walk with a friend.
- Kneel down and pat a dog.
- Read a poem or two to your mate or friend.
- Lessen your demands on others.
- Play some beautiful music during supper.
- Apologize if you were wrong.
- Talk together with the television off.
- Treat someone to an ice-cream cone.
- Do the dishes for the family.
- Pray for someone who helped you when you hurt.
- Fix breakfast for someone on Saturday morning.
- Give a soft answer even though you feel strongly.

- Encourage an older person.
- Point out one thing you appreciate most about someone you work with or live near.
- Offer to baby-sit for a weary mother.
- Give your teacher a break — be especially cooperative.

Let's make Christmas one long, extended gift of ourselves to others. Unselfishly. Without announcement. Or obligation. Or reservation. Or hypocrisy.

That *is* Christianity, isn't it?

Deepening Your Roots

Luke 21:1–4; Ephesians 2:8, 9; Matthew 2:11

Branching Out

You come up with three assignments:

1. _____
2. _____
3. _____

YEAR-END REFLECTIONS

*T*ime to reflect. That would be my answer to the question: "What do you like most about the year-end holidays?"

Oh, the food is good—those delectable, fattening morsels that make Thanksgiving, Christmas, and New Year's so special. So are the parties and the people . . . the songs, the smiles, the smells. Each weaves its way into the fabric of our minds in such a beautiful manner that we live in the warmth of them for days. Sometimes *months*.

But the best those traditional holidays can offer, in my opinion, is time to reflect. To stand in front of the full-length mirror of memory and study the scene. Thoughtfully. Silently. Alone. At length. To trace the outline of the past without the rude interruption of routine tasks. To walk along the surf or stroll through a mountain pathway, taking time to stop and listen. And think. To sit by a crackling fireplace with all the lights out, staring into the heat, and letting thoughts emerge, drift, and linger. To turn over in the mind a line out of a poem. To hear some grand music played at sufficient volume that all petty noises and worries are submerged beneath the waves of stimulating sound.

Maybe it's part of what Charles Wesley meant by being "lost in wonder, love, and praise." A kind of solitary worship. An extended, unhurried leisure yielding rich benefits and deep insights. Invariably, those occasions leave me feeling grateful to God. Often I end up thanking Him specifically for something or someone that He provided in the yesterday of my life that makes my today much more meaningful.

It happened again last week. The day had been relaxing and fun. Night fell. One by one my family slipped into sleep. I put a couple more logs into the fireplace, slid into my favorite chair, and read for well over an hour. I came across a few thoughts put together by a long-time leader in the World Vision ministry—Ed Dayton. His words sent me back many, many years. Ed mentioned watching the short film called "The Giving Tree," a simple, fanciful piece about a tree who loved a boy.

They played hide 'n' seek in his younger years. He swung from her branches, climbed all over her, ate her apples, slept in her shade. Such happy, carefree days. The tree *loved* those years of the boy's childhood.

But the boy grew and spent less time with the tree. On one occasion the young man returned. "Come on, let's play," invited the tree . . . but the lad was only interested in money. "Take my apples and sell them," said the tree. He did . . . and the tree was happy.

He didn't return for a long time, but the tree smiled when he passed by one day. "Come, play, my friend. Come, play!" But the boy—now full grown—wanted to build a house for himself. "Cut off my branches and build your house," she offered. He did, and once again the tree was happy.

Years dragged by. The tree missed the boy. Suddenly, she saw him in the distance. "Come on, let's play!" but the man was older and tired of his world. He wanted to get away from it all. "Cut me down. Take my large trunk and make yourself a boat. Then you can sail away," said the tree. And that's exactly what he did . . . and the tree was happy.

Many seasons passed—summers and winters, windy days and lonely nights—and the tree waited. Finally, the old man returned . . . too old, too tired to play, to pursue riches, to build houses, or to sail the seas. "I have a pretty good stump left, my friend. Why don't you just sit down here and rest?" He did . . . and the tree was happy.[27]

I stared into the fire. I watched myself pass in review as I grew older with the tree and the boy. I identified with both—and it hurt.

How many Giving Trees have there been in my life? How many have released part of themselves so I might grow, accomplish my goals, find wholeness and satisfaction, and reach beyond the tiny, limited playground of my childhood? So, so many. Thank you, Lord, for each one. Their names could fill this page.

Now I, like the tree, have grown up. Now it's my turn to give. And some of that hurts. Apples, branches, sometimes the trunk. My rights, my will . . . and even my grown-up children.

So much to give. Thank you, Lord, that I have a few things *worth* giving. Even if it's a lap to be sat on . . . or the comfort of a warm embrace.

The fire died into glowing embers. It was late as I crawled into bed. I had wept, but now I was smiling as I said, "Good night, Lord." I was a thankful man.

Thankful I had taken time to reflect.

Deepening Your Roots

Jeremiah 17:7, 8; Psalm 63:5 – 6; Philippians 2:1–11

Branching Out

1. Take a drive into the country and buy a bag or a crate of apples. Give them all away to those you see in the next forty-eight hours.
2. Give sacrificially today to someone else, but don't tell anyone what you did.
3. Find a beautiful tree and sit under it for awhile. Spend some time thanking God for the people He has brought into your life. List some of their names here: _____

   _____

   _____

❧ ❧ ❧

Growing Strong

Congratulations! You've grown strong. Now go celebrate.

CONCLUSION

Some verses from the Bible make us smile. We have enjoyed them together as we considered a few such verses through the pages of this book. Some references are penetrating and convicting as they cause us to look into the mirror of truth and face facts. We've considered a number of those, too. Others are comforting, giving us hope to go on, regardless. A few introduce us to brand new scenes we've never seen before. Maybe that has happened as you've worked your way through these pages.

There is one verse, however, that never fails to take us by the shoulders and shake us awake. It comes to my mind because it draws upon a word picture of seasons to make its point. You may recall reading it before.

> "Harvest is past, summer is ended, And we are not saved" (Jeremiah 8:20).

Does that describe *you?* If so, may I suggest that you come to terms with this need. Seasons follow a cycle: winter, spring, summer, autumn . . . so that the earth might enjoy all the things its Creator designed for it to enjoy.

Your life is, in many ways, the same. Multiple seasons, not a long, monotonous marathon of pointless futility; but variety, peaks and valleys, change and color. How tragic to move through the seasons without realizing their ultimate purpose! And what is that?

Go back to the verse. Read it aloud. The purpose is obvious: that we might be *saved* . . . that we might not trust in ourselves but in Jesus Christ, our Creator Lord . . . and, in doing so, receive from Him the assurance of abundant life now and eternal life forever.

Throughout this book I've been truthful with you. Now it's your turn to be truthful with yourself. Are you absolutely certain that you possess His gifts of forgiveness and purpose? You can have that assurance if your traveling Companion through the year is the Son of God. He alone can give meaning to the cycle as He enables you to grow strong in all the seasons of your life.

FOOTNOTES

Winter

1. Paul Tournier, *To Understand Each Other* (Atlanta: John Knox Press, ©️ 1967 by M.E. Bratcher), p. 8.

2. Samuel Butler, "The Art of Listening," *The Royal Bank of Canada Monthly Letter,* Vol. 60, No. 1, January 1979, p. 2.

3. Roy Croft, poem in article "Love without a Net," quoted in Jack Mayhall, *Marriage Takes More Than Love* (Colorado Springs: Navpress), p. 47.

4. J. Oswald Sanders, *Spiritual Leadership* (Chicago: Moody Press, 1967), pp. 59 – 60. Used by permission.

5. Sanders, p. 60.

Spring

6. Sir William Osler, *Familiar Quotations,* ed. John Bartlett (Boston: Little, Brown and Company, 1955), p. 744b.

7. Henry W. Baker, "Art Thou Weary, Art Thou Languid?"

8. Walter Martin, *Screwtape Writes Again* (Santa Ana, Calif.: Vision House Publishers, 1975), p. 16.

9. Richard Rogers and Oscar Hammerstein, "Climb Every Mountain," 1959.

10. Marilee Zdenek, *Splinters in My Pride,* Part 1 (Waco, Tex.: Word Books, 1979), [n.p.].

Summer

11. Bruce Larsen, *The One and Only You* (Waco, Tex.: Word Books, 1974), pp. 84 – 85. Adaptation by permission of Word Books, Publisher, Waco, Tex. 76703.

12. Leslie B. Flynn, *Great Church Fights* (Wheaton: Victor Books, 1976), p. 105.

13. Flynn, p. 104.

14. Bruce Larsen and Keith Miller, *The Edge of Adventure* (Waco, Tex.: Word Books, 1974), p. 156.

15. Dorothy Hsu, *Mending* (Ft. Washington, Penn.: Christian Literature Crusade). Used by permission.

16. F. B. Meyer, *Christianity in Isaiah* (Grand Rapids: Zondervan Publishing House, 1950), p. 9.

17. Alexander Solzhenitsyn, *The Gulag Archipelago*, quoted in Philip Yancey, *Where Is God When It Hurts?* (Grand Rapids: Zondervan Publishing House, 1977), p. 51.

18. J. Oswald Sanders, *Spiritual Leadership* (Chicago: Moody Press, 1967), p. 94.

Autumn

19. Charles L. Allen, *You Are Never Alone* (Old Tappan, N.J.: Fleming H. Revell Company, 1978), pp. 145 – 46.

20. Cathy Trost and Ellen Grzech, "What Happened When 5 Families Stopped Watching TV," *Good Housekeeping*, August 1979, pp. 94, 97 – 99.

21. Urie Bronfenbrenn, "TV and Your Child," *Christian Medical Society Journal*, Haddon Robinson, ed. (Richardson, Tex.: Christian Medical Society, 1978), p. 7.

22. Bronfenbrenn, p. back cover.

23. Kevin Lehman, *Parenthood Without Hassles — Well Almost* (Eugene, Ore.: Harvest House Publishers, 1979), pp. 139 – 40.

24. Philip G. Zimbardo, "The Age of Indifference," *Psychology Today*, August 1980, p. 72.

25. Zimbardo, p. 74.

26. John Bartlett, ed., *Familiar Quotations* (Boston: Little, Brown and Company, 1955), p. 475.

27. Shel Silverstein, *The Giving Tree* (New York: Harper and Row, 1964).

SCRIPTURE INDEX

Genesis
2:2—3:15 60
12:1—8 317
15:2—4 370
16:1—4 370
17:15—17 228
18:9—14 228
18:20 415
19:1—28 417
19:4 415
19:17 415
19:24—25 416
19:26 416
21:1—7 370
20:1—6 319
21:6 116
22 209
22:1—18 210
22:2 210
27:1—35 285
27:41—45 186
31:38—42 60
33:1—9 208
37:19 122
39:19—21 79
40:1—8 122
41:50—52 79
45:4—8 79
47:11—12 263

Exodus
1:15—22 206
2 52
2:1—10 206
3:10—4:14 408, 409
12 426
14 102
16 322
16:4 321
16:35 320
18:13—27 194

18:18—27 193
20:12 243
32:1—24 319
32:22—24 319

Leviticus
18:1—30 269
26:14 70
26:18 70
26:21 70
26:27 70
26:40— 46 70

Numbers
8:20—25 288
11 320
14:41—45 373
30:2 224

Deuteronomy
4:27—31 149
4:30 148
6:1 238
6:2 238
6:4—9 291
6:7 290
8:11—14 412
13 45
18:21—22 45

Joshua
1:1—5 389
1:6—8 213
1:6 398
1:7 398
1:8 212
1:9 398
6 274
6:1—22 228
14 317
14:1—15 317
14:6—12 200

Judges
11 52
12 52

Ruth
Book of 246
2:1—12 197

1 Samuel
13 372
15 146
15:1 145
15:3 145
15:13 145
15:15 145
15:20—21 145
15:22 146
15:23 146
15:24 146
16:1—7 109
16:7 108, 391
16:18—23 134
17:1—50 274
18:1 171
20:4 171
21:13 54
22:1—2 409
23:16 171

2 Samuel
1:17—27 191
16:13—14 329
22:1 134
23:10 151

1 Kings
1—11 105
1:20—39 155
2:1—11 288
2:1—4 243
3:3—15 243
3:3 105
3:16—27 359

Scripture Index

4:29—34 315
4:29—31 105
4:29 253
5:1—2 109
9:1—9 107
10:7 106
10:23—24 105
19 250
19:1—7 54
19:4 250
19:10 251
19:18 161
19:19—21 170, 171

2 Kings
9:11—10:36 33
9:20 33
10 34
10:15—16 33

1 Chronicles
4:9—10 48, 49
11:15—19 274
15:25—29 238
16:7—36 400
17:16—27 225
28:9—20 82
29:6—28 238

2 Chronicles
6:12—15 225
16:9 409
25:1—2 48
26:16—21 372, 373

Ezra
1:1—11 46

Nehemiah
1:1—11 200
2:1—5 200
2:11—18 194
2:17—20 58
6:15—16 58
8:1—12 216

Job
Book of 104, 260
1:1—5 386
2:9 104
12:10—13 384

13:5 302
15:3 169
16:3 222
18:2 169, 222
19:25—27 381
23:8—12 183
24:12 87
25 270
25:1—5 272
40 104

Psalms
Book of 211
1:1—6 213
5:3 86
6:6—7 151
8:1—9 272
15:1—2 224
18:1—3 282
18:16—19 282
19 375
19:1—4 374
19:12—13 372
23:1—3 329
25:15 356
25:16—22 157
27 395
27:1 395
27:3 395
27:4 395
27:5 395
27:6 395
27:13—14 395
30:9 400
31:1—2 280
31:9—10 280—81
31:10 281
31:11—13 281
31:14—15 352, 353
32:6—7 282
33:6—22 375
35:18 426
37:1—13 31
37:4—5 212
37:23—24 188
37:30—31 62
37:31 61

39:1 27
40:1—4 353
40:1—2 298
46 94
46:10 324
56:8 123
62:5—8 241
63:5—6 432
65 375
66:1—9 426
67 426
69:3 151
71:1—3 282
72 162, 163
73:1 180
75:6—7 386, 388
78:24—25 320
78:70—72 386
84:10—12 104
90:4 81
90:5 81
90:6 81
90:9 81
90:10 81
90:12 36, 37, 383
91:1 241
91:2 241
92:14 378
100:2 400
103:1—14 92
103:10 91
103:14 91
104 375
104:10-15 422
104:27—35 422
107:1—9 422
107:22 422
109:21—31 89
115:3 147, 292
119:9—16 62
119:9—11 61
119:97-104 213
119:67 299
119:71 299
126:1—6 116
127 407

127:1—5 359
130:5—6 353
131 94
139:5 292
139:16 292
139:13—17 108
139:13—16 120
145:1—14 37
145:3—7 235
145:13 225
147:1—11 89
149:1—5 400

Proverbs
2:1—10 315
3:1—15 107
3:5—6 212, 213
4:1—19 384
4:4 61
4:5—7 315
4:20—27 251
5:21—22 389
6:17 344
7:3 61
10:11—21 119
11:4 295
11:7 248, 347
11:16 347
11:24 326
12:18 28
13:4 60
13:19 59, 199
14:12 155
14:23 203
14:29 141, 302
15:1—7 119
15:1 302
15:13 115
15:15 115
16:1—9 177
16:31 378, 384
17:6 359
17:14 303
17:22 115
17:28 302, 303
18:1 367
18:12 79

18:24 108, 171
19:11 141
19:21 370
19:23 146
20:4 60
20:7 243
20:12 70
20:22 253
21:4 344
21:23 28
22:1 387
22:17—21 310
22:18 61
22:24—25 302, 303
23:1—2 302
23:5 295
23:21 363
23:23 363
24:10 385
24:30—34 138
25:6—7 389
26:13—16 138
26:23—26 361
27:1 175, 177
27:2 99, 257, 344
27:9—10 171
28:28 347
29:11 302, 303
29:25 146, 398
30:7—9 256
30:12 393
31:1—31 134
31:10—31 134, 203

Ecclesiastes
2:11 337
2:22—26 407
2:26 106
3:1 352
3:1—4 37
4:4 337
5:5 224
5:10—20 347
11:10 287
12:1 256, 287
12:6—7 256
12:1—14 256

12:9—11 309
12:12 151
Song of Solomon
6:9 342
Isaiah
9:6 46
13:17—22 45
26:3 315
30:15—18 94
32:17—18 94
37:36—38 45
39:5—7 45
40:11 428
40:21—31 322
40:25—26 342
40:28—31 151, 152
41 270
41:14—16 272
44:24—45 46
44:28—45:1 46
45:5—9 293
45:9 292
46:4 378
46:5—9 342
46:8—11 293
46:9—10 292
50:4 151
51:1 51
51:12—16 395
53:1—12 89
55:1—11 180
Jeremiah
Book of 29, 31
6:13—19 417
8:20 435
17:7—8 432
20 29
20:7—8 29
20:9 30
20:18 29
32:17—42 31
45:5 388
50:4 124
Lamentations
1:12—16 124
3:19—32 31

3:46—50 124

Ezekiel
20:21—31 356
22:30 409

Daniel
1 45, 387
1:8—16 363
2:19—23 353
2:21 351
3 398
4:28—37 149
4:29—37 299
4:35 147, 293
5 45
5:18—21 293
6:1—28 183
6:1—2 386
9:4—19 277

Hosea
1:1—11 305
1:2 304
3:1 305
3:1—5 305
6:1 305

Amos
Book of 121—22
7:10—17 408, 409
7:12—13 121
7:14—15 121, 386
8:11—13 215

Jonah
2:1—7 299
2:1—4 298

Micah
6:8 387

Nahum
1:1—3 149
1:3 147

Haggai
1:1—12 248
1:6 295

Matthew
1:18—25 43
2:1—23 43
2:11 430

4:1—11 380
4:1—10 62
5:13—16 111
5:16 67
5:47 48
6 414
6:1 391
6:2 392
6:4 392
6:5—15 169
6:5 392
6:7 168
6:16 392
6:19—21 302
6:24 65
6:25—34 407
6:33 347
7:1—5 393
11:25—30 241
11:28—30 151
11:28 324
12:33—37 339
13:1—29 322
15:1—9 349
15:2 218
18:21—35 185, 186
19:26 370
20:1—16 86
20:20—28 258
20:26—27 257
23 380
23:1—26 393
23:27—39 169
23:27—28 168
24:12 412
26:6—13 419
27:45—46 157

Mark
1:14—20 144
2:13—17 367
2:24 218
4:1—41 130
4:6 129
6 252
6:30—32 94
6:45—56 253

6:51—52 252
7:1—13 349
9:38—41 313
9:38 312
10:21—31 144
12:41—44 216
14:27—31 52
14:66—72 52

Luke
1:26—38 46
2:21—51 291
4:1—12 285
5:30 218
5:36—39 219
5:37—38 217
6:12 299
6:20—23 37
6:27—42 174
6:27—28 317
6:31 172
6:32—36 248
6:37—38 172
7:36—50 124
7:36—48 277
8:4—18 70
9:10—17 102
10:25—37 263
11:32 305
11:33—36 251
12:13—21 177
12:16—21 208
12:22—34 82
14:1—11 389
14:12—23 367
14:25—35 144
14:28—30 302
15:8—10 305
15:22—32 235
16:1—15 296
17:20—33 417
18:9—14 344
18:15—17 359
19:11—26 288
19:40 400
21:1—4 430
21:5—19 166

22:7—19 419
22:62 185
24:36—45 253

John
1:11 419
2:1—12 324
3:1—17 132
4 70, 380
4:1—26 70
5:4—43 248
7:1—9 324
8 380
8:15 174
8:32 264
8:36 264
9:1—41 251
10:40—11:23 324
11:5 170
11:17—44 191
12:42—43 344
13:1—17 73
13:34 34
14:6 240
15 414
15:13 171
15:15 109
16:5—22 191
16:33 31
17 380
17:20—26 339
19:25—27 206
21:4—14 222
21:19 142
21:20 142
21:21 142
21:22 143

Acts
2:42—47 404
2:42 403
2:43—47 367
3:17—19 326
4 158
4:22—23 159
4:25 158
4:26 159
4:32—37 158, 160, 319

4:36 158
5:1—4 319
5:40—7:22 169
6:1—4 367
8:23 185
9:26—27 170
10:34—43 277
11:1—18 313
11:25—26 170
13 159
13:1—39 160
13:1 159
13:13 159
13:42 159
13:44—48 216
15 159
15:36—39 159
15:40—41 170
16:25—26 298
17:6 218
17:22—31 154, 155
20:20—21 305
22—26 169
24:10—16 319
24:22 202
24:23 263
24:25 202
27:35 422

Romans
Book of 148
2:1—4 40
3:21—26 272
4 25
4:20 24
5:1—5 260
5:3—4 260
6:15 268
8 414
8:5—11 315
8:29 108
8:32 234
9:1—21 104
11:33 104, 176
12 414
12:2 315
12:3—8 122

12:3 108
12:9—13 141
12:10 257
13:7—8 302
14—15:7 40
16:1—27 163
16:7—15 161

1 Corinthians
2:4 310
2:6—13 310
2:19 360
4:18—21 347
4:21 428
6 65
6:12—19 363
6:12 63, 64
9:1—18 313
9:19 266
9:24—27 49
9:26—27 302
10:1—13 107
10:9—11 373
10:23—11:1 73
10:31—32 302
10:31 67
12 341
12:1—31 342
12:12—26 99
12:18 122
12:22 99
12:24 99
13 75, 76, 414
13:4 75, 260
13:5 75
13:7 75
14:40 138
15:1—58 381
15:52—58 228
15:58 57
16:17 326
16:18 326

2 Corinthians
1:8 54
1:1—11 54
3:1—18 266
3:17 264

4:1—18 54
4:16—18 251
5:6—10 256
5:17 132
6:1—13 144
6:3—4 259
6:6 259
8:1—15 208
8:7 48
10:1 428
10:1—18 307
10:12 306
11:13—15 165
12:7—10 152
12:14 296
13:14 90

Galatians
1:6 391
2:6 219
2:21 391
3:1—14 269
3:1 391
4:9 391
5:1 76, 264
5:4 264
5:13—15 76
5:13 86, 264
5:15 86
5:19—24 260
5:22—23 140, 259, 302, 427
6:1—5 307
6:1 428
6:3 344
6:7—10 58
6:7—8 269
6:9 24, 57
6:12—14 344
6:17 78

Ephesians
2:8 430
2:9 430
2:10 108
2:14 151
2:19—22 404
3:1—21 130

3:14—21 322
3:17 130
4:1 67
4:1—3 141
4:2 260, 428
4:12—16 404
4:12 403
4:25 224
4:26—27 302, 303
4:29 28, 302
4:31—32 186
4:32 40
5 399
5:1—33 111
5:1—11 269
5:14—17 203
5:18 399
5:19 399
5:29 108
6:1—4 243

Philippians
1:6 334
1:9—11 166
2:1—11 432
2:1—4 122
2:13 148
2:19—30 194
3:4 256
3:7—21 210
4:2—3 194
4:6—7 212, 299
4:8 356
4:10—13 208
4:12 208
4:21—22 163
4:22 161

Colossians
2:1—23 130
2:1—7 138
2:7 130
2:8—23 349
2:17 381
3:2 253
3:12—17 86
3:12 260
3:17 67, 224, 237, 336

3:22—25 60
3:23 336
4:2—6 111
4:5 82

1 Thessalonians
2:1—16 285
2:5—8 262
2:5—6 285
3:6—13 419
4:1—7 269
4:1 48
4:3 268
4:10 48
4:11—12 68
5:1—12 160
5:12—14 152
5:14 260
5:15—22 48, 49
5:16 337
5:22 268

2 Thessalonians
3:6—13 68

1 Timothy
3:2—3 302
4:15—16 25
6:3—10 296
6:17 234, 235

2 Timothy
1:3 319
1:7 395
2:1—4 414
2:22 302, 303
2:24 361
2:25 428
3:16—17 310
4:1—5 310
4:2 24
4:11 159
4:16—18 180

Titus
1:15 67
2:1—8 73
2:2—3 378
2:7—8 197

Philemon
8—18 76
20—21 326

Hebrews
2:18 107
4:9—11 232
4:12—16 188
4:16 272
5:1—14 253
5:8 96
6:1—12 25
6:13—15 353
10:19—25 65
10:20 218
11 99, 276
11:1—40 197
11:4 196
12:1—3 157
12:3 152
12:7—11 243
12:14 361
12:15 185, 361
13:1—6 246
13:4 269
13:6 398
13:8 24
13:15—18 319
13:20 90
13:21 90

James
Book of 414
1:1—12 97
1:2—4 182
1:3—4 24
1:14—24 68
1:19 70
1:21 428
2:1—12 307
2:10 188
3 414
3:1—12 119
3:2 92, 187, 188
3:6—8 26
3:14—16 361
4:7—12 174
4:13—17 370
4:13—14 175
5:7—11 260
5:11 260

1 Peter
1:1—5 132
1:3—9 79, 256
1:13—15 253
1:14—16 268
2:2—3 414
2:11—16 34
3:1—6 108
3:8—12 428
3:12 299
3:13—17 319

3:14—15 414
4:12—19 97
5:1—9 296
5:5 258
5:6 258
5:7 212
5:8 57
5:10 57

2 Peter
3 103
3:3—4 101
3:18 413

1 John
1 414
1:5—10 166
2:9—11 361
2:15—17 356
3:16—20 241
3:16—18 296
3:21—24 146
4:7—21 339
5:1—4 146

Jude
1—24 92
24—25 90, 91, 92

Revelation
2:4—5 412
3:15 414
3:16 414
19:7—9 367

SUBJECT INDEX

Challenges, 82, 95—97, 127—28, 136—37, 143, 169, 199—200, 221—22, 237—38, 248, 253, 255, 314, 315, 316, 317, 325—26, 335—36, 397—98

Children, 70, 71—73, 84—86, 93—94, 112, 113—14, 172—74, 209—10, 226—27, 233—35, 245—46, 247, 253, 314, 316—17, 323—24, 327—28, 354, 355—56, 357—59, 365—67, 382—83, 397—98, 400-401, 405—6, 422—24, 428, 431—32

Church, 90—92, 161—63, 217—19, 248, 264—66, 276—77, 279, 311—13, 363—64, 388—89, 399—401

Comforting, 189—91, 261—62, 299—300, 435

Consistency, 23—25, 35—37, 55—58, 66—68, 78—79, 98—100, 187—88, 205—6, 304—5, 321—22, 334

Criticism, 23—24, 78—79, 87—89, 112—13, 114—16, 117—19, 120—22, 142—44, 145—46, 150—52, 172—74, 184—85, 207—8, 218—19, 250—51, 281—82, 304—5, 311—13, 357—58, 390—93, 397—98, 428

Dependability, 23, 59—61, 66—68, 98—99, 170—71, 205—6, 223—25, 387, 398

Depression, 51—52, 54, 78—79, 103—4, 150, 156—57, 170, 184—86, 278—82, 283—87, 377

Despair, 29—30, 54—55, 127, 147—49, 150, 156—57, 170, 173—74,

239—41, 252—53, 278—82, 297—99, 334—35

Determination, 23—24, 31—32, 49, 55—58, 95, 130, 157, 169, 187—88, 199—200, 205—6, 259—60, 289—91, 321—22, 345—46, 368—70, 379—81, 395, 397—98, 406—7, 408—9, 413—14,

Diligence, 23, 55—57, 59—61, 66—68, 78—79, 98—99, 130, 205, 231—32, 253, 262, 289—91, 335—36, 413—14

Discipline, 23, 26—28, 55—57, 59—66, 69—70, 113—14, 129—30, 136—38, 169, 172—73, 202, 259, 309—10, 314—15, 355—56, 357—58, 383, 408, 423—24, 427—28

Discouragement, 29—30, 54, 57—58, 84—86, 98—99, 120—22, 127—28, 140—41, 150—52, 156—58, 170, 184—86, 194, 198—99, 223—25, 247—49, 280—82, 297—99, 334, 340—42, 351—53, 368—70

Doubt. *See* Faith.

Encouragement, 98—99, 114—16, 140—41, 158—59, 162—63, 170—71, 248, 262, 264—66, 274, 278—82, 287—88, 357—58, 368—70, 377—78, 428

Endurance, 23—25, 47—50, 55—57, 59—61, 65, 96—97, 129—30, 192—94, 259—60, 321—22

Enthusiasm, 47—50, 57, 61, 66—67, 306—7, 316—17, 341—42, 408

Excellence, 47—50, 59—61, 66—68, 195—97, 309—10, 340—42, 402—3

Failure, 35—39, 77—79, 86, 88—89, 91, 95—97, 150, 159, 187—88, 245—46, 273—77, 279—81, 340—42, 357, 368—70

Faith, 61—62, 67—68, 71—72, 90—91, 142—44, 147—55, 156—57, 176, 180, 198—99, 210, 231—32, 252—53, 274, 292—93, 294—96, 299—300, 321—22, 334, 335—36, 351—35, 368—70, 371—73, 374—75, 389, 395, 408—9, 423—24

Family. *See* Children.

Forgiveness, 39—41, 91—92, 132, 162—63, 172—73, 184—86, 188, 245—46, 270—72, 275—77, 304—5, 306—7, 311, 361, 380—81, 428, 432

Fulfillment, 198—200, 341—42, 405—6

Freedom, 40—41, 63—65, 75—76, 124, 198—200, 264—66, 311—13, 325—26, 346—47, 390—93, 418—19, 423—25

Friendship, 55, 85—86, 108—9, 170—71, 191, 226—27, 251, 278—79, 283, 338, 390—91, 428, 429—30

Grace, 39, 91—92, 104, 114—16, 132, 264—65, 267, 270—72, 275—76, 304—5, 320—21, 334, 390—91, 411—14, 424—25

Grief, 29—31, 95—97, 103—4, 123—24, 142—44, 147, 175—76, 189—91, 209—10, 259—60, 280—82, 289, 292—93, 333—34, 377, 423—24, 428

Growth, 95—97, 129—30, 170—71, 244—45, 335—36, 357—58, 383—84, 412—14, 431—32

Guilt, 40—43, 47, 113—14, 134—35, 187—88, 201—2, 207—8, 237—38, 247—48, 267, 275—77, 279—81, 283—85, 318—19, 324, 377, 405—6

Humility, 50—54, 142, 159, 207—8, 257—58, 270—72, 275—77, 283—85, 306—7, 343—47, 361, 372—73, 385—87, 390—93, 416—17, 424—25, 427—28

Hope, 31—32, 66, 82—83, 92, 104, 127—28, 132, 150—52, 190—91, 199—200, 218—19, 368—70, 432—33

Impatience. *See* Patience.

Jesus Christ, 23—25, 29—31, 42—43, 47, 49, 51—52, 65, 66—67, 70, 72—73, 90—92, 96—97, 102, 112—13, 123, 129—30, 142—44, 150—55, 157—59, 161—62, 168—69, 170—71, 185—86, 191, 208, 220—22, 223—25, 227—28, 240—41, 245, 251—53, 259—60, 262, 270—72, 281—82, 284—85, 289, 296, 305, 310, 312—13, 324, 346—47, 348—49, 366—67, 374, 380—81, 390—93, 413—16, 420—24, 429—30

Joy, 49, 90—92, 112—16, 133—35, 234—35, 294, 335—36, 365—66, 390, 400—401, 421—22

Judging. *See* Criticism.

Laughter, 38—39, 112—16, 227—28, 233—35, 287—88, 325—29, 365—66, 379—80, 420, 427—28

Leisure, 93—94, 113—15, 133—34, 231—34, 236—38, 247—48, 287—88, 325—29, 429—32

Liberty. *See* Freedom.

Loneliness, 29, 55, 133, 156—57, 244—45, 251, 285, 292—93, 334

Love, 42, 52—53, 86, 94, 105, 114—16, 120—22, 142, 146, 159, 161—62, 170—73, 176, 189—91, 209—10, 243—46, 259—60, 262, 304—7, 338—39, 346—47, 390, 408—9, 422, 427—28, 429—30, 432—33

Nostalgia, 209—10, 327—28, 333—
36, 358—59, 421—23, 429—32

Obedience, 142—44, 145—46,
264—66

Pain, 29, 77—79, 87—89, 95—97,
103—4, 142—44, 156—57, 175,
178, 182—83, 184—85, 189—91,
204, 209—10, 217—19, 260—63,
281—82, 298—300, 334, 335—36,
379—81, 385, 389, 431—32

Patience, 23—25, 70, 139—41, 181—
83, 192—94, 259—60, 289—91,
343—44, 372—73, 405—6

Patriotism, 71—73, 418—19,
422—25

Perspective, 38—39, 78—83, 93—94,
104, 114—16, 120, 127—28, 132—
35, 157, 175—76, 178—80, 198—
200, 211—13, 217—19, 237—38,
252—57, 292—93, 314—15, 323—
24, 333—34, 348—49, 377—84,
395, 409—14, 429—32

Praise, 99—100, 114—16, 212—13,
215—16, 333, 343—44, 374—75,
419, 422—25, 429—32

Prayer, 49, 90—91, 94, 98—99,
114—15, 123, 133—34, 136—41,
151—52, 168—69, 176, 192—94,
198—99, 211—13, 223—25, 252—
53, 255, 297—300, 338, 351—53,
372—73, 377—78, 383—84, 390,
391—92, 395—96, 403—4, 413—
14, 419—21, 423—25

Pressure, 40—41, 71—72, 93—94,
154—55, 181—83, 192—94, 223,
231, 236—38, 247, 289, 318, 324—
26, 360—63, 366—67, 405—7

Pride. *See* Humility.

Procrastination, 61—62, 65, 95—97,
136—38, 146, 201, 247—48

Reputation, 35, 304—5, 360—61

Rest, 93—94, 231—32, 248—49,
254—55, 287—88, 324—29, 362—
63, 395—96, 418—19

Risk, 44—46, 114—16, 264—66,
273—74, 316—17, 325—26

Salvation, 40—41, 70, 110—11, 132,
154—55, 157, 175—76, 202—3,
217, 221—22, 240—41, 380—81,
414—16, 432—33

Self-control, 63—66, 70, 289—91,
301—3, 324, 354—56, 357—58,
427—28

Sensitivity, 70, 74—76, 123—24,
158—59, 189—91, 244—46, 261—
63, 357—59, 426—30

Sin, 39—41, 49, 105—7, 120—22,
146, 187—88, 268—72, 275—77,
280—81, 302—3, 304—5, 380—81,
414—16

Struggles, 40—41, 52—55, 57—58,
77—78, 95—97, 142—44, 162—63,
181—83, 187—88, 198—200,
205—6, 250—51, 273—82, 315,
348—49, 397—98

Time, 70, 80—83, 93—94, 136, 175—
76, 181—83, 195—203, 255—56,
323—24, 333—34, 335, 351—53,
379—81, 382—84, 404—6, 429—
30, 433

Tongue, 26—28, 87—89, 117—19,
188, 189—91, 220—22, 223—25,
301—2, 314—15, 324

Trust. *See* Faith.

Trustworthiness. *See* Dependability.

Weariness, 23—25, 150—52, 167—
69, 176

Weeping, 38—39, 123—24, 156—57,
189—91, 227—28, 255, 283—85,
338, 379—80, 424—25, 431—32